Re]

In their   *izing Deviance* (1987) and *Negotiating Control* (1989), authors documented the politics of knowledge between journalists and news sources and how it shapes what is published and broadcast. In *Representing Order* they analyse the aggregate products of news: how topics covered, formats used, and sources cited vary by the distinctive features of each medium and by the market orientation of news outlets, and what different aspects of the knowledge-structure of society, and of social order more generally, are represented in various news outlets as a result.

The authors identify five components of representation in news discourse: visualizing, symbolizing, authorizing, staging, and convincing. Through these components, news representation involves a process of convincing others, for example in making statements by way of expostulation, remonstrance, or incentive that will 'bring the facts home' and thereby bear influence.

These five components of representation work in combination to constitute the news media's versions of social order. News represents order – morality, procedural form, and hierarchy – through constituting an active and influential discourse about the ordering activities of the people and organizations reported on. As such, news is used by people to order their daily lives, providing the preferred versions of social order upon which they take action. News becomes an agency of social control, not merely describing the crime, law, and justice processes but serving as an integral part of them.

Representing Order challenges the dominant ideology thesis. Its findings indicate that the news media provide a somewhat open terrain for struggles for justice, even though particular issues and institutional sources predominate. The documented variation by medium and market shows pluralism in meanings and values. In news content, as in the production of news, the authors find many signs that the news media provide space for meaning contests, struggles, and resistance regarding crime, legal control, and social justice.

Richard V. Ericson is Professor of Criminology and Sociology, University of Toronto.

Patricia M. Baranek is Manager of the Health Human Resources Policy Unit, Ontario Ministry of Health.

Janet B.L. Chan is a Lecturer in Sociology and Social Policy at the University of New South Wales.

Representing Order: Crime, Law, and Justice in the News Media

RICHARD V. ERICSON

PATRICIA M. BARANEK

JANET B.L. CHAN

OPEN UNIVERSITY PRESS

Milton Keynes

First published in Great Britain in 1991 by
Open University Press
Celtic Court
22 Ballmoor
Buckingham MK18 1XW

British Library Cataloguing in Publication Data

Ericson, Richard V. (Richard Victor) *1948–*
    Representing order: crime, law and justice in the news media.

I. Canada. Crime. Reporting
I. Title II. Baranek, Patricia M. III. Chan, Janet B.L.

070.44936497

ISBN 0-335-09753-7
ISBN 0-335-09752-9 pbk

Printed in Canada

Contents

Tables

Acknowledgments

Social-science research involves collaboration among many people in different institutions.

The Social Sciences and Humanities Research Council of Canada funded our work through two research-project grants (nos. 410-83-0748 and 410-84-0004) and through a leave fellowship (no. 451-84-3311) granted to Richard Ericson. The Humanities and Social Sciences Committee of the Research Board, University of Toronto, provided two research grants to facilitate data analysis and writing, and two travel grants to facilitate preliminary dissemination of results and exchanges with scholars abroad. Another important source of funding was the Ministry of the Solicitor General of Canada, through both its fund for independent research and its contribution program to the Centre of Criminology, University of Toronto. This book has been published with the help of a grant from the Social Science Federation of Canada, using funds provided by the Social Sciences and Humanities Research Council of Canada.

The University of Toronto has continued to provide an excellent supportive research environment for our work. At the Centre of Criminology we have benefited from the foundations for research laid by the first director, Professor J.Ll.J. Edwards, and the encouragement, advice, and support of successive directors, Professor A.N. Doob and Professor J. Beattie. We have also been assisted by the excellence of the Centre's library and librarians. Other colleagues, including the students in Richard Ericson's graduate seminars, helped us to develop many of the ideas expressed in this book.

Several people have made important contributions at various stages of the research process. Sophia Voumvakis was an excellent research assistant. She was patient, and offered a great deal of insight, during the main phase of data collection. Kevin Carriere assisted with specific data-collection tasks that arose during analysis, and we thank him also for his patience and insights. Sophia and Kevin have helped to make this a better book. Richard Ericson thanks Tony Doob for a discussion in his office one afternoon that clarified several methodological issues and inspired the continuation of a search for solutions to methodological puzzles that seemed intractable. We are grateful to Dr Michael Adena of INSTAT Australia Pty Ltd and to Ms Concetta Rizzo for their statistical advice. Mary Jackson is to be thanked for her good humour and patience in word-processing drafts of the manuscript.

Five scholars have enhanced the intellectual quality of this book by providing detailed comments on an earlier draft. These include two anonymous reviewers for the publisher and the Social Science Federation of Canada, as well as Professor David Altheide of Arizona State University, Professor Robert Menzies of Simon Fraser University, and Professor Paul Rock of the London School of Economics and Political Science.

Finally, we are grateful for our continuing association with a first-rate publisher. Virgil Duff and John Skelton have helped a great deal in seeing the manuscript through to publication. In the production of the manuscript the burden was eased considerably by the excellent copy-editing skills of Beverley Beetham Endersby and by the index preparation of Dianna Ericson.

RVE

PMB

JBLC

PART I

Theory and Methods

1

Representing Order

The eighteenth century was the age for analysing society as a machine, the nineteenth century was the age for analysing society as an organism, and the twentieth century is the age for analysing society as a communications network. Today an understanding of society, and the institutions of which it is comprised, must include analysis of what passes for knowledge and how it is communicated. Harold Innis, Marshall McLuhan, and Raymond Williams are among the prominent scholars who have taught us that effort to see through society and culture must include analysis of public conversations and the ways those conversations are communicated.

In this book we analyse public conversations about crime, law, and justice, and how they are communicated in the news media. We broaden our previous research in this field (Ericson, Baranek, and Chan 1987, 1989) methodologically, theoretically, and substantively.

In terms of methodology, we employ content analysis to examine news products in the aggregate. A limitation of our previous studies is that they present a series of case examples but no aggregate view. What is now required is a composite portrait of news products, and it is this mosaic that is crafted in the present volume.

In terms of theory, we explore how and why our public conversations are dominated by talk of crime, law, and justice. In our previous work we demonstrated that news is produced by journalists and sources in power/ knowledge relations involving imputations of deviance and efforts at control. In the present work we show that the aggregate product of this activity is representations of order. News of deviance and control represents order through constituting an active discourse about the ordering activities of the people reported on. As such news perpetually represents order – morality, procedural form, and social hierarchy – in ways that help people to order their daily lives. As an active *agency* of social control, stability, and change, news representations provide people with preferred versions and visions of social order, on the basis of which they take action.

In terms of substance, we focus on how news varies among news outlets that operate within different media and market orientations. In our previous research we learned that the format constraints of each medium and each market orientation have substantial influence on the practices of journalists and news sources. While detailing the strategies and techniques of journalists and sources in dealing with different medium and market formats, we did not analyse the medium and markets either as a central focus or in terms of aggregate data. 'It remains important to study variation among media (not only networks and newspapers but, importantly, wire services, radio, and local television) and among institutions within a single medium' (Gitlin 1980: 302). Are news organizations that operate within the same medium most similar, regardless of their market orientation? Are news organizations with a similar market orientation most similar, regardless of the medium in which they operate?

The methodological requirements and procedures for our analysis are addressed in chapter 3. In this chapter we initially elaborate our theoretical focus on news as a discourse that represents order. We then detail the differences in media and market orientation that inform our subsequent analyses of variation in news of social deviance, law, and justice.

News, Law, and Order

The news institution focuses upon what is out of place: the deviant, equivocal, and unpredictable. News operatives attend to the more calamitous happenings in other institutions that have proved difficult to classify or that contradict standard expectations in the social structure about rights and the distribution of power. The goal is to provide a set of classifications that are workable in that they establish the normal, reduce equivocality, and increase predictability – that is, to represent order.

News operatives pursue this goal through the use of social and cultural practices that have been well documented (Altheide 1976; Schlesinger 1978; Tuchman 1978; Fishman 1980; Ericson, Baranek, and Chan 1987). These practices include the use of formats – media, language, techniques (e.g., dramatization, simplification, personalization) – that make news discourse distinctive, and distinctively a part of common sense. The common-sense knowledge available in the news does not provide instruction on '*how things are*' as much as '*where they fit*' into the order of things (Hartley 1982; Hall 1979: 325).

In telling stories about where things fit, the news deals with three fundamental aspects of order. First, there is *moral evaluation*: whether something is in or out of order is judged in terms of whether it is good or bad, healthy or unhealthy, normal or abnormal, efficient or inefficient. As such, order is not a neutral concept. Second, order incorporates a conception of *procedure*. Order entails proceeding according to an established sequence or customary procedure. It is a method according to which things are understood to act or events to take place. When things or events do not proceed methodically, visualizations of deviance come to the forefront and procedural strays are identified. Third, order addresses *hierarchy*. Order means class, status, position, rank, and distinctions as to quality (higher and lower orders). It entails differentiation on the basis of special interests, occupation, character, excellence, and so on. News is fundamentally a discourse of morality, procedure, and hierarchy, providing symbolic representations of order in these terms.

Symbols are essential to the quest for order. Humans construct order in the form of symbols that can be referred to, deferred to, and used to accomplish everyday routines. Symbols have the practical 'capacity to inspire or to give meaning to individual or collective activity, to delegitimate other activity and to bring to bear the force of social control. In a word, symbols and symbol systems provide an important ordering impulse to social affairs and to the collective views of the world. Thus they are an essential part of the reality of everyday life' (Wuthnow et al. 1984: 37).

The act of making symbols, and of remaking them in the practical activities of everyday life, is captured by the word 'representing.' Humans perpetually represent the world around them in and through the available symbolic forms. Whether it is news discourse in newspapers, radio, and television; scientific discourse in scholarly journals; or legal discourse in case-law books, there is in common an effort to represent a world in which one's descriptions make sense.

News production involves five interrelated components that together define 'representing.' The components are visualizing, symbolizing, authorizing, staging, and convincing. Through dramatized descriptions, metaphoric language, and pictures, news depicts events that are called up in the mind (visualized) even while they remain invisible to the eye. News representations are symbolic in the sense that they embody, stand for, or correspond to persons, events, processes, or states of affairs being reported on. News representation involves authorization of who can be a representative or spokesperson of a source organization, of what sources are 'authorized knowers' (Tuchman 1978). In addition, journalists authorize themselves to represent the people, to stand in for citizens in making representations to powerful officials and bureaucracies on their behalf. News also 'represents' in the sense of being staged according to standard locations, scripts, props, and actors who are well-rehearsed in news-media formats and fictions (Ericson, Baranek, and Chan 1987). Through all of the components noted above, news representation involves a process of convincing others, for example, making statements by way of expostulation, remonstrance, or incentive that will 'bring the facts home' and thereby influence others. Representing order in the news always combines the five core ingredients of visualizing, symbolizing, authorizing, staging, and convincing.

Representing order entails consideration of the *conditions* necessary for the reproduction of morality, procedural form, and hierarchical relations. Of particular significance is an assessment of the extent to which threats or dangers to hierarchy are absent, for example, levels of crime or public protest. Representing order also addresses the procedures by which threats and dangers are minimized, including especially the rule of law and the police power of the state. Order is 'the condition in which laws or usages regulating the public relations of individuals to the community, and the public conduct of members or sections of the community to each other, are maintained and observed; the rule of law or constituted authority; law-abiding state; absence of insurrection, riot, turbulence, unruliness, or crimes of violence' (*Oxford English Dictionary*).

Order thus has legal meaning. Law is a conceptual device for the co-ordination of institutional activities. Law is a kind of 'order system' (Weber 1954: 13) that functions to allocate resources (by guaranteeing and protecting relationships, and by intervening to enforce policies and programs); to regulate and resolve conflict (by providing principles and procedures for doing so); and to keep the peace (by establishing rules of behaviour and enforcing violations with sanctions). News discourse is dominated by representations of law and legal relations in these terms. It concentrates on the allocation of resources, the regulation and resolution of conflicts, and peace-keeping. It focuses on procedural improprieties that raise questions of law; it assigns responsibility and thereby specifies who should be controlled by what legal procedures; and it relies upon legal officials and their documents to support the validity of its claims about what needs to be done to keep things in order. Contemporary with the society it reports on, news discourse represents order through a particular obsession with law.

There are many affinities between law and the news media in representing order. Both the law and the news media offer disciplinary and normalizing discourses (Foucault 1977), intertextually related to each other and to other disciplinary and normalizing institutions and discourses, whether religious, economic, or political. As Goodrich (1986: 147) observes, 'any common-law text belongs to a wider tradition and community of texts (intertextuality) and the values that such texts espouse. To a very great extent the so-called "logic of the Common Law" is precisely this tireless elaboration and affirmation of the values of legal community and legal order – the text is as much a sermon and an exhortation as it is in any strict sense an exercise of logical subsumption.' The legal text combines with others, including the news, to make authoritative imprints of order. With the news media, the law participates actively in the constitution of social order by functioning as 'social discourse, as part of a continuing political and administrative dialogue as to the terms and conditions of social life' (ibid: 20). As such, news of law serves as an influential vehicle through which the authority system can instruct people on what to *be* as well as what to *do*.

As disciplinary and normalizing discourses, law and news are both fundamentally concerned with *policing*, defined in the original French sense, as a mechanism for the moral health and improvement of the population. Law and news police the major institutions of society in terms of how the classifications, values, and procedures of these institutions fit with the expectations of various evaluators. This policing fosters a perpetual public conversation about what institutional arrangements are most appropriate.

In the process of policing, law and news articulate public morality. Morality is built into the classifications that members use for conducting their routine business. The very act of classification, including disputes about misclassification, involves questions of right and wrong and is therefore loaded with moral content. Morality is embedded in an institution's classification scheme, and it is this scheme that gives, and frames, a sense of justice. In policing classifications, values, and procedures, the law and news offer a sense of justice.

The news media and law also share an affinity in claiming that their policing is in the public interest. The basis of this claim is the appearance of neutrality. The consequence of this claim is that the news media and law are able to accomplish a degree of legitimacy and authority for their own institutions, while also selectively underpinning or undercutting legitimacy and authority of other social institutions.

Moral principles and justifications require publicity (Bok 1979: 96), especially as they are used in quests for legitimacy. Legitimacy is defined in terms of right and just actions. When justice and propriety can be imputed to actions, the legitimacy of those actions is in place. The importance of legitimacy is that it offers stability and order, not only in the narrow sense of preserving the status quo, but also in the sense of ensuring an adaptive capacity to cope with strains or changes in the environment. As Habermas (1975, 1979) states, legitimacy depends on the ability of authorities to make convincing *claims*, arguments that they are acting in accordance with social norms. Hence questions of legitimacy revolve around procedural norms, procedural propriety, and the search for and sanctioning of procedural strays. Especially regarding the legitimacy of the state, this obsession with procedure is expressed in terms of the constitutionality and legality of decisions. The news-media institution is pivotal to the ability of authorities to make convincing claims. It offers a pervasive and persuasive means by which authorities from various institutions can attempt to obtain wider consent for their moral preferences. Moral authority is always subject to *consent*, and legitimacy is always something that is *granted*. There is institutional space for choice in consenting to a given moral authority and in granting legitimacy, albeit circumscribed by institutional frames and their imprints on reality and morality.

The legal institution is also pivotal to the ability of authorities to make convincing claims. Public conversations about law are not only instrumentally directed at the solution and rationalization of particular problems, but also expressions of authority. Law justifies authority. Perfected, law makes authority appear natural, part of the order of things. Justifications of authority in law invoke not only core cultural values of justice, such as freedom and equality, but also core social institutions, such as the state and its policing apparatuses. Thus legal decisions are taken in the name of the state, the maintenance of particular moral standards, and the interests of the legal institution itself (e.g., the efficient administration of justice or so as not to bring the administration of justice into disrepute).

The news media and law also share affinities in their techniques of policing and moral brokerage. They share an orientation to conflicts that emerge during events, the individualization and personalization of conflicts, procedural form, realism, and precedent.

The news media and law share an event-orientation, examining conflicts as they arise on a specific, case-by-case basis. They both address moral principles deemed applicable to conflicts that emerge during particular events. That is, moral principles are articulated, delineated, sustained, and altered as they are grounded in the particular conflict, rather than summarized and synthesized into abstract concepts and rankings.

The news media and law also deal with moral principles through individualization and personalization. A lot of news consists of moral-character portraits: of demon criminals, of responsible authorities, of crooked politicians, and so on. The emphasis on individual morality is not only a dramatic technique for presenting news stories as serial narratives involving leading actors but also a political means of allocating responsibility for actions and attributing accountability. Moreover, in law enforcement, as in news, personalization combined with an event-orientation 'produces the appearance (or collective representation) that troublesome persons rather than troublesome social structures are at fault. This mystifies the social roots of trouble in a society that is structurally unequal' (Pfohl 1985: 353). By individualizing problems on a case-by-case basis, the news and law rule out systemic and structural accounts that might question the authority of cultural values, the state, and the news and legal institutions themselves. As Goodrich (1986: 204) observes with respect to law, 'It is of the very essence of legal rhetoric that it individualizes the issues before the court. Legal meaning is always to be attached to individual acts and legal explanation is correspondingly biographical and moral rather than sociological and contextualizing.'

The emphasis on concrete events and individuals involved in them is linked to another aspect of moral brokerage in both news and law, namely the emphasis on procedures. Both news and law can be described as social discourses of procedural propriety. Both are obsessed with institutional procedures and how they cohere with interests, morality, and accountability. This obsession is in keeping with the decreasing significance of absolute values or tradition in sustaining legitimacy, and the increasing significance of procedural propriety for claims of legitimacy. It is also in keeping with the search for responsibility and accountability, and the attendant emphasis on effects of actions more than on causes. As Wuthnow and associates (1984: 222) observe, referring to the work of Habermas on legitimation,

> the legitimacy of the modern state no longer rests on tradition or absolute values, but is rooted in conceptions of proper *procedures* – procedures deemed legitimate if they have been established according to norms of legality and constitutionality and if they conform to certain conceptions of citizenship and representation. They are intended to serve as mechanisms for negotiating policies oriented towards the common good. The modern period is characterized by a relatively high degree of reflection about these procedures. They are not taken for granted as the way things simply must be, but are consciously subjected to scrutiny to determine if they in fact produce desired consequences.

While legal procedures may have been established with reference to tradition or higher morality – God, truth, justice, community, democracy – such reference tends to be expressed rhetorically or is simply silenced in the drone of administrative discourse about procedural propriety.

The event-orientation, personalization, and obsession with procedure in the news are packaged realistically. While news events are staged and performed by actors in social dramas – for example, in news conferences, formally structured interviews, and photo opportunities – they are 'natural- ized' and presented as unmediated reality. While news is politically and socially constructed, includes elements that are fabricated and fictive, and presents evaluative differences as differences in fact (Ericson, Baranek, and Chan 1987), it appears as reality. That is, while news is based on the laws of social and moral constructs, it appears as if it is based on the laws of nature.

> The world *is*, naturally and of itself, what the mind-originated conventions of realism say it is ... a *story* may be fictional, but the way it is related tells it like it is ... realism requires that it be accepted not as *one* way of seeing, but as *the* way of seeing; realism's reference is not to bourgeois modes of thought but rather to nature itself ... Once the 'real' is established as such, it becomes a vehicle for the communication of messages which embody, not our 'real' social relationships, but rather cultural mythologies *about* those relationships. (Fiske and Hartley 1978: 161, 165, 170)

Law also operates in the mode of realism. Law 'justifies authority and makes it appear natural' (Goodrich 1986: 64) through conventions and techniques similar to those we have identified in the news. While law is politically and socially constructed (McBarnet 1981), includes aspects that are fictive (Fuller 1967; Scheppele 1990), and presents evaluative differences as differences in fact (Goodrich 1986), its realistic functioning in public culture erases these aspects. It functions as if facts naturally relate to laws without human and organizational mediation. It functions as if it is in pursuit of *the* truth – as if legal truth, and procedures for establishing legal truth, authenticate and guarantee 'the whole truth' rather than truth reduced to the genre capacities of the law report. It functions as if legal proof, which is largely a matter of formal procedure, and knowledge, which is largely a matter of the substance of the facts, are the same thing. To paraphrase what Fiske and Hartley are quoted as saying above: a law report may have fictional properties but the way it is related tells it like it is. Even though the law report is limited to its genre capacities, as realism it requires acceptance not as *one* way of seeing but as *the* way of seeing. As realism, the law report does not embody real social relationships but cultural mythologies about these relationships.

Presented realistically, the news and the law have the character of precedent, 'the repetition of a discourse or way of life and mode of belonging' (Goodrich 1986: 127–8). Precedent provides a vocabulary for classification of the world, and authority for that classification (Ericson, Baranek, and Chan 1987, 1989). It is common-sense knowledge about the order of things, a source of comfort about what seems right and real. Through repetitive formulas and ritualized texts, precedent literally 'brings home' a familiar discourse that people feel comfortable with and incorporate as a significant part of everyday life. Given all of the affinities between law and news, it is little wonder that the most familiar discourse today is a blend of news, law, and order.

The Representatives of Order

Order is a verb as well as a noun. As a verb, order connotes *agency*: giving orders or commands that are intended to produce morality, procedural form, and hierarchical relations. It connotes 'the *action* of putting or keeping in order; regulation, ordering, control,' and bringing 'into order or submission to lawful authority; hence, to inflict disciplinary punishment on; to correct, chastise, punish' (*Oxford English Dictionary*). It connotes people in *interaction*, actively seeking to co-ordinate and control each other's actions by identifying strays and responding to them through proper procedures.

News discourse involves journalists engaging sources in representing order through acts of visualizing, symbolizing, authorizing, staging, and convincing. As documented in our previous studies (Ericson, Baranek, and Chan 1987, 1989), representing is embedded in the micropolitics of power/knowledge struggles between journalists and sources. While news is a highly institutionalized form of knowledge, its institutionalization depends on the power/knowledge struggles of sources and journalists. Social order is reproduced in micro-episodes of conflict (Collins 1975), including discursive struggles or meaning contests over what is reported (secrecy and publicity) and how it is reported (the ordering and combining of words). And, while 'meanings are gained or lost through struggles ... what is at stake is ultimately quite a lot more than either words or discourses' (Macdonnel 1986: 51).

What is at stake is news as a power resource. The institutions and processes of the news media are entwined with political structures and processes more generally (Garnham 1986: 87). While access to the news depends on the possession of other resources of social, political, and economic power, the news resource itself is used to regulate the control and distribution of these other resources (Golding, Murdock, and Schlesinger 1986; Ericson, Baranek, and Chan 1989; H. Schiller 1989). The very condition of possibility of news as knowledge is in hierarchical roles and the power relations they entail in terms of control of resources. Analytically, the concern is not whether news as knowledge is true or false, but how it enters into power relations and serves to legitimate or to undermine these relations. In summary, sources and journalists do not merely report on politics, they constitute the news media as a political institution. In the representations that emerge from their discursive struggles, they construct the community, including especially its sense of order (Williams 1961).

As they engage discursive struggles in a particular institution, journalists become part of that institution, including its processes of social control. We have documented this thoroughly in the case of journalistic involvement in the legal institution (Ericson, Baranek, and Chan 1987, 1989). Journalists are directly involved in the activities of lawmakers and law-enforcers, joining with them as agents of social control. This social-control activity includes surveillance of deviant people and organizations, the identification of procedural strays, recommendations for controlling them, and direct social control through the stigmatic effects of publicity. The legal agencies themselves are included as objects of journalistic surveillance and control. The news-media institution intersects with the legal institution as part of the coercive apparatus as well as the ideological apparatus. 'No hard and fast line can be drawn between the mechanisms of hegemony and the mechanisms of coercion; the hold of hegemony rests on elements of coercion, just as the force of coercion over the dominated presupposes and reinforces elements of hegemony' (Gitlin 1980: 253).

Hegemony addresses how superordinates manufacture and sustain support for their dominance over subordinates through dissemination and reproduction of knowledge that favours their interests and how subordinates alternatively accept or contest this knowledge. The 'hegemonic' (Williams 1977) is produced out of transactions between superordinates and subordinates, and entails enormous labour, meets resistance, gets deflected, needs revision, and is never complete. The hegemonic process is at the core of transactions between journalists and sources. 'A lived hegemony ... is never either total or exclusive' (ibid 112–13), and is 'not so much the finished article itself, but the whole process of argument, exchange, debate, consultation and speculation by which it emerges' (Hall 1979: 342).

It is 'a lived hegemony' as a process, not as a 'finished article,' that appears in the news. The news provides a daily barometer of hegemonic processes. Through a focus on conflict and opposition, in and between major social institutions, the news provides 'indicative features of what the hegemonic process has in practice had to work to control' (Williams 1977: 112–13). The central aspect of this focus is reporting claims to authority and challenges to those claims, in the context of conflict over one or more of the following: the stratification of expert knowledge; the stratification of official knowledge; key values such as freedom and equality; rights associated with these values, such as rights to liberty and well-being; and just procedures to achieve these rights, including legal procedures. Daily news about procedural propriety, rights claims, value conflicts, official versus unofficial versions of events, and expert renditions of events testify to hegemonic processes at work. Since there is a high level of conflict and contradiction in the discursive struggles of news production in these terms (Ericson, Baranek, and Chan 1987, 1989), conflict and contradiction are also evident in daily news.

There are three general categories of participants in the news process. There are news sources, people who make news through their positions of institutional authority or involvement in newsworthy events. There are journalists, people who are mandated by their news organizations to make news in conjunction with authorized sources. There are consumers, people who make news through reading, watching, and listening to it, and locating its meaning in their own lives.

While research on relations between journalists and their sources stresses that 'both media and interpersonal interaction ... [are] part of the same system of "behaving" or responding to the behaviour of others' (Meyrowitz 1985: x), the point holds for everyone who reads, watches, and/or listens to the mass media. People spend several hours each day exposed to the mass media. Many people spend more time in 'mass-mediated' interaction than in direct 'live' interaction with other people. The mass media are just about everywhere – not at the level of production, in the sense claimed by some news organizations that their journalists are everywhere to reflect reality (Ericson, Baranek, and Chan 1987), but in the sense that news broadcasts penetrate all temporal and spatial arrangements in society. Television news appears on video screens in bars, in the home, and in prison cells. Radio news accompanies daily activities such as working, shopping, driving an automobile, riding in an elevator, sitting in a waiting-room, and waiting on the telephone for someone to deal with a business or service call.

News messages become part of the repertoire of extrasituational information used to engage in the transactions of everyday life. News words are also deeds, providing links to further action. 'Words build bridges to actions, and some people will choose to walk over those bridges' (Wagner-Pacifici 1986: 87). Knowledge derived from the mass media is used along with that obtained from person-to-person interaction and other sources as part of the person's 'information system' (Meyrowitz 1985), on the basis of which further action is taken.

These observations on the interactive nature of mass media suggest that there is substantial overlap among the roles of source, journalist, and consumer. News sources often function as journalists by, for example, submitting news releases that are published or broadcast verbatim, and producing commissioned features or regular slots or columns for news organizations. Sources are also avid news consumers, staying 'on top' of the news in order to manage the news in directions that will keep them 'on top' of the authority structure of their institution. Journalists often function as news sources by, for example, being interviewed by journalists from other news outlets and writing pieces for publications produced by the organizations they themselves report on. Journalists are also avid news consumers, obtaining most of their ideas for story assignment and angles from previous news stories. News consumers who are not regular news sources often function as news sources by, for example, calling in story ideas, using consumer-complaint columns or action lines, participating in phone-in segments on broadcast media, and being the subjects of 'person in the street' segments to show reaction to news stories. News consumers also function as journalists by, for example, writing letters to the editor and participating in popular news formats that allot them air time or column space to express their views.

There is heuristic value to thinking in terms of four broad categories of news sources: spokespersons for government institutions and organizations, spokespersons for institutions and organizations outside of government, individual citizens, and journalists.

The main research focus has been on sources in major institutions, especially those in government, because of their importance as authorized knowers to the mass media, and because of the significance of the news media to them. From the time of the founding of newspapers, governments have recognized the significance of news communication as an organizer of public opinion and as an agency of social control. Governments were active in buying and subsidizing newspapers, and journalists were also 'bought' (Burns 1979: 48–9). Governmental purchases of media power have continued to the present era, including the practices of keeping journalists on retainer (Royal Commission on Newspapers [RCN] 1981e: 61), buying advertising (Singer 1986), and establishing national broadcasting corporations (e.g., the Canadian Broadcasting Corporation and the British Broadcasting Corporation). While direct purchases are giving way to apparently more distant and benign public relations machines, behind this veil of administrative decency contemporary public relations perpetuates the same purpose of being close enough to the mass media to influence what they publicize.

Large corporations and interest groups have also realized the purchasing power of public-relations operations. Private capital is invested in the symbolic politics of news and advertising because sophistication in defending against bad news and trafficking in good news is seen as an essential part of achieving capital gains (Blyskal and Blyskal 1985; D. Schiller 1986; H. Schiller 1989; Garnham 1986; Ericson, Baranek, and Chan 1989: chap. 5).

Both government and private-sector organizations are oriented to public relations, including news, because public communications are an essential component of organizational enactment (on organizational enactment, see

Weick 1979, 1983; Meyer and Rowan 1977; Putnam and Pacanosky 1983; Rock 1986, 1988; Manning 1982, 1988; Ericson, Baranek, and Chan 1987, 1989). Organizations are first and foremost *images*, 'subjective congeries of experience which are bound and located spatially and temporally' (Manning 1982: 13). Thus 'most "objects" in organizations consist of communications, meaning, images, myths and interpretations' (Weick 1979: 156). These objects are used by members to create the ideology of the organization. Ideology gives organizational members their sense of place and power in interorganizational relations, their authoritative position.

'In so far as organizational work reproduces the larger order of authority in society, it reflects the position of the structure of meaning in class and power systems as well. Organizations are sources of hegemonic meanings, and tools by which interests are given shape' (Manning 1982: 131). As such, organizations provide the discourse and the platform on which members can perform their authority. The news media do their part by providing outlets for performances (Meyrowitz 1985; Ericson, Baranek, and Chan 1989). An adequate performance depends on variously avoiding news as well as taking part in it. Through both an ability to stay out of the news and an ability to shine when the news searchlight becomes a spotlight on their activities, sources enact their organizations and thereby help to establish their place in the hierarchy of authority. The power to stay out of the news, and alternatively to have access to the news, reflects social structure and hierarchy, and news content in turn communicates knowledge that is hierarchically and differentially distributed.

People appear in the news as individuals when there is no specification of an institutional role and status directly relevant to the story. The individual does not appear in the news as a representative of an organization, or as representative of the public in a statistical sense. Rather, the individual is typically used to make a representation on behalf of 'the public,' to express what are visualized to be public sentiments about government policy, a calamitous event, an industrial strike, etc. As such, the individual presents the fiction of 'the public' that is central to mass democracy.

Journalists function as news sources in authoring texts – working in material that makes the journalist himself or herself the original source of the material (Ericson, Baranek, and Chan 1987: chap. 7). This source function is evident when the anchor on radio or television news interviews a reporter from his or her own organization. It is also common practice for the anchor or reporter from a broadcast news organization to interview journalists of other news organizations, especially in foreign-news coverage. The Canadian Broadcasting Corporation's 'The Journal' uses this format frequently: its experts abroad are often journalists who happen to be posted to the place in question or who reside there permanently and are members of a local news organization. More pervasive are practices related to the use of already-published news produced by journalists from other news organizations: the radio-news practice of 'ripping and reading' news items from local newspapers; the use of syndicated videotapes, audiotapes, and print columns; and the use of news-wire material. As documented in chapter 7, journalists function as news sources, both directly and indirectly, with great frequency.

Journalists and their news organizations are key players in hegemonic processes. They do not simply report events, but participate in them and act as protagonists. Journalism is 'the art of structuring reality, rather than recording it' (Smith 1978: 168). The media institution affords journalists considerable power as *selectors* of which people can speak in public conversations, as *formulators* of how these people are presented, and as *authors* of knowledge.

As selectors, journalists influence which institutions and which particular spokespersons within institutions will be given access (space with opportunity for favourable representation), given mere coverage (space but with the risk of unfavourable presentation), or excluded (no space). Journalists have the power to 'certify' the 'authorized knowers' (Tuchman 1978) who serve as regular sources in the eternal recurrence of officially generated news, as well as the 'stereotyped persons' who are 'accorded a right to parade quickly through the pageant of the news' (Gitlin 1980: 284).

As formulators, journalists control the subtle aspects of source access and coverage. For example, on television, experts are usually presented in half-profile and/or with books or other authoritative signs of their office in the background. Those who are not experts, who represent other people's knowledge (including journalists) or a 'vox pop' opinion, are presented full-face and without the authoritative trappings of an office (often on the street). The line of questioning can differ substantially between opposing forces in a major conflict. The difference can be as subtle as addressing a union spokesperson by his first name (*Arthur* Scargill), while using the more distant and deferential prefix of 'Mr' for the management perspective (*Mr* MacGregor) (Tracey 1984).

As authors, journalists control the representations of sources as outlined above. However, they themselves are subject to substantial control. What appears under the newspaper reporter's byline, and before the broadcast reporter's sign-off, is material framed by the format and *Weltanschauung* of the news organization, media, and vocation of journalism. Nevertheless, journalists do struggle for and obtain considerable autonomy. Reporters actively resist efforts by powerful sources and by editors to censor their material (for notorious examples, see RCN 1981c), and they have made legal gains by having protection in this regard written into their contracts with management (RCN 1981d). News-rooms are characterized by resistance and conflict over control of the news process, not by a conveyer-belt consensus within a smoothly running media machine (Ericson, Baranek, and Chan 1987). Moreover, as Meyrowitz (1985: 324) points out, journalists form the one group in society who are able to use their institutional and organizational resources to control news-media threats to their position as authorized knowers. While sources in all other institutions are vulnerable to having journalists attack their authority – indeed, the greater their formal authority the greater their vulnerability (ibid; Ericson, Baranek, and Chan 1989) – journalists can use their powers of selection, formatting, and authorship to minimize such threats to themselves.

News consumers are participants in the news process (Ericson 1991). Ultimately, as McLuhan argued, it is consumers who give media its content. To the extent that news helps them to understand 'what is important ... who is important, where important things happen, when to expect specific things, and why to think about these things' (Robinson and Levy 1986: 45), consumers use the news to represent order in their own lives. They intentionally seek knowledge that will help them with the chores of everyday life (Blumler and McQuail 1969; Blumler and Katz 1974; Levy and Windahl 1985). News influences specific chores: who to vote for; whether to return a microwave oven to the manufacturer because of an announced product defect; whether to avoid certain places because of an announced crime wave. News is also used as entertainment, as a 'companion,' and as a form of 'background noise' to other more pressing activities such as doing the ironing or driving to work (for a review, see Robinson and Levy 1986).

Specific to our focus on news of social deviance, law, and justice, news is also monitored and used for its lessons in law. Many people learn about law from exposure to television and other media of popular culture, not from direct experience in the legal system (Macauley 1987). As a social discourse, the law is recognized as valid more through the ways it is 'mediated' in popular culture than through its formal procedures or substantive content as construed in legal culture (Mathiesen 1987; Goodrich 1986; Macauley 1987). In popular culture, no one is outside of the law. Law is there as a 'normal' part of public conversation in the media, to be represented as well as obeyed. Thus people experience the law not only in terms of constraint, but also as a form of knowledge that allows them to visualize realities, including the authoritative structure of society. As such 'law is not a bounded set of norms ... but part of a distinctive manner of imagining the real' (Geertz 1983: 173).

Consumers are interactive with the news process. This is obvious in the case of regular news sources who are avid users because they need to stay on top of how they are being represented in the news and to produce further material to sustain a reasonable representation. However, people who are not regular sources also interact with news operatives in such forms as letters to the editor; other letters or calls of complaint, correction, or information not intended for publication; the use of consumer action lines or media ombudsmen; and doing 'vox pop' interviews. The interactive capacity of the media is perhaps most fully demonstrated in the success of televangelism, which has built empires – including universities, fantasylands, and the largest cable-television network in the United States – out of its techniques of convincing people that they should send in donations along with their letters asking for help, guidance, and prayer (Gardner 1987; Hoover 1988).

There is a range of views regarding the participation of the consumer in the news process. Towards one extreme are those who depict the consumer as a mere spectator at the public dramas enacted by journalists and elite authorized knowers, and who argue that this role fosters political indifference among people. For them, the free market of public opinion is as much a fiction as the free market of the economy: the reality is that powerful institutions control the media system to inculcate their messages into the mass consciousness with little effective opportunity to answer back (Adorno and Horkheimer 1979; D. Schiller 1986; H. Schiller 1989). People are not quite relegated to the status of empty vessels waiting to be filled up, but they are depicted as no better than spectators left to cheer the heros and boo the villains of news melodramas (Wagner-Pacifici 1986). News is 'inert' and it leaves people 'inert' because it has 'no genuine connection to our lives' and therefore can provide 'something to talk about but cannot lead to any meaningful action' (Postman 1985: 68, 76). Growing tired of echoing news clips and of their own voices, people are discouraged politically and their voices become inactive (Robinson 1976). In the process they defer to officials and experts of the administered society who parade before them in the news media.

Towards the other extreme are those who view people as highly active and interactive in their uses of news. These analysts claim that the news media are better in some respects than other media in communicating certain types of knowledge (Berry 1983); that this knowledge is variously sought and used by different types of people for further action (Blumler and McQuail 1969; Singer 1973; Blumler and Katz 1974; Robinson 1976; Levy and Windahl 1985); and that news therefore is an active agency in both participatory and pluralistic politics among groups (Robinson and Levy 1986: esp. 51–4).

Both these positions are correct about the role of news consumers, depending on what group of consumers is being considered, the social and cultural context of that group, and the purposes of group members. A lot of confusion and vacuous debate derive from working with the fiction of the general 'public,' instead of being specific about which public is using the news in which context and for which purpose. There is a need to classify particular publics within the knowledge structure of society and to delineate differences among them in the making and use of news. 'The differential choices of, and responses to, media content predominantly reflect differences in social structure and in the social distribution of opportunity' (McQuail 1986: 135; see also Fiske 1987: chap. 5).

The question of how people use the news is obviously related to the question of the effects of news content on readers. There is a long tradition of fear that the popular news media, with their penchant for reporting crime, sex, and scandal, have ill effects on ordinary people (Murdock 1982; Pearson 1983). In the contemporary period these fears have been translated into media-effects research, which tries to show that bad news has bad effects on individual behaviour (for reviews, see Rowland 1983; Gunter 1987).

Counter to this are more recent cultural theories that bad news has the effect of reproducing consensus about social order. It does so through the ritualistic qualities of social dramas (Gusfield 1981; Wagner-Pacifici 1986); through the 'politics of signification' in which élite sources maintain a monopoly over the media as a resource in the hegemonic process (Hall et al. 1978; Hall 1982); and through a reliance on established channels of official discourse, which are already framed to support the status quo (Tuchman 1978; Fishman 1980; Altheide and Johnson 1980).

Both research that argues that bad news has bad behavioural effects and research that argues that bad news reproduces law-and-order ideology in favour of the powerful are too simplistic in their renditions of media effects. The effects of content from all media vary substantially. There is variation according to whether the consumer is directly involved in the story as a source. There is variation according to whether the events are local or distant. There is substantial variation in how people attend to particular news communications, and what they recall. For some people the news can serve as a vehicle for debunking the hierarchy of authority and have a democratic levelling effect rather than lead them to embrace the authority structure. It can function this way both by showing the faults, foibles, and foul-ups of the powerful and by failing to conceal the staged pseudo-ness of official events and social dramas. The media foster a pluralism in values, morality, and belief systems, and the effect can be a 'deinstitutionalization' of stable meanings that have traditionally shored up major social institutions. It is the variation and pluralism fostered by the different media and market orientations in news communications that we explore in this volume. Prior to beginning our explorations, however, it is necessary to delineate the formal differences among newspapers, television, and radio media, and between quality- and popular-market orientations.

2

Media and Markets

Medium Differences

In the news process, reality is not a solid but a fluid. All knowledge is mediated by a medium, whether print, television, or radio. The medium does not stand apart from the work as a technological apparatus through which news operatives simply transmit their messages. Rather, the medium is 'any process, technique or technology that produces something visible from something invisible ... Media provide a means to visualize, identify, and locate meaning. Although media rely on symbols for communications, they also do something more: media arrange, define, and communicate meaning' (Altheide 1985: 39). As such, the particular medium the news operative uses is integral to his or her work, and he or she helps to constitute its meanings and uses. While the medium constrains the formats in which knowledge can be presented, it is also a means of discovery, creativity, and innovation. While the medium frames discourse, it also accomplishes it.

In this section we contemplate how the newspaper, television, and radio news media each have a distinctive influence on news discourse. We consider how each medium influences the use of particular news formats, sources, knowledge, and topics. This consideration provides the necessary analytical framework for our empirical inquiry into how news of crime, law, and justice varies by medium.

FORMATS

How something is communicated precedes what is communicated. News-papers, television, and radio have distinct formats. Each medium has different procedures for the selection, transmission, and reception of knowledge. Each medium differs in how it transcends the limits of time and space to make news available, and thereby creates a different social environment and context for thinking. Format differences yield variation in content, and ultimately, different consequences for the knowledge structure of society (Altheide 1985; Meyrowitz 1985; Crisell 1986). Thus how communications are mediated by formats has an importance beyond particular expressions of economic and political power in news accounts. This is the importance of 'media power' (Altheide 1985).

The news reality of each medium is a matter of *how* it presents knowledge in its established formats, rather than of *what* it presents. Aspects of format fundamentally delimit and shape the news product: for example, the time available for a broadcast-news bulletin and the space available in a newspaper; the sequencing of broadcast-news items and the layout of a newspaper; the technologies associated with the medium; and the beats available as routine rounds for acquiring preselected material from sources that is itself formatted for the purposes of the reporter's medium. The format requirements are paramount. Content must always fit the format, and it is therefore always secondary to the format.

> Any medium's first commitment is to itself as a legitimate format for the definition, recognition, and communication of meaning ... Whatever defines a particular medium, e.g. sound for radio and visuals for TV, will essentially define and shape how the event's temporal and spatial features will be translated into those of the listener or viewer. Furthermore, whatever content is produced, e.g. people, places, things, will be subservient to and largely a result of these format considerations. And, whatever elements of format are deemed the most important will weigh disproportionately on the resulting messages. (Altheide 1985: 40, 56)

A fuller appreciation of media and formats can be derived from a detailed comparison of the capacities and limitations of newspaper, television, and radio formats as summarized in table 2.1.

A basic point of comparison, from which several other points follow, is that the newspaper is a visual medium, television both visual and audio, and radio audio. The fact that radio has no visual capacity and is therefore 'a *blind* medium' (Crisell 1986: 3) is fundamental. Television can transmit printed material: some cable-television stations present nothing but news in print, and newscasts use printed vistas to identify sources and to highlight key points in a story. Newspapers can use still photographs, graphics, and visually 'catchy' headlines, captions, and layouts. While television and

TABLE 2.1
A comparison of newspapers, television, and radio news formats

Newspaper	Television	Radio
Visual	Visual and audio	Audio
Weak validation of context	Strong validation of context	Some validation of context
Least redundancy/ simplification	Considerable redundancy/ simplification	Most redundancy/ simplification
Considerable imaginative work	Least imaginative work	Most imaginative work
Narrative/symbolic/ abstraction	Most dramatization/ entertaining/concrete	Considerable abstraction dramatization/ entertaining/concrete
Least personalization	Most personalization	Considerable personalization
Structure with space	Structure with time	Structure with time
Least immediacy/past tense	Considerable immediacy/ present tense	Most immediacy/present tense
Largest number of items	Intermediate number of items	Least number of items
Longest items	Intermediate length of items	Shortest items
Linear/sequential	Mosaic/episodic	Mosaic/episodic
Static	Dynamic/continuous	Dynamic/continuous
Consistent/permanent/ a record	Ephemeral/evanescent	Ephemeral/evanescent
Self-pacing	Imposes own pace	Imposes own pace
Individual/primary activity	More social/secondary activity	Most social/secondary activity

newspaper words and visuals can gloss a lot, radio words gloss everything because there is no opportunity for visual interpretation of individual character and interactional contexts.

As their medium lacks a visual capacity, radio journalists are more limited in their ability to convey connotative meanings. There is, of course, a great deal of connotative potential in the use of words alone. As Monaco (1981: 131) observes, 'If denotation were the only measure of the power of a language, for example, then English – which has a vocabulary of a million or so words and is the largest language in history – would be over three times more powerful than French – which has only 300,000 or so words. But French makes up for its "limited" vocabulary with a noticeably greater use of connotation.' A particular skill required of the radio announcer is to keep the audience engaged by dropping in witty and entertaining connotations as he or she talks (Goffman 1981: chap. 5; Crisell 1986). Nevertheless, radio talk, and especially radio-news talk, must be presented within a very limited, simple, 'perfected' form, not only to be engaged and understood, but also so as not to connote meanings that might give offence to some segment of the audience (Goffman 1981: chap. 5). While music and other background sounds can be used in radio news (Crisell 1986), they are not used often.

Language use in newspapers is similarly restricted, but the restrictions are not as great. The newspaper has considerable latitude in arriving at connotative meanings by contrasting and juxtaposing pictures, headlines, and stories in its page layouts. 'In both television and the newspapers – especially the popular tabloids – there is as much attention given to, and signification in, the spatial composition as the sequence of verbal/written signs. The composition within the TV screen puts different iconic signs together so that they modify or reinforce each other's signification. The same is true of the combination of headline and picture and story in newspapers. We read them simultaneously, and this is where a picture can indeed be worth a thousand ideological words' (Hartley 1982: 31).

The film and video technologies of television greatly enhance its connotative capacity. The television journalist can use camera angles, lighting, and background staging 'props,' and editing to connote meaning. The television journalist can also combine visuals with sound – words, music, background noise – to connote ideologically (Fiske and Hartley 1978, chap. 3; Ericson, Baranek, and Chan 1987: chaps. 7 and 8).

The visual capacity of television allows it to bind its messages to the context in which they were produced. Through the use of sounds from the context of production, radio also has some capacity in this regard. 'Quotes in a newspaper may have nothing to do with the place in which the words were spoken, but a recording of a speech also captures aspects of the physical environment in which the speech was made' (Meyrowitz 1985: 122). Newspapers are limited to the use of still photographs, and these provide a relatively weak means of tying messages to context.

The greater the capacity to bind messages to context, the greater the validation powers of the medium. Television appears most valid because statements made by its sources can be contextualized in the real places in which they were made. As politicians who preen themselves for television interviews know best (Ericson, Baranek, and Chan 1989: chap. 4), television can capture not only the offices and assembly rooms where important decisions are made, but also the source's dress, demeanour, and direct reaction to questions, from which readings of character are made. Television's capacity to bind messages to context and thereby validate its messages accounts for the fact that survey research in Canada, Britain, and the United States consistently shows that readers find television news more believable, fair, and influential than radio news or newspapers (Glasgow University Media Group [GUMG] 1976: 1ff; Royal Commission on Newspapers [RCN] 1981b: 35; Robinson and Levy 1986; Fiske 1987).

Radio, too, has some power of validation, although extra effort is required to accomplish it. The radio journalist must establish context by describing the environment in which events are occurring, and by using surrounding messages, source clips, and news items. Background sounds associated with the context in which statements are made also provide validity, although these are used indexically rather than iconically. Radio sounds require 'textual pointing – support from the dialogue or narrative' (Crisell 1986: 51). The context of all radio sounds is provided by the script, just as the context of all television sounds and visuals is 'anchored' by the script (Barthes 1977: 39). While radio and television are validated through the ability to use 'actualities,' it is the written text that directs one to the meaning of those actualities and anchors them in a framework.

Newspaper journalists have a limited ability to do the same thing, for example, by writing pointed captions for still photographs. A still photograph of a demolished car wrapped around a tree, with the caption 'Drunk driving tragedy,' can serve as a poignant reminder about the 'terror' of impaired driving. Without the caption, the picture would be polysemous and serve as a reminder of the 'terror' of uncertain signs. Outside the use of still photographs, which is limited (see chapter 7), newspapers must rely upon the visual aspects of their layout (juxtaposing stories, using bold-type headlines, etc.) to magnify the contexts of their stories and to give them force and validity. Popular newspapers in particular use layouts in this way, while quality newspapers rely more upon the authority of their sources to validate what it is they have to say and to lend authority to the newspaper itself.

Compared to most other cultural products, news is quite redundant and simplified. Newspapers are the least redundant and simplified because they have the capacity to present long and complex items in a literate mode. They present detailed features either singly or in a series. They also present stories on a continuing basis, using a wide range of sources (characters) in detailed and subtle narratives. Whether in features or in complex continuing stories, newspapers are more capable of introducing experts and their specialist knowledge than is television or radio news.

Television news is much more simplified and redundant than that in newspapers. It tends towards the concrete and dramatic and has great difficulty in being subtle. Its representations are sometimes 'cartoon stick-figure like' (Gitlin 1980). While television can use its visual capacity to establish context and to present written materials on the screen, this is of little help when it comes to detail and expert knowledge. It is difficult to watch and listen to detailed, specialized knowledge being conveyed because the television-audience member, unlike the newspaper reader, has no chance for retrieval, for introducing his or her own redundancy, unless he or she goes to the trouble and expense of recording the material and playing it over. While specialist knowledge is conveyed on television, it is revealing that 'ideas' programs – such as 'Realities' on TVOntario and 'Ideas' on CBC Radio – provide follow-up printed transcripts of what was said so that the reader can introduce his or her own redundancy at leisure. It is also revealing that in televised distance-education programs, such as those offered by the Open University and the BBC in Britain, the written textual materials are paramount and the broadcast materials are secondary. 'Paulu has pointed out that students of the Open University are expected to spend 65 per cent of their time reading and only 10 per cent of their time listening or viewing (1981: 270); more recently Bates has conceded that broadcasting is a relatively minor component of its teaching system (1984: 139)' (Crisell 1986: 114).

Lacking television's visual capacity, radio is forced to be even more simplified and redundant. 'Radio is the art of communicating meaning at first hearing' (Crisell 1986, quoting Lawrence Gillian of BBC Radio). Communicating meaning at first hearing is difficult because our ears are not terribly 'intelligent.' We tend to miss a lot and forget even more when what we hear is not augmented by something seen. Hence radio talk is reduced to being, as far as possible, simple, redundant, and without the errors typical in natural conversation. Radio is a kind of 'perfect speech machine' (Goffman 1981: chap. 5).

It is a general truth that much language is written down precisely because its meaning is too complex to be assimilated by ear ... And it is certainly the case that radio language will not be easily followed unless it is syntactically fairly simple or else fairly concrete in subject-matter ... [when] ideas and arguments become more abstract and their expression is premeditated, or when they require sustained explanation or specialist knowledge, the radio medium is less effective (McWhinnie 1959: 49–50). The BBC's Audience Research Department once tested a group of people on how much they could understand of a talk intended for the 'average' Light Programme listener: the average listener in the group could correctly answer only 28 per cent of the questions which were asked about the talk after it was broadcast (Silvey 1974: 141). Indeed it has been observed that the importance of the radio interviewer is not only as the poser of questions but as the interpreter of answers, the 'plain man' who in brief paraphrases renders the complex or specialist responses of the expert into language intelligible to the lay public (Cardiff 1980: 38). (Crisell 1986: 62; see also Goffman 1981: esp. 241)

The radio listener must make up for being blind by using his or her imagination. The visualization function of imagination is to an extent provided for by the visual capacities of television and newspapers. In relation to radio, however, the listener must supply the visualization, that is, making something visible to the mind because it is not visible to the eye. This includes imagining the setting, the characters, and even the facts of the matter. The listener must interpret the words as symbols of what they represent, and the voice (accent, stress) as an index of the character who is speaking. In radio, 'speech must be regarded as both typographic and photographic, as equivalent not only of the newspaper text but in many cases of its photographs' (Crisell 1986: 88). As Crisell (ibid: 116) also observes, radio 'is the only medium in which reality is in some sense directly presented yet must *at the same time* be imagined.'

While the visual capacity of television means that the television viewer has to do less imaginative work, there is still a considerable amount of visualization required (Fiske 1987: chap. 5). While television news *seems* to present reality more or less directly, it is nevertheless a highly mediated product that is produced out of considerable imaginative work by journalists and sources, and requires considerable imaginative work by its audience members. The following observation of Monaco (1981: 136–7) regarding the imaginative work required of the cinema viewer is equally applicable to the role of the television-audience member.

> Just as, in general, our sense of cinema's connotation depends on understood comparisons of the image with images that were not chosen (paradigmatic) and images that came before and after (syntagmatic), so our sense of the cultural connotations depend on understood comparisons of the part with the whole (synecdoche) and associated details with ideas (metonymy). Cinema is an art and a medium of extensions and indexes. Much of its meaning comes not from what we see (or hear) but from what we don't see or, more accurately, from an ongoing process of comparison of what we see with what we don't see. This is ironic, considering that cinema at first glance seems to be an art that is all too evident, one that is often criticized for 'leaving nothing to the imagination.' Quite the contrary is true.

Newspapers invite some conceptualization and abstraction, whereas radio and especially television must deal with the concrete and do so in a dramatic and entertaining way. Newspapers can be somewhat discursive, while radio and television tend to be more expressive and 'presentational' (Meyrowitz 1985: 93ff), providing 'experience' and tertiary understanding.

Television in particular is rich in its expressive dimensions, allowing a reading of people and how they answer that is unavailable to the other media, especially newspapers. As Meyrowitz (ibid: 103, 108) observes, it is therefore acceptable for a politician to appear on television reading a speech everyone knows was prepared by someone else, but it would not be acceptable for that someone else to appear on television reading a speech everyone knows was prepared by the politician. Moreover, television allows certain charismatic characters – such as the Polish Solidarity leader Lech Walesa – to become *powerful* communicators expressively, even though they are rather inarticulate discursively.

Newspapers try to convey reality by being 'realistic' in discursive terms, while radio and especially television try to convey reality by 'realism' in dramatic terms. Radio (Pietropaolo 1982) and television (Fiske and Hartley 1978; Fiske 1987) therefore are much more attuned to entertaining presentations. Television producers are directed to treat news as theatre and to keep the entertaining features uppermost (Epstein 1974; Cayley 1982). While snippets of information are dropped in along the way, and form the basis for doing the story in the first place, an entertaining angle and visuals provide the frame (Ericson, Baranek, and Chan 1987). Even serious matters must be treated in this way, 'lightened' more than 'enlightening,' 'livened' more than 'enlivening.' This is why, in Postman's (1985) view, television is contributing to the Huxleian nightmare that we are 'amusing ourselves to death.'

Personalization is part of the entertainment formula, especially in broadcast media. People tune in to radio and television to spend time with their favourite personalities, whether they be soap-opera stars, news anchorpersons, sports heroes, or regular news sources. In the broadcast-news media, there is also the tendency to simplify stories by personalizing them through the eyes of people involved. While newspapers also personalize to a considerable degree – for example, people like to read a regular column by their favourite opinionated columnist, and they like to read about their favourite television personalities in the newspaper – they arguably do so less often because the medium does not have the same expressive and dramatic dimensions of tertiary understanding available to radio and especially to television.

Television and radio use time as the major structuring agent, whereas newspapers use space. The auditory codes of television and radio exist in time, and give the sense that they are dealing in the 'here and now.' They are 'present-tense,' seeming 'to be an account of what *is* happening rather than a record of what *has* happened' (Crisell 1986).

Some of the differences among media in this regard relate to the practicalities of production. Newspaper production – even with the aid of electronic media such as word processors and computer-assisted editing and printing techniques – is still relatively cumbersome and slow. As a result, newspapers cannot compete in terms of immediacy. The very latest news has the least chance of making it into the newspaper ahead of broadcast media. While it has been argued that television is much more immediate than is the newspaper (e.g., RCN 1981b: 105), television journalists are encumbered by the need to obtain visuals and to edit them as scripted. To achieve a predictable supply, most of what television journalists cover is prescheduled and pre-scripted, and a lot of what they broadcast is prepackaged and days old (Epstein 1974; Schlesinger 1978; Ericson, Baranek, and Chan 1987).

Radio is most instantaneous and spontaneous. Radio can link an event and listeners very quickly. For example, radio can report a traffic jam quickly so that the knowledge is very helpful to listeners; by the time television and newspaper journalists are able to report it, the problem is likely to be over and therefore the knowledge is unhelpful. Moreover, radio listeners are often in a better position to receive the knowledge, since radio can be attended to in a greater variety of settings (e.g., while driving an automobile, while working) than can newspapers or television. Radio also has a 'rotating feature' (Altheide 1985: 54) whereby key items are repeated in frequent newscasts or special bulletins so that they are unlikely to be missed by anyone who is tuned into the station even for a relatively short time. Nevertheless, radio news is often less immediate than it seems. In face of limited budgets, radio journalists also do a lot of prescheduling and pre-scripting in a narrow range of preselected beats. While radio provides the illusion of 'fresh talk' (Goffman 1981: 172), the reality is usually scripted talk that narrows the speaker into the redundant grooves and recurrent paths of story themes and language.

The need to structure in time, and to hold audience attention through successive items, means that television and radio journalists are limited to a few items per newscast, and to brief items. In comparison, newspaper journalists have scope for a much larger number of items and for longer items, knowing that their readers will pick and choose among them. In a given day's news output, newspapers have a substantial number of items, television considerably less, and radio less still. Television and radio make up for this through other 'information programming' formats, including documentaries, talk shows, and investigative features. However, within the news genre itself broadcast media tend to limit themselves to a few items. For example, a ten-minute radio newscast, at 160–180 words per minute, is equivalent in words to only one and one-half columns of a newspaper (Crisell 1986: 71). The main evening television-news show typically contains fewer words than a single page of a broadsheet quality newspaper. While it is contentious as to whether more words provide more knowledge, it is clear that the brevity of broadcast-news shows and items indicates how limited they are in discursive potential.

The newspaper page layout allows for a mosaic-like, creative juxtaposition on a given page, although the overall presentation in print is linear and sequential, especially within the story. In contrast, television and radio are much more mosaic-like in their presentation as well as between items. They make a collage of very brief (ten- to fifteen-second) clips from sources and journalists to capture a sense of what has gone on and who the key players seem to be. While several items are sometimes combined into a 'wrap' with a theme, the presentation is still episodic and sometimes even strobe-like in effect. Reduced to the condition of advertising, and even overlapping with it (Fiske and Hartley 1978; Postman 1985), broadcast news paints an abstract mosaic of the world even while appearing to be closest to reality and to involve little imaginative work.

Television and radio have the related feature of presenting their picture of the world in motion. Their clips and items are presented continuously and therefore have a dynamic quality, in contrast to the newspaper, which is relatively static. This feature relates also to the element of immediacy raised earlier. In motion, television and radio seem to be very much in the present tense. Static, newspapers seem to be very much in the past tense. As Williams (1989) observed, while you can 'read all about it' in newspapers, the newspaper statement that 'a man was shot' has a less immediate and realistic quality than television-news pictures of a man *being* shot.

Researchers of broadcast news have shown that a lot can be read into it if only one takes the time to record it, stop its motion, and keep it still. When broadcast news is not captured in this way, it imposes its own pace, and people experience it as ephemeral and evanescent. All television-news sources have had the experience of having a friend say, 'I saw you on television last night but I can't remember what you said. What was it about?' The image lingers, but most of the details have evaporated. In contrast, newspapers are characterized by self-pacing. Readers can repeatedly review a permanent *record* that is consistent in presentation and tone. As a record, the newspaper functions not only as a reference work of the activities of contemporary élites (RCN 1981g; Ericson, Baranek, and Chan 1989), but also a rich source for social historians. Crisell (1986: 72–4) ably summarizes comparative dimensions of these elements.

> The language of newspapers is permanent: the reader sets her own pace and can reread what she has missed or cannot understand. This means that the press is capable of considerable linguistic variety. It can therefore divide the heterogeneous audience with which every mass medium is confronted into different intellectual levels by providing different kinds of newspapers for different kinds of reader ... The language of radio is evanescent. The radio newsreader sets an arbitrary pace and his words dissolve into thin air ... This means that however complex the material – and complexity is especially

likely in news, documentary and educational programmes – it must be expressed in language which is fairly simple and straightforward in style and diction. Since radio lacks the linguistic range of newspapers we would expect it to be less capable of providing different levels of output for different kinds of listeners and to remain confronted with a largely heterogeneous audience. This certainly seems to be the case with television, whose language code is also evanescent ... In both television and radio the heterogeneous nature of the viewers imposes constraints and restraints on the referential power of the message, but the nature of the contact makes a prior, even more basic imposition for it requires that the message should be relatively simple: and it must be even simpler in the case of radio since it is unassisted by visual codes and must therefore be apprehensible through ear alone.

The newspaper is read more as a primary activity and individually. While it may be read while doing other things – talking on the telephone, chatting to one's husband, listening to the radio, hectoring one's children, watching television – it is often read in isolation from all other social activities. In contrast, television and especially radio are typically used as secondary activities while doing something else, and this frequently includes being in the presence of other people. Most radios, and some television sets, are portable and can be used while driving, working, lying on the beach, etc. They accompany the flow of the day, providing a 'presence' and an 'aural environment' (Monaco 1981: 375) or 'sound' whose function goes beyond particular content. Meyrowitz's (1985: 90) observations on television in this regard are also applicable to radio.

A great part of the social significance of television ... may be less in what is *on* television than in the very existence of television as a shared arena. Television provides the largest simultaneous perception of a message that humanity has ever experienced ... Recognition of television's role as a new public arena solves a number of mysteries surrounding television viewing, including: why people complain so bitterly about television content but continue to watch so much of it, why many Americans say they turn to television for 'most' of their news even though – by any objective standard – there is remarkably little news on television, and why people who purchase video tape machines often discover they have little interest in creating 'libraries' of their favourite television programs.

SOURCES

We have already considered how media format requirements influence journalists in their selection and use of sources (pp. 16–17; Altheide 1985;

Ericson, Baranek, and Chan 1987). Media format requirements also influence sources in their selection and use of journalists (Ericson, Baranek, and Chan 1989; Schlesinger 1988, 1989). Through their procedures for controlling knowledge, different sources create different media environments, more suitable to one medium than others. For example, we found that, because of the nature of legal discourse, the fact that electronic media were excluded from the courtroom, and the ways in which reporters were effectively excluded from back regions where case settlements were negotiated, the court beat was primarily print-oriented (Ericson, Baranek, and Chan 1989). In contrast, on the police beat, the major-occurrence news releases, with updates on crimes and investigations, were especially attuned to the hourly update requirements of radio stations and therefore radio reporters were at the core of the reporters' subculture on the police beat (ibid). A further contrast was provided on the legislature beat, where politicians and their officials favoured television because of the assumed size and breadth of television's audience and the impact of its images (ibid). While radio reporters had a leading place on the police beat, they were referred to as mere 'spit collectors' at the legislature, indicating the fact that they picked up only residual material from interviews and questions framed by reporters working in other media. Different news requirements of different sources *vis-à-vis* medium format capabilities lead them to favour a particular medium, and variation in content across media is the result.

Each medium offers sources different formats for expressing their authority. Meyrowitz (1985) argues that a print-oriented society is supportive of hierarchy based on specialized and compartmentalized knowledge, whereas electronic media, especially television, tend to undermine claims to authority based on specialized knowledge and thereby foster a levelling and democratic effect.

> In a print society, the graded complexity of print data and the highly com-
> partmentalized nature of print audiences leads to high esteem for 'experts'
> (the 'top' in the field) and 'specialists' (people whose knowledge is focused
> in one tiny cluster of information about a particular subject) ... [In the elec-
> tronic society] messages from all bodies of knowledge are more equally
> accessible to all people. While such messages, especially as presented on
> radio and television, often offer more 'awareness' than 'understanding,' the
> new communication pattern works to undermine the stature of authorities
> whose knowledge and skills are based on isolated communication networks.
> (ibid: 326–7)

Meyrowitz's observations help explain the fact that while politicians and other members of the élite gravitate towards television to express their authority, they turn to the newspaper as a source of authority. When it comes to actually using knowledge available in the news in the course of their activities, members of élites who are regular news sources favour the quality newspaper. For example, in a survey of 602 élite decision-makers, 55 per cent said they relied on daily newspapers, especially the *Globe and Mail*, while only 22 per cent expressed a preference for television, 13 per cent for radio (mainly the CBC), and 10 per cent for periodicals (RCN 1981b).

KNOWLEDGE

The format requirements of a medium create an affinity with particular types of knowledge. Newspapers, television, and radio vary in the degree to which they each rely on knowledge that is primary (factual, asking 'What happened?'), secondary (explanatory, asking 'Why did it happen?'), tertiary (emotional, empathetic, asking 'What was it like to be involved in what happened?'), and evaluative (moral, asking 'Was what happened good or bad?'), and involves recommendations (asking 'What should be done about what happened?').

The distinction among these types of knowledge in any given news item is a matter of context, not syntax (Runciman 1983: 38). The journalist, like the novelist, uses various source clips, including his or her own, as part of a spoken dialogue to sustain a narrative. 'Whatever an individual character may say, its meaning will be determined not by his or her intentions or situation, but by placing of the interview in the overall context of the story. The terms he or she uses may be taken approvingly, or be contradicted and appear to be cynical, short-sighted, or bloody-minded ... All the individual voices, like individual notes in a musical score, are then orchestrated together with the overall news story. The effect of this on the narrative is to provide it with authenticity, the *reality effect*' (Hartley 1982: 109–10).

While the intended effect of the news story is to make consumers believe that they are witnesses to reality, reality is always inferential. What appears as iconic is actually the result of a process in which journalists and sources have necessarily gone beyond the knowledge apprehended by them, reconstructing it in ways that displace the observed world. The reality is that the news is embedded in the criteria of rational acceptability of news practice, and as such it is not mind- or discourse-independent. News discourse is not about objects; it constitutes objects. News reality depends on how the comments of journalists and sources have been contextualized in the narrative, and ultimately on how this contextualization is visualized by the consumer.

This context-dependency means that it is not a straightforward matter to specify what is a fact, explanation, empathetic understanding, evaluation, or recommendation. For example, depending on the context, the word 'inconsiderate' can be used as part of a statement of fact, explanation, evaluation, or prediction (Putnam 1981: 138–9; see also Dworkin 1986). The same can be said for many words that appear regularly in news discourse, including words taken from the discourses of professions that deal with social problems. For example, the psychiatrist's use of 'psychotic' and the sociologist's use of 'exploitation' vary in their knowledge-use, depending on their context within the text. Thus the term 'psychotic' can involve a mere report, an explanation, a prediction, and/or an evaluation (Runciman 1983: 38). As Putnam (1981: 139) observes, 'When we think of facts and values as independent we typically think of "facts" as stated in some physicalistic or bureaucratic jargon, and the "values" as being stated in the most abstract value terms, e.g., "good," "bad." The independence of value from fact is harder to maintain when the facts themselves are of the order of "inconsiderate," "thinks only about himself," "would do anything for money." '

These considerations indicate that even primary (factual) understanding can be polysemous. Reformulation of the factual depends on the methods people use to attribute meaning to the world, including especially the medium formats and language they use for what they observe. A fact cannot be photographed. In examining a photograph, we select certain features and express them in the forms and linguistic terms available to us. All factual empirical statements are entwined with interpretation (in the case of science, see Ryle 1949; Mulkay 1979; Brannigan 1981). In accomplishing primary understanding, the journalist does not simply reproduce the interpretations of his or her sources, he or she gives them a 'constructive interpretation' (Dworkin 1986: esp. chap. 4). That is, his or her interpretations contest and pass judgment on the interpretations of his or her sources. Similarly news consumers engage in 'constructive interpretation,' reading in an interpretation that contests and passes judgment on the interpretations of journalists. We know things only in terms of their significance to us. We always have to propound the world in which our description makes sense (Geertz 1983). Even the simplest facts are differentially interpreted in different contexts (Monaco 1981: 122; Fiske 1987: chap. 5). The reading or interpretation of facts gives them a fictive character, yet such fictions are essential to making sense of a communication and its context. As Crisell (1986: 124) observes with respect to radio, 'however factual the events which the commentator describes, they must be "created" in the listener's mind, very probably in a form which is in many respects different from the reality itself, and are in that sense a "fiction." '

Consider that statements that are descriptive on one level may also be read as evaluative. This is so because the very language we use to describe the world depends on our values (Putnam 1981). Thus descriptive terms may also bear evaluations and yet be assessed as 'fair comment' by journalists. As Hartley (1982: 27) observes, 'the sign *moderate* may be used to denote a politician or union leader, but it also connotes approval of their status and therefore of that individual. Much of the media's attention is devoted to giving people labels that denote their job or status, but these also connote the attitude or value they attach to it. The trick is to make multi-accentual connotation look like uni-accentual denotation.'

Another reason why factual or descriptive statements are read evalua-tively is because the facts that people construct are related to the moral conclusions they draw (Midgley 1982). The use of facts in making moral judgments best explains why sources take the news so seriously even though they are very sceptical about its factual accuracy (Ericson, Baranek, and Chan 1989). Sources are sensitive to 'the cultural significance of mass communication for assessment of one's moral qualities by others. In this sense all media reports are sanctionable as public documents and thereby call for an accounting (Scott and Lyman 1968)' (Altheide 1985: 192). The news is taken seriously because of its moral power, not because it is the best available source of primary facts.

The news media frequently value the facts through tertiary (emotional, empathetic) understanding, addressing the question, 'What is it like to be involved in what happened?' Sources provide 'emotional exhibitions' (Wagner-Pacifici 1986: 95) as part of the performance of their authority and how they wish others to value the facts of what happened. Television and radio have greater scope in this regard, including the use of emotive music on radio and emotive music and visuals on television (Epstein 1974: 242; Crisell 1986; Carriere and Ericson 1989: chap. 3). In the extreme, tertiary knowledge is a synthetic creation of sources and journalists that can intrude on or even extinguish other knowledge potentially available in the news item. When this occurs the news consumer is left with the feeling that 'we had the experience but missed the meaning' (T.S. Eliot, quoted by Gitlin 1980: 233).

The valuing of facts is also a matter of medium. News accounts involve technologically mediated metaphorical reconstructions that emphasize particular emotions and social and political realities. For example, on television 'an apparently direct or iconic representation of reality is more accurately a metaphorical reconstitution of that reality in the terms of the television medium. The similarity we perceive between signifier and signified should be thought of as a *constructed equivalence*; the metaphoric real world shown on television does not *display* the real world but *displaces* it' (Fiske and Hartley 1978: 48).

In contributing to the valuing of facts, each medium thus bears ideological functions (Elliott 1979; Altheide 1985; Meyrowitz 1985). 'For example, TV news information has a certain look and rhythm to it. As long as this is associated with news and the contexts of these special effects are not exploited, then it looks fine, complete, good enough, even true ... [It] can be regarded as a feature of rational ideology in its own right, and, therefore, is far more persuasive and consequential than run-of-the-mill political preferences' (Altheide 1985: 234). The medium itself takes on a familiar, credible, authoritative character that makes the knowledge it presents seem acceptable, as if what it offers is all that one needs to know. This ideological power of a medium can transcend political and economic power in framing how people see events and in influencing actions taken in relation to those events (ibid: 71ff; Meyrowitz 1985; Ericson, Baranek, and Chan 1987, 1989).

Market Differences

News formats, sources, and knowledge also vary in accordance with the market orientation of media organizations. Newspapers in particular pursue distinct markets. 'Popular' newspapers seek acceptance through seeming to be close to reality. Their formats thus incorporate iconic elements, including pictures, brief items on simple themes, strongly opinionated columns on simple themes, colloquial expressions, and parochial interests. These elements are combined in an entertaining and lively manner. The presentation of material in an entertaining manner does not contradict the sense of being close to reality, but rather underpins it. Playing on the heart, and on lower regions of the anatomy, popular newspapers are able to effect a sense of what it is 'really' like to be involved in a situation. Material that is lively also seems 'alive,' and thus real.

'Quality' newspapers, by contrast, seek acceptance through more 'literary' and symbolic means. Their formats include longer items, features, and continuing stories on complex matters affecting business and political élites on a national and international scale. There is a concern with being a source of record both at the moment and historically, resulting in close attention to language and to mechanisms for correcting errors that exhume accuracy and authority.

There are also newspapers that try to encompass both ends of the spectrum, to be all things to all people. For example, in Toronto, while the *Sun* is explicitly a popular newspaper and the *Globe and Mail* is explicitly a quality newspaper, the *Star* is a mass newspaper that includes elements of both and is read *in addition to* the others (RCN 1981c: 70–1). Instead of finding a particular limited niche in the market, the mass newspaper tries to be the market itself.

An appeal to the mass market is more characteristic of broadcast media, especially television, because of their medium formats. There is particular pressure on broadcast outlets to appear popular when advertising revenue is a consideration. For reasons we shall outline shortly, and document in substantive chapters that follow, television news is least able to offer distinct popular and quality products. However, as Crisell (1986: 48–9) has shown, there is scope within radio to make news distinctly popular or quality in character.

FORMATS

The need to sell markets leads to particular news formats. News that is relatively discursive, and unadorned with sensational and dramatic constructions, fails to hold readers and therefore fails to sell goods (Seaton 1980: 96–7). Hence news, like the advertising system that supports it, moves in the direction of non-discursive, entertaining formats of presentation. Fifty years ago the Gallup organization discovered that 'more people read comic strips than the news,' and this 'led advertisers to exploit emotional symbols and techniques' (Draper 1986: 15). The success of this exploitation in advertising has had a recursive influence on news producers who use the techniques of advertising to hold their readers for advertising. For example, the news focus on sensational crimes is in part explained by their entertainment value. A survey of newspapers in Ontario found that the greater the advertising space in the newspaper the greater the emphasis on crime news (Dussuyer 1979: 100). A television news producer informed us that 'news must be packaged in a glittering way so that viewers who have just finished watching Carol Burnett will stay tuned for the news. In noting that the 'Newshour' rating had gone up to 24 per cent of the audience in the previous eighteen months, this producer observed that Kellogg's does not spend most of its money on cornflakes, but rather on the cornflakes box' (Ericson, Baranek, and Chan 1987: 86).

Advertising offers no opportunity for assessing products on the basis of truth claims. Its claims are neither true nor false, just more interesting or less interesting, more imaginative or less imaginative, more beautiful or less beautiful. Television news in particular takes on these characteristics of advertising. It offers brief clips that show people making claims to authority, knowledge, and doing good, but this is largely presentational and non-discursive and as such does not allow for judgments of truth (Meyrowitz 1985; Postman 1985). Viewed this way, news is indeed a 'social hallucinogen' for a commercial culture in which the 'boundaries between news, entertainment, public relations and advertising, always fluid historically, are now becoming almost invisible' (D. Schiller 1986: 36, 21).

Advertising affects news organizations in other ways. In at least one newspaper chain in Canada, favourable news treatment for advertisers has been reinforced by promoting advertising managers to the publisher's chair and to other senior and influential positions that affect editorial content (RCN 1981b: 69; RCN 1981c: 100). People in the news business, of course, appreciate that news and advertising are entwined. For example, in commenting on a newspaper's decision to refuse two advertisements, the Ontario Press Council declared, 'Advertising is a form of news and the paper has a responsibility to publish advertising news whether it agrees with it or not' (RCN 1981b: 77). Ask an academic colleague why he bought a copy of the local popular newspaper and he will tell you that it has the best selection of advertisements for stereo equipment.

Distinctive quality and popular news products, and the organizational differences associated with them, may be more applicable to radio news, and especially to newspapers, than to television news. Research has shown repeatedly that television news production and products are similar. Epstein (1974) reported no substantial differences in the approach and coverage of the three national television networks in the United States, and the Glasgow University Group (1976) reported similarities in industrial news coverage among the BBC1, BBC2, and ITN channels in Britain. A study of television news comparing Ireland, Sweden, and Nigeria (Golding and Elliott 1979) concluded that there was a 'broad similarity of news production practices and of the news values embodied in the output of these three quite diverse societies, despite the distinctive relationships of broadcasting to the state in each case. The study presented broadcast news as an "international genre" with significant national variations, and argued for an understanding of news as ideology, in its emphasis upon consensus, in its alignment with the assumptions and preoccupations of the powerful, and on its inherent inability to provide "a portrayal of social change" or to reveal "the operation of power within and between societies"' (Golding, Murdock, and Schlesinger 1986: 4–5). These findings suggest that the format requirements of the television medium may predominate in limiting the range of what it is possible to present (Altheide 1985).

The format limitations of the television medium are a major reason why television news is directed at a mass audience. A newspaper can build its readership by appealing to an aggregate of minorities, each of whom will select and read only particular sections and items from the total volume available in the newspaper. Television must do the selecting of items for its audience and hold its attention through the newscast. Therefore television includes material that is attractive to the widest possible range of people, which means an appeal to the lowest-common-denominator mass audience. 'Whereas individual newspapers are assumed to be the competing parts of the market, individual broadcasters are assumed to be the market-place itself' (Epstein 1974: 64). Competition is for a share of the total audience – people with their television sets on during a time segment – rather than for a share of a more specialized or narrow market. Television has the greatest capacity for this popular appeal because of its pictorial strength, sense of realism, and simple language. Television news is accessible to virtually everyone, including young children (Meyrowitz 1985: chap. 13). The popular formula of dramatic, entertaining, simple, and short items is adopted by television journalists to fulfil the competitive requirements for audience share, and form takes precedence over content (Elliott 1978, 1979). Hence television journalists converge on similar topics, sources and story angles, and the popular/quality distinction is blurred.

Some of the format requirements of radio create a popular tendency in its newscasts. Like their counterparts in television, radio journalists must select items for their listeners, and hold their attention through the newscast with limited language and dramatic structuring. This means that radio news shows are relatively short and each item is brief; that coverage focuses on dramatic events and conflict; and that such techniques as alternating voices and sound actualities are used to strengthen the auditory appeal. These components combine to enhance the listener's ability to visualize what is being said, to make the radio news story as 'photographic' as it can be without the actual capacity to present a visual.

In spite of these tendencies, the radio medium does not preclude a quality orientation. Radio cannot be like the quality press. Its language is not that of the quality London *Times* or Toronto *Globe and Mail*. Because it is auditory, radio news must use a more limited vocabulary and a less complicated syntax than the *Times* or *Globe and Mail*. But neither is radio language that of the popular English *Sun* or Toronto *Sun*. Radio news has a greater need for a more objective, and a less individualistic, emotive, and opinionated tone than popular newspapers exhibit.

Crisell's (1986: chap. 4) detailed comparison of a popular newscast and a quality newscast, both emanating from the BBC radio network, shows clearly that the popular/quality distinction holds for radio. In language, presentation, content, and some aspects of format, popular and quality radio newscasts are very different. 'For all the linguistic compression which the medium imposes, its inability to editorialize and its need to use its voices not only for reportage but also as actuality, radio news does succeed to a remarkable extent in paralleling and evoking the differences between the popular and quality newspapers' (ibid: 99). For example, Crisell's analysis shows that in the popular radio outlet he studied, the newscast is presented as an enclave within an existing entertainment (pop music) show. It therefore tends to assimilate news to the wider broadcasting context of its entertainment programming. This assimilation is indicated, for example, by the title for the show – 'Newsbeat' – and by the fact that the show frequently ends with an item on pop music, such as an interview with a pop star. This packaging is based on the assumption that people listen to the station for the music, not the news, and so the news is in essence made part of a 'newsic' formula. In contrast the quality radio outlet studied by Crisell has a more discrete, self-contained, and much longer news show. The news show is therefore a program in its own right, rather than, in effect, an extended news summary. It is presented with greater detail and complexity on the assumption that people tune in because they want news, that they are seeking knowledge and detail rather than merely the station's 'sound.'

The format of newspapers allows their journalists to focus on various special interests, and thereby to increase circulation through the aggregate of interest groups who buy it for their particular purposes. Alternatively, newspapers can tailor their coverage to the interests of a single narrow or specialized group, who can be sold to advertisers whose products and services are of special interest to the group. These possibilities exist in particular because the newspaper is capable of linguistic variety, has a permanency to its language, and provides the self-pacing such permanency allows. The basic distinction is between the popular newspaper which is simple in structure and colloquial in its use of vocabulary, and gives more emphasis to emotive or tertiary understanding, and the quality newspaper, which tends towards great complexity in structure, 'literary' use of vocabulary, and primary and secondary (explanatory) understanding presented in an 'objective' tone.

While newspapers retain these flexible features of their format, there have been encroachments on the autonomy of their formats from the broadcast media, especially from television. All newspaper journalists have been affected by how television formats dominate particular beats, such as the legislature (RCN 1981b: 135; Meyrowitz 1985; Ericson, Baranek, and Chan 1989). They have also been affected by the peculiar conception of objectivity fostered in broadcast news, where an allegation is quoted from one source, a counterpoint is made by a spokesperson for the organization subject to the allegation, and truth is held to reside somewhere in between (Epstein 1974; Tuchman 1978; Ericson, Baranek, and Chan 1987). This approach has increased the expectation of impartiality in all media and has made the bias of newspapers appear increasingly improper (A. Smith 1980: 179).

Popular newspapers in particular have changed in tune with television formats. They are explicitly formatted in terms of television, and serve as a complement to television. The Toronto *Sun* has been described as the closest thing to television in print. Various executives in popular newspaper organizations have acknowledged the impact of television. 'John Hamilton, publisher of the Calgary *Albertan* at the time it was converted into a tabloid in 1977, said "Our format of tight editing rules related to young people brought up on television. They're used to brief presentation of news." Pierre Péladeau, whose two daily tabs have half Canada's tabloid circulation and enjoyed the fast growth of any Canadian newspaper in the 1970s, sees them as a complement to television' (RCN 1981b: 82). Entwined with this influence of television on newspaper formats is television's impact on newspaper marketing. The growth of life-style, entertainment, and sports sections of newspapers is associated with the spread of television, as is the 'zoning' of special supplements within a newspaper to different market areas. More fundamentally, television has become predominant in framing and demarcating the market that newspapers must feed into. 'The modern newspaper is essentially reaching out towards the *television* audience, a demographically defined audience, paid for by advertisers, which requires the kind of detail that turns into spectacle or reveals the panorama of events lying behind the reports that have already reached the audience in aural and/or visual terms' (A. Smith 1980: 241).

SOURCES

Market considerations, blended with media format requirements, have a substantial influence on the selection and use of sources.

Given their tendency towards non-discursive, entertaining, and simple accounts of events, outlets oriented to the popular market are likely to use fewer sources. They are also likely to rely more heavily on particular types of sources offering particular types of knowledge: officials who provide them with primary facts already formatted for their medium/market, and individual citizens who offer tertiary understanding that fits their 'vox pop' format.

The subtleties and nuances of source selection and use vary with the local market environment. In large urban markets with dozens of news outlets, there is sometimes a condition of 'overproduction.' This condition leads news outlets to pursue more unique stories with unofficial or minority-status sources in an effort to capture at least some of the market seeming to be different.

Advertising is a major factor in source selection. Those who advertise regularly are often given favourable treatment in news items and features about the wonders of their company and its products. This is especially the case with smaller, local newspapers and radio stations, and with feature sections of large newspapers such as those dealing with entertainment, travel, and real estate (RCN 1981b: 69; RCN 1981c: 100). Private-sector sources themselves treat the news accordingly, seeing access primarily in terms of their own marketing needs (Ericson, Baranek, and Chan 1989).

Sources in government are also oriented to their own marketing needs, blending news with advertising in the hope that the public will remain faithful to the belief that they are good public servants. However, with sources in government there is not a crude exchange of advertising revenue for news space that serves marketing functions, but rather a tit-for-tat subtle favouritism with particular outlets because their formats best fit the source's needs (Ericson, Baranek, and Chan 1989). For example, the police favour popular news outlets because these outlets offer a format suitable for communication of the primary facts of major occurrences at the core of police-defined newsworthiness (Ericson 1989; Wheeler 1986; Fishman 1981; Chibnall 1977). The police shy away from quality outlets because these outlets largely eschew the reporting of crime incidents in favour of a focus on police mismanagement and procedural propriety. Moreover, quality outlets, especially quality newspapers, search out a greater number of sources and a more diverse range of source types, and present them more discursively to make innuendo about police deviance. The police therefore perceive quality news outlets as a threat rather than as an ally, and erect different physical, social, and cultural barriers to the access of journalists from quality outlets than is accorded to journalists from popular outlets (Ericson 1989). The different needs of news sources and news organizations in terms of media/market format considerations are clearly reflected in content.

KNOWLEDGE

The news media have always been criticized for pandering to their readership to create and sustain a market share. John Stuart Mill described journalism as 'the vilest and most degrading of all trades because more of affection and hypocrisy and more subservience to the basic feelings of others are necessary for carrying it on, than for any other trade, from that of a brothel-keeper up.' In recent times there are complaints that journalism is done by market survey (RCN 1981b): deciphering what news readers want to fit with their 'life-styles,' which can in turn be linked to 'life-style' advertising. While reporters have little detailed knowledge of their readership (Schlesinger 1978; D. Clarke 1981; Ericson, Baranek, and Chan 1987), editors' expectations are framed by market considerations and they assign and edit accordingly (Seaton 1980). Hence news outlets with the same market orientation are likely to cover the same events, to talk to the same most influential sources involved in those events, and to formulate stories in similar terms. The result is pack journalism and convergence in news content.

These forces of convergence can also foster divergence. For example, the ascendancy of broadcast media has been accompanied by an advertising-driven need to appeal to a mass audience. In face of this need some newspapers try to appeal to a more limited readership that is attractive to particular advertisers. For example, quality newspapers take up an investigative and adversarial style that articulates with the institutional concerns of upscale readers who in turn are a market for upscale advertisers. The *Globe and Mail* has evolved to such a place within the Toronto news-media market. While finding a market niche in these terms leads to divergence in topics and sources on one level, on another level the product may not be different from more popular renditions of news. The popular news outlet continues its traditional formula identified by Mill, using salacious gossip, titillation, and sensationalism to allow its readers to be vicarious voyeurs, and then denouncing the very people and activities it preys upon (Roshier 1973). The quality news outlet does the same thing, only its targets are those prostituting themselves for the high life in established institutions (political corruption) more than those engaged in the low life of illicit prostitutions (vice and 'normal crime').

Ultimately the market orientation a news outlet tries to find for itself combines with its medium-format consideration to yield a distinct process of knowledge flow, system of knowledge, and type of knowledge. The popular format is characteristic of all television outlets because of medium considerations, and is chosen by particular radio and newspaper outlets for marketing purposes. It features particular knowledge: factual updating (largely bureaucratic constructs), evaluation and tertiary understanding (largely from the people as 'vox pop'), both of which are personalized and dramatized. Enclosed in these terms, the popular format is preferred by particular sources, especially the police, politicians, and others whose primary interest is helpful news and positive images (Ericson, Baranek, and Chan 1989). The quality format suits particular newspapers and radio outlets, but is available to television in a more limited way because of medium constraints. The quality news outlet features a more discursive presentation of knowledge: multiple institutional sources who offer greater depth in the form of explanation of events as well as evaluations and recommendations pertaining to legal change and political reform. Relatively more open in these terms, the quality format is preferred by particular sources, especially those who can benefit from particular instances of adversarial-style journalism to bring about the legal changes and political reforms they desire.

The market orientation a news outlet finds for itself also combines with its medium-format considerations to lead it in particular ideological directions. Popular news outlets tend towards strong ideological positions that are stated explicitly. For example, in their everyday crime reporting, they are strongly pro-police and pro–law and order; in their everyday international reporting they are strongly nationalistic and anti-communist. Quality news outlets offer their ideologies more gently. They appear more liberal, offering a greater number and wider range of sources and opinions, arriving at a particular ideological position only after a managed dialogue and debate.

Sources of Convergence

Our emphasis in this chapter has been on differences in media and market orientation of news outlets as these differences have a bearing on news formats, sources, knowledge, and topics. The emphasis on differences has provided an analytical starting-point for our empirical inquiry into how news of crime, law, and justice varies by medium and markets. However, we would be remiss if we failed to give weight to the many influences on news production that may yield similar news content across media and markets. We have already indicated some sources of convergence, including the important point that some factors that precipitate differences can also serve in contradictory ways to produce convergence. At this point it is worthwhile to make the sources of convergence more evident as they inform the empirical investigation that follows.

> We have the greatest, most sophisticated system for mass communication of any society that we know about, yet somehow mass communication becomes more and more synonymous with less communication ... We have the mistaken, conduit-metaphor influenced view that the more signals we can create, and the more signals we can preserve, the more ideas we 'transfer' and 'store.' We neglect the crucial human ability to reconstruct thought patterns on the basis of signals and this ability founders ... The conduit metaphor is leading us down a technological and social blind alley. That blind alley is mass communications systems coupled with mass neglect of the internal, human systems responsible for nine-tenths of the work in communicating. We think we are 'capturing ideas in words,' and funnelling them out to the greatest public in the history of the world. But if there are no ideas 'within' this endless flood of words then all we are doing is replaying the myth of Babel – centering it, this time, around a broadcasting tower. (Reddy 1979: 310)

Reddy articulates a pervasive sentiment that more media outlets have not brought better knowledge, and may be narrowing and trivializing public discourse (see also Postman 1985). In spite of the capabilities of each medium, and the competitive quest of news outlets for a different product that will secure a niche in the market-place, if anything the proliferation of news outlets may offer less diversity, not more. Why does the large urban news market-place – like the beer market-place or the automobile market-place – offer such a rich variety of brand names and yet end up being so bland?

One answer lies in monopoly capitalism and its relation to markets. In the case of newspapers, chains have become increasingly dominant, at least in the North American context (A. Smith 1980: 45–6; RCN 1981b: 9). The effect of the advertising-based chain monopolies has been to encourage journalism's peculiar version of objectivity, neutrality, and fairness, where overt and diverse opinion is reduced and blandness is produced. 'The professional code of the editor, and journalists as a whole, has been profoundly influenced by the evolution of the distribution methods of newspapers and their successive delineations of appropriate markets' (A. Smith 1979: 193). While 'narrowcasting' has expanded in recent years, the attitude in broadcasting is still " 'Least Objectionable Programming'' (LOP). That is, the key is to design a program that is least likely to be turned *off*, rather than a program viewers will activity seek out' (Meyrowitz 1985: 73). Even the Public Broadcasting System in the United States is dependent on corporate donors and therefore tends towards programming that will not offend and that is lacking in political relevance. It is difficult to show a direct link between advertising and particular features of news content. However, it is revealing that readers perceive the news as having been influenced by news organizations catering to advertisers. In survey research conducted for the Royal Commission on Newspapers (1981b: 36–7), 72 per cent of respondents said they believed newspapers play down facts in news items that might offend advertisers.

News outlets operating with different market orientations but within the same medium may converge in their coverage because of medium-format requirements. As addressed earlier (pp. 37–8), the format requirements of television make television-news production and products very similar, not only between outlets within a local market, but also between national networks and even in international comparisons. Television outlets compete head-on for a share of the total audience rather than dividing up into more narrow or specialized markets, and this inevitably leads all outlets into the popular formula of dramatic, entertaining, short, and simple items which are, in any event, most suited to the medium.

The impact of one medium upon another medium is also a source of convergence. As considered previously (pp. 39–40), television has had a major impact on newspapers. Some popular newspapers are explicitly formatted as the closest thing to television in print. They emphasize the visual, with display headlines, still photographs, and captions in bold type taking up more space in a story than the written narrative. More broadly, television has had a fundamental impact on newspaper marketing, essentially framing and demarcating the market that newspapers feed into.

Practices in news production also foster convergence. The knowledge-ability of journalists – the norms, values, and precedents of the craft – leads them to focus on similar topics, sources, and angles regardless of the medium or market orientation of their news organization (Schlesinger 1978; Tuchman 1978; Ericson, Baranek, and Chan 1987). The journalist's 'nose' for news seems to be the same, even if the details of what is required for each medium and market vary. It is the shared knowledgeability of journalists that leads to 'pack journalism': reporters covering news conferences, public hearings such as court cases or legislative proceedings, and continuing stories such as election campaigns, tend to focus on similar angles, use the same sources, and even reproduce the same 'quotable quotes.' It is as if journalists sometimes do no more than reflect a reality that is self-evident, at least to them. It is as if all that is required is to send one reporter to scoop up the facts, while the rest can simply polish them off and turn them into the symbolic gems required by their particular medium and market.

Pack journalism is compounded by the fact that journalists view existing news stories as their primary source of knowledge about newsworthiness (ibid). Broadcast journalists in particular rely on newspaper stories for their own ideas and assignments, with the result that 'newspapers are more of a source than a competitor' (Schlesinger 1978: 85). At some nth-level removed from what they are reporting on, broadcast journalists use newspaper reports verbatim, as background detail that they cite without attribution, for matching stories suitable to their medium, and as second-day leads that seek to further the story through a different angle, or at least a different twist. 'Newsmen come to see the print media as purveyors of *original* material while radio and TV extend or recirculate information, in the form of current affairs discussion or follow-up interviews. So newsmen turn to print media for information, and strengthen the pattern of dependence' (RCN 1981a: 2). As far as journalists are concerned, it is as if all one really needs to know is contained in the news, and one's only job is to repackage it in the different containers available in one's medium and market to make it appear new.

These journalistic practices are related to resources. The fewer the resources of a news outlet, the more it is dependent on a predictable supply of material from source bureaucracies and from other news outlets, and the greater the number of steps it is removed from the events reported on. Among the news media, radio stations tend to have the least journalistic resources and therefore are most dependent in this regard. Television stations are in an intermediate position, while newspapers have the most journalistic resources. Thus radio, with least resources, produces fewer items, shorter items, and more simple items that reproduce the bare essentials of stories as framed by sources and/or by previous newspaper stories. However, the limited aspects of radio news are not only a matter of resources. The radio medium is restrictive to the point where it may not be worthwhile for a radio organization to multiply the resources of its news division. Increased resources might not enhance its product greatly, and may even have a negative impact; for example, long items with multiple sources on complex matters might lead people to switch off mentally or literally.

A limited budget and therefore circumscribed content are characteristic of popular news outlets more than of quality news outlets. However, this is not a straightforward matter. For example, in our observation of the court beat in Toronto, we discovered that a popular newspaper and a quality newspaper each devoted limited resources to the beat, especially in comparison to a mass-market newspaper. As a result, the reporter for the quality newspaper and the reporters for the popular newspaper helped each other routinely, exchanging cases to cover, story angles and ideas, quotations from sources, and basic factual details. There was no similar exchange with reporters from the mass-market newspaper. The exchanges resulted in a convergence in coverage between the popular and quality newspapers (Ericson, Baranek, and Chan 1989: chap. 2).

Sources are another point of convergence (ibid). By restricting reporters to particular times and places, and by enclosing on knowledge, sources can effectively circumscribe news stories to a narrow range so that 'pack journalism' is the only possible outcome. While particular sources may favour particular media and markets on particular occasions, on other occasions they may offer a news release to all outlets, so that the only choice for those outlets is to report what everyone else has or not report at all.

In summary, there is a large number of medium and market considerations that yield both convergence and divergence in news coverage. We keep these considerations in mind as we embark upon our empirical investigation into how news formats, sources, topics, and knowledge vary across different media and markets. In this chapter, we have raised many of the relevant issues through an overview of the current state of knowledge. In the next chapter, we crystallize this overview into questions for research, and then describe the research project we designed to address them.

3

Reading the News

Research Questions

The theoretical considerations raised in chapters 1 and 2 point to a number of questions for research regarding how and why news outlets vary in formats; use of sources; topics of crime, law, and justice; and types of knowledge.

There is a need to specify particular differences in format in popular and quality newspapers, television stations, and radio stations, and how these differences affect news products. Another consideration is variation in the use of formats that all news outlets, regardless of medium or market orientation, have available. For example, how do news organizations operating within different media and markets vary in the extent to which their stories involve particular news types, sources, locations, initiating incidents, sides presented, and sides favoured?

There are several questions regarding how the representation and use of sources vary by medium and markets. Some of these questions also address variation in format across media and markets. Do news organizations operating in different media and markets vary in the number of sources they use, the types of sources they use, and the types of knowledge provided by their sources? Do news organizations vary in their use of different contexts for presenting sources? Do news organizations vary in the extent to which sources back up their statements with reference to evidence, and in the types of evidence referred to in this regard? How do news organizations operating in different media and markets vary in their use of visuals and sound in representing sources?

It is important to establish the proportion of total news content that involves crime, law, and justice stories, and how this varies by medium and market. A related question is how concordant stories of crime, law, and justice are across news outlets. Do most news outlets cover the same events and issues in crime, law, and justice in similar ways? Alternatively, are there some differences, for example, in terms of medium, with substantial overlap in broadcast news and a much greater variety in newspapers?

There are several key questions about the specifics of news topics of crime and deviance and how these vary by média and markets. Do news organizations operating in different media and markets vary in the areas and types of crime and deviance they focus on? Do they vary in their targeting of particular institutional contexts and fields in which crime and deviance occur? Do they vary in the types of knowledge about crime and deviance they emphasize? Do they vary in the types of explanations of crime and deviance they offer? Do they vary in their use of headlines, teasers, and leads, regarding the type of knowledge about crime and deviance these devices convey?

There are also several key questions about the specifics of news topics of legal control and justice, and how these vary by media and markets. Do news organizations operating in different media and markets vary in the extent to which they focus on legal control actions that have taken place, are projected, or are recommended? Do they give varying emphasis to particular legal control or justice models, styles, and mechanisms? Do news organizations vary in the institutional contexts and fields they present as being mobilized in legal control actions? Do they vary in their focus on institutional contexts and fields of persons involved in legal control actions? Do they vary in their selection of institutional contexts and fields as targets for legal control actions? Finally, do news organizations vary in the explanations or reasons for legal control actions offered?

Research designed to answer these questions involves an approach to cultural analysis explicated in our earlier research (Ericson, Baranek, and Chan 1987, 1989). Journalists and their sources re-create the texts of the social world, in effect producing texts about social texts. Our task is to understand the relationship of news texts, as an expressive cultural form, to social order, and to indicate the complex and variable nature of this relationship. In news content, journalists have already fixed meaning from the flow of events, and it is this fixation we seek to clarify and analyse. The questions raised above are essentially questions of intra- and intertextuality readable from news content. What is the relation of a text's parts to each other? What is the relation of the text to other texts? What is the relation of the text to those who participated in constructing it? What is the relation of the text to realities conceived of as lying outside of it? What empirical patterns are evident in these intra- and intertextual relations and what do these indicate about the meaning of news discourse?

In addressing these questions, our goal is to pick apart what is usually taken for granted. Through the very mechanisms by which news serves to represent order, it appears as common sense. Through 'simple truth ... artlessly apprehended,' and through 'things that anybody properly put together cannot help but think' (Geertz 1983: 10), news as common sense tells the consumer how to deal with the world. Our task is to make sense of the ways in which the news, mediated by journalists and sources, makes sense of our lives. This includes making evident not only the parameters of common sense, but also what it overlooks. This is the task of the critic, not the poet (Kermode 1966: 3)

Some critics might contend that reading the news for the common-sensical properties by which it represents order requires studying the people who consume it. We will deal with this consideration in more detail later in the chapter. An understanding of news content is necessary before we can pose meaningful questions regarding the effects of content on consumers. As Gitlin (1980: 14) has argued, 'Since the media aim at least to influence, condition and reproduce the activity of audiences by reaching into the symbolic organization of thought, the student of mass media must pay attention to the symbolic content of media messages before the question of effects can even be sensibly posed.'

Critics might also contend that the questions we have posed cannot be addressed adequately through a reading of news content, but instead must be grounded in an understanding of the process by which the news is produced. Many researchers (e.g., Hall et al. 1978) have tried to deduce social relations from a reading of the cultural form of news. Our view is that one can no more deduce fully what journalists and sources do from a reading of news content than one can deduce fully what law-enforcement officials do from a reading of statutes, law reports, and police occurrence reports (Ericson 1981, 1982), or what scientists do from a reading of journal articles, text-books, and reviews (Mulkay 1979: 69, 91). News, like law and science, is a socially constructed product that is highly self-referential in nature. That is, news content is used by journalists and sources to construct meanings and expectations about their organizations. This means that the analyst of news content must examine the meanings used by news producers in the con-struction of their product. We have, in fact, undertaken such an examination through a series of fine-grained ethnographies of journalists and news sour-ces at work (Ericson, Baranek, and Chan 1987, 1989). Our present analysis draws upon our previous work, especially in helping us to explain the aggregate patterns in news content that we identify. In our previous work, we dealt more with the phenomenological, subjective, and interactional processes by which the signs of news are constructed, while, in the present work, we move to the objectified signs of language, ritual, and classification available in news texts. This movement from contexts of production to patterns in texts provides us with a more complete view of sign or symbol use in action, and a more developed ethnography of modern thought.

Research Requirements

Our questions for research can be addressed most completely and adequately through a combination of research methods. As noted above, in our previous studies we analysed the 'operational data' of the news-production activities of sources and journalists. In the present study we need to add the 'presentational data' of news content and to analyse it systematically in terms of its variation across media and markets. These types of data are related. For example, it is possible to read news content for what it reveals about the parameters of news production. 'The spoken and visual vocabulary of news may be regarded as the outward and visible expression of newsroom codes and conventions and not as separate from them' (Glasgow University Media Group [GUMG] 1980: 409).

The 'presentational data,' or what is presented as news content, can also be analysed in several ways. Traditionally there has been a distinction between quantitative content analysis, which seeks to show patterns or regularities in content through repetition, and qualitative content analysis, which emphasizes the fluidity of text and context in the interpretive understanding of culture. Each of these approaches has strengths and limitations. Our purpose in this section is to show how the methodological issues and problems associated with quantitative and qualitative content analysis are entwined with the theoretical concerns, including considerations of epistemology and ontology, we raised in chapters 1 and 2. This discussion highlights the relative value of quantitative and qualitative approaches, and thereby indicates the value we assigned to each in designing our research.

QUANTITATIVE CONTENT ANALYSIS

Quantitative content analysis is a valuable means of revealing patterns in news content, and making evident previously unarticulated assumptions about how the news is structured and presented. It assumes repetition is the most valuable indicator of significance. Therefore the emphasis is on what can be reasonably classified so that it can be counted. Even narrative data are placed into predefined categories and thereby transformed into numerical data. Within this format, emphasis is on verification and reliability of data as classified. Data that prove recalcitrant because they are lacking in verification or reliability are discarded, rather than focused upon to discover alternative or new understandings.

Traditionally the patterns of regularities revealed in quantitative content analysis have been compared to other measures of reality. Since the main purpose of quantitative content analysis has been to comment on what is not presented, wrongly presented, and/or underrepresented, there is a need for data indicating the norm in relation to which the news content is compared. The basic questions in this regard concern the extent to which, and the ways in which, news mirrors reality. Does the cultural product reflect the social reality? For example, do the types of crimes, criminals, and disposition of cases covered in news stories reflect the patterns revealed in official statistics, or what the public thinks (e.g., Davis 1973; Roshier 1973; Jones 1976; Sherizen 1978; Ditton and Duffy 1982; Doob 1984)?

In setting out to show that news content in a particular area is distorted or biased in particular ways, quantitative content analysis is ideologically and politically charged. 'Content analysis, like the mass media generally, is the product of social conflict' (McCormack 1982: 145). A lot of research in this area has been sponsored by interest groups wanting to show how the news is slanted against their interests. News organizations also sponsor such research, especially when they themselves are subject to research indicating their content is slanted or distorted. One notorious example is the large research expenditures of the Independent Broadcasting Association and the British Broadcasting Corporation to counter the Glasgow University Media Group's analyses of industrial news on television (Towler 1984).

Quantitative content analysis has many limitations, several of which are made evident in our subsequent discussion of qualitative content analysis. A basic limitation is that content analysis can deal only with what has been disseminated. Only observational methodologies based in newsrooms and source organizations can tell us what is considered for inclusion but is not published, and why.

Quantitative content analysis is further restricted in that it is limited to what can be quantified. What counts analytically is what can be counted. This limitation leads to a concentration on aspects that are simple, measurable, and subject to standardization. Important dimensions are likely to be overlooked. Instead of searching for the anomaly and focusing upon its significance, the researcher looks no farther than what his or her predefined categories have told him or her to see. Magnification of the novel discovery gives way to standardization of the obvious category. In consequence, quantitative content analysis often results in a rather barren counting of repetition without adequate attention to its significance. In studies where there is no effort to theorize the significance of what is being counted, quantitative content analysis ends up as no more than 'repetition speculation ... since its practitioners are merely speculating about the significance of repetition ... Clearly, with no theory of significance, the method is *arbitrary* and *unsystematic*, and could not be anything else. Content analysis is based on empiricist thinking which provides that the truth is self-evident and visible – a provision which conceals the operation of its own highly political concept of ideology' (Sumner 1979: 69, 71). This is not to say that quantitative-content analysts are precluded from theorizing about the significance of what they count, as more sophisticated research has shown (for a review, see McCormack 1982). Rather, it indicates that most research in this tradition is obsessed with methodological concerns (validity, reliability, statistical significance) and ideological concerns (showing the news is distorted and slanted against particular political interests) to the relative exclusion of theoretical concerns (especially about the significance of what is being counted).

The narrow focus on standardizing categories and counting them also leads to simplification. The quantitative-content analyst is forced to reconstruct the common-sense categories in the news, instead of deconstructing these categories and analysing them in the particular. The analyst thereby reproduces the formats and language of journalists and of official news sources. This analytical task is easy, but not very enlightening. 'A thinker who classifies the phenomenon to be examined according to known and visible institutions saves himself the trouble of justifying the classification' (M. Douglas 1986: 94).

The most significant aspects of news content are not simple or easy to standardize. Indeed, the whole effort to standardize categories is thrown into doubt by the well-known fact that different people assign different meaning and significance to the same text. 'We know nothing of things beyond their significance to us' (Ames 1960: 4), as judged from where we 'sit' in space and time. Even the news – which is prepared to be simplistic and common-sensical so that it can be comprehended by someone with a primary-school education – is open to a wide range of interpretations and uses by different readers in various settings (Snow 1983; Robinson and Levy 1986; Fiske 1987; Ericson, Baranek, and Chan 1989; Ericson 1991).

The fact that even the simplest texts are open to multiple interpretation poses serious difficulties for quantitative content analysis. Surveys of news content, in keeping with positivistically oriented social surveys in general, are based on the assumption that everyone (respondents, readers, coders) has the same understanding of what he or she sees and hears. The research coders are trained to seek and to see things in common. If there are frequent 'misunderstandings' or 'misinterpretations,' then items are discarded, or simplified until a consensus is arrived at. In other words, a consensus is forged among coders through their training and accumulative experience. Obviously this is not the way people normally read the news.

The reality of reading the news is that people in various settings at different times give it significance according to their circumstances and their selves. The news fosters pluralism, varying opinion, and different uses, in different settings. This approach is the antithesis of that taken by researchers in most quantitative content analyses, which involve a methodological construction of consensus through prolonged discussion that culminates in forcing everyone either to 'see it this way' or to not see it at all. The failure of quantitative-content analysts to accept the reality of how texts are a matter of consumers' contexts means that their analyses are not only reified but fictive. Acceptance of the reality that news texts have differential meaning according to consumers' contexts is necessary for a full appreciation of what the news has to offer. As Molotch and Lester (1975: 240–1) state, 'Our general theoretical schema ... assumes that there can be no such thing as intercoder reliability, because each individual receives a unique observational world ... Our coders are competent social members, each of whom has a world as valid as any other. The intervention of such coders' worlds into the coding process is a fact which must be acknowledged, not obscured through assertions of objective intercoder reliability.'

These points about the socially constructed and interpreted nature of texts have implications for the effort by quantitative-content analysts to compare news texts with other textually mediated versions of reality such as official statistics or public-opinion surveys. These studies do not compare news signs and symbols in relation to some more basic and fundamental reality, but rather in relation to other signs and symbols that are themselves socially constructed. While it might be argued that some of these constructs are closer to the thing being observed than others (Wieck 1983), this is a complex matter. It is certainly problematic to assume that news accounts are at a more distant level of sign-reproduction than, say, official documents about an event. For example, a police reporter often has a more direct and detailed account of a crime from investigating officers than is available in police documents (Ericson, Baranek, and Chan 1989: chap. 3). News accounts may also be at a less distant level of sign-reproduction than public opinion surveys, in which the opinion of citizens is often based on what they have seen or heard on the news, and then textually mediated by the organizational practice of social science. Ultimately what is being compared in these 'Does the news mirror reality?' studies is the news genre as an institutional discourse and some other genre (e.g., legal, official) as an institutional discourse. The social constructs and appearances produced within the genre capacities and purposes of news discourse are compared with the social constructs and appearances produced within the genre capacities and purposes of another institutional discourse (e.g., police statistics). Ultimately a judgment is made about discrepancies in these appearances – for example, that the news is sensational because it dwells on violent crime – that does not reflect the distribution of types of crime as shown in police statistics. However, this judgment is vacuous because it is based on the association of appearances that have been generated in other contexts for other purposes.

Again, there is a need to appreciate the practices that lead to the appearances in terms of the genre capacities of each form of institutional discourse. This shifts the focus from a simple and standardized objectification of texts to an interpretive understanding of how people perceive and use texts. 'The relationship between observer and observed achieves a kind of primacy. It becomes the only thing that *can* be observed ... The true nature of things may be said to be not in things themselves, but in the relationship we construct and then perceive, *between* them' (Hartley 1982: 13; Hawkes 1977: 17). This relationship is at the core of qualitative content analysis.

QUALITATIVE CONTENT ANALYSIS

Qualitative-content analysts view written and electronically mediated texts as human action, and human action as a text. What is inscribed in written documents and electronic media is action, as is the process by which inscription takes place. As they participate in the construction of documented realities, actors are self-conscious that their actions are being inscribed as part of the overall performance of their roles. Thus they pay careful attention to the scripts, constructing interpretations that will spotlight a competent performance (Gusfield 1981; Geertz 1983; Wagner-Pacifici 1986; Ericson, Baranek, and Chan 1989). In this light, the role of the content analyst is 'to construct a "reading" of the text. The text itself is a sequence of symbols – speech, writing, gesture – that contain interpretations. Our task, like that of the literary critic, is to interpret the interpretations' (Carey 1979: 421).

> The great virtue of the extension of the notion of a text beyond things written on paper or carved into stone is that it trains attention on precisely this phenomenon: on how the inscription of action is brought about, what its vehicles are and how they work, and on what the fixation of meaning from the flow of events ... implies for sociological interpretations. To see social institutions, social customs, social changes as in some sense 'readable' is to alter our whole sense of what social interpretation is and shift it toward modes of thought rather more familiar to the translator, the exegete, or the

iconographer than to the test-giver, the factor analyst, or the pollster. (Geertz 1983: 31)

Qualitative analysis, aimed at understanding how human expression articulates social order, begins by picking apart the order that is presented to us as common sense. In the process, the analyst picks out what is relevant for analysis and pieces it together to create tendencies, sequences, patterns, and orders. The process of deconstruction, interpretation, and reconstruction breaks down many of the assumptions dear to quantitative analysts, such as the separation of theory and data, maintaining an objective language cleansed of subjective reference and claims to moral neutrality (Geertz 1983: 34). While the qualitative analyst tries to understand *with* the producers and users of texts he or she studies, he or she must engage in 'constructive interpretation' as he or she produces his or her own texts (Dworkin 1986: 62–5; Goodrich 1986). Interpretation, understanding, and application are all part of the same process in which the analyst makes judgments and ultimately presents claims that compete with those of the people involved in the practices he or she is analysing. This constructive interpretation is inevitable because the analyst is already dealing with the preinterpreted knowledge of those he or she is studying, and is not interested in simply reproducing their constructions. Inevitable also in this process is a melding of theory and data, subjective reference, and moral evaluation. The human action of reading and producing texts, in social-scientific analysis as in everyday life, selects and privileges meanings and thereby constitutes preferred texts. It is a social and political activity.

Recognition of the interpretive, subjective, and evaluative dimensions of textual analysis does not diminish the requirement of systematic evidence that is reliable and valid. As ethnographers of texts, qualitative-content analysts are primarily concerned with discovery and verification through quasi-experimental reasoning. They search for suggestive contrasts that 'may either test or extend a theory which has application over as much as possible of the range of events, processes or states of affairs which have been chosen for study' (Runciman 1983: 168; see also Glaser and Strauss 1967; Altheide 1987a). There is what Geertz (1983: 69) has termed an 'intellectual perpetual motion' from the concrete context of particular formats, meanings, styles, and images to general theoretical claims. Movement from the concrete to the general requires the detection and construction of regularities and patterns. This construction is usually accomplished through narrative description and commentary, although numerical data are also valuable. Whether numerical or narrative, the data are 'built up' into patterns over the course of the research through a process of reflexive and circular comparison, validation, and discovery. Many of these features are summarized by Hall (1975: 15).

[Qualitative-content analysts] point, in detail, to the text on which an
interpretation of latent meaning is based; they indicate more briefly the fuller
supporting or contextual evidence which lies to hand; they take into account
material which modifies or disproves the hypotheses which are emerging;
and they *should* (they do not always) indicate in detail why one rather than
another reading of the material seems to the analyst the most plausible way
of understanding it ... [They use] recurrence as one critical dimension of
significance though these recurring patterns may not be expressed in quan-
tifiable terms ... These recurring patterns are taken as pointers to latent
meanings from which inferences as to the sources can be drawn ... [The
qualitative-content] analyst has another string to his bow; namely, strategies
for noting and taking into account emphasis. Position, placing, treatment,
tone, stylistic intensification, striking imagery, etc., are all ways of register-
ing emphasis. The really significant item may not be the one which con-
tinually recurs, but the one which stands out as an exception from the
general pattern – but which is *also* given, in its exceptional content, the
greatest weight.

Qualitative-content analysts focus on each of the questions of intra- and
intertextuality raised earlier (pp. 47–8). Regarding how the components of
the same text are related to each other, analysts focus on, for example, how
news sources are juxtaposed and cited to 'drop' particular inferences and
innuendo. Especially in stories aimed at policing organizational life (Ericson,
Baranek, and Chan 1987, 1989), some sources are given a dominant place
in the lead and throughout the item, allowing them to frame both the
preferred definition of the problem and the control solution. Other sources,
'forced' into this frame, are variously used to underpin it or are themselves
marginalized, excluded, or shown to be part of the problem.

Qualitative content analysis is also capable of pin-pointing the subtle
ways in which news operatives combine different items and stories to create
new meanings and news themes. The newspaper layout juxtaposes stories on
the same page or on facing pages to suggest more than is available in each
item taken individually (for examples, see Hartley 1982; Voumvakis and
Ericson 1984). The same effect is achieved in the broadcast line-up by
'wrapping' several items into a segment to create a theme (for examples, see
Fishman 1978; Ericson, Baranek, and Chan 1987). Moreover, within the
same newspaper publication or radio or television broadcast, there are
different types of items – news stories, features, editorials, letters to the
editor, opinion columns, and advertising – that nevertheless are on the same
topic or themes and reinforce each other in the aggregate.

The same intertextual relation of different types of items occurs over
time in the presentation of continuing stories. Some stories continue for
months and even years, and questions of balance, range of opinion, and

which sources are setting the agenda become difficult to address because coverage intensifies and then lapses, and some sources and their version of events are in favour but then go out of favour. Researchers have shown that when analysing continuing stories and news themes, some patterns and systematic relationships can be captured only through qualitative research techniques. Quantitative content analysis, which promises to be systematic and to reveal patterns, would in fact miss systematic and patterned aspects if its random or stratified sampling techniques were used to study continuing stories and themes. This point is underscored, for example, in Altheide's (1985, 1987b) analysis of television coverage of the taking of American hostages in Iran; Chibnall's (1977) research on the 'violent society' theme in England; and various studies of particular moral panics, such as Hall and associates' (1978) analysis of the 'mugging' panic in England, and Ng's (1982) research on a sexual-assault-against-children panic in Toronto.

Qualitative content analysis is also valuable for comparing the content of different news outlets as they cover a continuing story or theme. Differences among news outlets in layouts or line-ups, priorities, and sources used are often difficult to capture quantitatively, and again may be lost if standard sampling strategies for quantitative analysis are employed.

Qualitative content analysts are also sensitive to the relation of texts to those who participate in construing and using them. Texts always escape their authors as they become used by different people in different contexts. Sources find their material taken over by journalists and put into different contexts; they are always taken out of context, literally. Journalists always find their material taken over by consumers, including sources and other journalists; they, too, are always taken out of context, literally. This means that an analyst of the text must remain sensitive to the various contexts in which it is used: once the text escapes its author, what matters is what it says to those who are using it rather than what the author meant to say or what influence he or she hoped it would bear. How does the regular source use it (Ericson, Baranek, and Chan 1989)? How does the journalist use it to produce more news (Tuchman 1978; Altheide 1985; Ericson, Baranek, and Chan 1987)? As Altheide (1987a: 74) directs, 'The aim ... is to place documents in context just as members do, in order to theoretically relate products to their organizational production.'

Sensitivity to the organizational contexts of textual reproduction also bears awareness about how the text is related to other constructions of reality. For example, it instructs about how news is intertextually related to official documents. To what extent does the news reproduce the performative and presentational character of official discourse (Altheide and Johnson 1980; Fishman 1980)? How do people represent themselves and their organizations in the news, compared to the representations they made in official forms and publications internal to their organization (Ericson,

Baranek, and Chan 1989)? Addressing such questions is part of the general task of the ethnographer to make evident how people represent themselves: 'searching out and analysing the symbolic forms – words, images, institutions, behaviours – in terms of which, in each place, people actually represented themselves to themselves and to one another' (Geertz 1983: 58).

The dimensions of openness and sensitivity in qualitative content analysis foster discovery, but not always solid evidence and analytical rigour. All readings, including those of media analysts, are subjective and speculative, particular and relative. All readers have to take the part for the whole, and the question becomes what they will fill in the blanks with. In this respect, qualitative content analysis is in the realm of literary and textual criticism, with attendant debates about the proper procedures for reading texts and which readings seem preferable. These debates centre upon 'preferred readings' and whose preferences win out, i.e., which readers are able to convince others that their readings are preferable and that these others should join them. In academic circles, as in other circles, such debates are partially settled by dimensions of knowledge/power, including cogent arguments about such things as evidence, objectivity, systematization of data, and generalizability of findings. This is illustrated, for example, in the reaction to the work of Hall and associates (1978) by media analysts representing different theoretical persuasions (e.g., Sumner 1981; Waddington 1986; Schlesinger 1988).

The fluidity of interpretation and ritual of debate are not exclusive to qualitative analyses, *vide* the money and psychic energy expended on efforts to discredit the work of the Glasgow University Media Group (1976, 1980, 1982; Towler 1984). Moreover, qualitatively oriented researchers with an ethnographic sensibility would predict such debates over the analysis of texts. These debates are not only healthy, but inevitable, given the fact that analysts must always engage in constructive interpretations that claim a superiority to interpretations of subjects or other textual analysts. Qualitative-content researchers do not exalt the reality of interpretive pluralism – particularism, subjectivism, idealism, relativism – but they do take pluralism seriously as a matter worthy of interpretive description and analysis. And, of course, to be honest, such interpretive description and analysis should be applied as much to their own work as to the work of other producers and readers of texts they may see fit to study.

Research Design

SAMPLING NEWS ORGANIZATIONS

Given our focus on how news content varies by media and markets, we selected for comparison a quality and a popular news outlet in each of newspapers, television, and radio in the Toronto region. This selection was based on our extensive knowledge of the Toronto news media, with reference to our own previous research in the region as well as various sources of secondary data (e.g., Royal Commission on Newspapers [RCN] 1981b, 1981g, 1981e; data from the Bureau of Broadcast Measurements; internal documents of some of the news organizations studied). Among the news outlets included in the content analysis were several we studied in depth as part of our observational research on news production (Ericson, Baranek, and Chan 1987, 1989).

All of the popular news outlets studied were oriented to the Toronto and region market only. While all of the quality outlets studied had national as well as Toronto regional publications or broadcasts, we examined only the news content they disseminated for the Toronto regional markets. Therefore news from the quality and popular outlets are comparable, at least in terms of the geographical area in which they operated. Our basic consideration in this connection was as follows: if people in the Toronto region compared what was available in a quality newspaper and a popular newspaper, the evening (6:00 PM) newscast of a quality television station and a popular television station, and the evening (5:00 PM) newscast of a quality radio station and a popular radio station, what would they find? What differences would be evident in the formats of presentation, sources used, topics of crime, law and justice, and types of knowledge presented?

In the analyses presented below, the news organizations are referred to as follows: NQ for the quality newspaper; NP for the popular newspaper; TQ for the quality television station; TP for the popular television station; RQ for the quality radio station; RP for the popular radio station.

SAMPLING NEWS ITEMS

In keeping with our theoretical interests in the wider news-media research program (see especially Ericson, Baranek, and Chan 1987: chaps. 1 and 2), we sampled items that addressed aspects of crime, deviance, legal control, and justice. Consistent with our earlier work, we operated with broad definitions, including, for example, acts of violence and issues related to the control of violence; interpersonal disputes; disputes within and between organizations; contentious public-interest issues in spheres such as health, welfare, and culture; contentious economic policies and practices, and economic crimes; contentious political policies and practices, and political crimes; conflicts in ideology and morality; and control or regulation of the above conflicts, disputes, or illegalities. Because of these broad definitions, additional rules were created to clarify the selection criteria. For example, stories related to public health and safety were not included if they merely described what happened (e.g., a fire, an accident, an epidemic) without either elaborating the event as a social problem or providing knowledge about the control action taken (e.g., inquest, charges laid). As we document in chapter 8, crime, deviance, legal control, and justice items constituted a substantial proportion of the total content in each of the outlets.

Details on the selection of news items from each of the six outlets are summarized in table 3.1.

The 33-day sampling period and the sampling ratios were established to yield a reasonable number of stories in each outlet for quantitative comparisons. The 33 days included weekdays (Monday to Friday) only in the period 6 June to 21 July 1983. Weekends were excluded because the broadcast-news outlets had different news shows on the weekends, and one newspaper did not publish on Saturday while the other newspaper did not publish on Sunday. The first of July was excluded because it was a holiday for some outlets. The 10 June news broadcast of TQ was cancelled because the station decided to replace it with continuing coverage of a political-party leadership convention; hence we substituted the broadcasts of 31 May for both TQ and TP.

Newspaper stories were sampled in pages because it was impractical to take a random sample of all the stories on each of the 33 days. We considered taking a sample of all crime, deviance, legal-control, and justice items in the newspapers for a few days only, chosen at random, but we decided against this approach because of the possibility of some unusual event's skewing a day's coverage by chance. Moreover, we decided it was better to extend the comparison to the same days studied for broadcast content. The specific steps in selecting newspaper items follow: 1 / we numbered all pages with news items (excluding full-page advertisements, cartoon supplements, sports scores, and photographs without an accompanying story); 2 / we determined the number of pages to include (e.g., if there were 50 pages we took 1/10, or 5 pages); 3 / we used a table of random numbers to select the actual pages to be analysed (if the same page came up twice, another number was selected; if the random number did not fall within the number of pages, another number was selected); 4 / for the chosen pages, all stories involving major elements of crime, deviance, legal control, and justice were selected.

For both television outlets, we videotaped the hour-long 6:00 PM newscasts for each of the 33 days. A schedule of each line-up was prepared, and the items with major elements of crime, deviance, legal control, and justice were identified. Two-thirds of these items were then selected randomly and transcribed verbatim, along with notes on the use of visuals. Opening 'headlines' and 'teasers' were treated as the equivalent of headlines in newspapers.

TABLE 3.1
News items samples

News outlet	Days	Approximate sampling ratio	Total number of items
NQ	33	1/10 pages	276
NP	33	1/10 pages	212
TQ	33	2/3 items	318
TP	33	2/3 items	213
RQ	33	all items	243
RP	33	all items	223
Total			1,485

For both radio outlets, we audiotaped the 12-minute newscasts at 5:00 PM for each of the 33 days. A schedule of each line-up was prepared, and the items with major elements of crime, deviance, legal control, and justice were selected. All such items were transcribed verbatim, along with notes on the uses of sound other than words, and all items were included in the sample.

In order to take into account differences in the readings of the three coders, as discussed in the next section, we divided the sample randomly into three roughly equal subsamples, and each subsample was coded by one coder. Each coder was assigned, randomly, 11 of the 33 days for each of the 6 news outlets. This procedure permitted comparison, for each variable or category coded, of the degree to which the results were dependent on the coder.

QUALITATIVE ANALYSES

The news media are too ubiquitous to be isolated from the flow of events and portrayed exclusively in quantitative terms. The news media are too much a part of the everyday life of journalists, sources, and consumers to be held apart, lifeless, in abstract quantitative analyses. The news media do not merely exist in everyday life, they help to constitute it. Thus, in understanding a cross-section of news items from different outlets and media, it is necessary to have an awareness of how that content is made by the various people who participate in the process, and of its relevance to them. We have such an awareness as a result of our detailed ethnographies of source organizations and news organizations (Ericson, Baranek, and Chan 1987, 1989), and we drew upon that research to understand the patterns we discovered in news content.

A qualitative, ethnographic approach was also taken to published or broadcast-news texts. A structured protocol for data collection combined with ethnographic notes is the best means of producing a theoretically informed analysis of news content (Altheide 1987a). Ethnographic readings of content result in the discovery of themes, patterns, and additional questions over the entire course of data-collection, often leading in new directions or to reconceptualization of the relevance of paths followed previously. Data are coded conceptually so that the same item is potentially relevant to a range of research topics. Along with journalists and news sources, qualitative researchers are aware of the fluid nature of text and context. These dimensions are captured in particular in the longitudinal qualitative analyses presented in chapters 4 and 5.

Indexes for qualitative analysis were developed by scrutinizing the 1,485 sampled items. This qualitative reading was conducted by Richard Ericson, and was separate from the quantitative coding process. The primary data were the newspaper items, and the printed transcripts of the broadcast items. Reliance on the printed transcripts of the broadcast items was based on the recognition that 'news is quintessentially a verbal genre,' and 'that words are the primary code in *all* the media' (Crisell 1986: 104, 143; see also GUMG 1976: esp. 121, 135–6; GUMG 1980: esp. 248, 332–3). One index included detailed notes summarizing the content and salient aspects of each sampled item, classified by news organization and data. Another index was constructed in terms of 42 research topics, noting under each topic the stories that related to the topic and the ways in which the stories were illustrative. A third index provided a key to continuing stories and news themes under consideration for comparative qualitative analysis, including details of what was covered by each outlet on each day within the continuing story or theme (see chapters 4 and 5).

QUANTITATIVE ANALYSIS

A structured protocol was developed for the purpose of quantitative data-collection by three coders. This protocol was not closed at any point in the data-collection process. The categories were built up inductively over the entire research process, with daily consultation among the researchers regarding new possibilities and problems with existing categories. As such, the protocol was constructed ethnographically, with openness to discovery and change as a first principle.

This approach to structuring the data means that our research is exploratory in nature and preliminary in consequence. At the end of the data-collection process, we had a very elaborate protocol with a fine-grained breakdown of categories within an item. Inevitably these categories had to be collapsed for statistical analyses, although we retained the more detailed breakdowns to preserve our appreciation of what went in the general categories. Throughout we struggled to balance the needs of generality, accuracy, and simplicity in our conceptualizations, while at the same time appreciating that our efforts to secure any two of these virtues entailed sacrificing the third one (Thorngate 1976; Weick 1979).

The coders were social scientists with extensive experience, including considerable experience in researching the news media. Prior to coding for the present study, Janet Chan and Pat Baranek had spent more than a year in field research on journalists and news sources, and Sophia Voumvakis had undertaken a newspaper-content study of a particular news theme (Voumvakis and Ericson 1984). Nevertheless, as is predictable from what we have said about the reading of news texts, there were substantial differences in interpretation over the course of data-collection. It is worthwhile to consider these interpretive differences because they are instructive about our theoretical claims concerning the nature of news as knowledge, and they also provide important lessons to other social scientists working in this field.

In spite of the knowledge we had gained from field research on the fluid and interpretive nature of texts and contexts, we spent considerable time and psychic energy trying to establish a protocol for quantitative data-collection that would lead us all to see the same things in reading news items. When categories proved recalcitrant to intercoder reliability, we initially followed the traditional route of discarding them, or reconceptualizing them in a way that would forge a consensus. However, through the painstaking and painful experience of taking this traditional route, we began to appreciate that we were following the wrong course. It became meaningless to 'test' the degree of intercoder differences using standard procedures of calculating the percentage of codes that were inconsistent between coders, because a different way of reading the story would result in dramatically different codes in many of the variables. In many instances, it was impossible to decide that one way of reading the text was more correct than another.

We began to appreciate that, for researchers, as for other readers of the news, reading is an individual exercise, and that, for quantitative analysis, variation in interpretations has to be respected. Researchers are no more able than other human beings to reproduce in one place at one time a meaning that was produced in another place at another time (Gadamer 1975). Researchers engage in 'constructive interpretations' (Dworkin 1986: 62–5; see also Runciman 1983: esp. 226–7, 280) in which they apply the intentions of the producers of texts to their own purposes and contexts. For the scientist as much as for other people, understanding and application are part of the same process. Any process of observation is active, involves categorization, is inferential, and is therefore not separate from interpretation. Moreover, 'judgements of observational adequacy seem to vary, like the meaning of propositions, according to the interpretative and social context' (Mulkay 1979: 49). That is, the researcher is constructing the material for his or her purposes, and even among a team of researchers with a common purpose, there is inevitably considerable variation in interpretation.

Research on the news media is especially instructive in this regard. All media depend on the reader's visualization, on his or her ability to imagine the facts (Crisell 1986: 11, 12, 46; Ericson, Baranek, and Chan 1987: 1ff). Even television, which relies on the primacy of iconic signs, in fact includes many significations that are arbitrary (Fiske and Hartley 1978; Fiske 1987). As addressed in chapter 2, even what appears as an iconic representation of reality is actually a 'metaphorical reconstruction' or 'constructed equivalence' so that 'television does not *display* the actual world, but displaces it' (Fiske and Hartley 1978: 48). Moreover, while news producers might work hard to communicate content that 'contains' their 'preferred meanings' presented simply and commonsensically (Knight and Dean 1982), this is no guarantee that people who consume it, including researchers, will see it that way. Consumers will express their own preferences, and will often remain unconvinced by the interpretations of others (Fiske and Hartley 1978: chap. 7; Robinson and Levy 1986; Fiske 1987: chap. 5). This was McLuhan's point in stressing that the consumer is, or provides, the content of media. The same point holds when the reader is a researcher. To repeat the wisdom of Molotch and Lester (1975: 240–1), 'The intervention of such coders' worlds into the coding process is a fact which must be acknowledged, not obscured through assertions of objective intercoder reliability.'

Again we emphasize that these problems are not peculiar to the reading of news texts. Indeed, because they have been rendered simple and commonsensical, news texts are probably easier to read than most other texts available to social scientists. Consider, for example, the historian who is faced with documents prepared centuries before for administrative purposes he or she can only imagine. Consider also the research team conducting systematic observation in natural field settings, where all sorts of people and paper may be encountered, and their research relevance raised or overlooked according to the peculiarities of team members (cf Reiss 1971a; J. Douglas 1976; Ericson 1982). '*The world is not the accomplice of our knowledge*, there is no prediscursive providence which disposes the world in our favour. We must conceive discourse as a violence we do to things, or in any case as a practice which we impose on them; and it is in this practice that the events of discourse find the principle of their regularity' (Foucault 1981: 67). The nature of things is in the relationships we interpretively construct and then perceive among them, and communicate in social-scientific discourse.

The situation faced by our coders was no different from situations we had faced in team field research, including our ethnographic research on news sources and journalists. Researchers observing an event often differ in their interpretations of what they observe and record as salient. Indeed, the strength of ethnographic research is precisely the recognition that social facts are not objective facts lying about like pebbles in the sand, but are socially constructed in processes of negotiation and power/knowledge. Reading news texts is no different. Indeed, the advantage of our present research over our earlier observational studies is that we could develop alternative, statistical means of at least estimating the variation in interpretation among coders and taking the estimated variation into account in our analyses.

As we detail shortly, the only reasonable approach to our materials was to treat each of our coders as news-consuming members of the public and then to incorporate their various interpretations in the aggregate into our overall understanding of news content. In essence, the pooled data from the coders represent what those news consumers derived from news texts in our sample. We do not make the claim that our coders were the same as any member of the public: as in other branches of science, trained observers do not see the same thing as the untrained (Mulkay 1979: esp. 46–7). The pooled data represent what three experienced, informed, and trained social scientists see in the news.

Additionally, it is clear that three coders are better than one. Consider that a lot of research involves a single researcher consulting texts, creating categories, and coding. For example, the historian scrutinizes official documents and ultimately offers his or her readings to his or her academic audience without, at the same time, having others consult identical or related documents to offer their readings. Other historians may do their own projects using the same or related documents, and inevitably they come up with different readings. This is the very stuff of academic differences, debate, and sometimes, progress. Similar comments apply to the solo ethnographer who spends a few months in an organization, reading their documents as texts and observing other signs as a basis for producing his or her own text of what is happening.

The method of pooling data from multiple coders and then taking their 'effects' into account through particular statistical techniques is also preferable to having data from multiple coders where the definitions of things to be coded have been narrowed and delineated in advance. Forged consensus in definitions would make the coders no different from members of the public responding to an opinion survey and asked to make fixed-choice responses. For discovery, it is far better to have members of the public, and coders as informed readers, communicate their own interpretations or readings of texts within more broadly set open-focused protocols.

In summary, we point to four advantages of the combined methodological approaches we adopted. First, we had the advantage of having as coders three trained and experienced social scientists, rather than only one person, and the pooled data from their readings are superior to a single reading. Second, we had an additional detailed reading for qualitative purposes by another experienced social scientist. Third, we had the advantage of our previous research on the news media, including detailed knowledge of news process and production in some of the same news outlets we were analysing regarding news content. Fourth, we undertook extensive statistical analyses to delineate how our coders as readers differed, and how this variation interacted with our primary analytical interest in how aspects of news content vary in relation to media and markets. This dimension is described in the following summary of the statistical techniques employed in our research.

The cross-sectional quantitative analyses presented in chapters 6, 7, 8, and 9 were conducted as follows: for some analyses we studied variation across news items, and these analyses were based on the news-items sample ($N = 1,485$). In other analyses we studied variation across news sources. Sources were defined as any person who was attributed as a source of knowledge in a news item, including spokespersons for organizations, individuals, and journalists themselves. In the sample of 1,485 news items, there were 5,175 sources. Our studies of variation across news sources was based on this sample of 5,175.

We wished to present a large volume of data in summary form. The approach arrived at was initially to analyse separately each variable under consideration. Each variable was dichotomized in terms of whether or not it appeared. The dichotomized variable was cross-tabulated separately with markets within each medium: with quality and popular newspapers, with quality and popular television stations, and with quality and popular radio stations. The dichotomized variable was also cross-tabulated with media: newspaper, television, and radio. For each of the cross-tabulations, tests of statistical significance were performed, for which we accepted as the level of confidence 0.1 on either the Cramer's V or PHI tests. The results for each variable analysed by markets and media were summarized in tabular form. We present how often a particular element appears in a news item, or among the total number of news sources, in each news outlet.

The next step was to take account of possible differences among coders as these might affect the relationship among variables. We decided to undertake log-linear analyses to clarify the extent of intercoder differences and the relationship among the tables (Bishop, Feinberg, and Holland 1975; Greenberg 1979). Log-linear analysis relies on relatively few assumptions and is especially useful for studying interactions among variables. Log-linear modelling is analogous to fitting a straight line through various data points; in this respect it is similar to regression analysis, except log-linear analysis is especially suited to categorical data. When a model fits well, that is, when the likelihood-ratio chi-square is not significant, we are able to say that the model in question is an adequate description of the data. There are, of course, always discrepancies between the observed data and the 'expected' data predicted by the model, but an 'adequate' model implies that these discrepancies can be ignored and treated as random errors. The 'expected' or 'fitted' data are seen as more reliable estimates of the frequencies because they are based on larger numbers (through 'collapsing' of categories where no significant differences are evident). This is usually the case unless the only adequate model is the 'saturated' or 'full' model, in which case the observed values and the fitted values are the same, i.e., there is no way of simplifying the interpretation of these data. The full model in our analysis is MEDIUM* MARKET* CODER* VARIABLE. X*Y is an 'interaction.' When it is significant, it means that variable X is not independent of variable Y. When X*Y*Z is significant, it means that not only is variable X not independent of variable Y, the relationship between X and Y also depends on variable Z.

The log-linear analyses allow us to make one of three conclusions about the presence of interactions with the dichotomized variables analysed. First the distribution of the variable X is independent of CODER, that is X*CODER is not significant. This can happen if X*CODER is found to be not statistically significant, or if it is, the magnitude of the difference is quite small. Since we are working with a large number of cases in this study, the chi-square statistics tend to be inflated, and statistical significance may not necessarily mean real significance. For the present analyses, we ignored all differences less than or equal to 10 percentage points. If X*CODER is not significant we can then draw conclusions about X and MEDIUM and/or MARKET according to the magnitude of the interactions.

Second, the distribution of X is not independent of CODER, and the difference is not small, but each of the three CODER samples exhibits the same or similar patterns with respect to MEDIUM and MARKET. If these differences with respect to MEDIUM or MARKET are large, we may then draw conclusions about X and MEDIUM and/or MARKET, in spite of CODER differences.

Third, the distribution of X is not independent of CODER, the difference is not small, and each of the CODER samples exhibits a different or inconsistent pattern with respect to MEDIUM and or MARKET. In this case, we have to accept that CODER differences permeated the results, although in some instances reasonable explanations are apparent for the differences. Thus, in considering formats (see chapter 6), CODER differences were explicable in terms of the sampling procedure. For example, in the sampling of newspaper stories it just so happened that one coder had a disproportionate number of editorial pages to code, resulting in a disproportionately large number of letters, editorials, and opinion columns in her subsample. Moreover, since the coding of the format variable was relatively straightforward (for example, Was the item a news story, a feature? Did the items originate locally, nationally, internationally?) the differences are unlikely to be attributable to variance in interpretations among the coders. Moreover, if the differences are largely the result of the chance occurrence of anomalous subsamples, then it is more reliable to pool the three coder subsamples together, which is the route we took for variables in chapter 6.

The tables include a 'significant differences' column to indicate the presence of statistically significant differences with each dichotomized variable analysed. This column denotes whether there are statistically significant differences (i.e., chi-square statistics significant at the 0.05 level with Cramer's V or PHI ≥ 0.10, when N is large) between the quality and popular newspapers (denoted as 'N'); between the quality and popular television stations (denoted as 'T'); between the quality and popular radio stations (denoted as 'R'); and among the three types of media (newspaper, television, and radio) (denoted as 'M'). This column also indicates whether, as a result of the log-linear analyses, there were significant interactions attributable to the coders (denoted by 'C'). The results of the log-linear analyses are not otherwise presented, but are available from the authors.

In order to understand the collective and relative influence of a number of related variables a series of stepwise discriminant analyses were undertaken (Morrison 1969; Tatsuaka 1971; Greenberg 1979). Stepwise discriminant analysis weights and combines independent measures in a way that forces groups (for example, popular and quality news outlets within a medium; or newspapers, television, and radio media) to be as distinct as possible so that one can predict the criteria according to which the groups are distinguishable. It is a cautious approach to the prediction of group membership without regard to the strictures of time order or causal structure of variables. This consideration, along with the nominal measure of the dependent variable, means that there are fewer restrictive assumptions necessary in discriminant analysis than in other statistical techniques. We simply wish to classify what characteristics most strongly predict whether the market orientation is quality or popular, and whether the medium is newspaper, television, or radio.

This discussion of analytical techniques has been formal and abstract because that is the quality of the techniques themselves. Greater clarity, and the value of the techniques, are evident in cross-sectional quantitative analyses presented in chapters 6, 7, 8, and 9. While the presentation of results inevitably bears the formal and abstract qualities of the techniques, we ground the quantitative analyses in qualitative materials, including case examples from the news items sampled here as well as insights from our observational research on news process and products. We proceed with the counsel of Gitlin (1980: 305) that 'it is late in the day for methodological exclusivity; in the act of interpretation and criticism, the proof of the pudding is in the eating.' We begin by digesting longitudinal qualitative materials from each of the six news outlets studied. In chapter 5, we analyse how a murder story was related in each outlet, and in chapter 6, we analyse how a story of law reform was played in each outlet.

PART II

Longitudinal Analyses

4

A Murder Story

In this chapter, we analyse how a story of murder was presented in each of the six news outlets. This story provided a popular narrative of a tragic event. It began with report of a body being found and the police investigation, and ended a few days later with reports of the funeral of the victim and the first court appearance of the accused. The news items reproduced and analysed here include everything a reader would have seen and/or heard about this murder if he or she had sampled the broadcast-news shows and newspapers as we did at the time.

As a popular narrative this murder story was given continuing coverage in the popular outlets. The popular newspaper (NP) treated it as a front-page item, the popular television station (TP) as a lead item, and the popular radio station (RP) as among its leading items. The quality television station (TQ) also provided substantial coverage of this story. As we document and explain, TQ's coverage was similar to that offered by the popular outlets because of the format requirements of the television medium combined with the television station's need to compete for a share of the mass audience market. In contrast, the quality newspaper (NQ) and the quality radio station (RQ) all but ignored the story, providing only 'briefs' with minimal primary facts.

Analysing this murder story longitudinally and qualitatively has methodological advantages in comparison to quantitative analyses (see chapter 3 and part III). A longitudinal qualitative analysis allows for deconstruction of the common-sense categories in the news, whereas quantitative content analysis tends to reconstruct them. It is especially suited to the quasi-experimental reasoning central to social science, allowing discovery and verification through suggestive contrasts. It entails the discovery of anomalous and peculiar detail of stories, and a focus on their significance. It takes into account emphasis, for example, position, placing, treatment, tone, stylistic intensification, and striking imagery. It reveals subtle aspects, including how an item is 'wrapped' with other items to create a theme and espouse an ideology; the particular sources used and how they are juxtaposed in stories to 'drop' innuendo or enclose on preferred readings; the priority given to items; and recurrence that may nevertheless not be expressible in quantitative terms. Moreover, in making evident these subtle aspects, longitudinal qualitative analysis clarifies the ways in which news texts are part of human action and help to constitute it. In this respect, longitudinal qualitative analysis is especially attuned to how human expression articulates social order, which is of central theoretical concern.

This murder story illustrates and substantiates the core thesis of our research. News of crime, law, and justice represents order through constituting an active discourse about the ordering activities of the people and organizations reported on. News of crime, law, and justice delineates the order of things, the procedures by which that order is accomplished, the organizational arrangements through which the procedures are invoked, the specific legal and policing provisions for reproduction of social order, and the identity of the human agents of this reproduction. In joining with the institutions they are reporting on to classify the tragic event and how it is dealt with, news operatives help to give shape to moral order and its articulation with social order. As such, the news media are as much an agency of *policing* as the law-enforcement agencies whose activities and classifications are reported on. In the face of signs of disorder, the news provides stable meanings that allow the individual to recognize, objectively, an order that stands outside of himself or herself as a source of authority and morality. Thus, in any given story of crime, law, and justice there is a lot more at stake than the resolution of a particular tragedy or trouble. The society's system of institutional authority and morality is at stake. Ultimately a single criminal act provides the occasion not simply for a primary factual account of what happened, but for a morality play of how what happened fits into the order of things.

Sensing Disorder: Murder, Investigation, Insecurity

A woman's body was found on a Saturday morning in the basement of a convenience store in the town of Alliston, north of Toronto. On the following Monday NP, TP, TQ, and RQ reported this tragedy. NP, TP, and TQ described not only what happened and what the police were doing about it, but also how the people of Alliston were reacting to it. NP kept its popular narrative alive by publishing another story on Tuesday that provided police accounts of the investigation and of how people were reacting.

We begin with the items in NP (figure 4.1). NP has been described as the closest thing to television in print because of its emphasis on the visual and the dramatic (Royal Commission on Newspapers [RCN] 1981b). This description is apt for the Monday item, as the headline and the photographs occupy more column-inches than the written text of the story. The headlines, pictures, and captions also do a lot of work in the item, indicating that a respectable woman had been severely beaten to death and that the police were now out in force to gather evidence and, it is hoped, to apprehend the culprit. The written text fills in details on these aspects, adds the fear and loathing of residents, and draws links to the recent murder of another woman in the same area.

These two items in NP are replete with signs of disorder. The community has been 'struck' with a violent crime signifying disorder. The assault on the victim has also pierced the rule of law. The breakdown of 'law and order' is dramatized in the language describing the assault. There was a violent struggle: 'she fought for her life,' 'she put up one hell of a fight – she tried to defend herself ... There was a lot of debris and a lot of evidence of violence.' There was a violent end: the body was 'blood-splattered,' 'she'd taken a vicious beating,' and she 'died of a fractured skull caused by blows from a blunt instrument.' The breakdown of 'law and order' is also dramatized through having sources draw links to other violent crimes. A female clerk at the store related several previous robberies there, including one in which she 'was held up at knife-point,' and then expresses her sense of disorder by saying 'It's getting pretty scary, that's for sure.' A female resident who lives near the store says, 'This used to be such a quiet town,' suggesting that it is now full of disquiet. She also draws a link to the murder of another woman in the area, expressing the fear that there might be 'some sicko running around.'

The community's sense of order is also disturbed by the fact that this assault was on a person of a higher order. She was respectable: according to the testimony of her fellow store clerk and her stepfather, she was 'quiet,' 'friendly,' 'a good person – easy to get along with.' She was successful: an 'honor student,' 'clever,' 'an Ontario Scholar,' 'a straight A student' who had gone on to higher education. She was innocent: although 22, she is described by the police as 'a girl,' and recognized by everyone as a person with a future. Such retrospective reconstructions of the victim's respectability are integral to representing order, especially as they magnify the dangerous character of those who prey on purity.

All of this is very disturbing. What can be done about it? The answer is that the police are on the case, and faith and hope rests with them. The police define all aspects of what happened and why it happened. The police even have a say regarding the fear and loathing of the local people. The

FIGURE 4.1 NP Monday, Tuesday

Honor Student Died of Blows to Head

She 'fought for her life'

ALLISTON – Karen Hunter tried to fight off her murderer before she was bludgeoned to death, say police.

An autopsy yesterday revealed the honors student, 22, died of a fractured skull caused by blows from a blunt instrument in an attack at the Becker's store where she worked late Friday night.

'The girl put up one hell of a fight – she tried to defend herself,' said Alliston police chief Larry Hembruff. 'There was a lot of debris and a lot of evidence of violence.'

The woman's blood-spattered body was found early Saturday in the store where she worked part-time while attending Georgian College.

'She'd taken a vicious beating,' said OPP Det. Insp. Joel McArthur.

Police say they are looking at several possible murder weapons, and won't know for a few days if Hunter was sexually assaulted.

McArthur said police are following many leads but don't have a suspect.

The motive for the murder was robbery, he said.

Betty Jenkins, who worked at Becker's on alternate nights with Hunter, said the store had been robbed several times.

She said there were two robberies between Christmas and February, and Jenkins was held up at knife-point three years ago.

'It's getting pretty scary, that's for sure,' said Jenkins.

Jenkins described Hunter as quiet, clever and friendly. She was an Ontario Scholar and went to Laurentian University in Sudbury.

She said she had wanted to be a translator, but changed her mind and enrolled last year in Georgian College to become a legal secretary.

Hunter's stepfather, Bob Greenhill, of Angus, said the family was 'shocked' at the murder.

'She had been a straight A student all the way through high school, she was a good person – easy to get along with,' he said.

Hunter's natural father died a year ago.

Meanwhile, as police combed the ravine behind the store and went door to door looking for leads, residents of the town are worried.

'This used to be such a quiet town,' said Helen Neilson, who lives a few houses from the store where the murder took place.

'When you think about the murder of Di Palma, and now this, I just hope there isn't some sicko running around,' she said.

The decomposed body of Lee Mari Di Palma, who had disappeared last December, was found May 14 about 12 km (7 1/2 miles) from Alliston, which is 32 km (20 miles) southwest of Barrie.

Police are still investigating the murder of the 31-year-old mother of one. They say the two murders aren't related. *[Monday]*

Alliston Slaying

Anger is growing

Alliston residents are 'upset and angry' over the brutal slaying of Karen Hunter, the town's police chief said yesterday as investigators continued their search for the killer.

Chief Larry Hembruff said residents 'are banding together' to help find the Becker's store killer in the town 32 km (20 miles) southwest of Barrie.

Investigators have interviewed 100 witnesses since Saturday when the Georgian College student's blood-stained body was found in the store.

Several items found at the scene, including a smashed pop bottle, have been sent out for forensic tests.

Hembruff refused to say if Hunter had been sexually assaulted and said police were still looking for the weapon used to kill the 22-year-old woman.

Police are considering the possibility the smashed pop bottle may have been the weapon used, but will not know until the forensic tests are completed.

'Nobody deserves that to happen to them,' he said.

'And everybody is helping out any way they can because they are mad and a little scared about what happened.'

An autopsy revealed that the honors student died of a fractured skull caused by blows from a blunt instrument.

Police said the woman received a vicious beating from her attacker.

Her body was found in the store Saturday morning.

Alliston OPP and town police are involved in the investigation of the death that has shocked the town.

Chief Hembruff is asking anybody who was in the Alliston Becker's store between 9 A.M. and midnight Friday to contact Alliston OPP. *[Tuesday]*

---

police observe that, although people are 'angry' or revengeful, they are not taking the law into their own hands but rather are converting their negative feelings into positive assistance through legitimate channels: 'And everybody is helping out any way they can because they are mad and a little scared about what happened.' The police are the embodiment of 'order' as a noun, systematic and methodical in their work. But they are also the embodiment of 'order' as a verb, in action to put things in order, to find a culprit and have him submit to lawful authority. This ordering is signified in a photograph of the police officers combing the ravine. Although it is a still photograph, the police officers are in action – walking, heads down, sifting for the minutest detail – signifying what people would like to think is the very essence of all criminal investigations by the police.

NQ had no coverage of this murder story on either the Monday or the Tuesday. This is the stuff of the popular newspaper. NP's stories seem to be close to reality and alive. This effect is accomplished through the use of iconic elements such as pictures, simple theme, a brief written text, and striking language. The result is a popular narrative told in an interesting and even entertaining way. The entertainment aspect does not contradict the sense of realism but rather underpins it. A morality play is on offer, constituted by the realism combined with the event orientation, personalization (moral-character portrait of the victim; reactions from the people), focus on procedures (of the police), and precedent (links drawn to other violent crimes to signify disorder). Sensationalism is also a part of this formula: the newspaper denounces the very activities and people it preys upon to generate its readership of vicarious voyeurs.

This is also the stuff of television news. Television has a much more limited discursive capacity than newspapers have and therefore has an even greater tendency to rely on a dramatic and entertaining presentation to create a sense of realism. At the same time, its realism is more powerful because it can be 'validated' through visuals that bind messages to context. As illustrated in the TP story on Monday (figure 4.2), the reporter uses a series of voice-overs to literally point to key scenes of the murder and investigation and how they should be read. Added to this 'being there' component is TP's personalization of the story through the authority of their 'crime specialist' reporter. This 'crime specialist' was a well-known personality, part of the daily menu of news on TP. He was repeatedly shown as working *with* the police in the fight against crime. He was a familiar, credible, and authoritative person working with an institution and through a medium that had the same characteristics. As such, he not only reported on social and political processes but helped to constitute them. Through the police and the television medium, he helped to construct the community, including especially its sense of order.

This personalization through the reporter as 'crime specialist' is the major difference between TP's coverage and NP's coverage. The TP reporter portrays himself as part of 'the scene.' He takes the reader 'in closer,' for example, to the back door of the store, behind which, at the bottom of the stairs, the body was found. He is pictured with the police, joining with them

FIGURE 4.2 TP Monday

Teaser: [Top of show; shots of police identification officer arriving at the store where the crime occurred] Beating death shocks town.

Anchor: [Wide-shot of store where crime occurred] Good evening. The brutal weekend murder of a young woman in Alliston has shocked residents of the small farming community north of Metro. But crime specialist [names reporter] says her killer left several clues for Alliston police.

Reporter: [Still photo of victim, with word 'Bludgeoned' slanted across the top left of the photo] 22-year-old Karen Hunter, an honours student going to Georgian College part-time, died sometime late Friday night, around closing time at the Becker's store on Alliston's main street. [Shot of store, then reporter's stand-up in front of the receiving door at the back of the store] Miss Hunter's body was found at the foot of some stairs just inside the rear receiving door on Saturday morning when a man came to deliver the Saturday *Stars*. Apparently the killer must have escaped out the back door because it was left open. [Shot of ravine] Police searched a nearby ravine for clues and another murder weapon, aside from things that appear to have been used in the struggle in the store. [Shot of police identification officer arriving at the store where the crime occurred] OPP crime-lab experts remained inside the closed store yesterday. [Reporter and police chief shown talking in front of the Alliston police station] Alliston police chief Larry Hembruff has called the OPP [Ontario Provincial Police] to help his small department solve it.

Police Chief: [head shot, in front of Alliston police station] We've interviewed ... I believe we're over seventy people now and we have another thirty interviews to do today. We've got three teams on the go with an Alliston officer and an OPP officer.

Reporter: [Voice-over a street scene] Allistonians were stunned by the brutal robbery-slaying. [Head shot of Carol Stoddard] You just moved up to Alliston recently?

Carol Stoddard: About a year ago, that's right. We wanted to move out of the city and get a nice quiet area. You know, kids to grow up in.

Reporter: It shakes you up then, I guess?

Carol Stoddard: Yeah, it's a surprise.

Unnamed man, about 60 years of age: Oh yeah, anything like this shocks a person. Especially a small town like this, where things, usually, a quiet atmosphere.

Reporter: [Shot of reporter and Lou Pacini talking in front of a 'Sam-the-Record-Man' shop] Record-store owner Lou Pacini is changing his operation because of this.

Lou Pacini: [Head shot in front of 'Sam-the-Record-Man' shop] I don't think a girl should be left alone in a store, especially at those hours. You know, I think there should always be at least two people.

Police Chief: [Head shot, in front of Alliston police station] We're asking that anybody that was in the Becker's store between 9:00 P.M. and midnight on June the 3rd, Friday night, to please call us at area code 705-435-4141 [Vista of telephone number, continuing into the following segment].

Reporter: [Stand-up, with Alliston town sign/service club sign in the background] The worst possible scenario is that Karen Hunter's killer is some desperado passing through town on highway 89. But even so police officers are hoping forensic experts come up with enough evidence to pin this crime on the right guy and soon.

[In Alliston, sign-off]

---

in soliciting the help of the public as possible witnesses in a format similar to the 'Crime Stoppers' program (Carriere and Ericson 1989).

Otherwise the coverage in TP is quite similar to NP's. Dramatic language is used in describing what happened. The same still photograph of the victim as used in NP is reproduced, similarly accentuated with the caption 'Bludgeoned' written in red and slanted across the top left of the photograph. A similar moral-character portrait of the victim as a respectable, successful, and innocent person is created.

However, TP does not produce a sense of disorder by having residents of the town draw links to other acts of violence and express their fears in this regard. Instead, residents are used to express the impression that this single violent crime has jolted them, threatening the peace and tranquillity they had come to expect in the town. The reporter found a woman who had moved from the 'evil big city' to this quiet little town only a year earlier in order to provide a more peaceful and better environment for her children. While she does not express her sense of disorder in the words of the reporter – 'stunned' and 'shakes you up' – she admits that the crime is 'a surprise.' In any case, this resident plays the part well through the suggestion that the evil city has cast its shadow northward. The next clip is of an elderly gentleman who represents tradition, the voice of experience as to the way it was. The elderly gentleman says he has experienced 'shocks' as a result of the murder. These 'shocks' express the sense that the rule of law has been pierced 'in a small town like this,' where there is 'usually, a quiet atmosphere.'

Given his role as a 'crime specialist' working with the police, the TP reporter gives special attention to the police investigation. He provides visuals of a ravine, although no police officers are there, and says that the police searched it. He shows Ontario Provincial Police crime-lab experts outside the store where the murder occurred. He obtains police accounts of the volume of interviews they have completed and have planned. He joins with the local police chief in encouraging citizens to call the police if they think they know something that might be of use. He includes a clip of a local merchant who indicates that new private security arrangements now seem to be in order: not allowing 'a girl' to 'be left alone in a store, especially at these hours.' Finally, he adds that the greatest fear for the police (but hardly for the townspeople!) is that the culprit is 'some desperado passing through town on highway 89.' This allows him to close with the hope that 'forensic experts come up with enough evidence to pin this crime on the right guy and soon.' The viewer is directed to put his or her faith in the special 'scientific' powers of the police as *the* source of hope that this 'desperado' will not strike again, piercing and shocking another community.

The TP story offers readers a particular way of imagining the real. The authorities – the police, the 'crime specialist' journalist, the television station and medium – are hard at work, doing everything they can to find the culprit and restore a sense of order. Moreover, even while their work is obviously directed at the rationalization and solution of a particular problem, it is also a testimonial to their authority. Already we have a renewed sense of order through the orderly ways in which the authorities have taken command of the matter. The viewer's perceptions are channelled into forms compatible with what has been authorized by the police and news operatives. This story bears witness to the authority of the police and news operatives to imprint reality, including their own pivotal roles in patrolling the thin blue line between order and disorder. Indeed, because their authority is represented and justified through an actual witnessing of their work on an important case, it appears to be natural. Any questioning of their authority is erased because the focus is on a single case and how it will be solved in terms of police and journalist investigative powers. In providing knowledge in this form – urging the viewer to acknowledge the authoritative apparatuses for ordering society – this story constitutes a social discourse of legal authority.

TQ's story (figure 4.3) on the Monday includes the same aspects. It opens with the anchor stating that 'police are working *frantically* to track down the killer,' and adding, 'they've *interrogated* seventy people in connection with the case.' This intensive police work is necessary because 'the brutal murder has scared the townsfolk.' The anchor's lead provides the

FIGURE 4.3 TQ Monday

Anchor: [Cell photograph of victim] Police are working frantically to track down the killer of a young woman in Alliston, near Barrie. So far they've interrogated seventy people in connection with the case. The brutal murder has scared the townsfolk.

Reporter: [Graduation photo of victim, as in cell] 22-year-old Karen Hunter died of a fractured skull caused by blows from a blunt instrument. [Shot of Becker's store] Karen's body was discovered Saturday morning in a basement storage room of the store where she worked. Police list the motive as robbery.

Police Chief: [Head-shot with top of police car in the background] The investigation, so far we've interviewed over seventy people as of this hour and we have four teams on the road and another thirty interviews scheduled. We've got everybody working around the clock on this thing, we want to get somebody as soon as we can, and yes the guys are working extra shifts just to cover 'til hopefully we make an arrest.

Reporter: [Shot of police officer leaving police van to go to the store where the incident occurred] The chief and other investigators say the girl was brutally beaten. OPP crime-lab members have spent much of the weekend and most of today at the scene. [Shot of reporter with face to entrance door of store, police officer on the other side of the closed door] The store remains closed, guarded by police. [Head shot of Brenda Bondy] Brenda Bondy, after this interview, provided police with information about a possible suspect.

Brenda Bondy: [Head shot of Brenda Bondy; the store where the incident occurred in the background] I seen a guy, he was standing on the corner. And, like, he had been there previous about two hours before. And like he was just hanging around.

Reporter: Could you describe him?

Brenda Bondy: Yeah, he was big, he had dark hair, he wore glasses.

Reporter: [Head shot of Tina Farr on street] As a result of the murder, many people are afraid.

Tina Farr: Everybody's staying in the house now and they're keeping the doors locked when they go in and they're making sure their windows are locked and secure and everything.

Reporter: [Stand-up with police vehicles in background] This town was already reeling from the shock of a murder-suicide which took two lives in March. Then there was the fire that destroyed four downtown

buildings two weeks ago. With the discovery of Karen Hunter's body here on Saturday many townsfolk are wondering what will happen next.
[Sign-off, Alliston]

---

essence of the story. The reporter is left to fill in the details of the authorities' hard work, including his own, directed at finding the culprit and alleviating the community's sense of disorder.

Following a brief description of the crime, the reporter uses a clip of the Alliston police chief, with his police car in the background, 'at the ready.' The chief reiterates that interviews with seventy people have been conducted and adds that thirty more interviews are scheduled. Unlike the anchor, who referred to 'interrogations,' thus giving the impression that seventy suspects had been processed, the chief uses the term 'interviews' to connote that these encounters involved the statements of witnesses or informants. The chief gives further emphasis to the extraordinary effort in stating that 'we have four teams on the road' and that 'we've got everybody working around the clock ... working extra shifts just to cover 'til hopefully we make an arrest.' The clip of the police chief is immediately followed by more signs of the police at work, with visuals of a police officer leaving a police van to enter the store where the crime occurred, voiced-over by the reporter stating that Ontario Provincial Police crime-lab members have been working over the weekend and are continuing their part of the investigation. This police work is depicted while the reporter reiterates that 'the *girl* was brutally beaten.'

The TQ reporter then plays his part in the investigation. Unlike the TP reporter, he does not picture himself close to the various scenes of the investigation, searching for physical evidence, nor does he give viewers the police telephone number and ask possible informants or witnesses to come forward. Instead he produces his own witness, a woman who says she saw a suspicious person. After presenting his own account from this witness, the reporter indicates that she then went to the police to offer the same information. Through this approach, the TQ reporter appears to have been directly involved in the investigative process, generating a witness account.

The reporter proceeds to underscore that all of this frantic work is necessary because 'the people are afraid.' Fear is expressed by a female resident who indicates that, in addition to all the frantic work of the public police, private security measures have intensified. '*Everybody's* staying in the house now and they're keeping the doors locked when they go in and they're making sure their windows are locked and secure and everything.'

As if this is not enough, the reporter closes by drawing his own link to other recent disasters in town over which there has been fear and loathing, intensifying the sense of disorder. 'This town was already reeling from the shock of a murder-suicide which took two lives in March. Then there was the fire that destroyed four downtown buildings two weeks ago.' With all of this, and now a tragic murder, who can help 'wondering what will happen next'?

TQ followed this item with an item on a dangerous sex offender who had escaped a closed custody facility in Toronto. This was more disturbing news, another reason to feel insecure. In its dramatic structuring and language, in its fear and loathing and attendant links to other problems, and in its displays of intensified policing, TQ was no different from TP and NP. They all employed the same recipe, albeit with some improvisation in the use of particular ingredients.

RP had no coverage of this murder story on the Monday. Given our knowledge of RP and its crime reporter at the time (cf Ericson, Baranek, and Chan 1989: chap. 3), a possible explanation is that RP was unable to commit its relatively scarce resources to this story. RP's crime reporter was required to submit several items each day from the Toronto police and court beats, and to update the items hourly. If he travelled to Alliston to cover the murder story, it would have taken all day, especially if he sought to generate actuality clips from the police and citizens. Nevertheless it is anomalous that RP did not include at least an anchor brief regarding this murder on the Monday.

An anchor brief was provided in RQ. It appeared sixth in the line-up, wrapped with another anchor brief stating that a man had been charged with murder after a man died during a fight in a Toronto rooming-house. The anchor brief regarding the Alliston murder (figure 4.4) states primary facts about the incident, the police attribution of motive, and the police investigation. Missing is the dramatic language, moral-character portrait of the victim, and actualities of reporters investigating with the police, characteristic of the television outlets and NP. This is a bulletin-type announcement, not a dramatic morality play fostering a sense of disorder and testifying to the forces of 'law and order.'

There are several characteristics of the radio medium that also explain why the radio outlets did not dramatize this item as a story of good and evil. The most fundamental characteristic is the lack of a visual capacity in radio. The fact that radio messages are apprehensible to the ear alone and as such are even more evanescent than television messages, combined with the need to direct messages to a heterogeneous audience, means that radio messages must be kept short and simple. Moreover, these characteristics – audio only, evanescence, heterogeneous audience, short and simple messages – combine to curtail the ability of radio journalists to convey connotative meanings.

FIGURE 4.4 RQ Monday

Anchor: Alliston police are investigating several leads in their efforts to solve the murder of a 22-year-old clerk. The body of Karen Hunter was found in the basement of the milk store where she worked late Friday night. Police say she was beaten to death with a blunt instrument and robbery has been reported as the motive. A police spokesman says investigators are waiting for results of a laser scan of the woman's body for fingerprints.

Television and newspaper journalists can connote a great deal through the juxtaposition of pictures, captions, headlines, story items, and source quotations. Television journalists can do even more through camera angles, lighting, staging, and editing techniques. Although the fact is that television journalists produce fictions (Ericson, Baranek, and Chan 1987: 335ff), their greater ability to bind their messages to context means that their items nevertheless appear most valid and real. If radio journalists tried to emulate the practices of television and newspaper journalists in the construction of connotative meanings – for example, through the use of dramatic language, juxtaposition of actuality clips, and background music and other sounds – their items would not only be sensed as inappropriate, but would be condemned as being in bad taste. In the extreme radio news messages would lose their authority, sensed as even more bizarre and disordered than the events being reported on. More than anything else, the comparative limitations of the radio medium explain why its coverage of the murder story at this stage was non-existent (RP) or limited to a factual anchor brief (RQ), rather than resonant with the popular narrative unfolding in NP, TP, and TQ.

Restoring Order: Arrest, Justice, Security

The popular narrative was advanced and brought to a conclusion through three rituals: a news conference at which the police announced that a man had been arrested and accused of the murder; the first court appearance of the accused; and the funeral of the victim. Each of these rituals provided an important occasion for restoring order. They offered moral lessons about what people should be as well as what they should do. They did so through the five key elements for deriving moral principles: an event-orientation, personalization (moral-character portraits), a focus on procedures (procedural propriety as a barometer of responsibility and accountability), realism (*the* way of seeing, a source of cultural mythologies), and precedent ('bringing home' a familiar discourse about what seems right and real, providing a mode of belonging). Through these elements, justice was displayed, and a renewed sense of security and order was conveyed.

As rituals, the news conference, court appearance, and funeral were structured performances in which actors played their parts by calling upon interpretations, meanings, images, and myths as institutional objects that were not their own. The actors communicated within the narrowed grooves of institutional meaning that defined the occasion, their qualifications to speak, their gestures and other permissible signs of the discourse, and the value of those signs. 'Religious, judicial, therapeutic and in large measure also political discourse can scarcely be dissociated from the deployment of a ritual which determines both the particular properties and the stipulated rules of the speaking subjects' (Foucault 1981: 61).

As the following news items show, the actors in these ritualistic performances were not only police, court, and church officials. Also included was a large supporting cast of the people of Alliston and, importantly, journalists. For their part, journalists also operated within the narrowed grooves of institutional meanings. However, journalists did not function simply as conduits for the institutional voices of their sources, reproducing a uniform product across media and markets. As we shall see, there was variation in the reports on these rituals. While journalists are left to interpret the preinterpreted symbols of institutional voices on such occasions, they must still engage in 'constructive interpretation' (Dworkin 1986) that expresses their news outlet's preferred reading. As central actors in these rituals, and in actively constituting them, journalists are circumscribed but not foreclosed in their use of institutional meanings. The following documentation of differences in coverage among the news outlets testifies to this fact.

The police arrested a suspect on the Monday, and on Tuesday they held a news conference to mark the occasion. The facts of the arrest and the charge of first-degree murder were reported in all six news outlets. The broadcast outlets had items prepared for their evening newscasts on Tuesday, and the newspapers published items in their Wednesday morning editions.

NP treated the arrest and charge of the accused as a lead item (figure 4.5). The story received front-page treatment, with a photograph of the victim captioned 'beaten to death' and a headline 'Arrest in milk store killing' leading the reader to page two. This boxed 'tease' was in red, with white lettering. It was wrapped with another front-page tease picturing a head shot of a two-year-old boy 'hit by a truck' and headlined, 'Tragic end to a park outing,' also leading the reader to page two.

On page two, there are photographs between the written texts for both stories. These photographs show two police officers checking a truck, in front of a pool of blood and a circle marking where a body was found; and a man in the rear of a car with his hands over his face. While these photographs 'belong' to the story about the boy struck by the truck, they function to draw the reader to the entire page, including the story of the arrest of the suspect in the murder case. In particular, the man in the back seat of the police car could be taken to be the suspect arrested for the murder, until the written text is inspected. While the photographs pertain to the story of the boy who died in the accident, they stand for the theme of the tragic death of youth with a future and emphasize the police investigation of these tragedies. Along with the headlines, these photographs tease the reader into both stories.

The writers give no hint that their story is based on a news conference held by the police, but the story has all the signs of this ritual. In contrast, television outlets are unable to disguise the fact that their material is framed within a news conference because of their need for visuals and talking heads from such occasions. The NP written text leads with the police account of the arrest and the identity of the accused. While it was evidently a tip from a citizen that was the essence of the matter, all the trappings of police work as the meticulous collection of physical evidence punctures the story: police divers have recovered the weapon and are still hard at work; blood-stained clothing belonging to the accused has been recovered; forensic tests on the victim continue; items found at the scene have been ruled out. These details provide witnessing about the likelihood that the accused is, indeed, the culprit.

The story also continues its witnessing of the victim's moral character. It reiterates through the still photograph of the victim used previously, and her status as 'a popular Georgian College student,' that she was respectable, successful, and innocent.

The main normative witnessing is now centred on the accused. While the accused 'is known to the police' (perhaps the most that can be said short of saying he has a police record), he has many attributes signifying respectability. He has had domestic stability, with daughters aged three and five, although he recently separated from his nuclear family. He has had employment stability, as witnessed by a former employer who says 'he was personable and honest' as an employee and 'the last person I would have suspected.' This character testimony, even well before the first court appearance, continues with a statement by a friend of the accused who says he saw the accused the morning the body was found and he 'didn't seem depressed ... He's an A-1 kid. He's never been in any trouble with the police.'

FIGURE 4.5 NP Wednesday

Dad of Two Accused of Beating Death

Arrest in clerk slaying

Alliston – A Bradford-area father of two appears in Alliston provincial court today charged with first-degree murder in the slaying of milk store clerk Karen Hunter.

OPP and Alliston police officials said yesterday a tip from a motorist who picked up a hitchiker with blood-stained clothing early Saturday in Alliston led to the arrest yesterday of James Edward Rogers, 30, at his parents' home in Riverdale Park, south of Bradford.

A Crossman pellet revolver, alleged to be the murder weapon, was found later by OPP divers in Soldiers Bay marina near Holland Landing, not far from the Rogers' home.

Police divers will continue searching the area today for more clues.

Blood-stained clothing belonging to Rogers was also recovered, police said.

OPP Det. Insp. Joel McArthur said forensic tests are being done to determine if Hunter was sexually assaulted during the attack.

Hunter, 22, a popular Georgian College student, was found lying in a pool of blood in the Becker's store in downtown Alliston early Saturday morning by newspaper delivery men who called police.

An autopsy revealed the honors student died of a fractured skull caused by blows from a blunt instrument.

Police believe Hunter was shot in the head with the pellet gun then beaten with it.

Several other items, including a smashed pop bottle, were found at the scene, but police have ruled them out as murder weapons.

Hundreds of tips
Although police received tips from more than 100 people, the key to the arrest was a motorist who contacted officers after hearing radio reports that they were looking for a man who'd been in the area at the time.

Alliston Police Chief Larry Hembruff said Rogers, an unemployed laborer recently separated from his wife Bonnie and two daughters aged 3 and 5, is known to police and has lived in Alliston during the past eight years.

Police are unsure whether Hunter knew her assailant.

Hembruff said he is concerned about security at Rogers' court appearance this morning at the downtown courthouse because of the anger in the town over the killing.

Shortly after Rogers is arraigned on the murder charge Hunter's funeral procession will move through streets near the courthouse at 1:30 P.M.

Lining the streets will be friends, relatives and town merchants who, in tribute to the young woman, will close their doors from noon to 3:30 P.M.

While the killing shocked this town of 4,700, 32 km (20 miles) southwest of Barrie, Rogers' arrest also came as a surprise to those who know him.

'Personable and honest'
'He's the last person I would have suspected,' said Don Robertson, owner of a Shell service station where Rogers worked two years ago.

'When he worked here, he was personable and honest.'

When he was in Alliston, Rogers lived with his family only a stone's throw from the Becker's store, friends said.

Rick Gossen, 37, lives across the road from Rogers near Bradford and was with two friends Saturday morning when they picked him up near Hwy. 11 and Bathurst St.

Gossen said Rogers 'didn't seem depressed. He didn't seem down in the dumps or anything,' when they picked him up about 11:30 A.M.

'He's an A-1 kid. He's never been in any trouble with the police,' said Gossen.

The other work done in this story is continuation of the subplot about the revengeful, 'angry' townspeople (see figure 4.1). The chief of police is cited as being concerned about security for the accused's first court appearance 'because of the anger in the town over the killing.' Moreover, 'shortly after Rogers is arraigned on the murder charge Hunter's funeral procession will move through streets near the courthouse at 1:30 PM.' This expression of concern about public order not only confirms the previous day's story headlined 'Anger is growing' (figure 4.1), but also sets up the next day's story, headlined 'Angry crowd sees accused dragged kicking into court' (front page) and 'Spectators jeer killing accused' (figure 4.11).

In contrast to NP's treatment of the arrest and charge of the accused as a lead item, NQ's report was a brief with three column-inches on page five (figure 4.6). This was NQ's only report on the entire matter. Based on police accounts, the NQ item reports when the crime likely occurred, where the victim's body was found, and the fact that the victim's skull was fractured. It also states the name and domestic status of the person charged, how the

FIGURE 4.6 NQ Wednesday

In Brief

Man charged in slaying

A 30-year-old man is to appear in Provincial Court in Alliston, Ont., today charged with first-degree murder in the death of Karen Hunter, whose body was found Saturday in the basement of the milk store where she worked. Alliston Police Chief Larry Hembruff said the charge against James Edward Rogers of River Drive Park, east of Bradford, was laid late Monday after a motorist reported taking a hitch-hiker from Alliston to Bradford early Saturday. Police now believe the 22-year-old Becker's Milk clerk was attacked as she was about to close the store, about midnight Friday. Examination of the body indicated her skull was fractured after being struck repeatedly with a pellet pistol. Chief Hembruff said a pistol believed to have been the murder weapon was recovered by divers from a river near Mr. Rogers' home shortly after his arrest. The accused is separated from his wife and two children, who live in Alliston.

police learned of the suspect, and the fact that the murder weapon has been recovered. This item eschews dramatic language and pictures, detailed character portraits of the victim or the accused, and detailed accounts of the police work involved. As such, it lacks the elements of a popular narrative with moral lessons, including personalization, a focus on procedures, realism, and precedent.

The popular narrative is very much alive in TP's same-day account of the police news conference (figure 4.7). Focused on the police news conference and 'framed' by it, TP's story on the Tuesday continues with the dominant feature of its coverage on the Monday: the 'scientific' police investigation and the 'involvement' of TP's 'crime specialist' reporter in it. TP's story also includes a moral-character portrait of the accused.

The story in TP appeared as the fourth item in the line-up, wrapped with three other crime and accident stories. A story about the toddler killed by the truck in the park was number two in the line-up. This was followed by an anchor brief reporting that a young girl had been sexually assaulted after a break-and-entry into her home in Toronto. The Alliston murder story was next, followed by an anchor brief regarding a dangerous sexual offender who had escaped from a closed facility in Toronto. So packaged, these lead items sustained the theme of pure and innocent young people being victimized by dangerous offenders 'on the loose.'

The anchor's lead offers a blunt reminder of the brutality of the murder, and follows with the introduction of the 'crime specialist' reporter. The reporter leads with a link to his Monday story and an effort to display investigative prowess. Pictured with the Alliston police chief outside the local station (i.e., working *with* police), he proclaims that his prediction of yesterday was correct: 'I told you last night the police had a lot of evidence in the murder of Karen Hunter and the suspect would be either a local resident or somebody passing through the farming community. It turns out all of that was correct.' It is difficult to imagine that such a 'prediction' would not turn out to be correct. The culprit was either a local or a stranger.

The police-centred narrative is sustained through a primary factual account from an OPP detective-inspector concerning the timing of the arrest, the identity of the accused, and the recovery of the weapon. Later, the reporter notes that a key tip came from a motorist who had picked up the accused as a hitch-hiker. This is followed by another clip featuring the OPP detective-inspector, who gives credit to the parts played by other unnamed witnesses, and uses the metaphor of a 'jigsaw puzzle' to describe how the police are working to put all of the pieces together. Later, the investigative prowess of the police is displayed further through visuals of police divers at work in the river where the murder weapon was found, voiced-over by the reporter pointing to their search for additional physical evidence. The reporter's 'closeness' to the police and investigation is signified in closing through visuals of the OPP detective-inspector and the Alliston police chief chatting to him informally after the news conference.

The other significant element in the TP story is the moral-character portrait of the accused. The reporter, 'in town,' notes that the accused lived there until his recent separation from his nuclear family. He uses a stand-up in front of the accused's regular pub to signify he had many friends in town although they now seem as if they do not want to know him. Later, the reporter talks to two men who live close to the accused's last residence in another town near Alliston. The reporter notes that the accused was raised in this area and was back living with his parents. The reporter has the first man give an account of the accused's recent employment history and changes in residence. Having 'pegged' the accused in terms of significant indicators of stability – domestic arrangements and employment history – the reporter uses a second man, unnamed, to express his surprise that the culprit turned out to be the person accused. The efforts of the TP reporter in this regard were similar to what was provided in NP (figure 4.5), although the employment- and residential-stability indicators seem less favourable in TP.

FIGURE 4.7 TP Tuesday

Teaser: [Second out of three teasers; shot of house] Arrest in Alliston murder.

Anchor: [Photograph of victim] We've learned the young woman, murdered last Friday night in Alliston, was shot with a pellet gun, and her killer had then used that weapon to beat her to death. Police have made an arrest and crime specialist [names reporter] says the 30-year-old suspect is a former Alliston resident.

Reporter: [Stock film from Monday's coverage showing the Alliston police chief and the reporter in front of the police station, with the word 'Charged' slanted across the top left of the shot] I told you last night the police had a lot of evidence in the murder of Karen Hunter. [Close-up of Alliston police chief] And the suspect would be either a local resident or somebody passing through the farming community. [Alliston street scene] It turns out all of that was correct.

OPP Detective Inspector: [Head-shot at the news conference] Late yesterday afternoon, on Monday, June 6, 1983, James Edward Rogers, 30 years, of [address] was arrested for the murder of Karen Ruth Hunter. [Cutaway to shot of Alliston police chief at the news conference] The murder weapon, a Crossman pellet revolver, has been recovered by the OPP scuba divers in the Bradford area.

Reporter: [Stand-up on an Alliston street] James Rogers moved from Alliston back with his family in Bradford after his marriage broke up here back in January. But he was known to come back and visit. [Points to a public tavern behind him] In fact, he was known to frequent this bar called The Cave. A lot of people in this small town, a lot of people, knew James Rogers, but his close friends were hiding today. [Stand-up in front of store where victim was found] One big lead in the case was from a man who said he picked up a hitch-hiker on highway 89 not far from the Becker's store and took him to the Bradford area. [Head shot of the OPP detective-inspector at the news conference] When he heard about the murder on Saturday he called police.

OPP Detective Inspector: We have that. We have other witnesses that have put the pieces together for us. Not only that one motorist, but other witnesses that have come forth, and like a jigsaw puzzle, the pieces are all fitting together.

Reporter: [Wide shot, reporter talking to Bill Trent] In [address] neighbours are stunned by the news. [Shot of exterior of house] Rogers grew up there and had just moved back with his parents. Bill Trent knows him.

Bill Trent: [Talking head, showing stream in the background] Come back from Calgary, three months ago. No job, looked for work, couldn't find any. Joined the circus in Bradford, and went with them for about three weeks I guess, and then reappeared here.

Young man: [Unidentified, talking head] ... shock to me [inaudible]

Reporter: [Stand-up on a bridge, pointing to the water, pan shot to the water] Yesterday divers found the murder weapon – the pellet gun – in the shallow waters of the Holland River, three blocks from the Rogers' home. [Wide shot of bridge, close-in to divers] Today divers were back in the river off the Bradford bridge, looking for something else they say is involved in the case. [Reporter, OPP detective-inspector, and Alliston police chief standing, chatting, in the room where the news conference was held] Rogers appears in court in the morning in Alliston, while friends of Karen Hunter bury her in the town tomorrow afternoon.

[Sign-off, in Alliston]

The major difference between the coverage of TP and NP at this stage is that NP sustains its theme of a revengeful and 'angry' townspeople, leading to a prediction that there might be serious trouble (collective violence) at the court building when the accused arrived for his first scheduled appearance. TP's reporter does not make a similar prediction. As a 'crime specialist,' he stays with his main theme of systematic police work and investigative success.

TQ did not sustain its popular narrative on the Tuesday. It continued the story by noting, in an anchor brief at the very end of the show, that a suspect had been arrested and charged (figure 4.8). This item was wrapped with another anchor brief stating that a toddler had been killed after being struck by a truck in a city park.

Given the play TQ gave to the murder story on the previous day (figure 4.3), it seems peculiar that it did not sustain the popular narrative through coverage of the police news conference on the Tuesday. On the basis of content analysis, it is impossible to explain why TQ chose to 'brief' this item. On the basis of our previous ethnographic observations of TQ, we can speculate on possible explanations. We know that at the level of production news is more procedure-related than content-related. The fact that this item was briefed has nothing to do with the newsworthiness of the event for TQ, but rather pertains to how TQ journalists were organized on the particular day. They may not have been informed about the news conference. They may have known about the news conference but decided not to assign a crew because of other priorities and limited resources. They may have dispatched

FIGURE 4.8 TQ Tuesday

Anchor: There has been an arrest in the beating death of Alliston store clerk
   Karen Hunter. Thirty-year-old James Edward Rogers of Bradford will
   appear in court tomorrow, charged with first-degree murder.

---

a crew but something went wrong: their equipment malfunctioned at the
event; the studio equipment malfunctioned in editing or during the show; the
crew did not make it back to the studio in time because their car broke
down, they were tied up in traffic, etc. Given the positioning of the item at
the very end of the show and its brevity, it is likely that either something
went wrong in production or the event was unknown to them up to a short
time before the show and the details were picked up from another broadcast
outlet's news show. In any event, given TQ's lead coverage of the story on
the Monday (figure 4.2) and on the Wednesday (figure 4.13), it is reasonable
to conclude that it briefed the Tuesday item in the face of such situational
contingencies, rather than because it normally 'briefed' such items 'for the
record' as was the case for both NQ (figure 4.6) and RQ (figure 4.10).

RP's crime reporter did manage to file a story on the Tuesday, having
missed Monday (figure 4.9). While the story leads with the fact that a person
had been accused of the murder, there is no indication that the reporter
actually attended the police news conference in Alliston. There is no
mention of him reporting from Alliston in the anchor lead or sign-off, and
no interview clips of police officials at the news conference, indicating that
the reporter prepared the story at his desk in Toronto. There is a voice clip
from a resident of Alliston, but this may have been recorded via telephone
after the reporter obtained the name of the source from another news outlet
or through personal contacts.

The RP story contained most of the features of popular narrative
developed in TP and NP. RP's crime reporter generally adopted the dramatic
language and focus on police investigation characteristic of his popular-
outlet counterparts in television and newspapers. However, because of the
limitations of the radio medium and RP's news format, the RP reporter was
less able than were his counterparts in television and newspapers to develop
a continuing popular narrative with long items and multiple sources.

In the RP item, the anchor and reporter use graphic and vivid language
of 'bludgeoning' and 'vicious pistol-whipping' to describe how the victim
met her death. The reporter also gives particular attention to the police
investigation, emphasizing the fact that the police and journalists mobilized

FIGURE 4.9 RP Tuesday

Teaser: [Lead teaser] The lead stories this hour. A man has been charged in connection with a weekend murder in Alliston ...

Anchor: A former resident of Alliston will appear in provincial court tomorrow charged with first-degree murder in the bludgeoning death of a milk-store clerk in that town last weekend. [Names RP's reporter] has the story.

Reporter: The suspect is 30-year-old James Edward Rogers who was arrested at his home [address] in Bradford, out of Alliston. He has lived in Alliston off and on for about eight years and moved to Bradford after separating from his wife and two children this past January. He had lived within a block of the Becker's store where 22-year-old Karen Hunter was held up and murdered last weekend. She would have known Rogers only casually as a regular customer. Miss Hunter was shot with a pellet gun. However, it was a vicious pistol-whipping with the butt of that gun which fractured her skull and caused her death. The gun was found by OPP scuba divers in water near the Holland Marsh. A resident of Alliston, Rhona Bolton, knew Rogers and his wife for almost eight years.

Rhona Bolton: My girlfriend lives in Toronto and she's nervous, you know, and then she comes up here and she's fine, but this happened now and you don't know where you can live. Like, where are you safe anymore?

Reporter: The extensive news coverage inspired over 100 tips from citizens. They included a motorist who drove a nervous hitch-hiker with blood-stained clothes from Alliston to Bradford early Saturday morning. This was the break in the case.

[Sign-off]

FIGURE 4.10 RQ Tuesday

Anchor: A 30-year-old man has been charged with first degree murder of a 22-year-old Alliston woman. Charged is James Rogers of Bradford. The body of Karen Hunter was found in the basement of an Alliston milk store on Saturday morning. Miss Hunter suffered a fractured skull after being repeatedly beaten with a revolver, according to police.

a large number of citizens as informants, including one citizen who provided 'the break in the case' by identifying a hitch-hiker he picked up who turned out to be a likely suspect. The RP reporter also addressed the police search for physical evidence by stating that a pellet gun believed to be the murder weapon had been recovered from a river. Consistent with the coverage in TP and NP, there is no suggestion here of the likelihood that the suspect told the police the exact location of the weapon as part of his statement of confession. Rather, it sounds as if police specialists, including trained scuba divers, used their investigative prowess to ferret out such evidence. This depiction of policing illustrates that legal and organizational restrictions on what can be communicated (in this instance, the suspect's statement of confession), combined with subtleties in how police work is therefore routinely described, result in the reproduction of police occupational ideology regarding their investigative techniques and prowess.

In contrast to TP and NP, and probably because of the limits on the permissible length of news items, RP does nothing to develop the moral-character attributes of the victim. Likewise there are no indicators of the moral character of the accused, other than the statement that he had recently separated from his wife and two children and moved to another town. Instead of using local people to account for the accused's character attributes, which was the approach taken in both TP and NP on Tuesday, the RP reporter includes a classic fear-and-loathing clip from a local resident more in keeping with the coverage on Monday in TQ, TP, and NP: 'My girlfriend lives in Toronto and she's nervous, you know, and then she comes up here and she's fine, but this happened now and you don't know where you can live. Like, where are you safe anymore?'

RP was also consistent with all the other outlets in sustaining the view that this murder was an act of stranger–stranger violence with robbery as the motive. The RP reporter does drop in the point that the victim 'would have known' the accused 'only casually as a regular customer' at the store. However, neither RP nor any of the other outlets ever raised explicitly the many possibilities surrounding the facts that the accused used to live very near to the store, had lived in the small town for eight years, and therefore probably knew the victim quite well. What specifically was the accused's previous relationship to the victim? 'Everybody' else in town seemed to have known the victim (figure 4.12), why not the accused? Why would the accused attempt a robbery at a store where he was almost certainly known as a 'regular' customer? This line of questioning is erased in favour of sustaining the impression that it was a stranger–stranger attack motivated by robbery. Such an impression adds sustenance to the popular narrative in two ways. First, it perpetuates the popular fear that 'you don't know where you can live ... where are you safe anymore?' Second, it underpins the popular belief that the police are well-equipped to turn a 'cold' case into a successful case cleared by arrest through shrewd, skilled, 'scientific' work.

As it had done on the Monday (figure 4.4), RQ broadcast an anchor brief on the Tuesday (figure 4.10). This account simply states that a named man of a certain town and age had been charged with first-degree murder in the beating death of a named woman of a certain town and age, after her body was found at a certain place and time. This primary factual account is even more sparse than the brief in NQ (figure 4.6), and it terminated RQ's coverage of the matter.

While RQ and NQ provided no further coverage, the other outlets searched for an ending to their popular narratives in the first court appearance of the accused and in the funeral of the victim. These rituals, which both occurred on the Wednesday, provided convenient 'pre-scripted' and 'precast' dramatic endings to the story. Nevertheless, the NP, TP, TQ, and RP scripts were not identical. The final script of each outlet reflected the particular 'constructive interpretations' (Dworkin 1986) their journalists had been developing all week long.

In the case of NP (figure 4.11), the accused's first court appearance was used to continue the theme of the townspeople turning their fear and loathing into anger and revenge against a dangerous man. NP's story on the Wednesday had predicted a large gathering at the court building and public-order problems (figure 4.5), and in their story on the Thursday, NP journalists did everything possible to show that the prediction was accurate.

As was typical of lead stories in NP, the photographs and headlines occupied more space in the story than did the written text. A huge photo-graph in colour, covering two-thirds of the front page, shows the accused as if he is being 'hauled,' literally, by a burly police officer. This photograph is framed by two caption/headlines, one in red with yellow backing, 'Alliston murder suspect,' and the other in red, 'Angry crowd sees accused dragged kicking into court.' The caption below provides a little more detail to lead the reader to the story on the next page. Included in this detail is the statement, 'In going into court, onlookers yelled insults as Rogers kicked out.' Taken together, this front-page material sets up the story by signifying the 'angry crowd' and an accused who seems to deserve the anger, being resistant to authority (having to be 'dragged kicking into court') and still violent (he 'kicked out').

On page two, the story leads with the elements depicted in the front-page headlines, captions, and photographs. The story is headlined 'Spectators jeer killing accused,' and leads with: 'While about 300 outraged residents shouted their anger, James Edward Rogers was dragged kicking by police into provincial court here yesterday and arraigned for the murder of milk store clerk Karen Hunter.' The next few paragraphs are punctuated with

FIGURE 4.11 NP Thursday

Spectators jeer killing accused

ALLISTON – While about 300 outraged residents shouted their anger, James Edward Rogers was dragged kicking by police into provincial court here yesterday and arraigned for the murder of milk store clerk Karen Hunter.

Rogers, 30, of Bradford, was remanded in custody by Judge Norman Nadeau until June 15 when he will appear again in Alliston on a first-degree murder charge.

A crowd of spectators began gathering outside the courthouse at about 8 A.M. yesterday. By the time Rogers arrived in an OPP cruiser two hours later, people swarmed nearby cat-calling and yelling insults.

Police blocked off the street where Rogers was brought to the courthouse and kept moving people away from the area for fear they would become violent.

During the brief walk from the cruiser, Rogers – a short, stocky man – kicked out at a group of 15 reporters and photographers.

Alliston Police Chief Larry Hembruff was slightly injured when he was kicked in the leg during the scuffle. A TV cameraman was also kicked.

Rogers was led into the tightly packed courtroom handcuffed to Alliston Deputy Police Chief Walter Kolodziechuk.

Rogers, sporting a moustache and collar-length brown hair, was dressed in jeans, a jean-jacket, and cowboy boots.

He sat silently in the prisoner's box, shielded from view by Hembruff and another policeman.

Rogers, who has yet to retain a lawyer, was represented during the five-minute hearing by duty counsel.

The crowd outside threw another barrage of insults at Rogers as he walked back to the cruiser returning him to Simcoe County Jail in Barrie where he is being held.

About an hour later, more than 250 mourners attended funeral services for the popular 22-year-old Georgian College student, whose slaying has left townspeople shocked and bitter.

'Karen was brutally and senselessly murdered. This is a senseless tragedy,' Rev. Peter Moffat told grieving relatives and friends at a 30-minute service.

'Our anger and outrage well up within us and threaten to overwhelm us. We are grieving as individuals and as a community.

'We are left in a state of shock and dismay. This happened not only to Karen, but to all of us.'

Moffat described Hunter as 'one in a million who could melt the hardest of hearts' with her pleasant manner. He said Alliston residents feel 'particularly vulnerable' for themselves and the lives of others in the wake of the killing.

Hunter's body was found in a pool of blood early Saturday at the Becker's store in downtown Alliston where she worked.

Police say Hunter's killer shot her in the head and bludgeoned her with a pellet gun.

Forensic tests are being conducted to determine whether she was sexually assaulted.

Rogers, a separated father of two, was arrested late Monday at the Bradford-area home of his parents.

A pellet gun was found by police in a nearby river.

Downtown businesses closed for three hours yesterday as a tribute to Hunter and part of the main street was blocked off briefly for the funeral procession.

Among mourners at the service and later at a brief grave-side tribute were Hunter's mother Doreen Greenhill, her stepfather Robert Greenhill, grandmother Dorothy Gauthier, sister Janice, and two of her three brothers, Colin and Brian.

Several fellow workers and classmates also attended the funeral.

---

additional statements about the 'angry crowd' – they '*swarmed* nearby cat-calling and yelling insults' when the accused arrived at the court building, and they '*threw* another *barrage* of insults' when he departed. The police are said to have been fearful that the crowd would become violent and, as a result, took preventative measures.

Based on our viewing of the television stories of this event, it appears that the preventative measures of the police precluded any resident's being anywhere near the accused. However, journalists did crowd near the accused as he was taken into court, and it seems that he reacted against them. As stated in the NP story, 'During the brief walk from the cruiser, Rogers – a short, stocky man – kicked out at a group of 15 reporters and photographers. Alliston Police Chief Larry Hembruff was slightly injured when he was kicked in the leg during the scuffle. A TV cameraman was also kicked.' This seems to confirm citizens' fear and loathing that this is a violent offender. However, it turns out that he was not reacting against the 'angry crowd,' as suggested by the construction on page one, but against loathsome reporters-as-vultures who prey upon those they denounce. Revealingly, while the television stories on this event refer to the 'anger' of the people and even the 'mob' that gathered outside the court building, they say nothing about the accused's actions. At one point in TQ's story (figure 4.13), the statement is made that 'there was no violence.' TP's story (figure 4.12) shows the accused being escorted from the police car to the court building. At one point, there appears to be the beginning of a 'scuffle,' but the visual suddenly moves to a long freeze shot of the accused *leaving* the court building, a shot almost identical to the front-page photograph used by NP. Apparently this is the point at which the accused reacted to the pack of journalists, but TP chose not to show the reaction or to make any reference in the script to such an occurrence.

The later portion of the NP story makes reference to the funeral of the victim. This account is introduced by recollection that the victim was respectable, successful, and innocent, as represented by the fact she was a 'popular 22-year-old Georgian College student' and by the photograph of her that had been used on each of the three previous days. The photograph also carries in a caption the blunt reminder that she was 'shot and bludgeoned.' The fear and loathing of the townspeople is now taken up through the institutional voice of religion and the church. The reverend who presided at the funeral is used to underscore not only the horrid crime, but also how it represents an assault on community order. The reverend says, 'Karen was brutally and senselessly murdered. This is a senseless tragedy ... Our anger and outrage well up within us and threaten to overwhelm us. We are grieving as individuals and as a community. We are left in a state of shock and dismay. This happened not only to Karen but to all of us.' Even the reverend's testimonial to the fine character of the deceased is contextualized by NP in terms of implications for members of the community. While the reverend described the victim as 'one in a million who could melt the hardest of hearts,' he is also said to have said 'residents feel particularly vulnerable for themselves and the lives of others in this time of killing.' Even the description of the funeral, and of those who attended, is inter-spersed with recollection of the body being 'found in a pool of blood,' 'shot ... in the head and bludgeoned,' possibly sexually assaulted, and with details of the police investigation and of the accused.

NP sustained the fear, loathing, and revenge of the townspeople to the very end, the funeral. This approach contrasts sharply with the constructive interpretation of the television journalists who covered the same events (figures 4.12, 4.13). They not only downplayed the 'anger' and sense of disorder of the people who gathered outside the court building, they gave emphasis to statements by the reverend that it is immoral and violent features of society that should be blamed and examined rather than the person responsible for this killing. The television journalists used the

FIGURE 4.12 TP Wednesday

Teaser: [Showing accused being taken into court building] 'Anger and Grief'
Anchor: [Still of suspect led by police officer in uniform and another officer
with an arm around him] In Alliston today murder-victim Karen Hunter
was buried. And the man accused of killing her appeared in court. Crime
specialist [names reporter] says emotions in the small town near Barrie
are running high.
Reporter: [Shot of people on street, side-banner 'Town Mourns'] About 200
townspeople gathered outside the city-hall court house/police station
building on Church Street for a glimpse of the suspect, 30-year-old
James Rogers, an off-and-on resident of Alliston, now of Bradford.
[Suspect getting out of police car, handcuffed hands over face, flanked
by two police officers] His arrival around 10:00 A.M. caused pushing
crowds and the odd jeer. [Move to freeze photo of suspect leaving court
building flanked by officers and cuffed to one] Rogers, a separated
father of two, was nabbed Monday in Bradford, charged with the pellet
shooting and beating death of 22-year-old Karen Hunter. He was
remanded until next week to give him time to hire a lawyer. [Shot of
accused and accompanying police officers returning to police car and
driving off] He left just as quickly for his Barrie provincial-jail cell.
He'll be back next week. ['Gone to Funeral' signs on the doors of two
stores] An hour later Alliston was shut down. Karen's fellow merchants
closed their stores along the three-block main drag to honour the slain
woman, a popular girl, working at Becker's and going to Georgian
College. [Shot of casket as it is carried out of the door of the funeral
home] She touched just about all of the 4,700 people here. If you had
a hankering for a late-night snack you probably remembered Karen's
pleasant ways and cheerful good night. [Shot of divers in river] OPP
divers continued looking for some other missing pieces of the Hunter
murder story in the Holland River near the suspect's Bradford home.
[Reporter stand-up in front of police van in front of the Becker's store]
Reverend Peter Moffat told the townspeople that we are all complicitous
in Karen Hunter's death. We're part of a society that puts profit before
people, that holds life cheaply, that condones subtle forms of violence
through pornography and even video games. He says the best thing
Allistonians can do now is to keep Karen's contagious spirit alive here.
[Sign-off, in Alliston]

FIGURE 4.13 TQ Wednesday

Teaser: [Lead tease at the top of the show; shots of crowds, police, a scuffle]
Mob scene in Barrie: accused woman killer brought to court.

Anchor: [Still photo of victim] James Rogers, the man accused of murdering
Karen Hunter, was met by an angry crowd when he appeared in court
this morning. Later, a clergyman at Karen's funeral tried to diffuse the
outrage. Here's [names reporter].

Reporter: [Shot of crowd near court building] A mob of people from
teenagers to grandparents stood waiting for the accused to appear.
[Police and accused rush past crowd and into the court building;
handcuffed accused covering his face] Police rushed him inside the
courtroom. [Shot of crowd near court building] But the crowd waited.
[Police and accused rush into car] A short while later Rogers reappeared. He's been remanded in custody. There was no violence. [Shot
of two women on street] But tension was high. [Shot of funeral-car
procession] Reverend Peter Moffat acknowledged the tension, the fear
and outrage in the community [Shot of men carrying coffin, funeral], as
he conducted Karen Hunter's funeral service. But he warned the
mourners not to let their feelings overwhelm them. He told them Karen
wouldn't want the community to be incapacitated by revenge. And he
asked them to take a critical look at the larger society [Shot of mourners
standing by] which he said tolerates and breeds violence. 250 people
came out to give emotional support to Karen's mother, stepfather,
grandmother, sister, and two brothers. [Wide shot of funeral, then
closing in] Many of these were shopkeepers on Alliston's main street.
[Still photo of victim, then sign on door 'Closed from 12–3:30 today for
funeral'] They closed their stores to show respect for a young woman
they admired.

[Sign-off, Alliston]

reverend to defuse the 'anger' and 'revenge' of the people, rather than to
fuel it as NP did in its coverage.

The coverage of the accused's first court appearance and the victim's
funeral in both TP (figure 4.12) and TQ (figure 4.13) was based entirely on
journalists' voice-overs. Rituals such as court hearings and funerals are not
occasions for source-interview clips on television. At the time it was illegal
to take either visuals or audio-recordings of court proceedings, and court
officials faced restrictions on what they could say until the case was decided

through the entire court process. Residents outside the court building might have been interviewed, but their reaction was better represented through visuals of the crowd, and later through the words of the reverend at the funeral. The visuals outside the court building offered sufficient action, including dramatic scenes of the police bringing the accused to justice. At the funeral it would have been improper to take an actuality of the reverend's eulogy or to interview him or individual mourners. The occasion speaks for itself. The solution for the television journalists was to voice-over many visual clips in rapid succession, relying on the visuals to do a lot of the description and in particular to convey tertiary understanding.

In TP's coverage only the anchor's tease and lead give particular emphasis to the 'anger' of the people and how their 'emotions ... are running high.' The reporter mentions that the accused's arrival at the court building brought 'pushing crowds and the odd jeer,' but these are neither seen nor heard. He makes no other reference to the collective behaviour of the crowd, which he describes in his opening statement as a gathering. As introduced previously (p. 101), the TP reporter 'froze out' the scuffle between the accused and journalists described by NP. We can only speculate on the reasons for this abrupt change of scene. The reporter may have sensed that his own pack of fellow journalists had precipitated the incident and, therefore, in fairness to the accused, decided to erase it. There may have been some question as to whether legal action might ensue, for which the television visuals of the incident might have served as evidence. Including the clip in the story might have prejudiced such a case. It may have been TP's own cameraman who was assaulted, interrupting his capacity to take visuals.

TP's coverage of the funeral is very different from NP's coverage. The reporter opens with visuals of the 'town' being 'shut down' to 'honour the slain woman, a popular girl, working in Becker's and going to Georgian College.' He adds his own statement about how she 'touched just about all of the 4,700 people here' as the pleasant clerk who served in the local convenience store. More significantly, his only reference to the eulogy is to say that the reverend said 'we are all complicitous' in the victim's death because 'we're part of a society that puts profit before people, that holds life cheaply, that condones subtle forms of violence through pornography and even video games.' While NP chose to attribute other statements to the reverend to sustain the individual pathology of the offender and what he had done to the community's sense of order, TP chose to use statements by the reverend that sustain a social-pathology view that evil causes evil, immorality breeds immorality. The message is that unless we all clean up our act, and unless we all contribute to moral repair work, there will be perpetuation of such violence.

TP's 'crime specialist' continued his thread that the police had worked hard and were successful through their investigative prowess. In this particular item, he barely had to say it because the visuals showed it. The police had their man, and they were shown, in action, bringing him to justice. And, even while the townspeople interrupted their normal routines to share in the ritual of the funeral, police investigators continued their normal routines, with scuba divers shown once again in the river, 'looking for some missing pieces in the Hunter murder story.' Moreover, the reporter recounts what the reverend said at the funeral about 'the violent society' through a stand-up shot of himself in front of a police identification-unit vehicle outside the Becker's store where the murder occurred. Here police effectiveness takes on the quality of affectiveness (Carriere and Ericson 1989). Our faith is restored through the police. Along with the 'contagious spirit' of people like the victim, the police manage to touch all of us.

In contrast to TP's, TQ's story gives much more emphasis to the 'angry' and revengeful feelings of the townspeople. This emphasis is accomplished through dramatic language rather than dramatic visuals. The lead tease at the top of the show states, 'Mob scene in Barrie: accused woman killer brought to court,' and the item opens with the anchor stating the accused 'was met by an angry crowd when he appeared in court this morning.' The frame is established with the statement that follows immediately: 'Later, a clergyman at Karen's funeral tried to diffuse the outrage.'

The reporter's opening account does not depict a 'mob scene' involving a 'crowd' that ranges in its emotions from 'anger' to 'outrage.' While the reporter refers to a 'mob,' and uses an isolation shot of two women to represent the contention that 'tension was high,' the visuals show a group of curious onlookers who say nothing and remain placid. After concluding 'there was no violence,' but contending 'tension was high,' the reporter moves to the funeral and opens with the statement that the reverend 'acknowledged the tension, the fear and outrage in the community.' This statement serves as a demonstration of what the anchor and journalist contended about the demonstration outside the court building, providing a bridge between the two rituals.

To this point the TQ story is more consistent with NP's than with TP's coverage. However, the TQ journalist then gives emphasis to the reverend's statements about not being revengeful, and about the need 'to take a critical look at the larger society which he said tolerates and breeds violence.' In contrast to TP's continuing emphasis on the police investigation, even during its coverage of the funeral, TQ's focus was on the funeral itself, maintained through visuals of the procession and proceedings voiced-over with accounts of who was in attendance and the numbers. The account here, as in the anchor's lead, is now personalized to 'Karen,' whom news consumers have come to know rather personally as the respectable, successful, innocent woman who represents, in tragedy, all that is pure and admirable.

While RQ did not broadcast a story on the Wednesday, RP included an anchor brief identifying the accused and his occupational status, and stating that he had appeared in court earlier in the day and was remanded for one week (figure 4.14). This item was fourth in the line-up, wrapped with two previous longer items: a report linking a person who had escaped from a closed facility with an entry into a residence and the sexual assault of a twelve-year-old girl there; and the sentencing of two men for a 'politically' motivated shooting in Toronto. RP's regular crime reporter covered the sentencing hearing, while a generalist reporter did the item linking the escapee to the sexual assault.

The comparatively scarce news resources of RP would limit the likelihood that a reporter would be sent out of town to cover the accused's court appearance and the victim's funeral. However, even if a radio station had reporters to spare, these events would have been extremely difficult to convey via the radio medium because of the absence of a visual capacity. As we have suggested regarding television, it was not appropriate on this day to obtain interview accounts from police and court officials, mourners, or other townspeople. However, it was also unnecessary for television journalists to obtain such accounts. Their visual capacity enabled them to show the police at work ('rushing' the accused in and out of the court building; still investigating in the river and at the scene of the murder), townspeople in a collective representation outside of the court building, and people in mourning at the funeral. Indeed, their visuals were so replete with tertiary understanding that voice clips from individual sources expressing what it was like would have seemed peculiarly redundant. The reporters from TP and TQ were able to sustain their own unusually long voice-over accounts through the use of a powerful range of visuals shown in rapid succession. At best, a radio reporter might have obtained the sounds of the townspeople gathered outside the court building, including any interesting 'catcalls' made as the accused was ushered by. However, a radio reporter could not use such sounds to sustain interest in any way equivalent to how the television reporters used their visuals. Moreover, he could obtain nothing from the funeral because it would be sensed as out of place and in bad taste to pick up either the reverend's eulogy or any other sounds in this context. Unable to portray these rituals in a visual manner, or to use words or background sounds to have readers visualize them adequately or appropriately, RQ opted for silence. RP did little more, carrying an anchor brief that stated primary facts about the accused and his court appearance in order to bring to a conclusion its lead item from the previous day.

FIGURE 4.14 RP Wednesday

Anchor: The man charged with last weekend's brutal murder of a young store clerk in Alliston made a court appearance in that town this afternoon. Thirty-year-old James Edward Rogers, an unemployed labourer from Bradford was remanded to June 15th whan a date is expected to be set for his preliminary hearing. Rogers faces a first-degree murder charge in connection with the beating death of 22-year-old Karen Hunter.

Representing Order: Morality, Procedure, Hierarchy

This murder story was presented as a continuing popular narrative in NP and the television outlets. A 'real life' story of murder and investigation close to home was the epitome of reporting for NP. As documented in chapter 6, NP normally used UPI wire copy of such tragic events in the United States to fill its columns and its readership's presumed desire for such material. When the event was close to home, it was 'played up' even more. The basic approach is to sustain a popular narrative through a blend of action and emotions. The victim is characterized as pure: respectable, successful, and innocent. This makes her death – described in graphic detail and with dramatic language – especially tragic and magnifies the dangerous character of the offender who preyed upon her purity. With the accused characterized as violent, dangerous, and less than human, his capture is especially heroic. The police are shown in action, both through prominent photographs and in dramatic descriptions of their efforts. The townspeople are also shown to be active, offering whatever 'bits' of information they can to the police, but also doing the emotional work of expressing sorrow, grief, anger, and revenge. The active senses of police investigative work and citizens' emotional work convey realism, making the reader feel close to the 'live action' of what is going on. This is, indeed, the closest thing to television in print. Moreover, it is only through the actions of *both* the authorities *and* the people that order can be restored and a feeling of security renewed. The police do their part by gathering evidence and bringing the accused to justice. The people do their part by making collective representations about justice: expressing fear and loathing, advising on private security arrangements, and attending the rituals of the court hearing and funeral. The journalists do their part by both helping the police with their investigations and helping the people with their expressions.

This approach in NP was repeated in the television outlets with some variation on particular themes and some medium differences in the capacity to convey the key elements of realism and tertiary understanding. As with NP, TP thrived on 'real life' tragedies close to home. Its approach to such tragedies was to give relatively greater emphasis to the police role in resolving them, with an active assist from their 'crime specialist' reporter. The leading actors in TP's crime stories were the police and TP's own 'crime specialist,' who always represented himself 'in close' with the police as they investigated. Combined with television's special qualities for conveying realism, this approach intensified the sense of action that was present to a much lesser degree in NP. TP's 'crime specialist' appeared as a familiar, credible, and authoritative person working with an institution (police) and through a medium (television) having the same characteristics. The authorities – the police, the reporter, the television outlet, and medium – were shown hard at work day in and day out, doing everything in their power to prevent and solve serious crime. This is unashamedly crime/police reporting as entertainment programming, reproducing popular myths about police 'scientific' investigation, crime, and criminality.

TQ's popular narrative was similar to TP in that it initially played up the police working 'frantically' in the face of the frantic townspeople, and its reporter was shown helping the police generate witnesses. However, lacking a familiar 'crime specialist' reporter similar to TP's, TQ's items were arguably less forceful and more 'forced' in this regard. Both TQ and TP included the feelings of the people, represented in their own words up to the point of the arrest of the accused, and in visuals with textual pointing by reporters on the day of the court appearance of the accused and the funeral of the victim. In the end, however, these visuals, combined with reference to selected statements of the reverend at the funeral, were used by both TQ and TP to downplay the angle of 'anger' and 'revenge' among the townspeople. In contrast, NP used other statements attributed to the reverend's eulogy, blended with reminders of the brutal slaying and police investigation, to sustain its main frame of 'community outrage.'

TQ's items were similar to those in the popular outlets because such stories fit so well with the dramatic-structuring capacities of the television medium. The visual capacity of television not only allowed for the realism and validation aspects described above regarding TP, it also allowed both outlets to display and thereby convey tertiary understanding in ways unavailable to newspapers or radio. The court appearance of the accused and the funeral of the victim could be shown as *spectacles*, with all of the ritual, drama, and tragedy associated with such *occasions* (Mathiesen 1987). From the perspective of television journalists, this story would seem a 'natural,' a 'real life' example of the rituals, dramas, and tragedies shown endlessly in their stations' entertainment programming. From the perspective of television business managers, this story would seem a 'natural' as a means of holding an audience in the competition for market share and advertising revenue.

RP made an effort to match the popular narratives in the television stations and NP but its accomplishments were much less. RP included one longer item with dramatic language, including a 'fear and loathing' clip from a female resident of the town to evoke similar feelings to those being expressed in the popular narratives in NP, TP, and TQ. However this effect was limited because of the characteristics of the radio medium itself: no visual capacity, evanescence, a heterogeneous audience, and the resultant need for short and simple messages combining to limit the ability to convey connotative meanings, including more subtle aspects of tertiary understanding. If an RP reporter had tried to overcome these limitations on the day of the court appearance of the accused and the funeral of the victim, his or her messages may not only have failed to represent order, but may have contributed to a sense of disorder by seeming out of place and in bad taste. Unlike his counterpart in TP, RP's crime reporter was limited to spot news with greater emphasis on primary facts (see also Ericson, Baranek, and Chan 1989: chap. 3).

Facing these same limitations of the radio medium, RQ did not even try to cover such events in terms of a popular narrative. Their only reports on this murder were bulletin-like anchor briefs, one announcing the murder and the police investigation, the other announcing that an identified man had been accused of the murder. RQ carried no advertising and therefore did not have to compete for a market share that would generate advertising revenue. Similar to NQ, it focused its reporting resources more on continuing stories about organizational deviance. For example, during our sampling period it sustained a popular narrative about corruption in a police force outside of Toronto (see chapters 8 and 9).

NQ also had an editorial policy that precluded treatment of such tragedies in the terms of popular narrative (Ericson, Baranek, and Chan 1987). If a murder occurred in Metropolitan Toronto, it was normally 'briefed' for the record only (ibid). In this context, since this particular murder occurred outside Toronto, it is anomalous that NQ carried even a brief stating that the accused was scheduled for a court appearance and providing some details about him and the investigation. This one brief was published probably because the murder and its investigation had been made a 'Toronto story' by other news outlets in Toronto to the point where NQ journalists felt they should at least publish what they normally included for such incidents in Toronto.

Focusing on the coverage in NP, TP, and TQ, we can summarize how popular narratives of this type serve to represent order. Readers are engaged in an active discourse of *ordering*. The focus is on the ordering activities of the people, and of the police and journalists working on their behalf. The narrative demarcates moral order, the specific legal and policing procedures for reproducing order, and the hierarchy through which those procedures are invoked. The narrative also constructs the identities of the human agents of this reproduction, including journalists who are pictured as *part* of these ordering activities. As such, journalists appear to join with other institutions involved in the reproduction of order, and serve as an agency of policing in this regard. Through well-established and routine journalistic devices – an event-orientation, personalization, a focus on procedures, realism, and precedent – news provides the essential elements through which readers can visualize moral principles and their connection to social order.

In a popular narrative of this type, there is a blending of fact and value, understanding and assessment. This blending occurs at the level of constructive interpretations by journalists and sources (cf Ortony 1979; Dworkin 1986) who, in the very process of describing the world factually, are bound to interpret and thereby falsify it, making it fictive in terms of their own values and understandings (Ericson, Baranek, and Chan 1987: 335ff). It also appears at the level of how the news is constructively interpreted by consumers. While facts are presented to them, they are blended with expressive, non-discursive (affectiveness) and procedural goals (effectiveness) (Carriere and Ericson 1989). These discourses of affectiveness and effectiveness are not a matter of what is true or false. Rather they provide a belief context, a reality that stands outside of the consumer 'objectively,' as a source of moral authority. As such, mass-communication messages, perceived by so many people, take on an objective standing, even if the objective meanings do not correspond to the facts (Meyrowitz 1985). Thus, in any given popular narrative of crime, law, and justice, there is a lot more at stake than the resolution of a particular tragedy or trouble. The society's institutional arrangements for moral authority are at stake.

The basic question always is: how does what happened fit with the order of things? A fitting answer is provided through notions, images, and myths about justice. Justice, as George Eliot (1863) once remarked, 'is not without us as a fact, it is within us as a great yearning.' Justice is a value we attribute to our social arrangements, 'the first value of social institutions, as truth is of systems of thought' (Rawls 1971: 2). As such, conceptions of justice are crucial to the co-ordination of activities through mutual trust and respect. Trust and respect are attributed to people in authority who seem knowledgeable (they know what they are doing and offer instruction to others), certain (they are predictable in their actions and offer predictability or reduced equivocality to others), and moral (in acting morally themselves they offer morality to others). It is such people who make the news as sources and journalists. Trusting and respecting their claims and associated ordering activities are essentially a matter of accepting the institutional position and authority from which they speak. 'The most profound decisions about justice are not made by individuals as such, but by individuals thinking within and on behalf of institutions. The only way that a system of justice exists is by its everyday fulfilment of institutional needs' (M. Douglas 1986: 124).

Popular narratives of crime, law, and justice, such as the murder story analysed here, display justice as the fulfilment of institutional needs. It is not only the heroics of individual decision-makers, but the strength of institutions and 'the system' that is on view: images of institutional success through its rituals of morality, procedure, and hierarchy. While particular authorities – journalists, police, church leaders, politicians – are shown to be hard at work, it is *authority*, more than their particular authority, that is reproduced. Furthermore, because the news consumer is actually witnessing it at work, authority seems 'natural.' This is where the realism of the television medium – and of the print medium to the extent it can adopt television formats – comes into play in service of justice. By showing authority at work, and by bringing it to life as real, popular narratives of crime, law, and justice establish authoritative ways of seeing the world. In the format of popular narrative realism, authority no longer embodies real social relationships as much as cultural mythologies about those relationships. These cultural mythologies, and the realism itself, are underpinned by the infusion of tertiary understanding that plays on the heart more than the head. In combination these elements secure the belief that institutional needs are being fulfilled and therefore that justice exists. It is this belief in justice that gives a sense of security, at least until the next popular narrative – news story, novel, film, television serial – is picked up at the beginning.

5

A Law-Reform Story

Law Reform

The minister of labour stood up in the Ontario legislature and announced that the government was introducing a bill to amend the Employment Standards Act. The amendment was intended to prevent employers from requiring employees and employment applicants to take lie-detector tests. In reporting this announcement, the six news outlets were not responding to an unscheduled event, as was the case in the murder story analysed in chapter 4, but rather to a 'news event' orchestrated by the government and channelled through the controlled news setting of an announcement in the legislature (this setting is analysed in Ericson, Baranek, and Chan 1989: chap. 4). The controlled-news-event format did not lessen the newsworthiness of the matter, as evidenced by the fact that the newspapers gave it page-one coverage and the broadcast outlets also gave it prominent play. The prominence given to a proposal to tinker with the details of a particular administrative law signifies that what is regarded as newsworthy regarding crime, law, and justice is not limited to dramatic violent events, such as the story of murder and investigation analysed in chapter 4. The present story brings to life what we show quantitatively in chapter 9: stories of administrative law, regulation, and compliance are as salient as stories that focus on criminal law, investigation, and deterrence.

This is a story of lawmakers at work. In the announcement the lawmakers are represented by a particular politician, the minister of labour, but the announcement is actually the culmination of a long process of deliberation by civil servants as well as other politicians in government and in opposition. These government officials are mobilizing the resources of government, its legislative powers, and eventually the powers of its employment-standards officers. Their regulatory target is private corporate practices – of business owners as employers, and of private security operatives contracted by these employers to administer lie-detector tests – as well as government practices in hiring and employment.

Why was such a seemingly unremarkable event as an amendment to the Employment Standards Act treated as so remarkable by all news outlets, regardless of medium and market orientation? At one level, it is because all of the news outlets were organized to record this announcement and to convey it to their readers. All outlets had reporters covering the legislature beat who were mandated to report on the government's major announcement of the day, whatever it was. They were there to participate in the government's ritual display of its good work: announcements of legislation with the public interest at heart. They accepted the performative statement of the minister of labour and its promotional quality for government in exchange for an easy, predictable supply of material that would fill their broadcast-news slots and newspaper columns.

At another level, such stories of law and regulation – even of a minor tinkering with an administrative act – provide a ritual occasion for journalists and their sources to foster moral education and preferred ideologies. As we shall learn, this law story was not presented as a morality play as was the murder story analysed in chapter 4. It was not heightened as popular drama, nor was it lengthened with a narrative structure that included an obvious beginning, middle, and ending. Rather, the minister of labour's announcement of a legal change provided the occasion for each news outlet to express its organizational voice regarding core values in society, and thereby to make its preferred ideology explicit. Each outlet showed appreciation for law as 'a strategic site for examining important aspects of a community's moral life. In law contemporary myths are made and stories about what *is* turn into stories of what *ought to be*. Law represents in a stylized way the concerns, the social organization, the aspirations, the political life of a particular society in a particular place and time' (Scheppele 1988: 316).

The following analysis reveals how the preferred ideology of each outlet is made evident through the angles chosen, the sources cited, and the news and opinion formats mobilized. The quality outlets essentially supported the consensus about the law expressed by the government and opposition parties in the legislature. The quality newspaper (NQ) used both its news and its editorial columns to consider various value positions. This served to rationalize the proposed law and underpin the consensus about it among the government and opposition parties. The quality television station (TQ) reiterated the consensus among all parties at the legislature without further exploration or rationalization. The quality radio station (RQ) also acknowledged the consensus that had been mobilized around this legal change, but left the thought that there might be room for further change by noting a possible contradiction in government policy in allowing public police forces to use lie-detector tests as an investigative tool. In contrast, each of the popular outlets created binary oppositions and an attendant sense of conflict to represent its respective ideology. The popular newspaper (NP) used 'on the street' interviews to show the consensus of the people that the law was a good thing, then challenged this with its editorial and letters-to-the-editor columns to point out that, in this case, the right of business owners to operate without governmental interference was of higher value than the individual's right to privacy. The popular television station (TP) sought the opinion of the private security industry and counterpointed this opinion with the consensus in the legislature, and with an opinion-slot editorial that not only was strongly supportive of the legislation but said it should be extended to restrict other forms of surveillance in the work place. The popular radio station (RP) took a similar approach to TP's, using a private-security-industry spokesperson to challenge the law and its advocates.

In making what they did of the minister's announcement in the legislature, the news outlets blended fact and value within both news and opinion slots. Outlets that used a point/counterpoint format, or presented alternative opinion beyond the consensus expressed at the legislature, did not always do so within a particular item but rather over the several items they included on the matter. These considerations, combined with the point that this law story was not presented in narrative form (as was the murder story analysed in chapter 4), suggest that the best approach to analysis is to examine the total coverage given by each news outlet in turn. Prior to analysis, however, some pointers can be offered regarding the values in this law story and their implications for the various readings of law offered by the news outlets.

The news outlets used the minister's announcement of the new law to advance their own views of the community's moral life and what ought to be. This particular law was especially newsworthy because it resonated with core values and their institutional expression. This resonance allowed each news outlet to articulate the values and its own position with respect to them.

A law preventing employers from requiring employees to take lie-detector tests is a story about the value of privacy as an institution. At stake here is limits on the right to know. The fundamental concern for privacy and the right to know in turn relates to other core values. The value of equality is central. Employers should not have access to special expensive resources to use in relation to employees that the employees themselves do not have recourse to *vis-à-vis* their employers. Employees should be subject to equal treatment by employers, without selective intimidation of some through the use of mechanical or electronic devices for assessing credibility. Rights with respect to privacy and equality inevitably entail considerations of liberty and freedom. What are the rights and freedoms of a person to limit what a prospective employer or employer knows of him or her, and to limit the means by which that knowledge is acquired? What are the rights and freedoms of an employer to protect himself or herself from crime and dishonesty in the work place? What are the rights and freedoms of the employer to conduct his or her business relations, including relations with employees and prospective employees, without undue interference from state regulation?

There are no settled answers to such questions, especially when liberty for one party can entail loss of autonomy for another. Indeed, it is the very unsettled nature of such questions that generates news stories about law that focus on whose autonomy should be strengthened and whose autonomy should be diminished. The unsettled nature of such questions also ensures varied opinion in different news outlets.

> The very act that serves as one person's expression of autonomy compromises another's autonomy. There need not be anything troubling or contradictory about this; after all claims of liberty of all sorts work the same way. One person's liberty ends at the edge of another's, so the wisdom runs, and the fact that one person's liberty may interfere with another's does not make the concept of liberty internally contradictory or meaningless. In fact, some restriction on action may actually enhance liberty. Setting the rules of the game opens up a sphere within which individuals may be free to act, a realm of action that, but for the rules restricting choices, would not exist at all. (Scheppele 1988: 305)

Also at the heart of a law story regarding the use of lie-detector tests in employment settings is the tension between science, technology, and efficiency, on the one hand, and human sensibilities concerning trust, intuition, and sensitivity, on the other. A 'lie detector test means an analysis, examination, interrogation, or test taken or performed by means of or in conjunction with a device, instrument, or machine, whether mechanical, electrical, electro-magnetic, electronic or otherwise, and that is taken or performed for the purpose of assessing or purporting to assess the credibility of a person' (Employment Standards Act, 1983, part XI-A, ss 39a[c]). As suggested by the range of things incorporated in this definition, and as shown in the following analysis, in this law story technology is characterized as inappropriate for the human assessment of credibility. As the story goes, the very need for such a technology is a sign of social pathology: of pervasive distrust and increasing social distance.

It is additionally troublesome that there are serious doubts regarding the validity and reliability of lie-detector tests. Even though they are illegitimate in this respect, they can be used to legitimate decisions in the name of 'science.' It is the technology that is untrustworthy, sold more on the basis of scientism than on that of its scientifically established efficacy. Lie-detector tests may be efficient in other respects. They may be efficient for the decision-maker who wants to relieve himself or herself of the more time-consuming and difficult task of assessing credibility in human terms. They may be efficient in discouraging the dishonest from even bothering to apply for employment in the first place. But, the story goes, such efficiencies do not stand up in light of a technology of questionable accuracy and with deplorable implications for trust, closeness, and bonding in organizational relations among human beings.

In summary, at the heart of this law story are moral lessons about the basis of trust in human relations. The values of privacy, equality, liberty, rights, freedoms, efficiency, and humaneness are all played out in terms of the central question of what constitutes legitimate procedures for establishing credibility and trust. This is a story about trusting people in organizations. How are employers to trust employees and prospective employees? How are employees and prospective employees to trust employers? This is a story about trusting government. How are we to trust a government that sees fit to regulate this aspect of business practice? How can a government claim to be legislating against an invasion of privacy when this law is itself an invasion of privacy? Finally, given our interest in understanding the news media, we should not lose sight of how this story can be read with respect to the trustworthiness of news. As we shall see in reproducing and analysing specific news accounts, the reader must judge and form opinions on the basis of his or her trust in the news outlets, their journalists, and their sources. For example, the reader is not presented with detailed scientific evidence about the efficiency of polygraph tests, or about public opinion regarding the use of such tests in employment settings in relation to other ways of knowing and establishing credibility. The reader is offered only the performative and promotional assertions of authorized knowers with a stake in the matter, and 'vox pop' attitudes used to make a representation of public opinion on the matter but not surveyed in a scientifically representative manner. The reader can judge only in terms of the trust implied by the institutional position and voice of journalists and their sources, because scientific evidence is not made available. In the news facts continue to be valued in the human terms of trust.

Rationalizing the Consensus

NQ's story on the minister of labour's announcement was featured on page one and continued on page two (figure 5.1). The story leads with the minister's justifications for the law. These justifications were repeated in the other five news outlets, and form the basis for the moral tales that each of them developed subsequently. The use of lie-detector tests in employment is to be illegal because 1 / they are 'scientifically invalid and inaccurate'; 2 / 'they constitute an invasion of privacy'; and 3 / 'they engender a sense of fear in the workplace.' The minister is later quoted as underscoring the third point by stating that although the primary use of such tests has been to verify information on application for employment forms, 'I think there is certainly intimidation involved.'

This report also accepts the minister's hint that the legislation is responding to a real problem as indicated by seventy complaints the ministry had received 'over the past few months.' The suggestion here is that the legislation is a response to growing popular demand in face of a practice that is 'degrading.' The minister is quoted as saying that he agrees with the complainants' claim that the practice is degrading and that the legislation is a democratic response to this claim.

The minister is also reported making the claim that the legislation is a pioneering effort in Canada, although it follows similar prohibition in some American states. He identifies the primary abusers as employers of people serving in 'the small convenience stores [and working with] coin-operated machines,' although he does not identify specific violators by name or corporate affiliation. The minister acknowledges that, although the legislation will not be passed for several months, he is seeking compliance now through the vehicle of publicity.

Having enumerated the minister's justifications for the law, the report turns to the leaders of the opposition parties for their reaction. The leader of the pro-labour New Democratic Party expresses agreement with the bill and claims that his party is to be given credit for it. He also urges broader consideration of all forms of surveillance in the work place. The leader of the Liberal party also acknowledges that the bill is a good thing. While these politicians express the consensus, they offer no reasons for doing so except by reference to vague values such as 'individual liberties.'

This NQ item closes by pointing to the fact that the new law will not apply to police use of lie-detector tests as an investigative tool. This is stated as a matter of fact, with clarification from the solicitor general that such police-administered tests are not compulsory, help people to prove their innocence, and are used infrequently. Although the story remains silent on the issue, inclusion of this aspect suggests the irony that what government claims is scientifically invalid and inaccurate, invasive of privacy, and intimidating in the employment context, is nevertheless a reasonable resource when used by its own law-enforcement officials for other purposes in other contexts. This thought was taken up in the subsequent NQ editorial on the matter (figure 5.3).

On 16 June, NQ published a story on a recent arbitrator's decision with respect to reinstatement of a government employee who had been dismissed for refusing a lie-detector test (figure 5.2). In this second-day item, a contemporary legal case is used to advance the story. The item offers a 'living' example of the kind of dispute that leads to the use of lie-detectors in the work place and the problems with such testing. NQ personalizes the issues raised in the minister's announcement through people involved in an actual legal dispute. This story and its approach were unique to NQ. In contrast, NP personalized the minister's announcement and justifications through on-the-street 'vox pop' interviews in which individual citizens gave their justifications for the legislation (see figure 5.5). The use of an actual legal case allowed NQ to include additional details that ultimately under-scored the wisdom of the legislation. The legal-case example also illustrated that legal precedent was in accord with the proposed legislation and its justifications. As such, this news item rationalized and strengthened the consensus that this new law was a good thing.

The item leads with the fact that the arbitrator's decision 'set a Canadian precedent in arbitration law with a ruling that the polygraph is not a reliable test of credibility.' This precedent is consistent with and supportive of one of the minister of labour's primary justifications for the legislation. The remainder of the story underscores this basic point by reference to previous legal decisions and data on predictive accuracy. There is reference to unspecified arbitration decisions in the United States regarding lie-detector tests, and a Supreme Court of Canada decision regarding the inadmissibility of polygraph-test results in criminal cases. There is reference to the fact that advocates of the polygraph claim that, under the best of circumstances, the polygraph has predictive accuracy of 70 to 90 per cent, although the scientific meaning of this claim and how it relates to other areas of government policy in which predictive accuracy of assessment is an issue remain unspecified (e.g., regarding dangerous offenders; see Menzies 1989).

Eight days after this legal-case story, NQ further rationalized and justified the proposed legislation in an editorial (figure 5.3). It is initially noteworthy that this editorial was presented under a quotation from Junius, which NQ placed at the very top of its editorial page each day: 'The subject who is truly loyal to the Chief Magistrate will neither advise nor submit to arbitrary measures.' Consistent with the wisdom of this quotation, the editorial writer advised acceptance of the proposed new law restricting the use of lie-detector tests in employment settings and rationalized the case by pointing to the arbitrariness of existing practices.

FIGURE 5.1 NQ 15 June

Bill to ban testing presented in Ontario

The Ontario provincial Government is the first in Canada to introduce legislation to ban the use of lie detectors by employers.

Labor Minister Russell Ramsay told the Legislature yesterday that the use of lie detectors in employment is unwarranted. 'Not only are they scientifically invalid and inaccurate, they constitute an invasion of privacy and engender a sense of fear in the workplace.'

The bill likely won't be passed into law until the fall, but Mr. Ramsay said he introduced the plan yesterday to deter employers from using polygraphs now. A number of U.S. states prohibit their use, but Mr. Ramsay told the Legislature that Ontario will be the first Canadian jurisdiction to ban them.

Over the past few months, the ministry has heard 70 complaints from people who either have been fired, not hired or angered because of the use of lie detectors by employers.

'They felt and I agree that it was degrading,' Mr. Ramsay told reporters. He refused to say which companies fired employees or didn't hire people because of lie detector tests. However, he said it has been a problem for a substantial number of people.

'It's primarily in the small convenience stores and coin-operated machines. Our experience was all they were seeking to do was get confirmation of information on an employee form,' Mr. Ramsay said. 'I think there is certainly intimidation involved.'

New Democratic Party Leader Robert Rae said his party has been pushing for a ban on lie detectors to ensure the protection of civil liberties. 'This is a good measure. We would like to see them move as well on the whole question of the electronic surveillance and the gathering of information after people are hired.'

Mr. Rae told reporters that the ban on lie detectors is 'yet another NDP measure. We're feeling good.' Recently, the province has introduced bills to ban professional strike-breaking and to allow the temporary takeover of poorly run nursing homes – measures the NDP has called for in the past.

Last year, Scarborough West NDP member Richard Johnston raised the problem of a woman who refused to fill in a medical questionnaire and take a lie detector test as part of an application to work for a coin-operated laundry firm.

Liberal Leader David Peterson said his party will support the legislation because there have been too many incidents of violations of individual liberties with the use of lie detectors.

The bill, which was introduced yesterday, prohibits anyone from asking an employee or potential employee to take a lie detector test or any electronic truth test.

If a test is given and an employment standards officer cannot settle the dispute, the officer can order a hiring, reinstatement or compensation up to $4,000.

However, the bill does not prevent people from taking lie detector tests as part of a police investigation. Solicitor-General George Taylor said such tests are not compulsory, but at times people ask for one to help prove innocence.

He said he didn't know how much faith police put in the tests, but said they are not used very often.

FIGURE 5.2 NQ 16 June

Fired for lie detector refusal, postal worker wins job back

A postal employee fired for refusing a lie detector test after accusing a supervisor of indecent assault has been reinstated by an arbitrator.

Kevin Burkett set a Canadian precedent in arbitration law with a ruling that the polygraph is not a reliable test of credibility.

The supervisor, who was acquitted of a criminal charge, passed a lie detector test he had volunteered to take after he had been suspended.

He had accused the employee at the Sarnia Post Office of having assaulted him. She was fired on allegations of unprovoked assault and a false accusation of indecent assault.

The two had been on bad terms previously.

Since the decision by Mr. Burkett, who is alternate chairman of the Ontario Labor Relations Board, labor Minister Russell Ramsey has introduced a bill to ban the use of lie detectors by employers in Ontario.

In the arbitration case, Mr. Burkett said the issue was one of the credibility of the supervisor versus that of the employee.

Mr. Burkett cited arbitration decisions in the United States on lie detector tests, and a Supreme Court of Canada decision upholding a lower court in refusing to allow a polygraph expert to give his opinion on the veracity of an accused person, based on a lie detector test.

A passage from the Supreme Court decision has been read as holding that polygraph evidence is inadmissible in all circumstances, Mr. Burkett stated.

He said the best that proponents of the polygraph are prepared to assert is that a properly administered test has accuracy of 70 to 90 per cent.

He said the risk of causing an injustice was such that he did not give any weight to the evidence of the polygraph expert that the supervisor had told the truth when he denied he had indecently assaulted the postal clerk.

But at the same time, Mr. Burkett said, the supervisor's readiness to take the test without any hesitation must weigh in favor of his credibility.

However, he commented that he could not choose between the two with respect to their apparent forthrightness, openness and powers of recollection.

There were major inconsistencies in the testimony of each. Mr. Burkett said he was unable to choose between the testimony of the two antagonists.

He said he was not satisfied on the balance of probabilities that the grievor engaged in an unprovoked assault on the supervisor, as claimed by Canada Post, or that she had falsely accused him of indecently assaulting her. But he was also not satisfied the supervisor indecently assaulted the grievor, as she claimed.

On the basis of those findings, he upheld the grievance and ordered the reinstatement of the clerk with compensation for nine months' lost wages.

He recommended that the supervisor–subordinate relationship between the two be ended.

FIGURE 5.3 NQ 24 June

Tell it to the machine

The suspicion with which the courts regard the polygraph – colloquially, though not entirely accurately, known as the lie detector – has by no means discredited it in the eyes of employers. Less fastidious than judges about the reliability of their information and ready to embrace almost any selection method that will spare them the need to make judgments of their own, some employers have turned to the 'scientific' method of choosing employees.

However, their freedom to dig into the lives of job applicants and to ply them with questions, some of an intensely personal nature, may be cut short. The swift endorsement by both opposition parties in the Ontario Legislature of a Government proposal to ban the use of lie detectors by employers indicates not just the prospect of swift passage for the measure but the widespread distaste there is for the practice.

The objection has nevertheless been slow to surface in legislative form. Ontario is the first province to assert that the use of lie detectors in employment is unwarranted – a step taken after 70 complaints in the past few months from people who had either been fired, not hired or simply angered by the method. Labor Minister Russell Ramsay said he agreed with them that it was degrading: 'It's primarily in the small convenience stores and (businesses using) coin-operated machines,' he said. 'Our experience was all they were seeking to do was to get confirmation of information on an employee form. I think there is certainly intimidation involved.'

A fairly free hand is allowed the polygraph in the United States where, by one estimate, about one million Americans were subjected to tests last year. Although no court in the United States will admit the tests as evidence without an agreement by both sides in advance, use by the police is widespread and a few months ago the House Judiciary Committee's Subcommittee on Civil and Constitutional Rights was informed that between 15,000 and 20,000 Defence Department officials were to be given polygraph tests. This was not to curb the unauthorized disclosure of information, said Gen. Richard G. Stilwell, deputy under-secretary of defence, but to improve counter-intelligence investigations.

There, as in Canada, uneasiness about the use of the lie detector stems not only from doubts about its accuracy but about the intrusions into privacy that seem to go with its use. Honesty may be tested, but so too are political beliefs, trade union activities, sexual proclivities and personal habits.

By no means everyone in the legal profession is convinced that the courts should disregard the changes in blood pressure, breathing and perspiration that occur in emotional response to questions from a skilled polygraph operator. Morris Manning, the Toronto lawyer who is chairman of the Criminal Justice Section of the Canadian Bar Association, says that polygraph evidence is as valid as comparison analysis of hair samples, which is accepted as evidence by the courts. 'As a defence lawyer, I would like to see the latest scientific tests made available to an accused person to ensure that a mistake is not made.'

Wherever the courts choose to go with the polygraph, the casual and intrusive use of the devices by employers among job applicants who have too much to lose to register strong objection, suggests that the protection contemplated by the Government is needed.

The first paragraph of the editorial suggests why employers find lie-detector tests attractive. Lie-detector tests ease both the process of making difficult decisions and the justifications of decisions. 'Science' proves to be both efficient and a ready-made legitimator of decisions. But the editorial undercuts this rationale in the very same paragraph. The suggestion is that employers are not careful in their use of such instruments in the way that, for example, judges at trial are when they consider the reliability of information *vis-à-vis* how it was obtained. Moreover, the word 'scientific' is placed in quotation marks to *suggest* that, in this instance, it is more a matter of scientism and what a technology offers by way of efficiency and legitimation.

The editorial follows with a reading of the consensus on the proposed law in the legislature. The consensus among the political parties at the legislature is said to indicate that there is 'widespread distaste' for the practice of using lie-detector tests in employment settings. There is no survey of other systematic evidence offered with respect to popular consensus on the matter. Instead, the editorial repeats what the minister said at the time of the announcement with respect to the level of complaints from employment applicants and employees regarding the 'degrading' and 'intidimating' aspects of lie-detector-testing procedures.

The editorial then proceeds to differentiate and distance us from the United States. In the United States, there is said to be widespread use in various settings, including police use and use for security checks among civil servants working in sensitive areas of government. Test results are admissible in U.S. courts with agreement by both sides in advance. In Canada, extensive use, including use in legal-dispute resolution, must be strictly limited because lie-detector tests are of dubious predictive accuracy and they represent a serious invasion of privacy. There is no mention of how the issues of predictive accuracy and invasion of privacy may also be of concern in the land of liberty to the south.

The editorial proceeds to acknowledge, through the institutional voice of the 'chairman of the Criminal Justice Section of the Canadian Bar Association,' that most scientific tests that are admissible as evidence in court have limitations in terms of predictive accuracy. The question is raised as to why lie-detector test results are inadmissible in Canadian courts when other tests or analyses with equally dubious levels of predictive accuracy are allowed. The point is made that all such tests or analyses might be of advantage to either side in a legal dispute. It seems that this paragraph is 'dropped in' to indicate that there is differing opinion and considerable doubt on the matter, but this equivocality is not taken up, nor are its implications addressed. The fragility of all of our scientific and legal powers of truth-finding, and their culturally specific nature (Geertz 1983), opens up a can of worms that news discourse simply cannot handle.

Instead of opening up the debate, NQ closes the matter with a concluding paragraph that supports the proposed legislation. In contrast to the legal profession (especially the criminal bar), to judges, and presumably also to police – all of whom are assumed to be fastidious about the reliability of information – employers who make use of lie-detector tests are assumed to exhibit the opposite qualities. Employers' use has been casual and intrusive, and by implication, of low visibility and lacking in accountability to the point where it constitutes misuse. The stakes are too high for employment applicants seeking a career – and who are inhibited from objecting to the practice, given their dependent relationship to the prospective employer – to go without the protection of the state. Thus rationalized, the legislation is a good thing, and NQ underpins the consensus.

The three items in NQ offer no detailed evidence regarding the validity and reliability of lie-detector tests. There is no comparison with other ways of assessing credibility in terms of levels of accuracy, intrusiveness, and intimidation. Instead the reader is offered the performatives of the minister of labour, other politicians, an arbitrator, and NQ's own journalists, all of whom have concluded that lie-detector tests are not the way forward in fact-finding, and in fact represent a regressive step that must be checked in law. As such, the accounts of all of these sources – whether expressed in the news columns or in the editorial opinion columns – meld fact and value. It is evident that the news columns are brimming with value positions in the very factual assertions that are made with respect to the minister's justifications for the new law. It is evident that the editorial in turn uses factual detail to express the value position of NQ's organizational voice.

NQ moved through a minister's announcement and a legal-case example to make its own judgment about an arbitrary practice and how it should be controlled legally. In selecting its preferred cast of characters, and using them to express its preferred values and outcome, NQ turned the matter into its own law story. In giving its reading to the ideology of a particular law, NQ helped to constitute not only the ideology of law but also its own ideological voice.

Expressions of Contradiction and Conflict

On 15 June, NP published a page-one headline tease, 3.5 by 1.5 inches, in a red box with white lettering; '*Aimed at Employers*: Bill to Ban Tests – page 3.' The story on page three (figure 5.4) included content very similar to that of the NQ story of the same day: the minister's justifications for the proposed legislation; details regarding the absolute rights of employees or potential employees to refuse tests; details of the penalties for violation; the reaction of the NDP leader (although not the Liberal leader); and the justifications of the attorney general (rather than the solicitor general) as to why there were no plans to prevent police forces from using lie-detector tests as an investigative tool.

The only significant difference between NQ and NP is that NP gives much more emphasis to the question of police use of lie-detector tests. The four

FIGURE 5.4 NP 15 June

Gov't to ban lie test on job

Precedent-setting legislation to prevent employers from forcing workers to take lie detector tests was introduced yesterday by Ontario Labor Minister Russell Ramsay.

The bill, an amendment to the Employment Standards Act, will also make it illegal for bosses to compel job applicants to take lie detector tests as a personnel screening method.

Ramsay, who said Ontario is the first jurisdiction in Canada to introduce such a measure, added he hopes the bill will become law by fall.

'In the government's view, the use of lie detector tests in the employment context is unwarranted,' Ramsay said. 'Not only are they scientifically invalid and inaccurate, but they constitute an invasion of privacy, and engender a sense of fear in the work place.'

The bill will enable the labor ministry to require an employer to pay up to $4,000 in lost salary and benefits if a company uses the tests improperly.

Employers will still be able to ask workers or potential employees to take tests voluntarily, Ramsay said, but they will not be able to distribute the test results to anyone.

In such cases, the person involved will have an absolute right to refuse, Ramsay said, meaning the refusal cannot be held against the individual in any way.

'I think the legislation will certainly discourage all employers from using it (the lie detector) under any circumstances,' Ramsay said.

Attorney-General Roy McMurtry said he agrees with Ramsay's bill, but added there are no plans to prevent police forces in Ontario from using the lie detector as an investigative tool.

McMurtry said in a judicial setting, there are stringent controls on the use of the tests, unlike work situations in which employees often feel compelled to take tests even if employers only suggest them.

In police situations, the operator of the test must be qualified and when the case goes to court, the test results cannot be used against the individual, nor can the refusal to take a test be interpreted as evidence of guilt.

McMurtry said he does see a role for lie detectors in cases in which a suspect volunteers to undergo the test in order to help police eliminate him or her as a suspect.

NDP leader Bob Rae, whose party has been pressing for such legislation, said he was pleased with the bill, but added more work needs to be done to protect employees from other forms of electronic surveillance.

---

paragraphs in NP on police use are remarkable for what they erase. The attorney general is reported to have said that 'in a judicial setting, there are stringent controls on the use of such tests, unlike work situations in which employees often feel compelled to take tests even if employers only suggest them.' Of course, judges and their rulings have no *direct* bearing on everyday police use of lie-detector tests as an investigative tool, and such use can hardly be construed as taking place in 'a judicial setting.' Moreover there is every reason to believe that suspects in police custody feel compelled to take lie-detector tests even if police only suggest them (cf Dell 1971; Baldwin and McConville 1977; Ericson and Baranek 1982), in a manner parallel to 'work situations in which employees often feel compelled to take tests even if employers only suggest them.' There is no evidence to indicate that employers do not use properly qualified technicians from private security firms to conduct their lie-detector tests for them. As are the police, private users are interested in lie-detector tests as an investigative tool to verify information and assess credibility, beyond the question of whether results can be introduced as evidence in trial courts. Just as the police want to use lie-detector tests to expedite their investigations by eliminating 'innocent' suspects, so employers want to use such tests to employ 'innocent' job applicants and to eliminate 'innocent' suspects when employee crime is suspected. In either case, one of the main uses of such tests is to take a refusal to be tested as a sign of guilt (cf Inbau and Reid 1967).

Although the NP story recounts the attorney general's justifications in a way that silences the invasive and coercive uses of lie-detector tests by police, it does at least leave a sense of contradiction in the reader's mind regarding government policing on the matter. One minister of government condemns a procedure as 'scientifically invalid and inaccurate, an invasion of privacy, and engender[ing] a sense of fear.' Another minister of government says a procedure so described is nevertheless acceptable if it is used in the 'different' setting of police officers judging guilt or innocence. While NP did not subsequently take up this contradiction and express it as a conflict between two departments of government, it did eventually express it as a conflict between state and private corporate interests and associated rights with respect to privacy, equality, and liberty.

FIGURE 5.5 NP 16 June

You Said It

Do you agree with the government decision to ban lie detector tests on the job?

Asked at the ManuLife Centre

Jim Garrity (student): Yes, because it hasn't been proven scientifically it is accurate. I think someone's past shouldn't have anything to do with the present situation. Maybe in certain positions but not with normal jobs.

Ken Winlaw (unemployed): Yes. I think they should ban it because I don't think they should be allowed to do a lie detector test on someone. I think it's unnecessary to do tests like that. It's an invasion of privacy as far as I'm concerned.

Connie Carrozza (student): Yes. It really is an invasion of privacy and also it hasn't been proved whether or not it is accurate. There's also other reasons, such as it can be psychologically damaging. I'm paranoid when it comes to that.

James C. Grossman (lawyer): I think that it depends on the matter of the industry. In a private industry it shouldn't be allowed but in a situation of national security, yes. But it shouldn't be the bellwether of whether they get the job.

Susan Liebman (dispensing optician): Yes. I think that's terrible. What they're saying is they're not going to trust the person going for the job. If they don't trust who they are going to hire then I don't think they'll put trust in anyone they do business with.

NP set up the conflict it visualized by including a second-day item in its regular 'You Said It' column (figure 5.5). This was a 'vox pop' column equivalent to 'streeters' on television. Passers-by were stopped by a reporter 'on the street' (in this instance, 'Asked at the ManuLife Centre,' a well-known shopping, office, and residential complex) and asked to consent to a still photograph being taken to be published along with a 'clip' on the question of the day. Photographs and 'clips' from five people were included to allow for majority opinion and 'democracy' in this form. This column even included a statement at the bottom each day: 'Got a question suggestion? We'll send you a [NP] T-shirt if we use it [address given].'

On this particular day, all five people were quoted as being in favour of 'the government decision to ban lie detector tests on the job.' These people *join with* the minister of labour, who also had his still photograph pictured with his account (figure 5.1), in expressing the popular consensus that a legal restriction on the use of lie-detector tests in employment settings is a good thing. Moreover, their justifications are the same as the minister's, with some elaboration: lie-detector tests are not accurate 'scientifically'; are an invasion of privacy; are potentially 'psychologically damaging'; are acceptable in some government contexts (e.g., areas sensitive to 'national security') but not in private-industry employment contexts; and are based on assumptions of distrust that do not create a positive milieu for employer–employee relations. As with 'vox pop' interviews generally (see Voumvakis and Ericson 1984: 53–5; Ericson, Baranek, and Chan 1987), these accounts from the people are not based on a representative sample in scientific terms, but on representations that NP wants made to advance its story. The reporter has selected prospective job applicants (two students and an unemployed person), an employed person, and an expert of sorts (lawyer), from among all those of varying opinion he happened to stop on the street. He has them express popular sentiments, the after-clap of accord, in support of the government's wisdom in developing the new law. Just as the government had mobilized political consensus among the opposition parties at the legislature before announcing the legislation, so NP quickly represented popular consensus through its regular 'vox pop' column reserved for the purpose.

NP had other purposes in mind. NP *used* the 'vox pop' to set up its own ideological readings of the law. These readings were given the next day in a lead editorial headlined 'Right to snoop' (figure 5.6). The editorial begins by stating that since lie detectors are 'unreliable' and 'pseudo-scientific,' NP agrees with the government proposal to restrict their use in employment settings, especially if it applies to the civil service. However, it then argues that the government's justifications for restricting the use of lie-detector tests by private-sector employees are not legitimate. While such tests are 'probably inaccurate and often mistaken,' 'so are the gut feelings of a businessman when he makes up his mind about an employee's truthfulness.' The basic argument is that such tests are no worse than 'gut feelings,' 'handwriting analysis,' 'astrologers,' 'a secretary's opinion,' 'a wife's instinct,' or any of the other methods created by the human imagination to read character. Logically, the lie-detector tests should be no more of a candidate for legal control than are these other means for construing credibility. Having reduced the lie-detector test to the level of these other means, NP is able to raise the question of the right of government to legislate against private uses of such devices. 'Where will the government draw the

---

FIGURE 5.6 NP 17 June

Right to snoop

We agree that lie-detectors are unreliable, still pseudo-scientific and it would probably be a very good thing if employers never used them on prospective employees, current ones or when hiring and firing.

So on merit, we agree with our provincial government's attitude towards lie-detectors. They don't like them.

In fact, we would applaud the provincial government if it outlawed their use in the civil service.

But we have the strongest objections to the new legislation proposed by Labor Minister Russell Ramsay to ban the use of lie-detectors by private employers.

When will this government understand its limits on interfering and *legislating* private business practices?

Yes, lie-detectors are probably inaccurate and often mistaken. But so are the gut feelings of a businessman when he makes up his mind about an employee's truthfulness.

So are half the factors a person uses to decide whether he believes or doesn't believe a person.

Will the provincial government outlaw the use of handwriting analysis in order to reveal personality characteristics by employers silly enough to consult graphologists?

Will we outlaw the use of astrologers, or a secretary's opinion or a wife's instinct?

Will we outlaw some of those foolish questionnaires that are supposed to reveal whether a potential executive is well-rounded enough for promotion?

Where will the government draw the line?

It is discouraging to see intelligent politicians like Ontario Liberal leader David Peterson echoing the praise of this proposed ban. Peterson says that lie-detectors have too often violated individual liberties.

According to Ramsay, the main areas in which these infernal machines are used and disliked are where employees handle coin machine collections.

Owners of such businesses have been trying to confirm information on employee forms by lie-detector tests.

Well, what about the individual liberty of the owner of that small business who wants to check out a prospective employee? Hasn't he the right to run his shop the way he sees fit – whether in a silly or a wise way?

Not, it seems, in Ontario.

---

line? ... what about the individual liberty of the owner of that small business who wants to check out a prospective employee? Hasn't he the right to run his shop the way he sees fit – whether in a silly or a wise way?'

Through this editorial, NP turned the story into a tale of itself as a minority voice in conflict with political opinion at the legislature and popular opinion on the streets. The opposition at the legislature is said to have been merely 'echoing' the government's sentiments about individual liberties, when the real issue is the liberty of business operators to do as they please in assessing the credibility of someone who is or will be affecting their resources. NP essentially converted the story into an opportunity for the expression of its organizational ideology supporting 'free enterprise' defined as freedom from government interference. While the government is free to set the terms and conditions for its own employees, including a ban on lie-detector tests for civil servants, it should not be free to dictate the terms and conditions of private business employment, including the use of lie-detector tests by private business operators. The employer's liberty is of higher value than the employee's liberty and government's effort to bolster the employee's liberty through law is therefore to be condemned.

This ideological position is consistent for a newspaper that banned its own employees from union membership and was frequently criticized publicly for the anti-union bias evident in its news and opinion columns (Royal Commission on Newspapers [RCN] 1981b). Even though NP's primary constituency was among working-class 'hard-hats,' its expression of such values was commonplace. Apparently NP's readers acknowledge the values of a social order that nevertheless can work against them, or at least like the feeling of a strong voice against government, no matter what is at stake.

NP closed the story by publishing a letter to the editor that supported the position of NP on the issue (figure 5.7). The letter repeats that business owners' rights should prevail, and congratulates NP for its 'rational thought' and its strong stand against popular and political opinion – 'the mindless herd which applauds every idiocy that hampers business, and tightens the stronghold of bureaucracy.' The letter is used to indicate that there is a minority opinion 'out there' that joins with NP to fight for the rights of private business in face of the 'irrational' majority of people (including those represented in the 'You Said It' column (figure 5.5) and of politicians (including those represented in the legislature story [figure 5.4] and the editorial [figure 5.6]). As was the practice with letters to the editor in NP, the last word went to the editors who stated, 'They are running out of areas to legislate.' This implies that the proposed legislation is trivial, almost a 'make-work' project of a bunch of people with little else to do. It also implies that the reach of governmental regulation is now so extensive that the government is reduced to legislation that is as petty as this proposal. The

---

FIGURE 5.7 NP 22 June

I was despairing that no one will denounce the invidiousness of the lie-detector ban legislation. Luckily your editorial 'Right to Snoop' (June 17) demonstrated once again that there still is a newspaper in Canada capable of rational thought, not following the mindless herd which applauds every idiocy that hampers business, and tightens the stronghold of bureaucracy. (They are running out of areas to legislate)   J. Draper

---

political consensus (figure 5.4) and the popular consensus (figure 5.5) were met with the political opposition of the newspaper in its editorial (figure 5.6) and letter to the editor (figure 5.7). While balanced within the point/counter-point format of news objectivity, these four items were also balanced within the ideological predilection of NP's subjectivity.

Acknowledging Political Consensus

TQ's only item on this law story was same-day coverage of the minister's announcement and the reaction of the opposition-party leaders (figure 5.8). The item was fourteenth in the line-up for the day, and it was not wrapped with either preceding or following items. As such, the item was treated as a routine and relatively unimportant report from the legislature-beat reporter. The entire matter was opened and closed in terms of a standard format used on the beat: government announcement, opposition reaction, end of story (Ericson, Baranek, and Chan 1989: chap. 4). One reason why this story was of low priority may have been that it lacked drama and conflict among the parties at the legislature. Moreover, unlike all the popular outlets, but consistent with the quality outlets, TQ decided not to construct a conflict by going to interested parties outside of the legislature whose liberties might have been affected by such legislation.

TQ chose to express the political consensus at the legislature from the outset. The anchor's lead begins, 'The Opposition has applauded a move by the provincial government to outlaw the use of lie-detectors.' This is but the after-clap of accord for a legal control sculptured in the back regions of ministry offices and legislative committees over a long period.

The reporter differentiates us from the United States, saying there is enough concern here about 'people's rights' to justify legal control over the use of lie-detectors in employment settings. The minister of labour is shown in the House justifying the legislation in terms of scientific criteria and assumed harms, and then in a scrum outside the House where he is said to have indicated that employers can still use lie-detector tests but 'the results of these tests should *not* be made public.' The latter statement is very ambiguous. It perhaps refers to a section of the act that was eventually passed indicating that an employee can take a lie-detector test voluntarily; and that a third party, for example, a private security firm hired to conduct such testing, cannot disclose test results to employers, which effectively prohibits private security firms from operating in this area.

39b – (1) An employee has a right not to take or be asked or required to take or submit to a lie detector test.

– (2) No person shall require, request, enable or influence, directly or indirectly, an employee to take or submit to a lie detector test.

– (3) No person shall communicate or disclose to an employer that an employee has taken a lie detector test, or communicate or disclose to an employer the results of a lie detector test. (Employment Standards Amendment Act 1983)

The clips from the two opposition leaders simply convey their agreement with the proposed legislation in terms of 'protection' and 'individual liberties.' The reporter closes with a statement that the legislation is not likely to be enacted until the fall, a mention of one of the sanctions that will be available in law, and a comment that police use of lie detectors is exempt.

In spite of the length of this item and the use of multiple sources, the story is kept very simple and a lot is erased. The story does little more than convey vague expressions of the values associated with the proposed law. The focus is even limited to the use of lie-detector tests to screen prospective employees rather than their use on employees, which the proposal also covered. There is no interrogation of the minister's justification regarding the scientific validity and reliability of the tests or how intrusive they are. There is no questioning of what 'voluntariness' might mean. There is no consideration of why the police use of lie-detector tests has escaped legal control, why they are allowed to continue using unscientific tests that invade privacy in circumstances where voluntariness is doubtful. There is no effort to obtain reactions from those affected by the legislation, either the people (as in NP) or private-security operatives (as in TP and RP). As presented, the story ends where it begins, with applause from the opposition. TQ claps also, and the story dies.

FIGURE 5.8 TQ 14 June

Anchor: [Tease] Lie-detectors used by personnel departments – it's to be outlawed.

Anchor: [Graphic with word 'Lie' written in bold letters, with an indicator to suggest a measurement device for liars] The opposition has applauded a move by the provincial government to outlaw the use of lie-detectors. The changes to the Employment Standards Act were introduced in the legislature this afternoon. Queen's Park reporter [names reporter].

Reporter: [Man administering test to another man sitting on a chair] The use of a lie-detector machine has become commonplace in the U.S. and increasingly it's being used in this country to screen prospective employees. [Dramatization. Close-up on person administering test then on the machine. Person tests machine] Employers are looking for answers to questions employees may not want to answer when they apply for work. [Wide shot of minister of labour in the House, then close-in] But the provincial government is worried about the use of the lie-detector and the abuse of people's rights. The minister of labour has tabled changes to the Employment Standards Act outlawing the use of lie-detectors.

Minister of Labour: In the government view, the use of lie-detector tests in the employment context is unwarranted. Not only are they scientifically invalid and inaccurate, but they constitute an invasion of privacy and engender a sense of fear in the work place.

Reporter: [Scrum of reporters outside the House, surrounding the minister of labour] Outside the House, the minister conceded that even with the changes he's announced, the use of lie-detector tests could still be an option for employers. But Ramsay says the result of those tests could *not* be made public.

NDP Leader: [Head shot] I think it's a good thing that the ministry's moved. I think there has to be basic employment protection for people applying for jobs and I'm glad to see the minister's finally moved.

Liberal Leader: [Head shot] We will support that legislation. We think it's a sensitive way to deal with the problem that's been growing in a number of years, for the last little while. I think it's a violation of individual liberties and I'm [pleased] that the minister's decided to move.

Reporter: [Stand-up outside the Parliament Buildings] With the legislature set to adjourn in about two weeks' time for the summer, it appears unlikely that the amendments to the Employment Standards Act will be law until the fall. But when they are, the provincial government will have the power to force employers in this province to reinstate or hire an employee who has been forced to take a lie-detector test. The amendments introduced today do not apply to the use of lie detectors by the police. [sign-off]

Science versus Politics

On the day of the minister of labour's announcement, TP carried a clip of his announcement as the fourteenth item in the line-up (figure 5.9). This item followed a much longer and more detailed report from the legislature-beat reporter on the topic of provincial government involvement in, and responsibility for, race relations. The clip from the minister is longer and includes more details than the clip used in TQ. The minister offers not only the justifications for the legislation in the name of science and of liberty, but elaborates on the requirement of voluntariness on the part of employees and the prohibition on the communication of test results. Presumably because the TP legislature-beat reporter decided to give priority to a race-relations story, TP treated the law story as a brief. No questions were raised. There was not even any indication of agreement with the legislation among the opposition parties.

Opposition to the minister's announcement was expressed two days later through a familiar figure, TP's 'crime specialist' reporter (figure 5.10). This reporter creates conflict by turning to a private-security polygraph operative and having him assert the true value of polygraphs in investigations. This angle was consistent with a central theme of the 'crime specialist's' reports: the role of technology in giving special powers to investigators in the fight against crime (see also chapter 4). As a self-styled crime specialist himself, TP's reporter turned the tale into one of the power of science versus the power of consensus politics.

The anchor sets up the conflict by proclaiming that 'polygraph experts are *furious* with the provincial government ... [and] are ready to fight a new bill.' After repeating the clip of the minister announcing the new law in the House, the reporter uses a clip from a 'doctor' who is a polygraph expert to assert that the political consensus at the legislature is wrong-headed. The political consensus represents legislating on the basis of emotion rather than on expert advice about the value of polygraphs in commercial settings. The reporter says that the expert indicated that he and his colleagues were not consulted by government, then includes another clip from his expert in

FIGURE 5.9 TP 14 June

Anchor: [Head shot] One more Queen's Park item of note tonight: the
government is moving now to banish lie-detector tests as a condition of
getting a job.
Minister of Labour: [Making a statement in the House. Vista slanted at top
left of screen, 'No polygraphs'] In the government's view, the use of lie-
detector tests in the employment context is unwarranted. Not only are
they scientifically invalid and inaccurate, but they constitute an invasion
of privacy and engender a sense of fear in the work place. The bill prohibits employers from requiring employees to take a lie-detector test and
gives employees the right to refuse to take such a test. The communication of test results is also prohibited. The term 'lie-detector test' is
broadly defined to include polygraphs and psychological-stress
evaluators.

which it is stated that polygraph examinations are used to verify information
pertaining to legal areas of inquiry for employers vis-à-vis employees.

The reporter concludes the item with a characteristically long clip in
which he voices-over a series of visuals. As we learned in chapter 4, it was
typically in this context that TP's 'crime specialist' reporter revealed his
own sentiments and values. He claims that 'police agents around the world
over the years have used [lie-detectors] as investigative tools.' By saying
'around the world' and 'over the years,' the reporter is indicating that global
wisdom, both comparatively and historically, suggests that polygraphs are
of investigative value in policing. The reporter is then shown connected to
a polygraph machine while he relates the story of an innocent accused
person who benefited from a polygraph examination. The line of argument
here is that the truth-tellers (including the reporter?) as innocents will be
protected, the guilty will be found out, and that is where the public interest
lies in the matter. The reporter then notes the contention that the real issue
of trustworthiness is whether the polygraph examiner knows what he or she
is doing and does it ethically. Like the skilled and upright police detective
(see chapter 4), the skilled and upright polygraph examiner 'is 90 per cent
of the equation.' The reporter returns to his 'if it has been used extensively
it must be fine for us too' line of persuasion by noting that there is pervasive
use by private corporations and government in the United States. This

combines with his other argument in the clip to set up the concluding sentence. The polygraph expert is said to have said that he hopes the bill will not be 'rammed through' (meaning passed undemocratically, without deliberation or debate) before he and his colleagues have the opportunity to present their expertise to the minister 'once and for all' (meaning that once the 'established' scientific value of polygraphs is appreciated the government will realize that the public interest resides with trustworthy policing agents who use such scientific powers to sort out the good from the bad).

The item in figure 5.10 is long on performative and promotional rhetoric and lacking in any direct evidence to support the claims. The government and the television audience are being asked to accept the use of lie-detector tests in employment settings along with other settings because their use is said to be accepted 'around the world over the years,' including especially by the leading government and leading corporations south of the border. The expert suggests that the legislators are being ignorant, misguided, and emotional in this matter, but he offers no evidence to support his own claims. The reporter raises the value of polygraph examinations in protecting the innocent as well as, by implication, sorting out the guilty, thereby suggesting that the real public interest is in the capacity of such devices to prevent and control crime. The urging is that the politicians curtail their unseemly rush to legislate and spend more time deliberating the matter.

While this item appears as news, complete with the mobilization of an expert's statements, its purpose is to express opinions contrary to the minister's justification for the proposed legal change. In turn, TP counter-pointed the 'crime specialist' reporter's opinion with an opinion piece formatted within a weekly opinion slot reserved for a particular commentator (figure 5.11). The commentator had previously served as a New Democratic Party member of the legislature for fifteen years, including a term of nine years as leader of the Ontario NDP. It is therefore not surprising that he took up the NDP position on the new law in his commentary, arguing not only that it was a good thing, but that the values behind it should be used to press for a ban on a wider range of surveillance techniques used against employees. Speaking to camera as a well-known figure in local politics and in political commentary in the media, he used explicitly emotive language to condemn the practice of electronic monitoring of organizational relations: it is 'ugly' and 'malevolent'; reflects the 'basest of human suspicions'; is 'notoriously unreliable,' reminiscent of 'Orwell's 1984,' and 'repugnant'; 'violates decent labour relations'; and is 'sick.' In other words, the commentator judges the lie detector as inhumane: modern distrust, alienation, and social pathology are at the core of the perceived need to use electronic technology to mediate human relations. The way to combat the malaise is to change our view of human nature: people are not manipulative and fraudulent at heart. A good

FIGURE 5.10 TP [1] 16 June

Anchor: [Shot of polygraph machine, then of man strapped to the machine] Ontario's small group of polygraph experts are furious with the provincial government. Crime specialist [names him] tells us tonight they are ready to fight a new bill which would ban employers from using lie-detectors.

Reporter: [Shot of minister of labour in the House, vista 'Polygraphs'] Labour minister Russell Ramsay's statement this week in the legislature did not catch the polygraphists off guard.

Minister of Labour: In the government's view, the use of lie-detector tests in the employment context is unwarranted. Not only are they scientifically invalid and inaccurate, but they constitute an invasion of privacy and engender a sense of fear in the work place.

Reporter: [Head shot of reporter and polygraph expert] But it doesn't upset them because experts like Toronto's Dr [names him] says the government's research is wrong.

Polygraph Expert: [Head shot] We have politicians, in fact politicians representative of all three parties in the province, who are acting out of ignorance, misguided information and some sort of gut feeling that there must be something inherently wrong with the use of lie-detectors in the commercial sense.

Reporter: [Head shot, then to head shot of polygraph expert, then to two-shot of them] [The polygraph expert] says they can tolerate a law which regulates licensing and leaves the polygraph as an option to a new employee. But Ramsay's people never bothered to ask the few recognized experts here anything.

Polygraph Expert: [Head shot] There's nothing illegal about what's being asked a job applicant in the interview process. It's merely a verification of those areas which the government has already defined by law as being legal areas of enquiry.

Reporter: [Shot of a polygraph machine] Even though the polygraph is not accepted as evidence in a court of law, it does have some applications. Police agents around the world over the years have used it as investigative tools. [Shot of polygraph machine connected to the reporter] Prosecutors and defence counsel have an interest in polygraphs as well. The classic case was a few years ago. Allen Basher, who was charged with the kidnapping of millionaire Fred Johnson and eventually acquitted. He eventually, after a court proceeding, took a polygraph and passed the test. [Shot of polygraph machine] The question of validity and ethics comes down to the polygraph examiner. He or she is 90 per cent of the equation. The American experience with lie-boxes is much more clear. [Shot of a man connected to a polygraph machine] Twenty per cent of the top 1,000 American companies have polygraph programs, half the major retailers. The U.S. Justice Department uses it extensively. [Shot of polygraph machine] [The polygraph expert] and his colleagues are hoping the new bill doesn't get rammed through 'til the fall. They are approaching Ramsay to give him the facts once and for all.

FIGURE 5.11 TP [2] 16 June

Anchor: [Head shot] Meantime our [names commentator] wants all electronic gadgets used to monitor workers banned.
Commentator: [Head shot] Well, it will please you to know that I agree with Russell Ramsay's new legislation. It's quite first-rate. It's quite frankly long overdue. There's something ugly and malevolent about using lie-detectors in the work place to try to measure the accuracy of employees' statements. It works from the basest of human suspicions that everyone is given to falsification, fabrication, distortion, and duplicity. When in fact virtually 100 per cent of employees would never work that way, would even intend to work that way. It's an ugly business to impose that kind of presence in a work place situation. And I am glad that polygraphs have been banned totally. As a matter of fact, as most people recognize, polygraphs can be, in some instances, notoriously unreliable. There are fascinating United States Supreme Court cases on the subject and a number of American jurisdictions have dealt with it in a similar fashion. I'm proud, in fact, that Ontario's the first jurisdiction in Canada to get rid of it utterly. But I'd go much further. There's that whole range of electronic monitoring, watching employees on TV screens, as though 1984 had arrived early somehow. Or using television cameras to monitor use of the washrooms and to chronicle it as the future purchase of discipline. Or indeed the whole business of checking, through computers, employees' credit ratings and employee personal information. It is all repugnant. It isn't necessary in work place relationships. It's just, frankly, in my opinion, sick and the sooner it's abolished the better.

---

beginning is the new law, which expresses Ontarians' view that people are to be treated as basically trustworthy and their credibility is to be assessed in human terms without mediation of technological hardware and the social distance, suspicion, and pathology it signifies. This is all the more important because lie-detector devices are 'notoriously unreliable' in any event. As did the 'crime specialist reporter,' the commentator makes reference to experience in the United States, only in this case to point out that Supreme Court decisions there have resulted in legal precedents similar to what is being embodied in statute law in Ontario. The claim is that legal wisdom here and there has it that the use of lie detectors in the work place must be legally controlled.

The emotive language in this commentary (figure 5.11) and the lack of any substantiating evidence for the claims made indicate that the appeal is to the heart as much as the head. The language invites readers to *feel* the intrusiveness of such devices and, it is hoped, to shudder at the thought that they might be subject to them, to the point where they acknowledge that the new law is a good thing and that it should extend its protective canopy over other aspects of work-place surveillance. The explicit opinion here counterpoints the explicit opinion of the 'crime specialist' reporter and his technical expert, leaving the reader to choose between the two sides in terms of his or her own values. Is respect for the basic trustworthiness of human beings and protection of individual privacy of higher value than the efficacy of such devices in classifying and sorting the innocent from the guilty, the good from the bad? Like the murder story in chapter 4, this is a story of good and evil, but in this instance the reader is left to create his or her own ending.

TP followed this commentary item with a teaser, 'A close-up on how computer technology can help paraplegics walk again. [Names reporter] will be talking to the man behind this breakthrough later.' This statement was voiced-over a visual of a paraplegic struggling to walk. The item was presented later in the show, and constituted good-news about the power of medical technology to help the handicapped. As such, it sustained the theme of the uses and abuses of technology and its role in the human condition and in inhuman conditioning.

In the 'crime specialist' reporter's piece and in the commentator's piece, TP offered long items with varied sources and a blend of news and opinion parallel to newspaper formats. There is nothing here to indicate that television, in comparison with newspapers, must necessarily eschew columnists and editorializing because of the need to turn over voice clips and visuals rapidly and to convey realism. This material was presented with explicit recognition of the ideologies involved. Indeed, one can assume that it was decided to present the story in terms of such a stark ideological

FIGURE 5.12 RQ 14 June

Anchor: The Ontario government has decided to prohibit employers from using lie-detector tests on their employees. Russell Ramsay, the minister of labour, says such tests are unscientific and degrading. With the details, [names reporter].

Reporter: Mr Ramsay has introduced an amendment to the Employment Standards Act prohibiting employers from requiring lie-detector or polygraph tests as a condition of employment. He says he's had about seventy complaints in the last few months from people who had been asked to submit to such tests. According to Mr Ramsay, lie-detectors are used by a number of employers, including convenience stores and operators of vending machines, to check the honesty of employees who handle money. The amendment prohibits the use of such tests on job applicants as well as on those already hired. Mr Ramsay contends that polygraph tests are scientifically invalid; they constitute an invasion of privacy, and engender a sense of fear in the work place. He says they are more widely used in the U.S. than in Canada, adding that Ontario is the first province to introduce a ban on the use of lie-detectors. However, the ban applies only to employers. Ontario police forces will still have the right to ask suspects to submit voluntarily to polygraph tests. The attorney general says police are careful in the way they administer the tests and he added that the results are not admissible in court. Roy McMurtry contends that lie-detector tests are merely a useful means of helping police conduct their investigations. [sign-off]

conflict to engage the reader in what was otherwise a routine announcement of a tinkering with regulatory law.

Transmitting the Government's Consensus

RQ decided to treat the proposed bill as a routine announcement of a tinkering with regulatory law. Its reporting was limited to a same-day account from its legislature-beat reporter (figure 5.12). The reporter included no clips from the two sources he referred to, the minister of labour and the attorney general. Instead, he recounted the minister of labour's House statement justifying the legislation and some details from that statement. Keeping the entire matter within the legislature, as did TQ, the RQ reporter turned to the attorney general to justify the fact that police are allowed to use lie-detector tests as an investigative tool. The *suggestion* here is a contradiction in policy between one branch of government saying lie-detector devices should be legally restricted because they are scientifically invalid and unreliable, an invasion of privacy, and degrading in the employment context, while another branch of government says that such tests are useful and acceptable when in the hands of the police. However the reporter does not take up this suggested contradiction and raise similar questions about police use as were raised about employers' use. Instead, the official justifications in the employer and police cases are taken at face value, and the story ends. The reader is left with a sensibility about the new law, and a sense of contradiction, but the reporter does no additional work for the reader to rationalize and resolve the sensibility or contradiction.

This item (figure 5.12) is a prime example of radio news as primary factual accounting of official statements. Even though he does so in his own words, the reporter transmits the government's official statements and conveys little else. Such items are what has given radio reporters the reputation of being 'spit collectors' (Ericson, Baranek, and Chan 1987, 1989). While the 'conduit metaphor' (Reddy 1979) is inappropriate in analysing any interpretive practice, it comes closest to being applicable in this type of news story.

Imagining Private Conflicts

RP also included only a single item on the proposed legislation (figure 5.13). This item originated with a news-service reporter covering the legislature beat. The reporter encapsulates the minister's justifications by saying that lie-detector tests are inaccurate and strain relations in the work place, and that the minister has received about seventy complaints. This was a very partial listing, excluding other justifications given by the minister, such as that lie-detector tests are invalid and constitute an invasion of privacy. Also erased is the opposition party support for the legislation. After including a clip from the minister referring to such tests as 'unprofessional' when used in employment settings, the reporter refers to a private security-firm owner who disagrees with the proposed law. For this person, polygraph examinations are big business – his firm has conducted '17,000 polygraph tests' and his reaction is that the legislation is irrational. The minister must be crazy: employers will lose *the* way to protect themselves from thieves in the company and the rights of criminals will be enhanced.

This RP story has the basic ingredients of the conflict set up in the other popular outlets: a government protecting the rights of employees and

FIGURE 5.13 RP 14 June

Anchor: [Teaser] Lie-detector tests as a means of screening job applicants will soon be illegal.

Anchor: Lie-detectors as a means of screening prospective employees are being outlawed in Ontario. That story from [names reporter].

Reporter: Labour minister Russ Ramsay says they are inaccurate, put unnecessary strain on the environment in the work place, and he's received about seventy complaints. The minister therefore has introduced legislation which will prevent companies from requiring employees or job applicants to take polygraph tests.

Minister of Labour: The results of the lie-detector test have been used in an unprofessional manner as far as employment is concerned or in, in asking questions of em-, of employees.

Reporter: [Names source], owner of a security company in Toronto which has done 17,000 polygraph tests, was stunned by the news and recommends the minister see a psychiatrist. [The company owner] says employers will have no way of protecting themselves from thieves in the company. He says government is preoccupied with the rights of criminals.

prospective employees versus the rights of employers to protect themselves against dishonest people. The main difference between RP and TP and NP is the brief manner in which RP asserts the conflict. Certain ingredients of the issue are not mentioned at all, e.g., scientific invalidity, invasion of privacy. Other aspects are stated more sharply, e.g., that this is to be read as a sign of a government that 'is preoccupied with the rights of criminals.' We learn what the government (but not the opposition) regards as a good thing and what a private business owner sees as disastrous not only for his interests, but for the interests of all business people. This law is a sign of the irrationality of government both because lie-detector tests have established uses (if they have been conducted 17,000 times they must be valuable) and because the law is expressing sympathy for people who deserve none (criminals). In 158 words and in one minute, we have an expression of private-sector business rights in conflict with the regulatory reach of government, and a law-and-order suggestion that government use of its legal apparatus should be directed at protection against criminals.

Representing Order: Morality, Procedure, Hierarchy

Law and legal change are perpetually newsworthy because they express dominant values and help constitute social organization. Indeed, this is why the legislature is a primary site for the assignment of beat reporters. However, not just any legal amendment is treated as newsworthy. A proposed law to restrict the use of lie-detector tests in employment settings is especially newsworthy because it resonates with dominant values and provides an opportunity for articulation of ideologies with respect to them. As formulated by the government and elaborated by news sources and news outlets, this particular act was productive of discourse about key words in social democracies: liberty, privacy, equality, efficiency, rights, and freedoms. It was also frameable within contemporary concerns about the human condition and the conditioning of humans: mechanical science, technology, and efficiency in tension with human trust, intuition, and sensitivity. It is the very unsettling and unsettled nature of such concerns that makes them newsworthy and that creates the opportunity for varied coverage across news outlets.

Our analysis reveals distinct differences in coverage in terms of market orientation. The quality news outlets accepted the consensus at the legislature that the new law was in the public interest. RQ limited its coverage to spokespersons for the government, describing only the minister of labour's justifications for the new law and the attorney general's justifications for continued police use of lie detectors as an investigative tool. TQ also kept the matter within the legislature, choosing to record the minister's statement of justification and to accord with it through clips of the opposition leaders saying it is a good thing. NQ arrived at the consensus through longer and more detailed passages. NQ moved from reporting the consensus at the legislature to rationalizing the matter through a news story on a legal precedent that was in accord with the new law, to an editorial that cited sources regarding uses of lie-detector tests in various settings as a means of indicating why such tests should be banned in employment settings if not in other settings. This was the quintessential NQ legal-control story, expressing 'the law as the repository of the results of rational argument generated in an effort to attract consent' (Scheppele 1988: 4).

The popular news outlets each created binary opposition and conflict by stepping out of the consensus at the legislature. NP's initial story signifying the consensus among the political parties was followed by a 'vox pop' piece in which five people joined in the after-clap of accord about the proposed legislation. Having set the matter up in this way, NP used its editorial columns to speak for the minority rights of business owners against the individual rights of their employees, all in the name of freedom from unwarranted governmental regulation. TP followed the minister's announcement with a point/counterpoint format. TP's 'crime specialist' reporter, with the aid of a private-security operative, expressed the value of lie-detector technology in crime prevention and control. TP's regular commentator, aligned with the NDP, countered with an equally opinionated and emotive piece emphasizing the inhuman implications of such devices and suggesting that other technologies like them should also be banned. RP imaged up its conflict sharply within the single item it broadcast. RP selectively construed the minister's justifications, and erased the fact of accord by the opposition parties, so that it could simplify the matter into the Minister calling private-security lie-detector operatives 'unprofessional' and a private-security operative countering that 'the Minister [should] see a psychiatrist.'

There is also variation by medium. The newspapers each used multiple items and varied formats. NQ used a front-page news item followed by a second-day-lead news item, and ended with an editorial a week later. NP used a front-page news item followed by a second-day 'vox pop' column and a third-day editorial, ending five days later with a letter to the editor. These items covered various topics and a range of sources, some of which were unique to the newspapers. For example, NQ had the unique story of a recent legal precedent consistent with the new law, and the labour arbitrator as the source. NP was the only outlet to question the individual citizen on the new law and its justifications.

Television was more limited, especially TQ. TQ ran one item, with the ministerial announcement followed by the consensual agreement of the two opposition-party leaders. TQ was similar to radio in giving the matter one-shot coverage with a very limited range of sources. In contrast, TP was more similar to the newspapers in providing three items, varied formats, and novel approaches and sources. TP's first item consisted of a clip from the minister in the House only. This was followed by an opinionated news piece from the 'crime specialist' reporter and a regular opinion-slot piece of the commentator with NDP loyalties. These two wrapped pieces were longer and more varied than anything the newspapers had on a single day.

The radio outlets did little, upholding their reputation as 'spit collectors' if not conduits when it comes to beat reporting. Each outlet had a single item with limited sources. RQ simply repeated what two ministers said in justification. RP also used two sources, only in opposition, choosing a dirt-collector or mud-slinging approach in which the minister called lie-detector operatives 'unprofessional' and a private-security operative called the minister crazy.

Our analysis reveals how in each outlet the facts were sculpted to fit particular formats and to espouse particular value positions. Taking the example of TP, we saw how the 'crime specialist' reporter made a series of factual claims revealing his value position: since lie-detector tests have been used around the world over time they must be acceptable; since lie-detector tests can protect the innocent, their use is especially worthwhile; since the real issue in validity and reliability is the skill and trustworthiness of the lie-detector technician, we can accept use if we have good people in the trade. In light of the above, it is evident that it is the government that is acting in an undemocratic and invasive manner by attempting to 'ram through' the legislation. The commentator then took his turn, using emotive language to have the audience member *feel* the intrusiveness of such testing procedures to the point where he or she agrees that the legislation is a good thing.

These accounts, consistent with what was on offer in the other outlets, were based on the performatives of journalists and their sources with promotional value for each – that is, the news consumer was left to accept their claims on the basis of who they were and how they appeared rather than in terms of any detailed evidence with respect to their claims. No one scrutinized the scientific evidence regarding the validity and reliability of lie-detector tests. No one examined the evidence regarding the seventy complainants mobilized by the minister of labour to express popular democracy concerning the matter. No one took a representative sample of public opinion on the law and its justifications; instead, there was at best NP's 'vox pop' representation of opinion as an expression of popular democracy concerning the matter.

As performatives for the promotion of ideologies and interests, these news items erased a lot. There was no detailed consideration of why the use of lie-detector tests is acceptable for some purposes and not others, and in some contexts but not others, although these considerations were at least touched upon in the NQ editorial. Why is something that *is* invalid, unreliable, invasive, and intimidating in the employment context *not* the same in the context of public police investigations? Why would a suspect being questioned by the police, as opposed to the job applicant being questioned by an agent of his or her employer, feel that in his or her situation there is greater scope for voluntariness, higher visibility and accountability, less intimidation, and less prospect for adverse inferences? There was no detailed consideration of what 'voluntariness' might mean in such contexts where the power imbalance is great and the stakes are high. If lie-detector tests are so invalid, unreliable, intrusive, and intimidating, why not ban them outright in the legislation rather than allowing them as long as the employee consents? Is the consent aspect crucial to upholding the values of freedom of choice and liberty over and above the practical difficulty of obtaining free consent in the contexts of use because of the power imbalance and stakes involved? There is no direct voice from a prime target of the legislation, business owners, and other employers who rely on lie-detector tests. Presumably in the face of the consensus already mobilized at the legislature and in the expressions of popular opinion in the media, business users of the tests would not want to have expressed their views in any event. With an eye to their own workers and unions, they may have taken the view that it is better to be silent than sorry. While NP spoke out, other business sources were silenced.

Of course, erasure occurs inevitably in the process of valuing facts. In a law story, the news institution coheres with the legal institution to meld the is and the ought, to 'provide a modern mythology, narratives that describe and justify. The way these legal narratives are accomplished – the way what is, in the world, blends imperceptibly into what ought to be, in law – illuminates how descriptions of fact reveal what is valued' (Scheppele 1988: 4). Legal narratives have news value because they engage us in modern mythology and its eternal dance between making sense and expressing sensibility.

Compared to the murder story analysed in chapter 4, this law story uses different modalities to represent order in terms of morality, procedure, and hierarchy. In the quality news outlets, high-status sources were used to articulate a consensus about the morality of a new procedural law that favoured human expression over technological obsession. In the popular news outlets, high-status sources, along with individual citizens in NP, were used to articulate a conflict about the morality of a procedural law that favoured individual citizens' rights over the rights of private-business owners and their private-security operatives.

In part II we have shown on the basis of qualitative, longitudinal case studies that there is substantial variation in how different news outlets construct crime, law, and justice stories to represent order. In part III we present quantitative, cross-sectional analyses to capture more systematically the differences among news outlets in formats, sources used, and topics covered. Complementing the analyses in chapters 4 and 5, the following analyses provide evidence that representing order – how order is visualized, symbolized, authorized, staged, and portrayed convincingly – is tied to the format requirements of the particular medium and market in which a news outlet operates.

PART III

Cross-sectional Analyses

6

News Formats

In this chapter, we consider how formats vary by medium and markets, and the implications of this variation for how the news represents order. Formats are the devices by which journalists are able to categorize, choose, organize, and represent knowledge as news. Many aspects of format are essentially invariant and autonomous features of mass communication. For example, broadcast-news journalists and their sources must present their statements in brief clips with simple language and the appearance of objectivity. Material that does not conform is not broadcast, and may even result in future exclusion of the source responsible, or dismissal of the journalists responsible for failing to practise the craft of journalism (Ericson, Baranek, and Chan 1987).

Restrictive requirements exist because formats provide the very basis of the ability to communicate, cementing 'events to organization to a medium (technology) to an audience' (Altheide 1985: 71). In solidifying segments of the communication process, formats allow everyone involved in the process to recognize something as news and to accept it as such. 'Formats give the look of familiarity and a relevance to an individual's encounter with a medium in a situation ... it is the look of order and disorder that media convey via their formats that invite (perhaps demand) the actor to, in turn, frame a definition of a situation' (ibid: 16). The source who wishes to maintain access to the news media, the journalist who wishes to be a competent practitioner of his or her craft, and the consumer who wishes to understand the content must work within the formats of news.

Format requirements mean that news is not more than that which can be itemized and contained within newspaper columns, a television news show, or a radio news bulletin. News is limited to its genre capacities. In this regard, news formats – like legal formats (Goodrich 1986), scientific formats

(Mulkay 1979), and literary formats (Knight 1980) – bear ideology. That is, ideology is produced as much by the format requirements of medium and market as by the specific substantive topics addressed in the content. Formats frame selection and omission of topics, sources, and narrative forms. They yield presentational forms that imply a particular epistemology and ontology.

As discussed in chapter 3, we are restricted by social-scientific formats. Hence, our analysis of news formats, while comprehensive, is limited in particular ways. In quantitative contrasts of how formats vary by medium and markets, we are limited to certain selected aspects that are comparable across all the news outlets and that can be counted. Aspects that are peculiar to only some of the organizations studied, or that cannot be captured numerically, are dealt with qualitatively through case examples and suggestive contrasts. Moreover, because the influence of format, as we have defined it, is so pervasive, we limit ourselves here to a few selected aspects. Other elements of format are considered in subsequent chapters. For example, chapter 7 is concerned with how sources themselves constitute format requirements, and how these intersect with other aspects of format to affect how order is represented in the news.

News-Item Types

In table 6.1 we document the extent to which each news outlet uses news or feature items, editorial or opinion columns, and citizens' opinion columns. These data indicate that there is significant variation by medium in the type of news items used.

Radio provided *no* separate format for expression of opinion either by their staff or by citizens, because radio news is very restricted in the time for the show (twelve minutes in both the quality radio station (RQ) and the popular radio station (RP)), and each item is quite brief (usually 100–150 words, sometimes fewer). Radio news is literally in a bulletin format. This should not be taken to imply that the radio medium itself is not capable of more extended and discursive presentations. Such presentations are offered in other show formats, including talk shows, 'phone-ins,' lectures, and commentaries. Indeed, while RP filled most of its air time with music and commercials, RQ was a commercial-free 'information radio' station with a range of current-affairs programming. Opinion formats on television were also rare. While the quality television station (TQ) and popular television station (TP) news shows were each an hour long, each item was quite brief (typically 150–200 words over ninety seconds). However, as in radio, these television stations provided other show formats for current affairs, including talk shows, and, on TQ, a weekly investigative-journalism show.

TABLE 6.1
News-item types

Type	Newspaper		Television		Radio		Sig. diff.
	Q	P	Q	P	Q	P	
News/ feature	203 73.6%	167 78.8%	310 97.5%	204 95.8%	243 100.0%	223 100.0%	M
Editorial/ column	33 12.0%	29 13.7%	1 0.3%	8 3.8%	0 0.0%	0 0.0%	M
Citizens' opinion columns	40 14.5%	16 7.5%	7 2.2%	1 0.5%	0 0.0%	0 0.0%	M/N
Total stories	276	212	318	213	243	223	1,485

Percentages are by column. Tests of significance based on tables with news-item types dichotomized into 'yes/no' for each of the categories. The last column indicates comparisons that show significant differences: chi-square statistics significant at the 0.05 level with Cramer's V or PHI ≥ 0.10, when N is large. Significant differences may occur between the newspapers (N); television stations (T); radio stations (R); or among the three types of media (M). The last column also indicates the presence of significant interactions with the variables being analysed and the coders (C) in a separate log-linear analysis.

While the information programming on radio and television provides for greater depth and discursive capacity than do news bulletins, it is arguable that broadcast media are nevertheless limited by their pacing requirements. Whether it is a television news show, drama show, or talk show, presentation is in 'a series of little vignettes lasting 20 to 30 seconds, with cues that more are on the way ... Commercials ... use essentially the same formula in casting a mundane concern, e.g. dandruff, into a scenario likely to be associated with "action programs," such as sex. Radio formats employ a similar pacing. Brief, punctuated introductions and transitions, with the avowed content, e.g. music or news, presented in brief chunks' (Altheide 1985: 142–3).

The small opening for opinion in the television stations studied was different in each case. TQ allowed for a minor component of citizens' input through a weekly letters' slot and through a media ombudsman segment. TP allowed for editorial opinion in a special segment. Two 'columnists' contracted especially for this segment gave very strongly opinionated statements on current issues. One person was strongly right-wing in his views on issues, while the other person was strongly left-wing. As Hirsch (1977: 29) observes about opinion segments in all news media, 'form comes to take precedence over content ... The product (a "column") is the important currency exchanged by the organizations, irrespective of its particular orientation.' Moreover, having persons who represent quite different positions on the political spectrum allowed TP to maintain balance, not within a particular segment, but over time, as the segment of the left-wing columnist was followed on another day by the segment of the right-wing columnist, and so on serially (see also pp. 171–2).

The need for the appearance of balance, and the associated connotations of objectivity and neutrality, is probably the major reason why the broadcast outlets did not give much scope for opinionated segments. Television and radio news is delivered in the voice of an individual journalist, and what might seem factual, truthful, and authoritative in print can 'sound idiosyncratic – be attributed to the newsreader, dismissed as propaganda, or even more likely, misunderstood as drama or comedy' (Crisell 1986: 82) on radio or television. As Crisell goes on to observe about radio, but with equal applicability to television,

> radio news is recognizable for what it is only when couched in quasi-objective language. Furthermore the nature of the medium produces a kind of *inversion* of the relationship between news and comment which exists in the press, and in so doing establishes the editor's presence in a quite different way. In the press, comment and opinion are felt to be at the heart of the enterprise, matters of much greater editorial impact than the accuracy of the news, which seems to be declared in the medium itself. We are accustomed to describe his leading articles somewhat loosely as 'editorials,' as though the editor had no responsibility for other parts of the paper, and to ask first of all what a newspaper's political views are – whether it is Conservative or left-wing, for example – and only secondly how comprehensive or accurate its news reportage is. In radio it is the reportage of the news which is felt to be at the heart of the enterprise and where a strong editorial presence is often established in the person of the newsreader or news presenter, while comment, speculation and argument are dependent, peripheral matters from which the broadcasting institution is at some pains to distance itself ... This means that much radio news is at an advantage over the newspapers in that on the face of it at least its editorial stance is non-partisan – a position brought about by the unavoidable presence of voices in the medium. This is not, of course, to say that radio news is never distorted or biased, only that to be recognized as news it must at least be objective in tone. (ibid)

We found that approximately one-quarter of the items in both the quality newspaper (NQ) and the popular newspaper (NP) were explicitly opinionated pieces rather than news or features. The two newspapers were similar in the proportion of their items given over to editorial and opinion columns. NQ included significantly more items in citizen-opinion formats than did NP, which is somewhat surprising given a 'vox pop' orientation in NP that is characteristic of the popular press in general. However, our findings may be an artefact of sampling, since by chance (using a table of random numbers) the editorial pages of NP, containing letters to the editor, were chosen frequently for our sample.

NP made extensive use of opinion columns, including those written by staff journalists, syndicated columnists, and individually commissioned columnists. This is typical of popular newspapers. Such columns provide a predictable and cheap supply of copy that is made popular through personalization of the writer.

Hirsch (1977: 29) observes that the most 'popular columns ... are featured, more so because to do so is economically rational than because they reflect the political or cultural preferences of the media.' However, NP seemed to provide for both economic rationality and its political and cultural preferences. While it did have some columns expressing empathy for underdogs who suffered injustices, including rights violations, it did not seek balance by having both right-wing and left-wing columnists, as was the case with TP. NP was explicitly right-wing, a fact well-recognized in the news business (Royal Commission on Newspapers [RCN] 1981b). For example, although its readership was solidly working-class, it had a strong anti-union bias; it did not allow its own workers to be unionized, and in the past it had been subject to calls for boycotts from labour unions (ibid). The anti-labour bias and strong right-wing ideology were especially apparent in the opinion columns of NP. For example, one column in our sample, headlined, 'Snuffing out the unborn,' was a strongly worded attack on allowing free-standing abortion clinics to operate, and on the practice of abortion generally. In this item, the columnist assailed the leader of the official opposition in provincial Parliament, who represented the left-of-centre New Democratic Party, for not taking a similar stand in the House: 'What a bizarre sense of priorities, to dismiss the massive killing of unborn babies as strictly a private affair, yet a few moments earlier talking of making it illegal for companies to hire scabs during strikes. One would have hoped that even Rae [the opposition leader] would place more weight on the life of a fetus than on the activities of a scab. How pathetic these people are.'

A question not addressed by these data is the extent to which the opinion columns, editorials, and letters to the editor of newspapers are distinct, and whether news outlets allow strong opinions from their journalists and sources to percolate into the regular news and feature items.

This matter is taken up more systematically at a later point, but at this juncture it is important to note that there is scope for explicit opinion in certain formats within newspapers. For example, newspapers have special feature sections – life-style, family, entertainment, travel, housing – that often blend advertising with feature articles on the wonders of the product. Moreover, in other features sections, especially sports, strongly opinionated statements are permissible: sports writers can berate teams' coachs or managers in the normal course of events, and even call for their resignation, in a way that is impermissible for a city-desk writer talking about the chief of police or the president of the local university.

Furthermore, newspapers use their journalists and sources interchangeably among news, features, and opinion columns. For example, in NQ, élite authorized knowers who are regular news sources are also given preferred access to the letters columns (Ericson, Baranek, and Chan 1989: chap. 6); are invited to write special feature articles; and, on occasion, even provide a regular column. Moreover, sources' opinion pieces are often 'wrapped' with the opinion pieces, news, and features of NQ's journalists to convey in no uncertain terms a preferred version of events and vision of eventualities. For example, on one double-page spread, NQ criticized federal government investments in, and subsidies to, private-sector and Crown corporations. The spread included several letters to the editor, an editorial, and a regular column by a full-time staff member. The government-mismanagement theme was also sustained in regular news stories, accomplishing a blend of fact and opinion in the hope of particular 'public opinion' control effects on the federal government.

Consideration of how all news media 'wrap' items to sustain a narrative and theme provides a further caution regarding the distinctiveness of individual news items. Often a single item constitutes no more than a segment of a narrative that is sustained by wrapping it with other items. This is especially the case with broadcast news, in which wraps of connecting items are seen as an important way of creating narrative structure so that the audience member will not turn off (for examples, see Ericson, Baranek, and Chan 1987: part III). However, it also appears in the page layouts and lead phrases of newspaper items. For example, newspaper 'briefs' are sometimes written as separate items, but they are in fact connected and can as easily be, and often are, written together as a single larger item. In NQ, one brief item from the Middle East was followed by another that included the phrase 'in other Middle East developments yesterday.' These two briefs were treated as separate items, but facing differing contingencies at the time of layout editors could have just as easily combined the two items into one. As Palmer (1978: 205) has observed, 'The necessary distinctions made by newsmen cannot hide the essential interdependence of news categories.'

News-Item Sources

In table 6.2, we document variation among news outlets in the sources of their news items. 'Reporter' refers to any journalist working for the particular news outlet as a regular reporter, columnist, or broadcast anchor. This category includes any journalist who is part of a syndicate, chain, or network in which the particular news outlet is a member, e.g., reporters for network or chain affiliates, syndicated columnists, and free-lances hired for specific assignments. 'Wire service' refers to any print or broadcast-news service cited in the story. This category does not capture the many instances in which newspaper reporters use wire materials in their stories without citing the source (Ericson, Baranek, and Chan 1987), nor does it capture items for which broadcast journalists use print wire material as the basis for assignment, statements by the anchorperson, and voice-overs of video feeds without attribution to the wire source (ibid; Roscho 1975: 69, 70). Broadcast-news outlets rely heavily on Canadian Press (CP) wire material but often use it without attribution. 'The extent of CP's importance is probably not widely understood, because the system is designed to disguise it. Radio and TV stations, especially, downplay their reliance on print and on CP in particular, and accentuate those elements that make their programming appear distinctive' (RCN 1981a: 1; see also RCN 1981b: 143). Finally, we include 'citizens' as sources of news items, a category coincident with the one used in the previous section regarding citizens' input.

Table 6.2 indicates there were significant differences by medium in the use of reporters, wire-service material, and citizens as item sources. The most evident trend is that the vast majority of broadcast items derive from journalists associated with the particular broadcast-news organization, whereas roughly one-half of newspaper items (55 per cent in NQ, and 43 per cent in NP) derive from sources other than reporters, mainly the wire services, but also citizens. These differences are probably exaggerated by the tendency of broadcast-news organizations to disguise their use of wire material. The differences are best highlighted through detailed consideration of each news outlet.

RQ relied on the voices of its reporters almost exclusively. This reliance is explained by the fact that the particular RQ newscast we studied was primarily oriented to coverage of local events, leaving national- and international-event coverage to the separate newscast of the national network of which it was a member. Moreover, to the extent that this particular RQ newscast did include news from elsewhere, it could rely on items produced by network journalists rather than on wire feeds.

RP made greater use of wire material, although still only for a small minority of its items. As a local private station, RP relied on the 'News

TABLE 6.2
News-item sources

Type	Newspaper		Television		Radio		Sig. diff.
	Q	P	Q	P	Q	P	
Reporter	124	125	226	190	242	196	M/N/R
	44.9%	59.0%	83.6%	89.2%	99.6%	87.9%	
Wire	112	71	45	22	1	27	M/R
service	40.6%	35.5%	14.2%	10.3%	0.4%	12.1%	
Citizens	40	16	7	1	0	0	M/N
	14.5%	7.5%	2.2%	0.5%	0.0%	0.0%	
Total stories	276	212	318	213	243	223	1,485

Percentages are by column. Tests of significance based on tables with news-item sources dichotomized into 'yes/no' for each of the categories. The last column indicates comparisons that show significant differences: chi-square statistics significant at the 0.05 level with Cramer's V or PHI ≥ 0.10, when N is large. Significant differences may occur between the newspapers (N); television stations (T); radio stations (R); or among the three types of media (M). The last column also indicates the presence of significant interactions with the variables being analysed and the coders (C) in a separate log-linear analysis.

Radio' services for national stories, and on the National Broadcasting Corporation radio service for stories from abroad. RP used wire material without direct attribution quite frequently. Typically the anchor gave a brief summary of a situation abroad without any indication as to the source of the material. However, even when a clip from a correspondent for a news service was used, there was usually only a sign-off with the correspondent's name and the location of the story, but not the news-service affiliation (e.g. 'John Smith, Washington' rather than 'John Smith, NBC Radio News, Washington').

The two television stations varied little in their proportionate use of item sources. Both stations made relatively little explicit use of news-service feeds, and the vast majority of their items originated with their reporters. TP was slightly more reliant on its reporters. TQ made slightly greater use of attributed news-service feeds, a fact attributable to its greater emphasis on foreign news, using a combination of its own network correspondents and news-service correspondents.

The TQ newscast we studied was primarily local in orientation, using its own staff of reporters and camera crews to produce stories in and about the region. However, as a member of a national network, it had the resources of its affiliate to enable it to include national and international stories in the line-up. In our observational research, we found extensive contact and collaboration between the assignment editor for TQ and assignment editors for the national and French-network affiliates that were also located in Toronto (Ericson, Baranek, and Chan 1987; see also Fairhurst 1983). Among the 266 TQ items originating with their associated reporters, 25, or about 10 per cent, were network feeds: 15 from Ottawa, 4 from other Ontario-based affiliates, 2 from Vancouver, and 4 from foreign correspondents of the national network. Occasionally place was irrelevant, and the news-service source was somewhere along a line that seemed extensive and unmeasurable. For example, in one story, a national-network reporter did not sign off from a designated place, and the entire story consisted of stating what a United Press International reporter had said about a meeting in Poland between the Pope and state authorities.

TQ made use of wire feeds from several news services: the National Broadcasting Network (20) and the Columbia Broadcasting System (2) of the United States, the British Broadcasting Corporation (4), VisNews (3), and several that remained unspecified or were combinations of more than one source (16). Two of the NBC-fed items were also used by TP, giving them identical coverage. A lot of the NBC feeds were simply voice-overs by NBC reporters. In some instances, these materials were edited to better fit the format of TQ, a practice that is common when the news-service format and the user format differ (Epstein 1974: 185), or when the user wants to make it appear that it has put more into the story than is actually the case (D. Clarke 1981: 30–1). Indeed, in a TQ seminar for journalists we attended, there was considerable discussion about the need to edit foreign-service feeds to 'Canadianize' the account: to eradicate perceived bias and to tailor the material to the presumed needs of the TQ audience (Ericson, Baranek, and Chan 1987). In the TQ wire-service items sampled here, there are instances in which the TQ anchor frames the story, followed only by a clip from a source provided via a news service; instances in which the TQ anchor voices-over video feeds provided by a news service; and instances in which a TQ reporter frames a news-service feed by providing details both before and after the presentation of the feed.

TQ sometimes made use of a blend of news-service feeds and local stories to constitute a theme for a particular newscast. For example, in one show, eight items were wrapped on the theme of East-West relations and the question of nuclear arms. Included were four news-service feeds: regarding a visit of the West German chancellor to Moscow; a visit of the American vice-president to Denmark, where he defended the U.S. nuclear-arms policy in Europe; a defection of two Soviet citizens to Sweden; and an anti–nuclear arms protest at Greenham Common in England. These news-service items were combined with the following four local items to constitute the show's theme for the day: an employee going to a Labour Relations arbitration hearing regarding his right to wear an anti–nuclear arms protest button at work; a program to teach 'nuclear awareness' at local schools; a story on the plans of local anti–nuclear arms protesters, including the re-establishment of a camp on the lawns of the legislature building and the expectation that they would be arrested; and, a 'feature' panel discussion involving the anchor-person, a local member of the Parliament of Canada, the deputy-chief of the local police force, and a representative of a group called the Against Cruise Testing Coalition. This example of constituting a theme illustrates clearly that journalists' own structuring devices affect whether and how news-source material is used. News items from anywhere will be used as they help to constitute a theme, suitably edited, contextualized, and lined up to sustain a narrative over the course of a news show.

TP was a privately owned station oriented to the local market, and had no network affiliations to draw upon for stories outside the local area. TP's limited foreign-news coverage derived almost exclusively from NBC feeds: among the 22 TP wire-service feeds in the sample, 21 came from NBC and 1 from BBC. Similar to TQ, TP sometimes voiced-over news-service feeds. Similar to RP, TP also sometimes used news-service feeds without indicating the reporter's affiliation, perhaps giving the impression that its own reporting resources were more substantial (see also D. Clarke 1981).

The differences among radio and television outlets in the use of wire-service material are illustrated in the coverage all four broadcast outlets gave to the fact that the Parliament of the United Kingdom had voted against reinstatement of the death penalty. TQ and TP both used a feed from NBC to report the story, which included visuals of Westminster, statements by members of Parliament, and a 'person on the street' interview. Lacking the capacity for such colour, RQ and RP both reported the story with an anchor brief only, and without giving any indication of the source of the information.

In the newspapers we studied, we found that a little more than one-third of their material was designated as being from wire services. This appears to be well below the average for newspapers. For example, a study of newspapers in 37 Ontario communities found that 63 per cent of items originated with wire services (Dussuyer 1979: 41). NQ was slightly more likely than NP to use wire-service material, because NQ has a greater national and international news emphasis. Although NQ had a more substantial network of its own reporters in other Canadian cities and abroad, it also made heavier use of wire-service material to report on national and international events. In particular, there were a lot of 'briefs' on stories from abroad that were composed from wire material. NQ also made use of long features supplied by news services abroad, especially from the New York Times Service.

Among the 112 wire stories in the NQ sample, the main sources were Canadian Press (35), Reuters (29), Associated Press (15), New York Times Service (11), and Associated Press and Reuters combined (8). Among the remaining 14 wire stories were 4 that combined material from the above-mentioned agencies. More than one-third of the CP stories were from Ottawa, with no other location predominating. The Reuters stories originated from 20 different countries, and the AP stories from 8 different countries. Compared to NP, NQ used a greater variety of wire services, a greater range of locations indicated by place lines, and was more likely to combine multiple wire sources into one story. Five stories in NQ combined the wire-service material with 'staff,' including a very long, prominent item designated 'AP/CP/staff.' The NQ sample also includes 24 items that appeared to be constituted exclusively by wire-service material, but no attribution was given by which we could confirm the source.

Wire-service material is widely regarded as the most straightforward and factual news available. As such, it can even provide a standard against which a reporter's account of the same event is judged (Fishman 1980: 91). However, leading quality newspapers are also standard-bearers that reciprocally influence the wire services. Gitlin (1980: 99) observes that, in the United States, the New York 'Times alone can become the critical mass that certifies a story's significance – and even its frame. Likewise, the wire services by themselves can certify the story, leading editors to assign reporters to it.' In Canada, a similar role has been attributed to NQ and to one or two other newspapers. According to the Royal Commission on Newspapers, Canadian Press sometimes does not 'recognize the value of a story until it turns up in the Globe and Mail or the Star' (RCN 1981a: 24–5). Elsewhere, the commission notes that Canadian Press derives a lot of its copy from leading newspapers, and that while 'it now generates about 60 per cent of its own copy, its news priorities tend to be heavily influenced by the Globe. Le Devoir plays a similar role in Quebec and for the French media' (RCN 1981e: 20).

Through our direct observations of journalists at work as well as the news content sampled here, it is evident that the use of wire material varies substantially according to the credibility of the source. If the news organization has a share in a domestic wire service, then the copy is often taken at face value and even incorporated into stories without attribution as to the source. There are exchange-of-information agreements between a newspaper's reporters and wire-service reporters on particular beats (Ericson, Baranek, and Chan 1989: chap. 4), as well as wholesale use of wire-service material for complete news items and for particular background facts and quotations from news sources.

Particular foreign wire sources are treated with more scepticism. If the material is used, it is more likely to be attributed to the service. In the extreme, foreign news outlets that are not connected to the major news services nor otherwise part of the media establishment are treated with a great deal of scepticism. Their political affinities are sometimes specified along with other evaluative terms, in effect warning the reader that the information should be treated with caution. The purpose seems to be to distance the newspaper from the account. Thus some newspaper accounts of foreign events actually make it quite explicit that there has been reliance on many wire-service mediators of reality and that something may well have been lost or distorted in the process. Consider the following excerpts from an item in NQ, headlined 'Gunmen battled Syrians in Lebanese port city' and attributed to the Reuters news agency.

> More than 20 shells or rockets crashed around the towns of Antellus and Dbarye, *state television said* ... *The right-wing Christian Falangist radio* said the shells were fired from mountain positions held by the Syrian Army and its Lebanese leftist allies ... In the Syrian-held Bekaa Valley in eastern Lebanon, *local radio stations* reported another clash involving Syrian troops. *State-run Beirut radio* said two people were killed and several wounded when the Syrians intervened to stop a quarrel between civilians in the town of Majdel Anjar. *Right-wing media* put the death toll at five, including some Syrian soldiers, but the cause of the clash was not clear. (our emphasis)

When news outlets and wire services close to home are used, it is either without attribution as to source or with straightforward designation of the name of the source outlet. At home, and especially in the reporting of primary factual details of the type in the item above, the information is stated as factual without reference to the news outlet or wire service from which it was derived. It would seem peculiar, indeed, to have a reference such as 'the state-run Canadian Broadcasting Corporation says that a man carrying a gun tried to enter the parliament building yesterday,' or 'the right-wing Toronto *Sun* said that the police exchanged gunfire with a gang of bank robbers yesterday.' The NQ report quoted above is distanced textually as foreign: it not only makes it clear that every factual detail reported has been mediated by foreign media, but also that the most important additional information for understanding these facts is the political affiliation of the media source that provided them. H. Schiller (1989: 167) strikes at the heart of these attribution practices: 'In quoting or referring to reporting emanating from non-market economies, the US media not infrequently preface the account with a warning – similar to the cautionary words on a cigarette package – that the information comes from a "state-controlled" press.

Would it not be equally appropriate to preface domestic reporting with the indisputable point that it customarily comes from privately-owned billion-dollar companies?'

While the data in table 6.2 indicate that NP news items were more reporter-based than were those in NQ, NP still relied on wire-service material for one-third of its items. Except for 5 items designated as 'specials,' all NP wire-service items came from the American agency United Press International (53), or from United Press Canada (13). Around the time of the content survey, UPC was 80 per cent owned by a newspaper group of which NP was a partner, and 20 per cent owned by UPI (RCN 1981b: 128).

The 13 UPC items were about events in only 4 Canadian cities, Ottawa (5), Vancouver (4), Winnipeg (4), and Edmonton (1). The 53 UPI items were about events in 19 different countries. However, the United States was predominant, with American locations being the place line for 29, or 55 per cent of the UPI items. No other country accounted for more than 3 place lines. These data support contentions that reliance on wire-service material means reliance on American-mediated and American-based items (e.g., RCN 1981a: 36). The bulk of wire copy in NP derived from very limited news services and places. Inevitably, such material bears the ideological imprint of the wire service's format, personnel, and preferred places (Boyd-Barrett 1979; D. Schiller 1986).

The UPI stories in NP focused on two themes. One theme was events, political developments, or speeches that conveyed anti–communist sentiments in general, and anti-Eastern-bloc-nation sentiments in particular. This was in keeping with political ideology presented in NP's columns and editorials. UPI wire material provided an additional basis for doing the same thing. The other theme was bizarre and violent crimes, including especially mass killings, all but one of which occurred in the United States. As we address in more detail in chapter 8, NP often used serious crime as a staple product for representing order. What NP couldn't find locally they made up for with the perpetual supply of such wire material from elsewhere.

News-Event Locations

Some analysts argue that the location of news events is of little significance because medium format requirements mean that the routines of news production and the resultant products are similar across Western nations. For example, the constraints of television-news production mean that medium-driven, standardized formats are used, resulting in 'news from nowhere' (Epstein 1974). Similarly wire-service material used by radio stations and newspapers is prepared in accordance with standardized formats; it derives from 'nowhere' and can be used anywhere. Electronic media in particular have deconstructed traditional conceptions of place. Socially and culturally, geographical location is becoming less important and information environments more important, with an emergent feeling that one has 'no sense of place' (Meyrowitz 1985).

However there are certain aspects of location that are related to the formats that can be cited, the topics selected, the sources cited, and the knowledge conveyed. For example, because of resource limitations and language barriers, foreign correspondents for television tend to use fewer source clips than do their home-based counterparts, and to do reports that are entirely voice-overs of visuals produced by their own crews or by television operatives in the country concerned. In his research on American television coverage of the hostage-taking of American citizens in Iran, Altheide (1985) found that coverage varied across four place lines. Altheide attributes this variation to differences in the availability of sources and visuals, and to aspects of timing, in each place.

Another consideration, introduced in our discussion of wire-service material, is the imperialism associated with material based in one culture flooding into another culture. This is a major problem in entertainment programming, with American-produced material circulating throughout the world. In Canada, it is often argued that while the situation is bad regarding entertainment programming, we have strength in our news and current-affairs programming and that this is crucial to our national identity, and indeed to our sovereignty. The argument is advanced that the availability of American television stations close to the Canadian border, and via cable-television and satellite transmissions, makes it especially important to produce a distinctive Canadian news product that will keep citizens focused on events as interpreted by Canadian journalism (e.g., Canadian Broadcasting Corporation [CBC] 1978). There seems to be some success in this regard, as '89 per cent of [television] news-watchers watch Canadian news ... while 95 per cent of all drama is foreign' (ibid). However, if a substantial proportion of the news material in Canada is already mediated by foreign, especially American, news agencies, media imperialism may remain intact. Given the substantial proportion of American-produced wire material used by the newspapers and television stations we studied, there is reason for concern in this regard.

In table 6.3, we document that there is significant variation in news event locations by medium and market.* Focusing initially on newspapers,

---

* 'NA' was coded if there is no particular news event involved (e.g., a particular issue is discussed). 'Canada' includes something happening in Canada or between Canada and another country (e.g., free trade between Canada and the United States). 'Foreign' includes something happening in a particular foreign country, or between foreign countries.

TABLE 6.3
News-event locations

Locations	Newspaper		Television		Radio		Sig. diff.
	Q	P	Q	P	Q	P	
Toronto	27	64	94	119	87	90	M/N/T
	9.8%	30.2%	29.6%	55.9%	35.8%	40.4%	
Ontario	26	32	33	22	98	32	M/R
	9.4%	15.1%	10.4%	10.3%	40.3%	14.3%	
Canada	89	32	53	18	40	55	M/N/
	32.2%	15.1%	16.7%	8.5%	16.5%	24.7%	T/R
Foreign	120	67	131	52	16	43	M/N/
	43.5%	31.6%	41.2%	24.4%	6.6%	19.3%	T/R
Not applicable	14	17	7	2	2	3	M
	5.1%	8.0%	2.2%	0.9%	0.8%	1.3%	
Total stories	276	212	318	213	243	223	1,485

Percentages are by column. Tests of significance based on tables with news-event locations dichotomized into 'yes/no' for each of the categories. The last column indicates comparisons that show significant differences: chi-square statistics significant at the 0.05 level with Cramer's V or PHI $\geq$ 0.10, when N is large. Significant differences may occur between the newspapers (N); television stations (T); radio stations (R); or among the three types of media (M). The last column also indicates the presence of significant interactions with the variables being analysed and the coders (C) in a separate log-linear analysis.

we find NQ is the outlier. Its items originate largely in international settings (44 per cent) or national settings outside Ontario (32 per cent), rather than in Toronto (10 per cent) or elsewhere in Ontario (9 per cent). This finding gives substance to NQ's claim that, even in its Toronto edition, it pursued a national focus as well as an emphasis on world events. In contrast, NP was much more oriented to events in Toronto (30 per cent) and Ontario (15 per cent), but less oriented to national (15 per cent) and foreign (32 per cent) events. In this regard, NP is more similar to what Dussuyer (1979) has documented as the norm for 37 Ontario newspapers: their orientation is local (28 per cent) and provincial (32 per cent) more than national (11 per cent), with a considerable degree of foreign coverage primarily through the use of wire copy (29 per cent).

Histories of journalism have documented that popular-newspaper readers are not interested in foreign-news coverage unless it can be made relevant to their own local knowledge. In one of the more colourful statements in this regard, Bell (1927, quoted by Palmer 1978: 216) asserted,

As to the great majority of uneducated and unintelligent classes ... people of this sort don't want news unless it is of something they can imagine happening to themselves ... As to a place where they have never been and know no one who has ever been there – nothing can interest them about it. A whole population might be destroyed in Peking or Macedonia, but it would not interest them as much as a fight in a street in which their aunt once lived! As to whether the street fight is true or not – that is indifferent. The contradiction of the next day would be quite as interesting as the assertion. Feeble jokes, tidbits of sorts is what they want.

The fact that almost one-third of NP's items originated from foreign locations seems on the surface to belie this viewpoint. Substantial space is given to foreign-news stories, and to commentary on international events in editorials and regular opinion columns. However, as we have already observed regarding the wire material in NP, most of their foreign-news items are supplied by UPI, and most UPI items are consistent with the right-wing, anti-communist ideology of NP or, alternatively, with NP's penchant for shocking violent crimes, which are rare locally but prevalent on the wires. Thus, NP's foreign material is made relevant to local people in the same way as are items culled from locations closer to home. The formula is to play on the hearts as well as the heads of the readership, making them shocked and appalled at the threats to order posed by 'foreign' ideologies and 'pathological' individuals. It does not matter where this affective material comes from since it is apparently effective in maintaining a slice of the market for NP.

TQ had by far the greatest proportionate coverage of foreign events of any broadcast-news outlets studied (41 per cent). Its foreign coverage was based on a combination of feeds from the national network to which it belonged, foreign-network video feeds, and print wire-service material. Its provincial (10 per cent) and national (17 per cent) news coverage was considerable, but reduced by the fact that national coverage was dominant in a later separate newscast of the network. Local coverage (30 per cent) was about the same as for NP, but considerably less than that available in the other broadcast-news outlets. In contrast, TP gave by far the greatest attention to local events (56 per cent) of any outlet. It had carved out a Toronto 'city' orientation for itself in the market, and the location of the majority of its news events confirms this orientation. TP gave much less attention to national (9 per cent) and foreign (24 per cent) events than TQ. Its foreign coverage was essentially limited to NBC feeds, and to reading to camera information that was probably derived from print wire services or newspapers.

RQ is an anomaly among the sampled outlets in the extent to which it sustained a provincial focus (40 per cent). Most of its remaining items were locally based (36 per cent), leaving little room for national (17 per cent) and foreign (7 per cent) coverage. RQ obviously left national and foreign coverage to the separate newscasts it picked up from the national network of which it was a member. However, since RQ and TQ were part of the same network and could each rely on national newscasts to give more coverage to events outside Toronto, it is curious that, in local newscasts, TQ nevertheless sustained substantial foreign coverage while RQ all but ignored it. The answer may lie in the particular within-medium competitive market of each and/or in their network-ascribed division of labour in the information-service side of their operations. RQ was an 'information radio' station with virtually no music and no commercials. This particular newscast was simply designated for local and provincial events and issues. TQ was highly competitive with TP, and with two other television stations that offered newscasts over the same time period. Its audience was known to be relatively older and interested in international events, and in order to sustain this market segment, TQ proceeded to oblige with substantial foreign as well as local coverage (Ericson, Baranek, and Chan 1987: esp. 84–6).

Similar to TP, RP was local in ownership and orientation. Exhibiting what Crisell (1986) has termed the 'newsic' formula, RP blended pop music with short newscasts at frequent intervals. RP provided 'vox pop' in its news and pop 'sounds' in its music in an effort to be popular for advertisers. Hence RP carried far more Toronto-based stories (40 per cent) than stories emanating from elsewhere, although it did sustain considerable national (25 per cent) and international (19 per cent) coverage, both through the use of audio feeds from news services and through anchor briefs, presumably derived from newspapers and print wire services.

Overall, it is clear that the popular news outlets were predominantly local in orientation. The quality news outlets were more varied. NQ and TQ offered substantial foreign coverage, as one would expect from quality outlets. However, given that the particular newscast of TQ we studied was also mandated to cover local events, it also had a substantial proportion of Toronto-based items. RQ is an anomaly, being more local and provincial than national and international, but this can be explained in terms of the place of the particular RQ newscast we studied *vis-à-vis* the overall information programming of RQ.

News-Event Initiating Incident

In table 6.4 we record the initiating incident for the news items in each outlet. A *scheduled event* includes anything that appeared to have been planned in advance for media coverage, e.g., a news conference, a demonstration, the launching of a new program or service, and a recurring event. An *unscheduled event* includes anything that appeared to have been reacted to by journalists without prescheduling, e.g., spot news of serious crimes, accidents, or disasters. An *other media/continuing* item includes anything

TABLE 6.4
News-event initiating incident

Initiating	Newspaper		Television		Radio		Sig.
event	Q	P	Q	P	Q	P	diff.
None	36	27	9	11	19	16	M
indicated	13.0%	12.7%	2.8%	5.2%	7.8%	7.2%	
Scheduled	96	77	171	95	126	121	M
event	34.8%	36.3%	53.8%	44.6%	51.9%	54.3%	
Unscheduled	63	74	68	56	63	56	N
event	22.8%	34.9%	21.4%	26.3%	25.9%	25.1%	
Other media/	81	34	70	51	35	30	M/N
continuing	29.3%	16.0%	22.0%	23.9%	14.4%	13.5%	
Total stories	276	212	318	213	243	223	1,485

Percentages are by column. Tests of significance based on tables with news-event initiating incident dichotomized into 'yes/no' for each of the categories. The last column indicates comparisons that show significant differences: chi-square statistics significant at the 0.05 level with Cramer's V or PHI ≥ 0.10, when N is large. Significant differences may occur between the newspapers (N); television stations (T); radio stations (R); or among the three types of media (M). The last column also indicates the presence of significant interactions with the variables being analysed and the coders (C) in a separate log-linear analysis.

that appears to follow from stories already published or broadcast in the outlet concerned or in other news outlets.

It was sometimes difficult to judge what had initiated the news item. The 'other media/continuing' category is especially problematic because it sometimes depended on the particular coder's knowledge of continuing stories in the news to determine whether the particular item was a follow-up to previous stories. One coder recorded this category much more often than did the other two. Moreover, it was sometimes impossible to ascertain the initiating incident. When the initiating incident was not evident in the content of the news item, we recorded *none indicated*. As documented in table 6.4, the lack of any indication of the initiating incident was most common in newspapers and least common for television. Indeed, the characteristics of each medium affected our recording of this variable. Television visuals usually provided enough cues to determine whether the event was scheduled, unscheduled, or continuing. The lack of visuals for radio and nearly all newspaper items meant that, if the reporter did not state what had initiated coverage of the incident or tie the event into a story covered previously, it was usually impossible to determine what had initiated the coverage.

The data in table 6.4 reveal that broadcast news outlets are much more likely than newspapers to report on scheduled events. This confirms the findings of ethnographic studies (e.g., Epstein 1974: esp. 31; Schlesinger 1978: esp. 68; Ericson, Baranek, and Chan 1987: esp. chap. 6) regarding the particular need of broadcast journalists to rely on scheduled events. Scheduled events give broadcast journalists a predictable supply of stories. While a predictable supply is also a concern of the newspaper journalist, it is especially important to the television journalist who is additionally responsible for an expensive camera crew and the need to obtain reasonable visuals quickly. Moreover, both television- and radio-news outlets have very limited resources compared to major daily newspapers. Broadcast-news producers are especially dependent on their reporters to yield something each day to fill the show. The easiest way to meet this demand is to attend events already organized by sources to fulfil the requirements of broadcast journalists.

Table 6.4 also indicates that radio-news outlets are especially unlikely to cover other media/continuing stories compared to television news and newspapers. This finding is related to our earlier observation that, in their news formats, radio stations focus exclusively on news items and do not provide for editorials, opinion pieces, letters from citizens, and so on (see table 6.1). These later item types, common in television news and especially newspapers, are almost all 'other media/continuing,' in that they are responding to previous news items and issues in the news.

The two radio stations were remarkably similar in their proportionate use of scheduled events, unscheduled events, and other media/continuing stories. The two television stations were also quite similar in this regard, although TQ had slightly more scheduled events, reflecting its emphasis on institutional reporting, while TP had proportionately more unscheduled events, reflecting its spot-news and 'on-the-street' emphasis. However, it is clear that both television stations relied much more on a combination of scheduled events and continuing stories than on unscheduled events. The television medium dictates that scheduled and continuing stories will be more suitable to formatting requirements, while spot news may often appear to be old news by the time it is broadcast because radio is capable of communicating it more quickly.

Between the newspapers, NQ gave significantly more coverage to 'other media/continuing' news items. This is a reflection of NQ's orientation to major issues, and 'investigative' policing of events related to those issues, over long periods. In contrast, on a proportionate basis, NP included more unscheduled-event news items than did NQ. This reflects NP's emphasis on events involving crimes, accidents, and disasters, including the material it culled from local events of this type, as well as its use of UPI wire material on horrendous and calamitous events elsewhere.

Sides Presented and Side Favoured

The question of what sides of a conflict or controversy are presented in the news, and whether a particular side is favoured, has been central in debates about journalism. Journalism professionalized through a commitment to objectivity and impartiality. This commitment was fostered through techniques such as citing sources with opposing viewpoints and allowing the news consumer to infer implicit bias (Roscho 1975: 29–30). Journalism continues to value the appearance of impartiality embedded with the truth claims of its sources (ibid: 56; Epstein 1974: 265). And, in spite of the advance of adversarial journalism in newspapers (A. Smith 1980), broadcast-news organizations cling to the ideology of objectivity. For example, a policy handbook of the Canadian Broadcasting Corporation (1982: 92) states: 'the basic purpose of radio and television news broadcasts is to report on events, to be a fair witness to the reality of the day. It is evident however, that in the very mirroring of reality, attitudes can be influenced, perhaps in the long run shaped. This is why the Corporation, in the reporting of news, insists that journalistic choices be based on the most rigorous standards of accuracy, fairness, balance and impartiality, all of which are the essential ingredients of objectivity.'

In modern journalism the appearance of impartiality is crucial for the legitimacy of the news-media institution. Only if it appears relatively 'neutral' can the news media, similar to the legal institution and the state itself, translate power interests into the public interest (Hartley 1982: 55). 'The impartiality, objectivity, neutrality and balance which form the bedrock of editorial ideology are no sham. They are required if news is to act alongside the other agencies in naturalizing dominant ideology and winning consent for hegemony ... The purpose of news ideology is to translate and generalize, not to choose this opinion or that. In other words, news naturalizes the (fairly narrow) terrain on which different sectional ideologies can contend – it constantly maps the limits of controversy' (ibid: 61–2).

The professional ideology of objectivity is also functional at the level of everyday news production (Roscho 1975: 42; Phillips 1977: 70; Ericson, Baranek, and Chan 1987: part III). The reporter who is required only to obtain a statement from one source, and then to record a counter-claim from another source, can produce stories quickly and routinely without requiring extensive knowledge of the matter in dispute. From the viewpoint of supervising editors, these features in turn allow flexibility in assignment of stories, since any reporter can work on anything within this format. Moreover, the editors and reporters are freed from the practical and legal difficulties of sifting evidence and judging truth claims. In the 'strategic ritual of objectivity' (Tuchman 1978), a point is followed by a counterpoint, and truth is left to reside at a point somewhere in between, dependent on the visualization of the consumer. A related consideration is that consumers are less likely to be offended because they know that they have participated in constituting truth and ideology rather than having them imposed. However, in truth, the professional ideology of objectivity is directed at the enhancement of professional autonomy, strengthening the authority of news and thereby enclosing on it. If news is seen as lacking in objectivity it is then seen as open to negotiation for control (Wagner-Pacifici 1986; Fiske 1987; Ericson, Baranek, and Chan 1987, 1989).

There are various techniques for producing objective-looking stories. The creation of different types of items – e.g., news, features, and editorials as discussed earlier – is one device that seems to separate fact from opinion. Another device is the use of a narrative form – a beginning, middle, and end within an item, in wrapped items, or over a continuing story – that erases historical and social structural contexts (see chapters 8 and 9). A third device is the aforementioned bifurcated structure of presenting two sides to a story.

In order to capture this third device for producing objectivity, we coded the number of items in each news outlet that presented two or more sides within the given item. The results are presented in table 6.5. In the total sample, 448, or 30 per cent, of news items had two or more sides presented, although all but 5 of these 448 items presented two sides only. NQ had 2 items with three sides, and 1 item with four sides. TP and RQ each had one item with three sides. Except for these outliers, Epstein's (1974: 227) observation that news 'dialogue ... is limited to two sides' certainly holds for the large number of items surveyed here.

Table 6.5 indicates that sides are somewhat more likely to be presented within newspaper items, compared to television and radio items. Between the two newspapers, there is no difference in the proportion of news items in which sides are presented. Within television, TQ had significantly more news items in which sides were presented than did TP. Within radio, RQ had somewhat more news items in which sides were presented than did RP. An additional consideration is whether, having presented two sides to a story, a news outlet indicates that a particular side is to be favoured. As documented in table 6.5, only the newspapers blatantly 'took sides,' and they did so for only a small minority of items. NQ favoured a side in 15 items, which is 14 per cent of NQ items in which sides were presented and 5 per cent of all NQ items. NP favoured a side in 14 items, which is 18 per cent of NP items in which sides were presented and 7 per cent of all NP items. Most of these were features and opinion-column pieces in which one side was described in 'straw man' fashion and then lambasted with the favoured viewpoint of the author.

With one exception in TP, broadcast-news outlets showed no favouritism towards one side while presenting two sides to an issue within a given news item. When the 'strategic ritual of objectivity' is used within a broadcast

TABLE 6.5
Sides presented/side favoured

	Newspaper		Television		Radio		Sig.
	Q	P	Q	P	Q	P	diff.
Sides presented	104	79	96	44	72	53	M/T
Yes	37.7%	37.3%	30.2%	20.7%	29.6%	23.8%	
Side favoured	15	14	0	1	0	0	M
Yes	5.4%	6.6%	0.0%	0.5%	0.0%	0.0%	
Total stories	276	212	318	213	243	223	1,485

Percentages are by column. Tests of significance based on tables with sides presented and tables with side favoured dichotomized into 'yes/no.' The last column indicates comparisons that show significant differences: chi-square statistics significant at the 0.05 level with Cramer's V or PHI ≥ 0.10, when N is large. Significant differences may occur between the newspapers (N); television stations (T); radio stations (R); or among the three types of media (M). The last column also indicates the presence of significant interactions with the variables being analysed and the coders (C) in a separate log-linear analysis.

item, the result is the appearance of impartiality. The lack of an editorial or opinion segment in all broadcast outlets except TP also contributes to these findings. In the case of TQ and RQ, these findings give weight to an assertion in the policy handbook of the national network they both belonged to that 'the Corporation takes no editorial position on its programming' (CBC 1982: 6).

The most remarkable finding is that, within the vast majority of news items (70 per cent of the total sample), there is not a presentation of two or more sides. One explanation of this fact is that news operatives are not committed to impartiality and balance within a given item, but only across items presented on the same day or over time. For example, the policy handbook for journalists of TQ and RQ says that 'those responsible for journalistic programming must avoid a cumulative bias or slant over a period of time and must be mindful of the CBC's responsibility to present the widest possible range of ideas' (CBC 1982: 9).

Taking the example of TQ, there were many individual items that were heavily slanted in favour of one side in a controversy, without any reaction whatsoever from the other side. However, at a different point within the same show, there was another item that provided for the viewpoint of the other side. For example, a very long item on an industrial strike was pro-union and very critical of management and the police. This is suggested by the anchor lead, which began, 'The strikers at Gabriel Shock Absorbers in Etobicoke are bruised, but determined to fight back. Their picket line was smashed by a wedge of policemen this morning.' This lead was followed by visuals of violence on the picket line, and then shots of four different persons on the picket line, each making strong statements such as, 'They're [the police] there to serve and protect, what they do is serve the company, not us!' These statements were followed with voice-overs by the reporter that basically supported the workers' contentions, such as, 'There were several minor injuries to the workers, none to the police' and 'the President of the union is accusing Gabriel of trying to bust the union and, he added, that some of the replacement workers escorted in today are professional strike-breakers.' There was no direct quotation of police or management officials within this item. However, later in the show there was a feature item on strike-breaking, with an in-studio interview between the anchor and a lawyer who acted for the managements of companies involved in labour disputes. This interview focused on the legal provisions that allowed management to use replacement workers during a strike, with the lawyer stating in conclusion that, unless there is 'equilibrium' between manage-ment's 'right' to carry on their business and the workers' 'right' to seek a better lot, 'industrial development here in Ontario will be somewhat inhibited to say the very least.'

TP had a regular opinion slot filled on an alternating basis by a left-wing commentator and a right-wing commentator, thus providing a sense of balance over time but certainly not within a given item. These opinion-slot items were very biased and strongly worded, more typical of what was found in NP than in broadcast journalism. For example, one piece from the left-wing commentator began with him saying that he was going to engage in a 'socialist rant.' He proceeded to criticize a speech by the prime minister televised the previous night, calling it a 'shameless piece of theatre,' and 'fundamentally dishonest' regarding the explanation given for economic problems. Following criticisms of the explanation given, the left-wing commentator stated, 'And there wasn't a thing in that statement last night worth a tinker's damn in terms of creating jobs for the unemployed. And then there was that usual finale, a conspiratorial finale, the business about groups of people, unnamed, greedy, ready to grab, ready to turn the nation back into fragmentation. Those were his words, but no names, just the usual fear-mongering.' Two shows later the right-wing columnist had his turn, likening the attitudes of the left-of-centre New Democratic Party leader to the political deviance of Yasser Arafat and other 'pinkos.'

Numerous studies show that people have turned anti-union and that they want less government, not more of it. One leading pollster made the com-ment to me recently that nothing reveals how out of touch UAW [the United Automobile Workers] is with public opinion than their decision to strike Chrysler Canada last year. He says that any union which today asks more rather than less is totally out of touch just as the manufacturer who thinks there is a killing to be made in buggy whips. Yet Ed Broadbent continues to breathe pink fire, and like Yasser Arafat, he's under siege by a lunatic fringe of his own organization who believe the fire is neither pink enough or hot enough. Undeterred by the catastrophe that has befallen France since socialism, Broadbent and the NDP are now speaking of nationalizing at least one Canadian bank. Now fortunately the NDP has all the impact of a sophomore debating society. It never has formed a national government, and judging by the polls, which just underlines what I said at the outset, it is unlikely that they ever will. It is nevertheless frightening to think that some Canadians think that way.

There is no balance or impartiality here. It is only by examining the total news product over time, and in this case the alternating vitriolic diatribes of the left- and right-wing commentators, that one can visualize a sense of balance. Within single items, the norm is a decided one-sidedness.

Strongly worded, opinionated statements were a part of the daily menu in NQ and NP. The editorials and opinion columns in NQ displayed a range of concerns and interests, with an emphasis on the rights of citizens and empathy for the underdog who was suffering at the hands of government or corporate bureaucracies. For example, an editorial in NQ said a farmer who falsely reported his assets to a bank did not deserve a sentence of imprisonment, arguing that the bank was also responsible to a degree, and that economic recession at the time should also be taken into account as a mitigating factor. While NP columnists also took up the case of 'the little guy versus bureaucracy,' on occasion NP editorials and opinion columns were decidedly right-wing, and sometimes critical of organizations and policies designed to help 'the little guy.' NP was persistently critical of the union movement (see also RCN, 1981d: esp. 86–7, 101), and also carried an opinion column stating a case against affirmative action programs. NP also included many items that expressed strong sentiments against communism, against the USSR, and against the need for American commitment to de-escalation of nuclear arms. NP trafficked in a partisan ideology, choosing opinion to fit the narrow grooves of its political preferences more than providing a 'terrain on which different sectional ideologies can contend' (Hartley 1982: 62).

A substantial proportion of items in each news outlet included only one source and therefore one version of the matter addressed (for quantitative comparisons, see chapter 7). Often it was a matter of the news outlet conveying the views of a prime member of one of its primary constituencies. For example, the business section of NQ frequently included items that reported what one corporate official said about a particular business sector or aspect of the economy. Thus one item, headlined 'Slow-growth period may follow upswing,' and 22 column-inches in length, consisted entirely of quotations from a speech given by the chairman of the Canadian Chamber of Commerce to a conference of the Canadian Institute of Plumbing and Heating. TP, with its 'vox pop' orientation, included a large number of items in which a citizen only was quoted as she or he was 'fighting' government authorities or corporate officials over a particular issue or problem. In many of these single-source stories, reporters themselves added expressions of affinity with the source's views.

In television, the reporter's role in expressing particular views became especially marked when the entire item consisted of a voice-over of video. This was evidenced in a number of CBS- and NBC-fed stories from Poland used by both TQ and TP. These stories focused on the Pope's activities, the activities of Solidarity leader Lech Walesa, and security-force activities, all voiced-over without direct quotations from sources. The recurrent theme in these voice-overs was that communism as practised in Poland is not popularly supported, that the Polish people have their hearts in political rights (via Solidarity) and religious freedoms (via the Catholic church) rather than in the oppressive Communist Party (represented by its security forces). Regardless of how much these items captured the essence of what was going on in Poland at the time of the Pope's visit, the point here is that the only voice of interpretation was that of American network reporters who voiced-over video feeds.

Television anchors also offered preferred readings before and/or after video feeds. Consider the following TQ use of a feed from NBC in which the only voices heard are those of the anchor and the NBC reporter.

TQ Anchor: [Voice-over still photograph of Andropov] Turning to international news. The suspense is over. Soviet leader Yuri Andropov came out to see West German leader Helmut Kohl today after bowing out of yesterday's meetings. Observers say the Kremlin's chief's left hand was shaking. More on the meeting between East and West from [names NBC reporter].

NBC Reporter: [Voice-over wide shot of meeting between Kohl and Andropov, pan shot to each leader] When West Germany's Helmut Kohl and Soviet Union's Yuri Andropov posed for photographs today, there were smiles across the tables. But later there were tough words. The Soviet leader warned West Germany would face an increased military threat if new American missiles were deployed on their soil. Kohl defended U.S. and German missile policy and added the Germans were not missile fanatics and that there was still time for Washington and Moscow to reach agreement in Moscow.

[Voice-over shot of Kohl walking down a corridor and shaking hands with Andropov] The give-and-take of tough talks continued at other meetings but

it is obvious that the Soviets don't like much of what Kohl is saying.
[Voice-over shot of Kohl in a scrum giving a statement to reporters] Many
of his remarks, including the rejection of Soviet facts on U.S. negotiating
policies, have been censored in Soviet news reports.

[Voice-over shot of soldiers placing wreath on tomb, Kohl, Andropov, and
others standing nearby] Kohl took the time to remember the dead of past
conflicts between the two countries.

[Voice-over shot of Kohl placing wreath on tomb at a different site] There
were flowers placed at the tomb of an unknown soldier honouring the Soviet
dead of the Second World War. And there were more flowers at another site
– this one set aside as a memorial to German prisoners of war who died on
Soviet soil. Two reminders of the dark past – NBC news.

TQ Anchor: [Voice-over still photograph of Kohl] A final note on Helmut Kohl's
tough talking in Moscow. Apparently it isn't being much appreciated. Pravda
is printing texts of his speeches without controversial passages. Western
diplomats say that it is a sure sign that Kohl is not making his hosts happy.

This piece of television-as-visual-radio reveals the subtleties of how
journalists, as the only voice in the item, take sides. The reporter and the
anchor emphasize Kohl's 'tough talking,' and the fact that he was censored
in the Soviet press, suggesting that East-West conflict is not only about
military arms but also about thought policing. The irony, of course, is that
neither the NBC reporter nor the TQ anchor offers one word from the
'controversial passages' of Kohl. They, too, have censored Kohl's remarks,
substituting the language of conflict by asserting that there were 'tough
words,' and 'tough talk,' with the result that 'Kohl is not making his hosts
happy.' The inference is that East-West conflict persists in spite of this
meeting between Kohl and Andropov.

News organizations have various justifications for becoming one-sided,
and for mobilizing their resources in favour of particular control actions and
remedies. When a news organization undertakes a piece of investigative
journalism, for example, it will reduce its concern with impartiality, favour
particular sources, and publish highly speculative material (Herman 1986).
NQ undertook long-term 'investigative' stories, aimed at policing organizations and individuals, in the hope of serving the public interest as well as
sustaining the interest of their reading public (Ericson, Baranek, and Chan
1987). The television stations studied also took up particular causes and used
their media power to advocate on behalf of particular interests. For example,
TP took up the protests of the Canadian Civil Liberties Association against
a federal bill that provided for a new Canadian security and intelligence
service and enabling laws for its operatives. The only sources cited for a
long item were the head of the CCLA, followed by the attorney general of

Ontario, and a spokesperson for an anti–nuclear weapons group, all of whom expressed strong opposition to the bill. No representatives of the federal government were cited, although the reporter said he placed a call to the federal solicitor general but his call was not returned. The item closed with the telephone number of the CCLA, presented as a vista on the screen, with the head of the CCLA stating, 'The Canadian Civil Liberties Association is planning some action to combat this bill and to cut back on some of the power they're talking about. If there are people who are interested ... please call us at [phone number].' It is clear that TP conceived its role in this case as an active mobilizer of resistance to a federal government bill that it found offensive.

News organizations argue that they are bound to take into account 'weight of opinion' along with fairness and impartiality. For example, a policy handbook for TQ and RQ states that 'programs dealing with matters of public interest in which different views are held must supplement the exposition of one point of view with an equitable treatment of other relevant points of view ... Equitable in this context means fair and reasonable, taking into consideration the weight of opinion behind a point of view, as well as its significance or potential significance' (CBC 1982: 8). This statement echoes the recommendation of the Annan Committee (1977) in Britain, and its translation into the policy of the BBC. What 'weight of opinion' means in practice is that concern for impartiality can be dropped if it is in the 'public interest' (Bennett 1977: 38; Schlesinger 1978: 163ff; Hartley 1982: 51). What is meant is that marginal groups – especially those that threaten parliamentary democracy, such as the IRA (ibid) – are excluded. However, as in the above-noted case of TP siding with the Canadian Civil Liberties Association against the federal government's security bill, it can also mean using authoritative sources outside the central state to mobilize citizens against a particular act of the state. Journalists and their sources are too concerned about making moral judgments, and effecting social control on the basis of those judgments, to avoid taking sides. In the news, 'All writing slants the way a writer leans, and no man is born perpendicular although many men are born upright' (E. Black 1982: 17, referring to a statement by E.B. White).

Discriminating News Formats by Medium and Market

In previous sections, we have considered selected aspects of news-formats individually, and how each one varies by medium and markets. It is also instructive to consider the collective and relative influence of the news-format characteristics as they relate to medium and markets. This can be accomplished through a series of stepwise discriminant analyses. The following analyses weight and combine four elements of news format (news-item types, news-item sources, news-event locations, and sides presented) as independent measures in a way that forces the groups – media (newspapers, television, radio), and the market within each medium (quality, popular) – to be as distinct as possible so that one can predict on what criteria the groups are distinguishable.

The stepwise discriminant analysis of news formats across medium types is presented in table 6.6. The best predictor of the medium is the news-item source. Some additional predictive influence comes from adding in turn the news-item type, the news-event location, and sides presented. Newspaper stories are distinguished as giving more coverage to foreign-news events and as presenting two or more sides. Television stories are distinguished as originating with reporters, being news/feature items, and giving coverage to foreign-news events. Radio stories are distinguished as originating with reporters and being news/feature items.

The stepwise discriminant analyses of news formats within markets are presented in table 6.7. From table 6.7a we learn that the best predictor of markets within newspapers is the news-event location. Some additional predictive influence comes from adding in the news-item types and the news-item source. NQ is distinguished by its coverage of foreign-news events. NP is distinguished by its greater use of news/feature items, and its greater reliance on reporters as the source of its items. From table 6.7b we learn that the best predictor of markets within television is the news-event location, with some additional predictive influence deriving from whether sides are presented. TQ is distinguished in terms of its coverage of foreign-news events and its greater emphasis on presenting two sides within an item. From table 6.7c it is evident that the best predictor of markets within radio is the news-event location. Some additional predictive influence is derived from adding in the news-item source and whether sides are presented. RQ is distinguished by its greater reliance on reporters as the source of its news items, and by its greater emphasis on presenting two sides. RP is differentiated in terms of its coverage of foreign-news events.

In this chapter, we have established important components of format peculiar to each news outlet. Each news outlet had a distinctive form of presentation, and attendant epistemology and ontology, because it operated with medium and market criteria that differed from the others.

NQ gave considerable space to items that were explicitly opinionated, especially letters to the editor. It was also most reliant on wire-service material, and used a much broader range of wire-service sources and place lines than did the other news outlets. A related component is that NQ had the greatest proportion of items originating in international or national as opposed to provincial or local settings. NQ was also the most likely to

TABLE 6.6
Stepwise discriminant analysis of news formats by medium

Variables	F	Discriminant function 1 standardized coefficients	Discriminant function 2 standardized coefficients
Source of item:			
Reporter	114.32	0.71	0.39
Type of item:			
News/feature	87.82	0.61	0.00
Location:			
Foreign	26.43	–0.17	1.08
Sides presented:			
2 or more sides	6.57	–0.17	–0.01
Centroids:			
Newspaper (N = 488)		–0.92	–0.06
Television (N = 531)		0.28	0.22
Radio (N = 466)		0.65	–0.20
Percentage of cases correctly classified:			
Newspaper	61.7%		
Television	22.2%		
Radio	85.0%		
Total	54.9%		

Wilk's lambda = 0.6731; chi-square = 585.98 (d.f. = 8; $p < 0.01$)

include continuing stories, indicating a greater emphasis on issues and investigative journalism. While NQ was similar to the other news outlets in not presenting different sides to a story within a majority of its items, along with NP it was the most likely to do so.

NP had a similar proportion of explicitly opinionated items as NQ, but differed from NQ in that many of these items derived from regular columnists, and most were explicitly right-wing. Although NP used a considerable amount of wire material, its stories were more likely to derive from staff reporters than were NQ's. NP was more similar to the broadcast-news outlets in this respect. Virtually all NP wire stories came from either UPI or UPC. NP used a very limited range of place lines in Canada, and foreign place lines were dominated by American locations. NP's wire stories were also predominantly on two themes, which it pursued relentlessly in all contexts: anti-communism and violent crime. NP was more local in orientation than was NQ, and when it did provide foreign news it was, again, mainly on the themes of anti-communism and violent crime. NP's local-news emphasis meant that it offered more unscheduled events than did NQ, especially,

TABLE 6.7a
Stepwise discriminant analysis of news formats within markets:
newspapers

Variables	F	Discriminant function standardized coefficients
Location:		
Foreign	4.37	–0.61
Type of item:		
News/feature	4.00	0.54
Source of item:		
Reporter	3.59	0.53

Centroids:		
Quality paper (N = 276)		–0.16
Popular paper (N = 212)		0.21
Percentage of cases correctly classified:		
Quality paper	44.9%	
Popular paper	63.7%	
Total	53.1%	

Wilk's lambda = 0.9679; chi-square = 15.79 (d.f. = 3; $p < 0.01$)

TABLE 6.7b
Stepwise discriminant analysis of news formats within markets:
television

Variables	F	Discriminant function standardized coefficients
Location:		
Foreign	20.97	0.90
Sides presented:		
2 or more	10.58	0.65

Centroids:		
Quality television (N = 318)		–0.19
Popular television (N = 213)		–0.28
Percentage of cases correctly classified:		
Quality paper	65.7%	
Popular paper	60.1%	
Total	63.5%	

Wilk's lambda = 0.9510; chi-square = 26.54 (d.f. = 2; $p < 0.01$)

TABLE 6.7c
Stepwise discriminant analysis of news formats within markets: radio

Variables	F	Discriminant function standardized coefficients
Location:		
Foreign	14.52	−0.70
Soure of item:		
Reporter	11.86	0.63
Sides presented:		
2 or more	1.60	0.24

Centroids:		
Quality radio (N = 243)		0.25
Popular radio (N = 223)		−0.27
Percentage of cases correctly classified:		
Quality radio	93.0%	
Popular rdio	23.8%	
Total	59.9%	

Wilk's lambda = 0.9373; chi-square = 29.94 (d.f. = 3; $p < 0.01$)

crime, accident, and disaster events. NP was about as likely as was NQ to offer two sides to a story within an item, and just slightly more likely to take one side over the other. However, it bears emphasis that none of the outlets provided more than one side in the majority of their items. Balance was more likely to be provided over time rather than within a given item, and frequently there was no balance at all but rather an adversarial approach aimed at policing wrongdoing. Journalists and their sources are too concerned about making moral judgments, and effecting social control on the basis of those judgments, to avoid taking sides.

TQ offered virtually no space for explicitly opinionated items. This practice is in keeping with broadcast-news formats and their constitution of objectivity: because broadcast news must be formatted primarily in the voice of the individual journalist, what seems factual and authoritative, although opinionated, in print, can appear idiosyncratic, biased, propagandistic, and even laughable in the broadcast media. Most TQ stories originated with their own reporters, although there was some explicit use of news-service material from their own affiliates and a variety of foreign sources. TQ had the most foreign-location coverage of any of the broadcast outlets and rivalled NQ in this regard. In keeping with broadcast news generally, TQ relied in particular on scheduled events. TQ presented two sides to a story within an item more than did the other broadcast-news outlets, but in keeping with those outlets it never took one side over the other in such items. More common were items that took one side only. Although these one-sided items were formatted as news, they were often expressions of strong opinion as a consequence of the way the script was constructed and sources were used. On occasion such items amounted to explicit advocacy.

The television medium conduces news outlets towards similar forms of presentation within the popular mode (see especially chapter 4). Hence, with a few exceptions, TP was quite similar to TQ. TP used less news-service material than TQ, which was a result of TP being a local privately owned station without a network affiliation and having a local-news-event orientation. With one exception, all TQ news-service material came from the National Broadcasting Corporation of the United States.

RQ offered no space to explicitly opinionated formats. It was reporter-centred, relying on the voice of its own reporters almost exclusively. RQ was the most provincial in focus of all the news outlets, and it also presented a lot of local-news events. It largely eschewed national and international news, leaving such coverage to the separate newscasts of the national network of which it was an affiliate. RQ offered few continuing stories, relying instead on the spot-news format typical in radio.

RP also eschewed explicitly opinionated pieces and relied heavily on the voice of its own reporters. However, RP was more likely than was RQ to make explicit use of wire-service material. While RP was primarily oriented to local-news events, it included more national and international news than did RQ because it did not have separate network newscasts for such material. Like RQ, RP had relatively few continuing stories and relied heavily on spot news.

In the following chapter we examine components of format that pertain to the sources used by each news outlet. The number of sources used, the institutions sources represent, and how sources are represented by journalists are important components of format that vary substantially in terms of the medium and market of news outlets.

7

Source Formats

News outlets use a variety of sources of knowledge for their stories, but their sources are not always evident in news content. Sometimes the only 'voice' is that of journalists, even though the knowledge they are using has been obtained from elsewhere, for example, from other news stories, wire copy, news releases, and individuals who remain off the record. Only observational studies of journalists and sources involved in news production can reveal the nature and extent of practices in this regard (Ericson, Baranek, and Chan 1987, 1989). However, many sources of knowledge are made explicit in news content. The 'voice' of the journalist-as-author is usually evident, and his or her news-organization affiliation is always clear. Often other 'voices' are cited directly or are referred to as attributed sources.

In this chapter we focus on sources of knowledge evident in news content. Our analysis is based on a sample of 5,175 sources who provided knowledge in the 1,485 news items surveyed. The basic concern is to identify the sources of crime, law, and justice news used by different news outlets. What are the characteristics of the authorities, the members of the deviance-defining élite, who reproduce the normalizing and disciplinary discourses in society?

News is very important to regular sources because it helps them to enact their organizational environments and to constitute their authority (Ericson, Baranek, and Chan 1987, 1989). Environments are actively created by actors who produce knowledge about them (Weick 1979). Knowledge provides a basis upon which actors establish coherence between their organization and their identity, and also serves legitimating functions *vis-à-vis* others in the organizational environment. The essence of organizational work is the production of knowledge, of images and symbols with objectivated meaning, as these function to provide identity for members and legitimate their activities to others. Organizations are constantly being rationalized and cast into rhetorics, so that they exist 'as images, as subjective congeries of experience which are bounded and located spatially and temporally' (Manning 1982: 130). Image-making in the news is crucial for organizational enactments. Effort to publicize certain events while remaining secretive about others influences organizational routines, affects careers, and promotes both change and stability (Ericson, Baranek, and Chan 1989).

Source organizations, through their designated spokespersons, also become 'authors' of the news. They work hard to produce knowledge, and to police it, so that they can sustain their preferred versions of events and visions of what should be done about them. As producers of social discourse, actors in the news participate in every part of the social drama. They write scripts, perform, and do critical reviews, each one seeking to implant his or her own vision of a happy ending. However not everyone is able to perform his or her authority equally. News organizations have their own legitimating justifications, one of which is that 'weight of opinion' can be used to imbalance accounts of events. News operatives assign particular organizations and their actors to leading roles, cast some as only supporting, treat others as mere extras, and leave most as spectators. The question of which types of organizations and actors are assigned these various places in the news and how this varies by medium and market is central to this chapter.

Sources in official positions use the power of the news media to establish publicly the symbols of their administration. They do so by focusing on aspects of deviance – procedural impropriety, mismanagement, wrongdoing – and its correction through disciplinary mechanisms, especially law. This perpetual social discourse of crime, law, and justice provides a 'continuing political and administrative dialogue as to the terms and conditions of social life' (Goodrich 1986: 19–20). Arguably, it is this dialogue that provides people with their sense of the validity of law (ibid: 17; see also Mathiesen 1987; Macauley 1987), and of other institutions. As such, this social discourse is an important vehicle for justifying the authority of institutions and making them appear natural. People are to acknowledge their institutions as authoritative, and to obey them, more than to know them. All institutions (Meyer and Rowan 1977), as exemplified by the law (Atiyah 1982), function in terms of the images and myths their members re-enact in their institutional environments.

In what follows, we analyse how various sources of knowledge about crime, law, and justice are represented in the news, and the social discourse that results. We sustain our focus on types of medium and market, asking whether this representation varies in different news outlets operating with different format constraints and different news-consumer considerations.

Number of Sources

In table 7.1, we document how many sources, other than journalists, were used in the news items sampled within each outlet. We also summarize these data by indicating at the bottom of table 7.1 the mean number of sources other than journalists used in each item, as this varies across the six outlets studied. The data on the mean number of sources per item indicate statistically significant differences by medium. Newspapers (2.7/item) use more sources on average than television stations (2.0/item), which in turn use more sources on average than radio stations (1.7/item). These differences are expected in light of the greater discursive capacity of the newspaper medium. Newspaper journalists, compared to their counterparts in broadcast journalism, have much greater scope for producing longer items with multiple sources.

The newspapers had very few items in which no other sources of information were cited or referred to. In contrast, the broadcast outlets, and especially the popular television station (TP), had a substantial number of items without reference to other sources of information. The extremes in this regard are the quality newspaper (NQ), with only 2 per cent of its items lacking reference to other sources, and TP, which had no reference to other sources in 21 per cent of its items. As documented below, in the section on types of sources, broadcast outlets frequently use their own journalists as sources. For example, the anchor interviews a reporter from his or her own outlet, or the anchor or reporter provides a statement on his or her own. In a substantial number of items, this is all there is, as indicated by the data presented here. The popular broadcast-news outlets in particular included a number of items with no sources other than their own journalists talking to camera or microphone.

Radio was the medium that used a single source most often. One-third of all items in the quality radio station (RQ), and 42 per cent of items in the popular radio station (RP), involved reference to one 'outside' source of information. Isolating RP, we find that 56 per cent of their items involved a journalist alone, or only a single outside source referred to. In contrast, the two newspapers each had about 27 per cent of items that referred to a journalist alone or only a single outside source. This finding underscores the fact that radio news is restricted. Its items are brief, and the number of voices are limited so that the audibility of the message remains clear and does not regress to mere background noise in the listener's mind.

On the other end of the scale, the radio outlets rarely had items with more than three outside sources cited (only 11 per cent in RQ and 4 per cent in RP). In contrast, both television (22 per cent in the quality television station [TQ] and 20 per cent in TP) and especially the newspapers (34 per

TABLE 7.1
Number of sources cited*

Number of sources	Newspaper Q	P	Television Q	P	Radio Q	P	
None other than journalist	6 2.2%	11 5.2%	43 13.5%	45 21.1%	21 8.6%	31 13.9%	
One	68 24.6%	46 21.7%	89 28.0%	61 28.6%	83 34.2%	93 41.7%	
Two	62 22.5%	48 22.6%	64 20.1%	39 18.3%	74 30.0%	59 26.5%	
Three	46 16.7%	40 18.9%	52 16.4%	25 11.7%	38 15.6%	32 14.3%	
Four or five	45 16.3%	46 21.7%	56 17.6%	34 16.0%	18 7.4%	7 3.1%	
Six or more	49 17.8%	21 9.9%	14 4.4%	9 4.2%	9 3.7%	1 0.4%	
Total stories	276	212	318	213	243	223	1,485
							Sig. diff.
Mean no. of source/item	2.7	2.6	2.1	1.9	1.9	1.5	R
Std deviation	1.5	1.4	1.4	1.5	1.2	1.0	
Mean no. of source/item	2.7		2.0		1.7		M
Std deviation		1.46		1.47		1.14	

Percentages are by column. The last column indicates comparisons that show significant differences, i.e. one-way analysis of variance with F ratio significant at 0.05 level. Significant differences may occur between the newspapers (N); television stations (T); radio stations (R); or among the types of media (M).
*Excluding journalists

cent in NQ and 32 per cent in the popular newspaper [NP]) had a substantial proportion of their stories with four or more outside sources cited. These data indicate that radio journalists restrict the number of information sources within an item, while television journalists have more scope in this regard, and newspaper journalists even greater scope.

These differences are significant, but should be assessed in light of the fact that broadcast journalists work within a format of very brief items, but often link successive items in a wrap to sustain related items or a theme (Ericson, Baranek, and Chan 1987: part III). Taken together, the several items in a wrap cite many different sources, offering a range of perspectives on the matter addressed. For example, a wrap might begin with a report of an assault on a woman, follow with 'fear and loathing' reactions from other women who live in the area, obtain an account from the police as to the progress in their investigation, and conclude with an item on self-defence courses available to women. A newspaper covering the same matter might include all of these elements within a single item. Our analysis in terms of individual news items does not capture these media differences in how items are formatted to construct a 'larger' story or theme (cf Altheide 1976, 1987a).

Although radio is more restricted in its use of multiple sources, there were occasions on which very long items with several sources were used. For example, in the RQ sample, there is an item reporting on the recommendations of a jury following an inquest regarding a teenage boy who died of a skin disease. This item cited or referred to seven sources other than the reporter and anchor, included three sources in extended clips, and was 670 words in length. In terms of length, complexity, and sources used, this item was more substantial than any of the items offered by the other news outlets on this matter.

Combined with the fact that radio offers information-show formats that are long and use a range of sources, we conclude that the differences documented in table 7.1 have more to do with how radio operatives structure the news segment of their programming than with the inability of the radio medium per se to handle longer stories with a large number of sources (see also Crisell 1986: part two).

Turning to comparisons within each medium, table 7.1 makes evident the fact that there was little difference between NQ (2.7/item) and NP (2.6/item) in the number of outside sources used on average. This is surprising, since the quality-newspaper format seems to allow for longer items, more features, and greater complexity, including the use of multiple sources. In contrast, the popular newspaper uses short items and many still photographs. It is only in the extreme of using six or more sources that NQ stands out, with 18 per cent of its items in this category, compared to 10 per cent of the items in NP. There was also little difference between TQ (2.1/item) and TP (1.9/item) in the number of outside sources used on average. However, the differences in radio are statistically significant. RQ (1.9/item) used more outside sources on average than did RP (1.5/item). As noted earlier, RP more often than not used only a journalist or one outside source in its items, and very rarely used four or more sources. In contrast, RQ used a journalist alone, or only a single information source, less often than did RP, and made greater use of items with four or more outside sources cited.

Source Types

In this section we analyse the use of five general types of sources in crime, law, and justice news. First, we examine journalists as sources of knowledge, including journalists representing a particular news outlet itself, as well as those representing other outlets who are interviewed or cited as sources. We then consider government officials, including those representing the criminal-justice system, public administration, and other government agencies. Next we analyse sources from private-sector organizations, including private corporations, occupational associations, political groups, and community organizations. Consideration is then given to the individual citizen, without organizational affiliation, as a source. Finally, we attend to sources who were referred to but not identified in the news item. An enumeration of these types of sources, as the frequency of their use varied in the six news outlets studied, is presented in table 7.2.

Prior to discussing each type of source and variation in their use, two preliminary observations are helpful. First, the frequency with which a source is cited is not instructive about how the source is represented. Some sources appear relatively frequently, but are not represented favourably, instead being portrayed as deviants whose authority is being discredited by the news media in conjunction with preferred sources (Gitlin 1980; Glasgow University Media Group [GUMG] 1980; Tracey 1984; Herman 1986; Schlesinger 1988; Ericson, Baranek, and Chan 1987, 1989). Second, the distinction between public- and private-sector sources is problematic, given the complex relations among government and non-government organizations, as exemplified in the media institution itself. Nevertheless, the public-private distinction is sustained by journalists themselves, affecting what they attend to and how they classify their items (Tuchman 1978: 163–4; Ericson, Baranek, and Chan, 1987, 1989: esp. chap. 5).

The data in table 7.2 indicate that the bulk of knowledge sources about crime, law, and justice are journalists themselves, or government officials. News of crime, law, and justice is primarily based on the accounts of government institutional definers, and/or the accounts of journalists themselves. Journalists work in relation to the 'sacredotal' (Blumler and Gurevitch 1986: 88–9) institutions that can be counted on to imprint a designation of the deviance and implant a preferred control solution that represents the dominant value system. Relegated to a minor role, at least statistically, are private-sector organizations, and even more so, individual citizens. While supporting the generalization in the existing research

TABLE 7.2
News-source types

Type	Newspaper		Television		Radio		Sig. diff.
	Q	P	Q	P	Q	P	
Journalist of organization	146 13.9%	141 18.9%	459 38.7%	297 41.4%	365 43.1%	285 45.3%	M
Other journalist	127 12.1%	84 11.3%	54 4.6%	33 4.6%	6 0.7%	18 2.9%	M
Criminal justice	31 3.0%	79 10.6%	64 5.4%	40 5.6%	71 8.4%	44 7.0%	N
Public administration	60 5.7%	30 4.0%	60 5.1%	30 4.2%	42 5.0%	43 6.8%	
Other government sources	332 31.6%	148 19.8%	191 16.1%	76 10.6%	151 17.8%	115 18.3%	M/N
Private corporation	82 7.8%	60 8.0%	95 8.0%	63 8.8%	76 9.0%	34 5.4%	
Occupational association	43 4.1%	21 2.8%	32 2.7%	11 1.5%	35 4.1%	11 1.7%	
Political organization	38 3.6%	12 1.6%	26 2.2%	9 1.3%	4 0.5%	7 1.1%	
Community organization	47 4.5%	25 3.4%	85 7.2%	41 5.7%	41 4.8%	22 3.5%	
Individuals	78 7.4%	119 16.0%	73 6.2%	96 13.4%	37 4.4%	38 6.0%	N/T
Unspecified	56 5.3%	25 3.4%	20 1.7%	18 2.5%	14 1.7%	11 1.7%	
Don't know	10 1.0%	2 0.3%	26 2.2%	4 0.6%	5 0.6%	1 0.2%	
Total sources	1,050	746	1,185	718	847	629	5,175

Percentages are by column. Tests of significance based on tables with news-source types dichotomized into 'yes/no' for each of the categories. The last column indicates comparisons that show significant differences: chi-square statistics significant at the 0.05 level with Cramer's V or PHI $\geq$ 0.10, when N is large. Significant differences may occur between the newspapers (N); television stations (T); radio stations (R); or among the three types of media (M). The last column also indicates the presence of significant interactions with the variables being analysed and the coders (C) in a separate log-linear analysis.

literature that the news media favour governmental sources, and themselves, there is some variation in this regard that is best highlighted through a detailed comparison of differences among news outlets in representing each source type.

JOURNALISTS

Journalists frequently insert their own statements as a source of knowledge in the news item. This is often done at the beginning and end of an item, especially to frame it, and also in the process of shifting from the comments of one outside source to another. Frequently the journalist does not make evident the source of his or her knowledge, although we know from observational research (Ericson, Baranek, and Chan 1987) that usually his or her knowledge is derived from news accounts published previously and, to a lesser extent, from other sources who remain off the record.

In table 7.2 the category 'journalist of organization' refers to journalists who provided knowledge on their own, without reference to its source. The data indicate that this practice occurs frequently, especially in broadcast-news organizations. While this knowledge source is a small minority of all sources in newspapers (14 per cent in NQ and 19 per cent in NP), it is by far the greatest single source in television (39 per cent in TQ and 41 per cent in TP) and radio (43 per cent in RQ and 45 per cent in RP).

These data indicate that, in broadcast news, journalists dominate. In particular, the anchorperson is at the fulcrum of the show and provides a lot of knowledge without attribution to others. The anchor embodies the authority of the broadcasting outlet. His or her 'personality' indexically guarantees the 'impersonality' or objectivity of the outlet. The anchor's stature is enhanced by his or her ability, in conjunction with the news producer, to control the show and what is ultimately broadcast. The anchor can stage a performance that exhumes authority and credibility, without the negative criticisms and counterpoints that are sustained against other regular news sources.

With an assumed authoritative voice, the anchor can make statements without attribution to any source and without use of a reporter's account. Moreover, when an outside source or a reporter is used, the anchor can frame the account by comments before and after the clip. As the embodiment of the outlet's objectivity and authority, the anchor has latitude to give a reading to the outside source and reporter clips included in a news item. He or she can editorialize, alternatively lending weight to or undercutting what other voices have to say.

The anchor is especially dominant on radio newscasts. The bulk of the items in the radio line-ups consisted of some combination of anchor-only statements, anchor statements with a clip from an outside source, and anchor statements with a clip from a reporter for the outlet. For example, among the seven items in our RP sample for one day, three were statements by the anchor only, three were statements by the anchor and then a clip from a single outside source, and one included an anchor statement followed by a statement by an RP reporter who in turn used a clip of an outside source. Both RP and RQ made frequent use of an interview format that involved the anchor as the interviewer and the outlet reporter as an interviewee. In these items, the reporter was in effect formatted in the same way as any other source. This approach was used most often as a way of summarizing the proceedings in a court case, inquest, inquiry, or other hearing. Often this was at a stage in the proceedings when witnesses or officials were probably unwilling to be interviewed, preferring to wait for the official conclusion of the case before agreeing to interviews. However, the anchor-reporter interview format was also used when actuality clips from outside sources seemed readily available (e.g., at public demonstrations, at news conferences). Regardless of the event and setting, the approach was similar. The reporter offered his interpretation, and the anchor actively intervened with his or her statements and questions to further the interpretation. The only difference from interviews with outside sources was that the anchor and reporter always agreed on the interpretation. The following RQ item is illustrative.

Anchor: Dr Henry Morgentaler held a news conference in Winnipeg today. He faces charges there of conspiring to procure an illegal abortion. Seven other people face similar charges. RQ reporter [first and last name] was there and he's on the line. [Reporter's first name], what did Dr Morgentaler tell the press?

Reporter: I think he wanted to make a couple of points. Number one, he's appealed to Manitoba's attorney general, Roland Penner, to drop the charges laid against the four nurses and two counsellors at the abortion clinic. He said he was absolutely stunned when they were charged and it's the kind of move which simply isn't worthy of an NDP government. He described it as reactionary. He also restated his offer to let the province take over the clinic and run it themselves because there's definitely a need for this type of service here, he says, and he did say he'll proceed with his plans to open a clinic in Toronto tomorrow no matter what. He stated in fact he expects to be charged by a Tory government in Ontario. He did not expect wide-ranging charges against all the staff from the NDP government in Manitoba.

Anchor: What you were saying at the beginning is a little reminiscent of his experience in Quebec, the first time he was charged there, isn't it?

Reporter: Exactly, and I think that's why he's so confident and plans to proceed in any event. He keeps stating that he's been acquitted by three juries in Quebec. That was the beachhead – he's moving out from there. But he really considers the clinics in Ontario and in Winnipeg to be the next step, the step which, if successful, could guarantee such services to women across Canada. He's in a bit of a hole. He says he needs $500,000 for his defence fund. They've raised only 10,000 so far. There was also a brief appeal at the beginning of the news conference for money so they are planning on running up some pretty, you know, pretty high legal charges but they're in trouble right now.

Anchor: But planning to fight it all the way?

Reporter: Exactly.

Anchor: O.K., thank you very much [reporter's first name] [Reporter's first and last name], [RQ] reporter in Winnipeg. And as [reporter's first name] mentioned, Dr Morgentaler is opening his Toronto abortion clinic tomorrow morning.

The only thing on offer here is the authoritative interpretations of the RQ anchor and reporter. It is their voices, not the voices of Dr Morgentaler or his staff members, that tell us the 'couple of points' Dr Morgentaler wanted to make. It is also the journalists' voices that frame the conflict, drawing upon the metaphors of military and legal battles: establishing 'the beachhead,' building the 'defence fund,' and 'planning to fight it all the way.' The only guarantee available to the reader is that the story emanates from an anchor who is known as an authoritative news voice of RQ, and that the reporter's account is authenticated both by being there and by being in accord with the 'trusted' anchor.

The television outlets studied used a similar format, although to a lesser extent. For example, on each of the two days before the release of a major report on the problem of violence against women, TQ broadcast stories that consisted entirely of anchor and reporter statements to camera and voiced-over stock visuals. It was only upon official release of the report on the third day that outside source clips were used. TQ and TP each had a format in which a news item, or series of items, was followed by in-studio conversation between the anchor and a reporter for the outlet. TP sometimes used NBC feeds on foreign-news topics, followed by an in-studio discussion between the anchor and a reporter for TP, in which events in the foreign culture were converted to local culture. A TP reporter framed the account of a NBC reporter's voice-over account, and this account was followed by further interpretive work from the TP reporter and anchor. Distanced N-levels from the realities reported on, these items appeared, rather ironically, in a feature segment titled 'Closeup.'

Occasionally correspondents from local news outlets were interviewed directly as experts. For example, the NP business editor was interviewed in-studio by a TQ features journalist regarding the economic impact of asbestosis suits again asbestos-producing companies. Occasionally clips produced by one television reporter at the scene of a scrum or public demonstration were also shown by a competitor. For example, TQ used a clip of a TP reporter questioning a lawyer about a case he was involved in. The TP story on the same matter did not use this clip.

The data in table 7.2 indicate that the newspaper medium made frequent use of other journalists as sources, while radio outlets rarely used sources of this type. The greater proportionate use of outside journalists as sources by newspapers is attributable to several factors. The newspapers used wire copy that sometimes included the byline of the reporter for the wire service. They used syndicated and other outside columnists on a regular basis. They also used outside feature writers and guest writers from other news outlets. While the proportionate use of other journalists by radio and television outlets is low, we know from our observational research on the practices of journalists (Ericson, Baranek, and Chan 1987) that broadcast outlets routinely use material produced by journalists from other news outlets without attribution.

GOVERNMENT SOURCES

Previous research emphasizes the dominance of government sources in the news. For example, Sigal's (1973) survey of the *New York Times* and *Washington Post* revealed that 78 per cent of all stories involved government officials, domestic and foreign. Others have shown that in various types of reporting – for example, on environmental disasters (Molotch and Lester 1975), industrial strikes (GUMG 1976, 1980), political movements (Gitlin 1980), and routine crime occurrences (Fishman 1980) – government institutions predominate in setting the agenda and sustaining preferred accounts. Often the official imprint of a government agency is required before something is regarded as news at all.

As documented in table 7.2, government sources (criminal-justice, public-administration, other) were cited more than private-sector organization sources (private-corporation, occupational-association, politicalorganization, community-organization) and individual citizens. On a proportionate basis, government sources were cited in the newspapers and on radio about twice as often as private-sector-organization sources. In television, however, government sources were cited only marginally more often than were private-sector-organization sources.

Criminal-justice sources appear frequently in the news. NP (11 per cent of all sources cited) in particular gave substantial place to the knowledge of criminal-justice sources, especially in comparison with NQ (only 3 per cent of all sources cited).

The data in table 7.2 fail to capture the full range of source types who provided knowledge about the criminal-justice system or about persons involved in it. In a separate analysis of law-enforcement coverage, we identified all sources who provided some knowledge about the system or its participants. While the vast majority of these law-enforcement sources addressed criminal justice, a few were also involved in civil litigation. The total number of sources in this law-enforcement group is 529, incorporating the types distinguished below (for comparable data, see Sherizen 1978: 220).

Police officers were cited or referred to 93 times, constituting 18 per cent of the law-enforcement group. The chief of police or his deputy were cited 33 times; persons with the ranks of inspector through staff superintendent were cited 10 times; staff sergeants and sergeants were cited 27 times; and constables were cited 23 times. On a proportionate basis, NP cited twice as many police officers as did NQ. NP mainly cited lower-ranking officers, while most of NQ's citations were at the level of chief or deputy-chief. Exactly the same pattern appeared between TP and TQ. These data indicate that the popular newspaper and television outlets were more oriented to police news, and to the views of officers on the beat, than were the quality newspaper and television outlets.

Crown attorneys were cited or referred to 45 times, constituting 9 per cent of the law-enforcement group. In its law-enforcement coverage NP cited a Crown attorney 10 times, while NQ did so only once. TQ, which had a regular court reporter, cited Crown attorneys much more often than did TP, which did not have a regular reporter on the court beat. RP, whose police reporter also covered the courts, used Crown attorneys as sources more frequently than did RQ, which did not have a regular reporter assigned to either police or courts.

Lawyers were cited or referred to 75 times, constituting 14 per cent of the law-enforcement group. Among these, 47 were representing persons who were defendants in civil litigation, or criminal suspects, accused, or offenders; and 28 were representing persons who were plaintiffs in civil litigation, or complainants or victims in criminal cases. Within-medium analysis indicates that NP compared to NQ, and TP compared to TQ, cited lawyers for civil defendants or defendants in criminal cases much more frequently.

Judges and justices were cited or referred to 70 times, constituting 13 per cent of the law-enforcement group. Included in this category are 9 from the Supreme Court of Canada, 21 from provincial-level supreme courts, 11 from county courts, 18 from provincial courts, 3 justices of the peace, and 8 from courts abroad or where the level of court could not be determined. The only within-medium difference of note is in television, with TQ citing judges much more often than did TP. Again, this is related to the fact that TQ had a regular court reporter, while TP did not.

Only 6 correctional officials were cited or referred to, constituting 1 per cent of the law-enforcement group. Among these officials, 3 were line-level correctional officers, and 3 represented management. These data are in keeping with the findings of others that, when the news media cover criminal justice, it is primarily in relation to the police and courts, while corrections is all but excluded from consideration (Sherizen 1978; Graber 1980; Garofalo 1981).

The most significant aspect of our findings about sources of law-enforcement news is the place given to citizens. This aspect is addressed further in our discussion of individuals as news sources. Citizens who were witnesses or informants regarding law-enforcement matters were cited 22 times, constituting 4 per cent of the law-enforcement group. Citizens who were plaintiffs in civil cases or victims in criminal cases were cited 71 times, constituting 13 per cent of the law-enforcement group. Each of the popular outlets, but especially NP compared to NQ, gave particular emphasis to victims. Citizens who were criminal suspects (14), accused (32), and offenders (including prisoners) (25) were also cited 71 times, constituting 13 per cent of the law-enforcement group. NP also cited these citizens more frequently than did NQ; otherwise, there were no substantial differences across the news outlets studied. Finally, the family and friends of criminal victims (52) and suspects, accused, and offenders (24) were cited 76 times, constituting 15 per cent of the law-enforcement group. Again NP stood out in comparison to NQ, citing 21 sources of this type while NQ cited only 4. The television stations each cited 18 sources of this type, joining with NP in providing the fear and loathing, and tertiary understanding, available through these sources. In contrast, the radio stations were similar to NQ in rarely seeking accounts from this type of source.

Returning to the data in table 7.2, we find that sources categorized as being in public administration – involved in administrative branches of government such as Crown corporations, health or educational administration, tribunals, task forces, public inquiries – constituted a very small proportion of the total sources cited or referred to. There were no significant medium or market differences in the use of sources of this type.

In table 7.2, we record the fact that there was substantial use of 'other government sources,' namely politicians and civil servants involved in local, provincial, national, or international capacities. In this category there are significant differences. The newspaper medium made much greater use of this type of source than did television and radio. However, within the newspaper medium, NQ accounted for the much greater use of politicians and civil servants, while NP used them only marginally more than did the broadcast outlets. NQ stands out as giving by far the greatest attention to the institutional voices of politics. Almost one-third of all knowledge sources cited or referred to by NQ were in this category. Excluding journalists as knowledge sources, 43 per cent of NQ outside sources were politicians and civil servants in various branches of government.

PRIVATE-SECTOR SOURCES

In comparison to knowledge sources from the media institution and from various branches of government, private-sector sources – representing private corporations, occupation associations, political organizations, and community organizations – were used less frequently. On a proportionate basis NQ and NP used government sources more than twice as frequently as private-sector sources. RP used government sources almost three times as frequently as private-sector sources. In RQ, TQ, and TP the proportionate use of government sources compared to private-sector sources was somewhat greater, but less marked than in RP and the newspapers.

Table 7.2 reveals that, except for the low figures in RP, the news outlets were about equal in their proportionate use of sources from private corporations. This finding supports the contention that the news media give relatively little attention to the 'business world' (Tuchman 1978: 163–4; Royal Commission on Newspapers [RCN] 1981c: 21). NQ did not have greater proportionate reference to or citation of knowledge sources in private corporations, which is surprising since NQ had a substantial separate business-news section and seemed to favour private corporate sources in its letters-to-the-editor columns (Ericson, Baranek, and Chan 1989: chaps. 5 and 6). While NQ's private corporate sources tend to be executives and experts cited in the business section regarding corporate difficulties, take-overs, and the state of the economy, the corporate sources in other outlets represent the view of corporate executives and managers on specific labour troubles, especially strikes.

The power of private corporate sources over the news includes especially their power to keep things out of the news (Ericson, Baranek, and Chan 1989: chaps. 5 and 6). At a different level, private corporations have significant control over the news system via ownership and consequent ability to channel news operations in the direction of knowledge 'intelligence' that serves their interests (Clement 1975: chap. 7; RCN 1981b; D. Schiller 1986; H. Schiller 1989). However, a lot of news about the private corporate world is about procedural deviance and wrongdoing in that sphere, aimed at achieving a degree of compliance through negative publicity (see chapters 5 and 9).

Another private-sector source listed in table 7.2 is occupational associations, including both labour unions and professional groups concerned with the interests of their members. There are no statistically significant medium or market differences for this category, although it is evident that quality outlets in each medium cited occupational association sources more frequently than did popular outlets. Existing research that analyses particular industrial disputes indicates that, while labour sources can receive even more frequent citations than management, they may be given less print space or broadcast time than management and policing officials (e.g., GUMG 1980: esp. 81, 162), and be treated more critically by journalists in interviews (Tracey 1984). Our data indicate that when analysing the coverage of occupational-associations in general across a range of issues and disputes, rather than one specific dispute, there is little difference in the citation rates of their members compared to corporate officials. Moreover, our qualitative readings (see the example at pp. 170–1; see also Ericson, Baranek, and Chan 1987) suggest that there was space for occupational association members to receive sympathetic interviews and access from journalists.

The category 'political organizations' includes groups defined as marginal or radical by the political authorities in the jurisdiction concerned. Surveying the news media cross-sectionally at a particular time, rather than studying how one political movement struggles in the media searchlight over time (e.g., Gitlin 1980), reveals that these sources are used infrequently relative to other types, especially in radio. NQ, in keeping with its general focus on political sources, cited marginal political organization spokespersons more often than did the other outlets, but these sources constituted less than 4 per cent of the total NQ sources cited or referred to.

The other private-sector category included in table 7.2 is community organizations, within which we included a range of formally organized, non-profit groups such as religious organizations, charitable organizations, and citizens' reform groups focused on a single issue. These organizations are reported on as they confront the state with major issues, and they are also a major source of knowledge 'intelligence' for the state regarding the specific social issues they organize to deal with (Rock 1986; M. Clarke 1987). Sources of this type received more citation or reference than any other private-sector sources with the exception of corporate sources. While their proportionate use did not vary significantly across news outlets, they tended to be cited more by the quality outlets. This is somewhat surprising, given the orientation of popular outlets to local grass-roots politics. In particular, NP and TP had a 'vox pop' thrust, yet this did not include a larger proportionate representation of community-group sources than was available in NQ and TQ.

INDIVIDUALS AS SOURCES

NP and TP sustained their 'vox pop' orientation through the citation of individual citizens. As documented in table 7.2, NP (16 per cent) made much greater proportionate use of individuals as sources than did NQ (7 per cent). Similarly, TP (13 per cent) cited individuals much more frequently on a proportionate basis than did TQ (6 per cent).

Compared to sources who speak from an institutional position, individuals have a minor place in the news. Moreover, individuals appear at best as a *representation* of what journalists think they stand for in a story, rather than as *representative* of public opinion on the matter addressed in the story (Tuchman 1978: 212). Hence individuals are rarely given an introduction or a caption, as is customary with most institutional news sources. They are simply to stand for what 'the public,' or a segment of it, is visualized to think about a matter. Moreover, the matters addressed by individual citizens are usually already framed in the terms of established institutions.

While newspapers have a long history of reserving space for individual opinion, such as in the letters-to-the-editor columns, granting individuals access to broadcasting is a recent phenomenon. Bridson (1971; cited by Crisell 1986: 181) observes in the case of British broadcasting that the idea that a 'man in the street should have anything vital to contribute to broadcasting was an idea slow to gain acceptance. That he should actually use broadcasting to express his own opinions in his own unvarnished words, was regarded as almost the end of all good social order.' This view has changed, especially with the advent of non-news formats such as phone-in shows on radio and television (Singer 1973). However, our data indicate that in the news individuals are cited infrequently relative to the institutional voices of authorized knowers, especially in the quality broadcast outlets (TQ and RQ) operated by the national network. Thus it is ironic that this network has taken the view that 'the air belongs to the people, who are entitled to hear the principal points of view on all questions of importance. ... The air must not fall into the control of any individuals and groups influential because of their special position' (Canadian Broadcasting Corporation [CBC] 1982: 6). However, the network has also asserted the need for professional journalistic control of news, and the selection of institutional authorized knowers, citing with favour the British Annan Report (1977): 'Broadcasting is not mass conversation. Broadcasting is a form of publishing ... If everyone is talking, who is listening?' (CBC 1978: 423).

Individuals as sources were used in the following ways. First, they were used to provide 'public reaction' to events already framed by institutional sources in the news. This use was routinized in the letters-to-the-editor format in NQ, NP, and TQ, which allowed individuals to react to and add to continuing news stories (see also Ericson, Baranek, and Chan 1989: 333–76). It was also depicted through regular news stories. For example, under a story citing various institutional sources regarding proposed divorce-law reform and its priority in the federal parliament, NP published a separate story headlined 'It's too hard on the kids,' in which three women in the process of divorce proceedings or already divorced were cited as saying divorce-law reform is a good thing because it would ease the problems created by the cumbersome legal procedures. This was a variation on a special column in NP titled 'You Said It,' in which several citizens were asked their opinions of legislative changes, reform proposals, current events, etc. (see chapter 5).

The television equivalent was 'streeters,' 'vox pop' interviews asking people for their reaction to issues or events, a favoured format for TP. For example, following a telephone interview with an 'expert' commenting on the Pope's visit to Poland, TP used on-the-street interviews with three members of the Toronto Polish community seeking their comments. On another occasion, in light of an announcement of changes in the membership of the Ontario cabinet, six people were asked what portfolio they would choose if the opportunity arose for them to join the cabinet. This was classic 'vox pop' of the type, 'If you had the power, what would you do?' Material of this type distinguished the use of individual sources by NP and TP in comparison to their quality-market counterparts.

Individual citizens were also used to criticize policies or practices that had a direct negative impact on them. Business or professional practices that disadvantaged citizens, especially more vulnerable citizens such as the elderly or disabled, were attacked by using individuals affected to tell what the practice did to them. Government policies that failed to help particular types of citizens were also criticized through the eyes of citizens represent-ing the types concerned. Sometimes this was done through clips of individual citizens who were making individual representations before government bodies. For example, TP broadcast an item shot at a meeting of the commissioners of the city transit commission. Three citizens, each representing a different constituency – senior citizens, high-school students, and disabled veterans – were shown standing before the commissioners, making their respective pleas for lower fares.

A third use of individual citizens was to express their emotions regarding a critical event they were involved in or close to. As addressed earlier, crime victims, and family and friends of crime victims, were fre-quently called upon to express the agony of the event and the psychic state it had left them in. This was a favoured approach in each of the popular news outlets studied. These sources were also used by journalists to express particular views on official decisions, which in effect bolstered the reporter's ideology. Typical was a story in RP that covered the sentencing of a man convicted of murdering three people. Coverage consisted of underscoring how horrid the murders were, and then using a woman who was the mother of one victim and grandmother of another victim to express the view that the sentence of life imprisonment with no eligibility for parole for twelve years was too lenient.

Anchor: A Mississauga couple whose daughter and grandson were among three people murdered by their son-in-law are upset with what amounts to a twelve-year prison term. [RP]'s [reporter's first and last name] reports on today's sentencing.

Reporter: The trial judge perhaps said it best when he told [names offender], 'You destroyed the very people who loved you and would have protected you.' Court was told the 31-year-old accountant was depressed and he panicked when he was caught embezzling $56,000 from his employer. He used the money to bankroll the stock market and a life-style he couldn't keep up. He inexplicably stabbed his 29-year-old wife [named] twenty-one times. He then put a blanket over the face of his eight-month-old infant son [named] and stabbed him nine times in his crib. The parents of [wife's name], [parents named], are not happy with the life sentence given their son-in-law on three counts of second-degree murder. [Offender's name] will be eligible for parole after twelve years, and day parole before that.

Victims' mother/grandmother: Well, let's put it this way, my daughter and grandson are dead forever. So he should be the same way.

Reporter: There was also a third innocent victim: 58-year-old motorist [named] died when [the offender] tried to kill himself in a bungled car accident. [Reporter sign-off]

Individuals were also used to provide tertiary understanding of other experiences. For example, following a long feature article on the pros and cons of giving birth at home and in hospital, NP included a separate item personalizing the matter through the eyes of a woman who had given birth both at home and in hospital.

Another way in which individual citizens were included was as peculiar characters, out of the mainstream. Thus both NQ and TQ carried long feature pieces on a woman who was an ex–psychiatric patient. She had decided to make her home in a tent near a busy highway, and to use it as a base to make signs to passers-by that they should join her fight for 'rights' and 'peace.' It is revealing that even the stories about this marginalized member of society focused on her statements about the excesses of government power. When individual citizens were given a voice in the news, it was to address institutional arrangements and practices.

UNSPECIFIED SOURCES

News reports sometimes refer to unnamed sources as providers of knowledge without any specific indication of their identity or organizational affiliation. As Gitlin (1980: 81) has observed, 'the citing of unnamed "observers" or "experts" is conventionally a way for reporters to address either their own opinions or the opinions of other reporters, officials or cronies they credit.' As indicated in table 7.2, some outlets, especially the newspapers, and NQ in particular, made frequent reference to unspecified sources. These references were varied, mentioning, for example, 'analysts,' 'reports,' 'observers,' 'intelligence sources,' 'authorities,' 'experts,' 'specialists,' 'professionals,' 'critics,' 'groups,' and 'diplomats,' as knowledge sources.

References of this type are meant to indicate that the knowledge provided is not the interpretation of the reporter, but rather of knowledgeable others who, for whatever reason, must remain anonymous. An example is provided in the following anchor's lead to a TQ item.

Anchor: NDP leader Ed Broadbent has rejected any suggestions that there is a 'get Broadbent' move in Western Canada. The NDP leader was reacting to a document released by former Saskatchewan premier Allan Blakeney and Alberta NDP Grant Notley, suggesting certain goals the party should hold. *Some analysts* suggest the document's principles are aimed at unseating Broadbent.

It would have appeared as too interpretive and aggressive, in other words as too 'political,' for the anchor to have asserted on her own, 'The manner in which an NDP Party [*sic*] document was released indicates that members in western Canada are out to unseat party leader Ed Broadbent.' Regardless of who the 'analysts' actually were – other journalists, political scientists, other NDP members, members of other political parties, or no one – it facilitated the appearance of objectivity to make this reference to them.

An associated practice on television was to include a talking-head clip from a source without identifying the source by name or organizational affiliation in an introduction or a vista. Persons speaking in formal settings such as legislatures were sometimes shown in this way, as were people interviewed in 'streeters.' In these cases, however, the person's role could often be inferred by the visuals presented in a way that was not possible for unnamed newspaper or radio sources. This raises the question of the contexts in which the sources are presented, a topic that requires separate treatment.

Source Contexts

The context in which a person provides knowledge is often revealing of his or her character and status, which in turn provide indicators of social structure. When people are involved in face-to-face encounters in particular, much is revealed by the signs given off by the other person in his or her place. What is evident in the news media in this regard is more limited, since the important signs of a person's office or station in life have already been selectively staged and contextualized by the source, and mediated further by reporters. Nevertheless the same general relation among context, character, and status holds for the source appearing in the news. 'Every culture, and certainly ours, seems to have a vast lore of fact and fantasy regarding embodied indicators of status and character, thus appearing to render persons readable. By a sort of prearrangement, social situations seem to be perfectly designed to provide us with evidence of a participant's various attributes – if only to vividly re-present what we already know ... It is in these processing encounters, then that the quiet sorting can occur which ... reproduces the social structure' (Goffman 1983:8).

Each medium differs in its capacity to reveal context and identity. In the newspaper items, the contexts in which sources were quoted were almost invariably made evident in descriptions offered by the authors of the items. Although the newspapers could have indicated context by the use of still photographs, they did so very rarely. In the television items, the vast majority of the contexts in which sources were quoted were made evident through visuals. This is one way in which television visuals are especially significant. With the capacity of visuals, television made little use of reporters' statements to provide the context in which the source was speaking, and virtually no use of sound alone (other than reporters' statements) as a device for providing contexts. Radio, lacking the capacity for visuals, used anchor and reporter statements, and to a much lesser degree background sounds, to help the reader visualize contexts. These considerations explain why the contexts in which sources were cited or referred to were much more evident in television news than in newspapers or radio news.

In table 7.3 we document the various contexts in which sources were quoted and how these varied in the six outlets studied. The context that appeared most often in each outlet was 'author,' meaning that the source was identified as the author of the item itself. Typically this identification included the author's name and organizational affiliation. Examples of authorship contexts include journalists identified as producing a story or column; broadcast anchors announcing items to camera and microphone; and persons identified by name, place, and sometimes organizational affiliation as the authors of letters to the editor. The vast majority of authors were, in

TABLE 7.3
News-source contexts

Type	Newspaper		Television		Radio		Sig. diff.
	Q	P	Q	P	Q	P	
Author	285	234	517	323	366	299	M
	27.1%	31.4%	43.6%	45.0%	43.2%	47.5%	
Interview	31	10	120	120	14	8	M/T
	3.0%	1.3%	10.1%	16.7%	1.7%	1.3%	
Official	40	68	174	75	111	62	M/N
meeting	3.8%	9.1%	14.1%	10.4%	13.1%	9.9%	
Citizens'	49	29	91	58	23	17	M
meeting	4.7%	3.9%	7.7%	8.1%	2.7%	2.7%	
Statement/	29	15	37	30	14	13	
press release	2.8%	2.0%	3.1%	4.2%	1.7%	2.1%	
Drama/	5	10	20	11	9	3	
actual events	0.5%	1.3%	1.7%	1.5%	1.1%	0.5%	
Document	71	28	49	14	40	18	
	6.8%	3.8%	4.1%	1.9%	4.7%	2.9%	
Media report	76	33	9	5	2	3	M
	7.2%	4.4%	0.8%	0.7%	0.2%	0.5%	
Location sig.	0	0	87	98	51	12	M/T/R/C
org. context	0.0%	0.0%	7.3%	13.6%	6.0%	1.9%	
Location not							
sig. org.	2	10	122	115	9	1	M
context	0.2%	1.3%	10.3%	16.0%	1.1%	0.2%	
Total sources	1,050	746	1,185	718	847	629	5,175

Percentages are by column. Tests of significance based on tables with news-source contexts dichotomized into 'yes/no' for each of the categories. The last column indicates comparisons that show significant differences: chi-square statistics significant at the 0.05 level with Cramer's V or PHI ≥ 0.10, when N is large. Significant differences may occur between the newspapers (N); television stations (T); radio stations (R); or among the three types of media (M). The last column also indicates the presence of interactions with the variables being analysed and the coders (C) in a separate log-linear analysis.

fact, journalists, either reporters or broadcast anchors. Hence, the data show similar trends to what we have already analysed for journalists under news-source types (table 7.2). Close to one-third of newspaper sources and almost one-half of television and radio sources were contextualized as authors of the news items. The greater proportions in the broadcast-news outlets are attributable to the fact that all of their news items are visibly authored because the presenter (anchor) or presenters (anchor and reporter) are identified.

The next category, 'interview,' was defined in terms of whether the source was depicted in a one-to-one interview with a journalist, without any other indicator of context. As revealed in table 7.3, there were significant medium differences. Television contextualized sources in interviews with journalists much more often than did radio or newspapers. Moreover, there were significant market differences within television, with TP using the interview context much more often than did TQ on a proportionate basis. This finding is explained by TP's particular reliance on in-studio discussions and 'vox pop' interviews. With its visual capacity, television can show these people making representations 'head-on' with journalists, but otherwise stripped of organizational context or identity. In interview formats of this type, the citizen interviewed comes close to appearing as an author of information, except, of course, that his or her accounts are framed and contextualized by the journalist's questions.

'Official meeting' refers to places in government institutions where regular proceedings are held and which are open to members of the public. Included in this category are the courts, legislatures, legislative committees, and public hearings of commissions or boards of inquiry. The data in table 7.3 document the fact that these contexts were presented much more often by the broadcasting outlets than by the newspapers. However, official-meeting contexts are likely underrepresented in the two newspapers because newspaper reporters often fail to mention that they have derived their information from these contexts (Ericson, Baranek, and Chan 1987). NQ was especially unlikely to cite sources in official-meeting contexts, while NP was closer to the broadcast outlets in its proportionate citation of sources in this context. While we have established previously that NQ was oriented to extensive coverage of the major institutions of government, it accomplished this through the use of documents, other media reports, features, and editorial columns more than through coverage of official meetings. In contrast, the other outlets tended to rely on scheduled events because such events provided them with a predictable and regular supply of stories in the face of limited resources. This reliance on scheduled events is especially the case with broadcast outlets, which have few reporters, and whose reporters are expected to produce daily to meet the production needs of their producers (Schlesinger 1978; Ericson, Baranek, and Chan 1987: chap. 7). TQ and RQ had a particular burden in this regard because as national network–affiliated quality outlets they were expected to undertake institutional reporting. With limited resources, they ended up relying on official-meeting contexts for doing so to a much greater extent than did NQ.

'Citizens' meeting' – prescheduled meetings, conventions, rallies, or demonstrations – provided another context in which television sources were cited much more frequently than newspaper or radio sources. This finding is related to the television outlets' slightly greater coverage of community organizations (see table 7.2). It is also related to the fact that television journalists attend rallies and demonstrations more often than do their counterparts in newspapers and radio because of the possibilities for dramatic visuals. An additional explanation is the one noted regarding official meetings: prescheduled citizens' meetings provide a predictable context in which the commitment of a reporter and camera crew is likely to yield a usable story to fill the show.

The latter explanation also applies to the use of material from scheduled news conferences and/or formal news releases. While the differences are not great among the news organizations in this regard, television outlets also use this context slightly more often, probably because it, too, provides a routine supply of usable items. An additional consideration is that news-conference contexts are visible on television. It is possible that the newspapers and radio stations derived material from sources' news-conferences and news-release contexts without saying so, thereby deflating the frequency with which such contexts actually contributed to their items.

It is well established that journalists deal primarily with realities already constructed and mediated by their sources through meetings, documents, and structured interviews. Hence it is not surprising that the news outlets rarely portrayed sources in the contexts in which the events described were actually occurring. Even the television outlets – which had the capacity to show 'live' events, and could be expected to be drawn to them because of their potential for good visuals – actually had very few sources shown in the context of the actual unfolding of events being reported on. TP had a 'live eye' mobile truck, and advertised that its news crews were 'everywhere' to capture news as it happens. As it happened, among TP's 718 sources, only 11 were cited in contexts where the events described were occurring at the time.

It is also well established that reporters rarely make use of the documents of source organizations, except those that have already been textually mediated by the source organization for news purposes (Ericson, Baranek, and Chan 1989). NQ cited sources in the context of organizational documents more than the other outlets did. The quality outlets in each medium had a tendency to cite sources from documents more than did their popular outlets counterparts. The institutional emphasis of quality outlets includes a greater scrutiny of official documents.

A 'media report' was a reference to a previous report in other media in which the source was quoted, in effect, treating other media as a document in which a source was quoted. There was a substantial medium difference in this mode of contextualizing sources. The newspapers, especially NQ, used this mode frequently, whereas the broadcast outlets rarely emphasized this mode. However, recall that newspapers are more likely to make evident their use of other media reports, while broadcast outlets frequently use such reports without revealing that they are doing so.

A 'location signifying organizational context' refers to a field location in which the source is providing knowledge that also reveals something about the organizational context in which the source is speaking. Newsroom or broadcast-studio contexts are excluded from this category. Included are such things as a source standing outside a well-known building, such as the courts or city hall, signifying the institutional context of the report. Included also is reference by the source to the fact that he or she is in a particular field context such as the courthouse or city hall. Table 7.3 makes evident that the newspapers never explicitly contextualized sources in this way, while radio did so occasionally. RQ used this mode of contextualizing sources significantly more often than did RP, because RQ had more stories covered by reporters in institutional field locations. The television outlets presented this mode most often, a fact explained by their visual capacity to represent field locations as background to talking-head accounts. TP used this mode significantly more often than did TQ, a fact explained by TP's orientation of being on the streets of the city, even if it was only to represent people and things indexically or symbolically rather than iconically.

A 'location not signifying organizational context' refers to a field location in which the source is providing knowledge, but the organizational context in which the source is speaking is not evident. The newspapers and radio outlets rarely quoted sources in this manner, but the television outlets did so frequently. Most of the television items in this mode consisted of talking-head accounts from sources who were in some unrecognizable place, whether on the street or in an anonymous building. The use of sources speaking from nowhere was in keeping with television's use of 'streeters' and related formats to have the source express a viewpoint deemed to be characteristic of his or her group or social category rather than his or her status and affiliation in a formal organization or institution. TP's greater reliance on 'vox pop' 'streeters' explains its greater use of sources contextualized in this way.

Types of Knowledge Provided by Sources

As introduced and conceptualized in chapter 2, the types of knowledge available in the news include primary (factual, asking 'What happened?'), secondary (explanatory, asking 'Why did it happen?'), tertiary (descriptive, asking 'What was it like to be involved in what happened?'), evaluative (moral, asking 'Was what happened good or bad?'), and recommendations (asking 'What should be done about what happened?'). In this section, we consider the extent to which these types of knowledge were offered by sources, and whether particular types of knowledge were associated with different types of sources, as these varied across the six news outlets studied. Our analyses 'freeze' types of knowledge out of the various narrative flows in which they were contextualized. This is done to meet our analytic purpose of understanding how often particular types of knowledge appear in crime, law, and justice news, and who are the sources of this knowledge. These data are presented with the caution that they cannot capture the subtleties of sources and context, nor the overlap among types of knowledge in a given usage. Such subtleties are only analysable qualitatively (see chapters 4 and 5; see also Ericson, Baranek, and Chan 1987, 1989).

In table 7.4 we present the frequency with which sources provided each type of knowledge in the six news outlets studied. These data indicate that the news outlets do not vary significantly in the proportions in which their sources provide each type of knowledge. A more detailed consideration of each type of knowledge, and the types of sources who provided it, affords additional understanding not available in these data.

PRIMARY KNOWLEDGE

Table 7.4 documents the fact that primary knowledge is the type provided by sources most often. In each outlet close to one-half of all sources provided knowledge of this type, with a range from 39 per cent in NQ to 48 per cent in RP.

In table 7.5, we document the extent to which each source type provided primary knowledge. We find that the vast majority of journalists of the news outlets themselves offered primary knowledge. There was significant variation in this regard, with television journalists providing primary knowledge most often in comparison to radio and especially newspapers. Within radio, RP was similar to the television outlets in this regard, while RQ was lower and in line with the newspaper outlets. These data suggest that, in television, in particular, journalists offer the factual details and use outside sources to provide other types of knowledge. This conclusion is augmented if we include the extent to which 'other journalists' were also used extensively, especially in newspapers and television, to provide primary facts. The vast majority of primary knowledge is transmitted by journalists themselves without reference to, or direct citation of, other sources.

Only a minority of the criminal-justice sources provided primary knowledge. In television especially, criminal-justice sources were rarely used to provide primary knowledge. There are also significant market differences. All three popular outlets, but especially RP compared to RQ, were more likely than were their quality-market counterparts to use criminal-justice

TABLE 7.4
Types of knowledge provided by sources

Type	Newspaper		Television		Radio		Sig. diff.
	Q	P	Q	P	Q	P	
Primary	409	313	525	330	374	300	
	39.0%	42.0%	44.3%	46.0%	44.2%	47.7%	
Secondary	120	108	163	69	76	52	
	11.4%	14.5%	13.8%	9.6%	9.0%	8.3%	
Tertiary	28	44	65	52	12	11	
	2.7%	5.9%	5.5%	7.2%	1.4%	1.7%	
Evaluation	237	136	227	114	119	90	
	22.6%	18.2%	19.2%	15.9%	14.0%	14.3%	
Recommendation	140	84	75	56	74	61	
	13.3%	11.3%	6.3%	7.8%	8.7%	9.7%	
Total sources	1,050	746	1,185	718	847	629	5,175

Percentages are by column. Tests of significance based on tables with types of knowledge provided by sources dichotomized into 'yes/no' for each of the categories. The last column indicates comparisons that show significant differences: chi-square statistics significant at the 0.05 level with Cramer's V or PHI ≥ 0.10, when N is large. Significant differences may occur between the newspapers (N); television stations (T); radio stations (R); or among the three types of media (M). The last column also indicates the presence of significant interactions with the variables being analysed and the coders (C) in a separate log-linear analysis.

sources as providers of primary knowledge. These data are consistent with our ethnographic research on the police beat, which revealed that reporters for popular outlets, and especially popular radio stations, including RP, were oriented to using police sources for factual updates on crime incidents (Ericson, Baranek, and Chan 1989: chap. 3).

Sources representing public administration or other aspects of government also offered primary knowledge with some frequency. Again television was much less likely than were radio and the newspapers to cite or refer to public-administration sources as providers of primary knowledge. The radio and newspaper outlets were more oriented to letting the institutional voices of government state the primary facts themselves, whereas in television journalists stated the facts, and government sources were used to provide other types of knowledge. The same trends are evident regarding individual citizens as sources. When individual citizens were cited as newspaper sources, about one-half of them offered primary knowledge. In television and radio, however, citizens only offered primary knowledge in about one-fifth of all citations. These differences between the newspapers and

TABLE 7.5
Primary knowledge and source types

Source type by primary knowledge	Newspaper		Television		Radio		Sig. diff.
	Q	P	Q	P	Q	P	
Journalist of organization	96 65.8%	98 69.5%	371 80.8%	225 75.8%	237 64.9%	214 75.1%	R/M
Other journalist	85 66.9%	57 67.9%	36 66.7%	26 78.8%	3 50.0%	11 61.1%	
Criminal justice	12 38.7%	35 44.3%	10 15.6%	10 25.0%	14 19.7%	17 38.6%	R/M
Public administration	21 35.0%	8 26.7%	6 10.0%	3 10.0%	10 23.8%	14 32.6%	M
Other government sources	74 22.3%	36 24.3%	28 14.7%	17 22.4%	52 34.4%	22 19.1%	R/M
Private corporations	18 22.0%	8 13.3%	26 27.4%	12 19.0%	16 21.1%	4 11.8%	
Occupational association	7 16.3%	5 23.8%	6 18.8%	2 18.2%	16 45.7%	3 27.3%	M
Political organization	14 36.8%	3 25.0%	6 23.1%	1 11.1%	2 50.0%	1 14.3%	
Community organization	12 25.5%	2 8.0%	14 16.5%	11 26.8%	14 34.1%	5 22.7%	
Individuals	46 59.0%	54 45.4%	16 21.9%	19 19.8%	6 16.2%	9 23.7	M
Unspecified	21 37.5%	6 24.0%	6 30.0%	3 16.7%	4 28.6%	0 0.0%	
Don't know	3 30.0%	1 50.0%	0 0.0%	1 25.0%	0 0.0%	0 0.0%	
Total sources	1,050	746	1,185	718	847	629	5,175

Percentages are by column. Tests of significance based on tables with primary knowledge offered by source type dichotomized into 'yes/no' for each of the categories. The last column indicates comparisons that show significant differences: chi-square statistics significant at the 0.05 level with Cramer's V or PHI ≥ 0.10, when N is large. Significant differences may occur between the newspapers (N); television stations (T); radio stations (R); or among the three types of media (M). The last column also indicates the presence of significant interactions with the variables being analysed and the coders (C) in a separate log-linear analysis.

broadcast media are especially marked because of the letters-to-the-editor format in newspapers, a forum in which individual citizens author items that almost invariably include primary knowledge along with other types of understanding and assessment (Ericson, Baranek, and Chan 1989: 353–5).

The fact that primary facts on television are especially likely to emanate from reporters is related to parsimony of television news items. The factual object of the story is constituted by the anchor and/or reporter. If other sources are mobilized at all, it is usually not to augment the facts, as much as to explain and evaluate them, or to offer an account of what it was like to be involved in the factual events reported.

SECONDARY KNOWLEDGE

Returning to the data in table 7.4, we find that secondary knowledge or explanation was not very prevalent in any of the news outlets. While sources in newspapers and quality television offered more explanations than did those in popular television and radio, the medium and market differences are not significant. Secondary knowledge was provided within the range of 8 per cent of RP sources and 15 per cent of NP sources.

These findings are consistent with the research literature. Explanations are seen by journalists as making stories too boring and as working against the need for simplification (Hartley 1982: esp. 98; Ericson, Baranek, and Chan 1987). Explanations are also inconsistent with the event-orientation of news, which focuses on what happened and who was involved to the relative exclusion of explanations. Moreover, when explanations are offered, it is usually in terms of 'natural forces (e.g., floods, earthquakes) or by the immediately preceding actions of particular individuals or groups' (Murdock 1973: 164; see also Chibnall 1977). This tendency to 'explain' events in terms of recent related events is typically associated with sustaining a continuing story or news theme. As such, it usually means that the news explains things away rather than explains them, as a precursor to recommending a control solution. In a separate analysis of what types of sources offered secondary knowledge and how this varied across the six outlets studied, few significant differences were revealed. Proportionate to other types of knowledge they provided, newspaper journalists were significantly more likely than were television and especially radio journalists to provide explanations on their own. This is to be expected because, as we have seen, newspapers offer more scope for journalistic analysis through their editorial and opinion columns. Even so, only 17 (12 per cent) of NQ journalists and 18 (13 per cent) of NP journalists offered secondary understanding. TQ journalists were similar in proportion to newspaper journalists (50, or 11 per cent), while TP journalists (20, or 7 per cent) were closer to radio journalists

(15, or 4 per cent, in RQ and 15, or 5 per cent, in RP) in rarely, relative to other types, offering secondary knowledge.

The other source type of note in the provision of secondary understanding was the individual citizen. While radio rarely cited individuals, when it did they sometimes provided secondary understanding (9, or 24 per cent of individuals, in RQ, and 5, or 13 per cent of individuals, in RP). The newspapers, especially in their letters columns, also gave scope for the explanations of individual citizens (13, or 17 per cent of individuals, in NQ, and 15, or 13 per cent of individuals, in NP). While TQ offered some scope for individual citizens' explanations (9, or 12 per cent of individual sources, in TQ), TP did so very rarely (4, or 7 per cent of individual sources, in TP). While TP pursued a 'vox pop' orientation, it did not allow individuals much scope for explaining the events they were asked to address.

TERTIARY KNOWLEDGE

Table 7.4 indicates that tertiary knowledge was also rare, especially in radio. Tertiary knowledge was provided within the range of only 1 per cent of RQ sources, and 7 per cent of TP sources. While the differences between outlets are small, they are nevertheless in the expected direction. The popular newspaper and both television outlets used sources who provided tertiary understanding much more often than did the quality newspaper and the radio stations. Tertiary understanding is especially suited to the television medium because of its visual capacity: it can show the person and aspects of the experience described at the same time that the person gives his or her description. The visual-display possibilities in NP, combined with its popular 'human interest story' orientation, account for its frequent citation of sources providing tertiary knowledge. In contrast, the radio outlets, while able to carry the verbalized experiential description of persons involved in an event, lack the capacity to underscore the experience with visuals and therefore generally avoid conveying this type of understanding.

A separate analysis to ascertain what source types provided tertiary understanding revealed few significant differences, because of the small numbers involved. Tertiary understanding was offered with some frequency by television journalists (by 21, or 5 per cent of TQ journalists, and by 10, or 3 per cent of TP journalists), and a few times by newspaper journalists (by 4, or 3 per cent of NQ journalists, and by 4, or 4 per cent of NP journalists), but very rarely by radio journalists (by 2, or less than 1 per cent, in each of RQ and RP).

An example of reporters offering tertiary understanding is provided in the case of an abortion-clinic opening in Toronto. Prior to the official opening, reporters were invited to tour the facilities, and a large number of outlets accepted the invitation and had their reporters prepare 'What is it like?' descriptions of the facility. While radio stations also responded in this instance and had their reporters give their accounts of what it was like, these accounts were obviously limited in comparison to those of the television stations, which included visuals of the building, offices, operating equipment, personnel, and so on.

The television stations sometimes had their reporters offer tertiary understanding in the context of an in-studio interview with the anchor. This typically entailed a retrospective 'analysis' of a news event or situation the reporter had witnessed or covered previously. For example, TP televised an NBC item on the Israeli-Lebanon conflict, focusing on Israeli casualties. This was followed by an in-studio interview between the anchor and a TP journalist who had just returned from a three-week tour of the Middle East with an organization called 'Professors for Peace.' The interview was dominated by questions from the anchor that begged answers conveying tertiary understanding.

1 'You were in Lebanon, were you afraid ...?'
2 'Did you see any action at all at any time – any firing of arms?'
3 'You were in Israel, tell us about the atmosphere, the feeling of the people
  – I mean, it's gone on for so long, they're so overtaxed, I mean, they're
  tired of it all, did they, how do they feel?'
4 'One of the purposes of Professors for Peace is to go over there to try and
  understand the horrendous problems. They're not coming up with instant
  solutions but to see if there are some long-term – and I know it's
  extraordinarily complex. But did you leave as a group the feeling of op-
  timism, or did you leave with a depression and how are we ever going to
  figure this out? Which way did you go?'

The same type of question was put to individual citizens, the only other type of source that provided tertiary understanding with some frequency. For example, TQ broadcast a feature item in which refugees who had just arrived from El Salvador were asked to express what it was like for them and others there, and previous refugees from El Salvador were asked to describe their experiences in Canada including problems with housing and employment (further examples are included in chapter 4).

When the television outlets used individuals as sources, a considerable number (14, or 19 per cent, in TQ, and 22, or 23 per cent, in TP) provided tertiary understanding. Individual sources in NP (20, or 17 per cent) also provided tertiary understanding with some frequency, while individual sources in NQ (8, or 10 per cent) did so infrequently. Very few individual sources in radio (1, or 3 per cent of individuals in RQ, and 4, or 11 per cent of individuals in RP) were used to provide tertiary understanding. Experiential descriptions from individuals, especially of the fear-and-loathing variety, were largely limited to television and the popular newspaper.

EVALUATION

Table 7.4 indicates that, next to primary knowledge, evaluations were most frequent. Evaluations occurred with greater proportionate frequency in newspapers compared to the broadcast outlets, especially radio, with a range of 23 per cent of NQ sources to 14 per cent of sources in both RQ and RP.

In a separate analysis, summarized in table 7.6, we ascertained which source types contributed evaluations and whether this varied by news outlet. Regarding journalists, we find that journalists for newspapers provided significantly more evaluative knowledge on a proportionate basis than did their counterparts in television, while television journalists were more significantly evaluative than were radio journalists. These data confirm that newspapers, and especially qualities, offer more scope for their journalists to be explicit in asserting moral evaluations of the issues and events they report. These data are also consistent with the views of sources in the local media culture that NQ is especially evaluative, while radio in particular is the best medium for circumscribing the account to primary facts without risking the explicit interjection of journalists' evaluations (Ericson, Baranek, and Chan 1989).

Journalists do not have to state explicit evaluations themselves to get across their moral messages. The research literature on morality news is replete with examples of how journalists accomplish their preferred versions and visions of morality, while maintaining an air of objectivity, through the selection of institutional sources who are only too willing to make moral statements consistent with the journalists' moral sentiments. This is accomplished through the 'embedding capacity' of our speech. 'Words we speak are often not our own, at least our current 'own' ... We can as handily quote another (directly or indirectly) as we can say something in our own name. (This embedding capacity is part of something more general; our linguistic ability to speak of events at any remove in time and space from the situated present.)' (Goffman 1981: 3).

The data in table 7.6 indicate that source types other than journalists themselves were drawn upon frequently for evaluations. Focusing upon criminal-justice sources, it is evident that both NQ and TQ used these sources more than their popular outlet counterparts to make evaluations. This is related to the emphasis in these quality outlets on the organizational aspects of the administration of justice – efficiency, management, and procedural propriety – while the popular outlets used criminal-justice sources more for factual details about crime incidents and police investigative operations (Ericson, Baranek, and Chan 1987, 1989: chaps. 2 and 3).

TABLE 7.6
Evaluation and source types

Source type by evaluation	Newspaper		Television		Radio		Sig. diff.
	Q	P	Q	P	Q	P	
Journalist of organization	27 18.5%	16 11.3%	33 7.2%	29 9.8%	12 3.3%	8 2.8%	M
Other journalist	11 8.7%	9 10.7%	3 5.6%	5 15.2%	1 16.7%	0 0.0%	
Criminal justice	9 29.0%	5 6.3%	11 17.2%	3 7.5%	6 8.5%	9 20.5%	N
Public admin- istration	10 16.7%	7 23.3%	10 16.7%	3 10.0%	7 16.7%	8 18.6%	
Other government sources	68 20.5%	30 20.3%	64 33.5%	20 26.3%	48 31.8%	26 22.6%	M
Private corporation	19 23.2%	7 11.7%	30 31.6%	12 19.0%	10 13.2%	9 26.5%	
Occupational association	11 25.6%	11 52.4%	12 37.5%	0 0.0%	8 22.9%	7 63.6%	N/T/R
Political organization	11 28.9%	1 8.3%	4 15.4%	0 0.0%	0 0.0%	1 14.3%	
Community organization	18 38.3%	9 36.0%	29 34.1%	15 36.6%	16 39.0%	12 54.5%	
Individuals	42 53.8%	36 30.3%	18 24.7%	24 25.0%	5 13.5%	4 10.5%	N/M
Unspecified	11 19.6%	5 20.0%	7 35.0%	3 16.7%	4 28.6%	6 54.5%	
Don't know	0 0.0%	0 0.0%	6 23.1%	0 0.0%	2 40.0%	0 0.0%	
Total sources	1,050	746	1,185	718	847	629	5,175

Percentages are by column. Tests of significance based on tables with evaluation offered by source type dichotomized into 'yes/no' for each of the categories. The last column indicates comparisons that show significant differences: chi-square statistics significant at the 0.05 level with Cramer's V or PHI ≥ 0.10, when N is large. Significant differences may occur between the newspapers (N); television stations (T); radio stations (R); or among the three types of media (M). The last column also indicates the presence of significant interactions with the variables being analysed and the coders (C) in a separate log-linear analysis.

In the case of 'other government sources,' the broadcast outlets, especially television, gave greater scope for evaluations than did newspapers. Broadcast outlets tend to use these sources more for explicit evaluation of social problems as these articulate preferred control solutions (see chapter 9). As we have seen already (table 7.5), newspapers make greater use of the institutional sources for primary knowledge of the matter being reported on.

Table 7.6 documents marked differences in the extent to which the news outlets had occupational-association sources providing evaluations. There are significant market differences. When NP and RP cited occupational-association sources, more often than not the knowledge provided was evaluative. The same does not hold for NQ and RQ, whose occupational-association sources provided evaluations in only a small minority of instances. The differences are even more marked in television: 12, or 38 per cent of TQ's occupational association sources provided evaluations, compared to none in TP. This is explained by the fact that TQ had a number of journalists sympathetic to labour and eager to provide the evaluations of labour spokespersons in opposition to management. Our ethnographic research revealed major ideological differences and open conflicts in the TQ newsroom in this regard (Ericson, Baranek, and Chan 1987). The previously quoted item, which cites several strikers on a picket line condemning the actions of police and management, illustrates how TQ journalists allowed scope for evaluations by occupational association members (pp. 170–1).

Another illustration is provided in the following excerpt from a TQ in-studio panel discussion. In the context of proposed legal changes affecting the job security of civil servants in British Columbia, and the institution of substantial cut-backs in the BC civil service, which were described by the anchor as 'almost breathtaking in its severity,' the panel included only pro-labour sources: the British Columbia New Democratic Party campaign manager for the previous election, and the head of the Ontario Public Service Employees Union (OPSEU). These sources offered strongly worded evaluations of the cut-backs, as illustrated by the following quotation from the head of OPSEU.

It's a technique or a formula for revolution – a revolution because it will create class war, something we haven't had too much of in this country, but this is a formula for class war ... I wouldn't put too much faith in going to the Supreme Court of Canada on this issue, because in the long run, of course, we'll all be dead, and by the time the Supreme Court get around to dealing with this matter, a lot of rights will have been taken away ... They're inviting this kind of class conflict. It can't just come from the deficit. It must come from their own philosophy, their far-right philosophy, it must come from that and that's a lesson for us in this province that we beware of the ... people in the Conservative Party.

Table 7.6 also indicates that when individual sources were used, it was often to offer evaluations. Evaluations were especially frequent among individual sources in newspapers, accounted for in part by the letters to the editor. The large number of letters to the editor in the NQ sample accounts in part for the fact that it provided for more evaluations from individuals than NP. The 'vox pop' orientation of NP and TP meant that a lot of their individuals providing evaluations were citizens formatted in on-the-street interviews. 'Streeters' also account for most of the TQ individual citizens who offered evaluations. Relative to television and especially the newspapers, the radio outlets gave very little scope for evaluations by individual citizens. Radio provides for citizens' opinions outside the news format, for example, through phone-in shows. In radio news, there was no regular citizens' opinion slot nor were 'streeters,' which provide for evaluations by individuals, used often.

RECOMMENDATIONS

Table 7.4 indicates that only a small minority of sources provided recommendations for action, with a range from 13 per cent in NQ to 6 per cent in TQ. A separate analysis of source types offering recommendations revealed that recommendations were provided most often by other government sources (mainly politicians), persons in public administration, members of occupational associations, members of community organizations, individuals, and journalists of the news outlets studied. The news outlets did not vary significantly in their use of source types to provide recommendations, except regarding their use of their own journalists. A few newspaper journalists offered recommendations (14, or 10 per cent of NQ journalists, and 8, or 6 per cent of NP journalists), primarily in the context of editorials and opinion columns. A few recommendations were also offered by TP journalists (6, or 2 per cent), again because TP provided for a regular opinion slot. In contrast, TQ and the radio outlets each had less than 1 per cent of their journalists' clips include a recommendation. The newspapers also made some use of outside journalists to provide recommendations (4, or 3 per cent in NQ, and 7, or 8 per cent in NP), and TP did so once, but TQ and the radio stations never did so. In summary, the newspapers allowed a small opening for journalists to recommend some social-control measures, television outlets did so only rarely, and radio outlets almost never did so.

EVIDENCE USED BY SOURCES

In order to investigate further the knowledge provided by sources, we analysed whether sources add anything to their statements to substantiate their claims. Do sources provide knowledge sources that add weight to the credibility of their claims? In developing quantitative data on this question, we allowed for the possibility that one news source might refer to multiple additional knowledge sources. This produced a sample of 4,662 responses, including 1,691 in the newspapers (NQ = 970, NP = 721), 1,765 in television (TQ = 1,112, TP = 653), and 1,206 in radio (RQ = 676, RP = 530).

In the vast majority of instances sources provided no additional sources of evidence to back up their claims. In the newspapers, no additional knowledge source was cited in 89 per cent of the cases, with little difference between NQ (90 per cent) and NP (88 per cent) in this regard. In television, no additional knowledge source was cited in 91 per cent of the cases, with virtually no difference between TQ (91 per cent) and TP (90 per cent) in this regard. In radio, no additional knowledge source was cited in 93 per cent of the cases, with no difference between RQ and RP in this regard. All news outlets were remarkably similar in that about 90 per cent of the time no additional evidence or evidentiary sources were cited by their news sources.

When other sources of knowledge were referred to, they appeared as follows: other source persons were quoted by 4 per cent of the newspaper sources, 1 per cent of the television sources, and 2 per cent of the radio sources. One reason why the newspapers were higher in this regard relates to their inclusion of letters to the editor, in which the letter writer usually cites one or more additional sources (Ericson, Baranek, and Chan 1989: 347–9). Research studies or official statistics were cited by 3 per cent of the newspaper sources, 1 per cent of television sources, and 2 per cent of radio sources. Other media reports were cited by 1 per cent of the newspaper sources, and no sources in any of the broadcast outlets, except for three sources in TP. Case examples were cited by 1 per cent of sources in each medium.

The only source of knowledge in which there was more substantial variation by media was organizational documents. These were cited much more often by television sources (6 per cent) than radio (2 per cent) or newspaper sources (2 per cent). These findings seem somewhat anomalous, since the newspaper medium has greater space and capacity to reproduce quotations or segments of organizational documents than does television- or radio-news formats. However, what is revealed in the cases for television is that the television outlets often *displayed* documents by actually picturing them on the screen as well as using vistas to quote some key phrases. This practice, along with having sources quote from documents or actually refer to them, accounts for the more frequent reference to documents in television news. In radio also, sources occasionally made statements that included additional knowledge from documentary sources, or actually included evidence from 'verbal documents.' An example of the latter practice is evident in the following RP story, which focuses upon a government's public-relations campaign for political gain associated with the announcement of a job-creation program.

Anchor: Housing minister Claude Bennett has provided some new details on a program announced long ago and spending, he's spending lots of money getting the message out. Here's [names reporter from news service]

News Service Reporter: We all learned in treasurer Frank Miller's May 10th budget that 12,500 temporary jobs will be created for recent school graduates. The government will pay up to $100 a week in salary per worker to the private sector. Now Housing minister Claude Bennett has unveiled the program details with a fanfare. He's sent video-cassettes and tape recordings to radio and television stations across the province in the form of news reports. Here's a sample.

Sample: Mr Bennett is optimistic that the Young Ontario Career programme will offer permanent entry for youth into the work-force in time for the growing economy to absorb them. This is [government's 'reporter' named] in Toronto.

News Service Reporter: Bennett has also distributed an impressive information kit on the program to reporters here at the legislature. It contains a news release, a copy of the minister's statement, a brochure, a poster. Liberal leader David Peterson condemned the public-relations exercise saying the government is more concerned with image than substance. [sign-off]

In this story the reporter treats the PR package clip from the minister of housing as a document to illustrate how the government was attempting to 'sell' its good work. Normally radio reporters are restricted from presenting actual government documents in evidence because such documents are not tailored to the radio medium. However, in this instance the availability of a packaged audio cassette made it possible for the reporter to treat it as a documentary source from a government organization. Of course, RP could have taken the cassette at face value to report on the good work of government as was intended by the PR staff of the ministry of housing; instead, RP used it as a document in evidence to support its view of the PR practices of the government.

The example above illustrates that, even with limitations imposed by the medium and by news formats, reporters and their sources had some capacity to offer additional evidence in support of their knowledge claims. The question that needs to be addressed is why, given some capacity in this regard, they failed to use additional sources of evidence in the vast majority of instances. Why is it usually sufficient for the news source to make a statement without evidentiary sources to bolster the claim?

In answering this question we must consider that what is at issue in knowledge claims by news sources is not so much the truth as 'what people accept as criteria and evidence of information, completeness, and, ultimately truth' (Altheide 1985: 51). It is the aspect of what sources, journalists, and consumers will accept as evidence that is most significant, and it is this aspect that makes questions of how news is formatted so important. Our data indicate that in all news outlets there was a presumption that the credibility of the product could be sustained without frequent reference to evidentiary sources. Sources and journalists are apparently able to perform in a way that makes their claims seem reasonable and authoritative even without substantial evidence.

The specific mechanisms by which credibility is accomplished have already been analysed in detail in our ethnographic research on news production (Ericson, Baranek, and Chan 1987, 1989). Sources' statements can be taken at face value because of their own credibility as occupiers of elevated positions in their respective organizations and institutions. Similarly, journalists can be taken at face value because of their own credibility within the news outlet that employs them, and because of the credibility of the news institution itself. Of course, this credibility must be worked at, and not all sources and their organizations, or journalists and their news outlets, are equal in this regard. Nevertheless journalists and sources capitalize on each other's credibility so that they can routinely state their case, without substantial evidence, in an authoritative voice (ibid). This process is similar to what occurs in other fields of cultural production. For example, scientists, and those who use scientific expertise, assess scientific publications on the basis of the reputations of the scientists and research institutes who author them. The voice of authority, constituted on the professional, organizational, and institutional levels, makes a knowledge claim easy to accept (Mulkay 1979; Gusfield 1981).

Particular features of a medium also lend credibility to those who communicate through it. For example, it is well established that television is the most credible medium to the public. This fact is explained by the visual capacities of television, which make its messages seem iconic even if they are not. Information programming on television seems to be relatively unmediated, to be as close to reality as any medium can get.

Another consideration is that news operatives have long recognized their limited capacity to validate the news they produce. This is why they fall back on the strategic ritual of objectivity, in which sides are presented and then it is left up to the reader to decide where the truth resides. All they can do is rely on credible people who have a stake in making reasonable claims, and otherwise leave it up to the consumer to visualize whose claims appear the most reasonable.

Additional evidence in support of knowledge claims is also unnecessary in the routine case because of the nature of news discourse itself. The news is not after truth, but truth reduced to its genre capacities. The news genre systemically produces representations that are dramatic and thematic. It does not seek to systematically produce representative data that might satisfy a social scientist. As indicated in particular by how it covers politicians and their events (Boorstin 1962; Postman 1985; Meyrowitz 1985: chap. 14; Edelman 1988; Ericson, Baranek, and Chan 1989: chap. 4), the news is more concerned with the politics of the image than with the polity and its truths.

Another consideration in explaining why journalists and their sources do not need to cite evidentiary sources relates to the power of news as a text. Entwined with the previous points we have raised is the fact that news texts take on a life and power of their own, and are not dependent upon further detailed reference to other evidentiary texts and their voices. In contrast to gossip, for example, which is local knowledge that is very people- and context-specific (Shibutani 1966), news texts escape the intentions of their authors and disperse into myriad settings simultaneously to take on new meanings and new lives. News texts have the power to mediate social organization (D. Smith 1984; see also Wheeler 1986). Indeed, public-relations and advertising specialists in government (Merton 1946; Diamond and Bates 1984), as well as in the private sector (Blyskal and Blyskal 1985), have long recognized the transcendent power of news texts in accomplishing 'mass persuasion.' Freed of a demand for an evidentiary base, the news can traffick in the versions and visions of reality of its preferred sources.

Visuals and Sound in Representing Sources

The representation of a source in the news cannot match what would be available to us if we could interact directly with the source. In interaction, the setting, context, gestures, facial expressions, and speech (accent, emphasis, pauses, etc.) provide rich details that not only allow considerable scope for reading the meanings of the person, but can be acted upon for clarification, elaboration, and exploration. In the news media, only selected aspects of the setting, context, gesture, facial expressions, and speech can be communicated. The news can offer only extracts of the fuller picture available from the source. The news source's position is truncated, at best adequately represented but not substantially elaborated.

The ability to communicate aspects of setting, context, gestures, facial expressions, and speech varies substantially across media. Newspapers are limited to sight, and radio to sound, while television can use both. In the following analysis, we consider how the news outlets represented sources, given the visual and/or audio capacities available to them.

NEWSPAPERS

Newspapers are limited to representing sources in ways that the reader can see. In practice, there is a reliance on words, although these may be displayed differently with various sizes and weights of type and the use of colour. Still photographs are also used, but these are treated as optional (Hall 1981) and appear with only a tiny fraction of newspaper stories. In a survey of crime stories in Ontario newspapers, Dussuyer (1979) found that only 5.6 per cent of the stories were accompanied by a photograph.

In the newspapers we studied, there was a substantial difference in the use of photographs. Among the 1,050 NQ sources, only 25, or about 2 per cent, were pictured in a photograph. Moreover, 10 of the 25 photographs were of NQ journalists (mainly regular columnists), with no other source type predominant. In contrast, among 746 NP sources, 73, or almost 10 per cent, were pictured in a photograph. In proportion to the frequency with which they were cited in NP, the source types pictured most often were those representing political organizations (25 per cent), individual citizens (17 per cent), private corporations (13 per cent), and NP journalists (12 per cent).

These data indicate that NP was especially likely to give a face to sources outside of government. One explanation of this fact is that many of these sources lacked the ability to appear credible based on an officially authorized position, and the photograph was a way of lending weight to their representations. Another consideration, especially in light of the number of individual sources pictured, is that photographs are important to the 'vox pop' orientation of NP. Photographs personalize accounts to the views of the individual source, whereas the absence of photographs leaves the account in the more distanced and anonymous voice of the spokesperson for a bureaucracy.

In contrast to NQ, NP used other visual devices to display its stories and the place of its sources within them (see chapter 4). On the front page, it used massive bold headlines, a very large photograph in colour, and a few dramatic words, to attract the reader to the newspaper and, it is hoped, into it. Similar displays, combining bold headlines, pictures, and words, appeared elsewhere in the newspaper. This is comparable to what is available in television: putting 'different iconic signs together so that they modify or reinforce each other's signification ... We read them simultaneously, and this is where a picture can indeed be worth a thousand ideological words' (Hartley 1982: 31).

Pictures in newspapers, as in television, bring events and those involved in them to life. A picture grounds a story in an actual happening. It also bears witness to the people involved in the event and their moral character. While a news picture is a result of an ideological procedure of selection

(Ericson, Baranek, and Chan 1987), it appears unmediated and to be reflecting the real world. While printed statements from sources are obviously perspectival, pictures appear less so. They add a sense of objectivity to the news, and are an important part of its discourse of factuality (Tuchman 1978; Hall 1981).

News pictures are also an important means by which the event reported on is personalized. Personalization makes complex matters simple by seeing them through the eyes of a person involved or affected (Ericson, Baranek, and Chan 1987: 141–3). Especially when a news item features the views of a particular source, a photograph often accompanies the item to further personalize it. Similarly, some newspaper columnists are pictured each time they appear to indicate the 'personality' of the person offering the opinion, as well as to distance this format from the less personal and more institutional and objective formats of news and features columns. Regardless of whether a journalist or other news source is involved, personalization involves 'the isolation of the person from his relevant social and institutional context ... Photos play a crucial role in this form of personification, for people – human subjects – are par excellence the content of news and feature photographs ... A newspaper can account for an event, or deepen its account, by attaching an individual to it, or by bringing personal attributes, isolated from their social context, to bear on their account as an explanation' (Hall 1981: 236–7).

TELEVISION

Television can represent sources in direct speech and other sounds, as well as in a range of visual possibilities, including printed words, graphics, sketches, still photographs, and moving pictures. The combination of sight and sound in television makes it seem especially grounded as a witness to reality. It appears to bring us closer to the real world of face-to-face interaction, allowing us to read many more aspects of setting, context, gestures, facial expressions, and speech than are available in newspapers or radio.

In television, the visual aspects seem to dominate. Some television-news analysts have argued that sight takes precedence over sound (including the written script or news text). Altheide (1985: 110) observes that 'visuals are disproportionately weighted in the news equation: actors, action, and objects that can be filmed are the foundation of network news. Indeed, we believe that news reports are based on what is visually available.' Epstein (1974: 241–2) reports that because television news items are brief and the audience is assumed to have 'zero knowledge about a subject,' journalists must engage in 'selecting news pictures which can be expected to have "instant meaning." ' This seems to be in keeping with the observation of Barthes (1972: 110) that 'pictures ... are more imperative than writing, they impose meaning at one stroke, without analyzing or diluting it.'

In the extreme, the spoken words of television are said to be overwhelmed by the visuals, 'drowned in the visual soup in which they are obliged to be served' (Raphael 1980: 305). The dominance of the visual is especially evident in advertising, in which 'the visual frequently stands on its own, undescribed and unexplained. The language of ads becomes condensed, allusive, conversational, or poetic. It is the visual that conveys the story, use, or reason for consumption' (Draper 1986: 16). The same may be said for television news, which trafficks in visual images that are left to the viewer's imagination to decode, while its words are reduced to brief clips and 'fragmented conversations' (Postman 1985; Fiske 1987).

In contrast, the words of journalists and sources have been shown to be significant for understanding television news. Precisely because a visual alone would leave people to rely exclusively on their imagination, embroidering the evidence of their visual sense, television sources and journalists carefully prepare their verbal scripts to ensure that their own meanings provide pointers as to how the pictures should be understood. This use is analogous to that served by captions for newspaper photographs. Indeed, ethnographic research in television newsrooms indicates that scripts are sometimes prepared in advance by the reporter, albeit with constant visualization of what pictures might fit the script (Ericson, Baranek, and Chan 1987). Similarly, television news sources carefully script and stage their appearances so as to ensure that their words cohere with how their deeds are pictured (Ericson, Baranek, and Chan 1989: chaps. 2–5). As a result the television-news format is analogous to an 'illustrated lecture' (Gitlin 1980: 264) or 'visual radio' (Gans 1979) in which the verbal serves as a meta-discourse for the visual. Journalistic codes in the production of talk are more significant than visual codes, and they constantly instruct the reader how to read the visuals (Glasgow University Media Group [GUMG] 1980).

Stills

Stills, including photographs and sketches of sources, were used when other visuals were unavailable (see also Ericson, Baranek, and Chan 1987). For example, because cameras were not allowed in courtrooms, sketches of the participants were used. When an anchor talked about a source in a brief, for example, about an activity of a political leader, a still photograph of the person was sometimes used rather than a voiced-over video of the activity or a stock video of the leader. Sometimes, when a source was contacted for a telephone interview because he or she was too far away or otherwise unavailable for a face-to-face interview, a still photograph of the source was voiced-over with the interview clip. Voiced-over photographs were like talking heads, except the heads were not seen to be actually talking.

Among the 1,185 TQ sources, 48, or about 4 per cent, were pictured in still photographs or sketches. In proportion to the frequency with which they were cited in TQ, the source types represented in stills most often were those representing political organizations (27 per cent), criminal-justice organizations (from courtroom scenes) (11 per cent), other government organizations (9 per cent), and private corporations (8 per cent), as well as individuals (7 per cent). Among the 718 TP sources, 24, or about 3 per cent, were pictured in stills. In proportion to the frequency with which they were cited in TP, the source types represented in stills most often were those representing public administration (10 per cent), private corporations (8 per cent), and community organizations (7 per cent), as well individuals (6 per cent).

Talking Heads
The predominant way in which sources were represented in television news was as talking heads. Among the 1,185 TQ sources, 640, or 54 per cent, were represented in this way. In proportion to the frequency with which they were cited in TQ, the source types represented as talking heads most frequently were TQ journalists (87 per cent), occupational-association members (56 per cent), community-organization members (54 per cent), government officials other than those in criminal justice and public administration (38 per cent), individuals (37 per cent), and private corporate officials (34 per cent). TP used talking heads proportionately more often than did TQ, with statistically significant differences between them in this regard. Among the 718 TP sources, 445, or 62 per cent, were represented in this way. In proportion to the frequency with which they were cited in TP, the source types represented as talking heads most often were TP journalists (91 per cent), occupational-association members (64 per cent), individual citizens (55 per cent), community-organization members (54 per cent), government officials other than those in criminal justice and public administration (45 per cent), government officials in public administration (43 per cent), and members of private corporations (43 per cent).

These data can be compared to the findings of the Glasgow Group (GUMG 1976: 125): 'across all bulletins, 61 percent of material ... does contain *talking heads* ... the news is, by professional criteria, visually extremely unexciting. Basically, despite still photographs, graphics and the rest, most of it is *talking heads* in studio or on location.' The predominance of talking heads belies the view that television news is 'everywhere,' an 'eyewitness' to reality 'as it happens.' In fact, television news consists predominantly of journalists, and selected sources, pictured as witnesses to events that have occurred at a different time and in a different place. In this regard, talking heads serve the same witnessing function as still photographs accompanying the printed accounts of journalists and their sources in newspapers (Hall 1981: 241). The advantages of talking heads over still photographs are that the person can be pictured in action (talking, gesturing, and making facial expressions) and in a 'fuller' setting whose props (an office, books, certificates, desk piled with documents, etc.) signify additional attributes about the person and his or her context.

Our data reveal that, especially in TP, non-governmental sources – individuals, and members of community organizations and occupational associations – were proportionately more likely to be pictured as talking heads. This finding testifies to the 'vox pop' orientation of television, and of TP in particular. Just as NP was more likely to give a face to sources outside of government through still photographs, so the television outlets used talking heads more often when the source was not speaking from an official position. Apparently, in television, the official voice can be more readily cited or referred to by the journalist without a direct account from the source, while the individual citizen or member of a citizens' interest group is usually represented more directly in a personalized visual and verbal account.

Voice-overs

Television news sources often appear on a video segment but with someone else talking about them and their activities. Usually the voice is that of the journalist who points to how the video segment showing the source should be understood. Like the caption for the newspaper photograph, the journalist's words indicate how the source's deeds are to be understood. The journalist rarely describes the shots iconically, but rather frames them indexically and symbolically.

As discussed in chapter 6, voiced-over video segments of source actors and actions was *the* mode of presenting stories from abroad. News-service video feeds were voiced-over by the reporter for the news service, or by the news outlet's anchor. Stock videos were used frequently. For example, a stock shot of a foreign head of state was often used for an anchor brief that reported a statement made by him or her. A stock shot of a major demonstration or violent confrontation was often used in reporting the aftermath, including official meetings or a court case about it.

While these practices in voicing-over visuals are typical in foreign coverage and network news (see also Altheide 1985: chap. 5), they are also common in reporting local events (Ericson, Baranek, and Chan 1987: chaps.

7 and 8). It is sometimes impossible, and often inconvenient, for television crews to capture local events and sources in 'actualities.' As often as not, they are captured in the more distant reportage of stock visuals and reporters' accounts of what the source said and did. Moreover, even on the rare occasions when the source can be pictured while engaged in the activity reported on, it is often better journalistically to have the reporter voice-over the video, pointing to the significance of how the source was displayed. The source's words may not be reducible to a short clip. The source's words may be inconsistent with his or her deeds as videotaped. The journalist's narrative may be better served by having his or her script dominate, pointing to the significance of how the source has been pictured in his or her own terms. 'Even in the few cases where overheard (ie. more observational and less interventionist) film is concerned, there is still the commentator to set up how such shots shall be seen and understood by the audience ... such commentary does not tend iconically to describe the shots, but rather forces the viewer to see the shots indexically or even symbolically within a framework of understanding thereby established by the professionals' (GUMG 1980: 332).

Among the 1,185 TQ sources, 352, or about 30 per cent, were pictured in a video segment with a voice-over. In proportion to the frequency with which they appeared in TQ, the source types pictured on video but voiced-over most often were those representing community organizations (57 per cent), individual citizens (55 per cent), private corporate members (52 per cent), persons in public administration (48 per cent), members of political organizations (46 per cent), and government officials other than those involved in criminal justice or public administration (44 per cent). In proportion to the frequency with which they were cited in TP, the source types pictured on video but voiced-over most often were identical to TQ, although in slightly different proportions and rank order: those representing community organizations (66 per cent), private corporate members (51 per cent), persons in public administration (47 per cent), individual citizens (45 per cent), members of political organizations (44 per cent), and government officials other than those involved in criminal justice or public administration (44 per cent).

When the journalist appears on the television screen it is almost always as a talking head, personalizing authorship in a way that is unavailable to newspapers and radio. Journalists rarely voice-over themselves or other journalists, but instead appear speaking to the camera directly. In contrast, news sources other than journalists are almost as likely to be voiced-over as they are to appear as talking-heads, with the journalist pointing to the sources' relevant attributes and activities. These data indicate the television journalists' dominance in and over the story.

Sound-overs
In addition to using such filming devices as camera angles, lighting, and cutting, television can create connotative meaning through the use of sounds. However, television news has traditionally limited the use of sounds other than the voices of journalists and their sources. This limitation is related to the fact that it is rarely possible to be present at the event being reported in order to capture its 'natural' sounds. Furthermore, it is 'unnatural' to introduce background sounds that seem to fit because there is a risk that they will expose the fictive quality of television news and cast it more explicitly into the realm of entertainment programming. This concern also explains why the use of music is sparse in television news, and why when music is used it is generally a 'beat' or 'pulse' that seems empty of myth content (GUMG 1980: 231).

There were differences between TQ and TP in the use of background sounds as part of representing source actors and activities. TP occasionally used music and other audio inputs to create a 'mood' for its news items. This is one reason why TP's news operation was referred to by practitioners as 'disco journalism.' A vivid description of the practice was given by a police-officer source we interviewed (Ericson, Baranek, and Chan 1989: 120). Talking of how TP 'really dramatized' an item reporting on an increase in bank robberies in the city, he observed that 'they showed hooded gunmen rushing into a bank and music, the drama-type music with beating drums and everything behind it. And it showed flicks, and these were actual pictures taken during robberies from bank cameras and it almost made them look as if they were moving like a jerking movement with the accompanying music.'

More typically the background sounds on TP and TQ were those associated with the context in which the source was represented. For example, stories from the scenes of demonstrations or strike picket lines included the singing or chanting of citizens involved. Stories of accidents, disasters, and crime incidents included sirens and other noises signifying emergency personnel at work. This explains the fact, detailed below, that most sources represented through background sound were individual citizens, members of occupational associations (workers), representatives of private corporations (management), or members of community organizations.

With its popular orientation and 'disco journalism' style, TP used background sounds to represent sources significantly more often than TQ. Among the 1,185 TQ sources, 173, or fewer than 15 per cent, had background sounds associated with their appearances on the screen. In proportion to the frequency with which they appeared in TQ, the sources pictured with background sounds most often were individuals (23 per cent), private corporate members (21 per cent), members of community organizations (20 per cent), and officials in public administration (20 per cent). Among the 718 TP sources, 131, or more than 18 per cent, were pictured with background sounds. In proportion to the frequency with which they appeared in TP, the sources who had background sounds associated with their appearances most often were individuals (28 per cent), members of occupational associations (27 per cent), government officials other than those in criminal justice or public administration (20 per cent), and representatives of private corporations (19 per cent).

Voice-clips
Television-news outlets also use audio-clips without picturing the source. In this approach they are very similar to radio, except that the journalist (usually the anchor) is pictured in the studio while the source's voice is heard.

TQ used voice-clips alone much more often than TP. Among the 1,185 sources cited or referred to in TQ, 83, or almost 7 per cent, were quoted in voice-clips without a visual of the source. The vast majority of these sources were journalists, especially journalists for other news organizations. In proportion to the frequency with which they were referred to or cited in TQ, the sources used most often with voice-clips only were journalists for other news organizations (67 per cent) and TQ journalists (7 per cent). Among the 718 sources cited or referred to in TP, only 25, or fewer than 4 per cent, were quoted in voice-clips only. Again most of these were journalists representing other news organizations (16/33, or 49 per cent of these sources used in TP). In contrast to TQ, only 4/297, or just over 1 per cent, of TP journalists were presented through voice-clips alone.

Television Language
Television news derives much of its authority from the sense it gives of being close to reality. This sense is derived primarily from television's visual capacities, but it is intensified through the use of language that also seems realistic in that it is 'hard-hitting,' dramatic, and colloquial. While TP used such language more often, there was little difference between the television outlets in this regard (for detailed comparisons, see chapters 4 and 5). In contrast, as we learn in the next section, the radio outlets differed substantially in the use of language, with RP being similar to the television outlets.

Examples from reporting on criminal justice typify the hard-hitting, popular, colloquial use of language. Legislation was referred to as being 'rammed through' the legislature. Police searches of premises were referred to as 'raids.' Heavy sentences for criminal offenders were described in terms of the accused being 'slapped' or 'slammed' with the sanction. For example, a TQ report on the fact that a retail store had been fined one million dollars for misleading advertising referred to the store as a retailing 'giant' that had to 'cough up' the fine 'slapped' on it by a judge.

Anchor leads in particular included graphic language to draw readers into the story. These leads were the functional equivalent of the bold headlines in the popular newspaper. Sometimes they were accompanied by visuals that made evident the fact that television language is most realistic when it blends the verbal and visual. For example, TQ presented an item reporting on two developments in protests against nuclear armament: the removal of protesters from the grounds in front of the legislature; and, a national railway ticket-seller who lost a case before an arbitration board regarding his right to wear a 'No Nukes' button at work. This item began with a statement by the anchor, 'The anti-nuclear lobby suffered two more body blows today ...' This graphic statement was accompanied by a graphic in the background picturing a big boot kicking the peace symbol.

In talking about their work, and in official manuals that try to lay down what they are doing, journalists sustain a distinction between true and false. For example, a TQ policy manual (Canadian Broadcasting Corporation [CBC] 1982: 30) instructs, 'Journalistic programs must not as a general principle mix actuality (visual and audio of actual events and of real people) with a dramatized portrayal of people or events.' If it is deemed necessary to do so 'the dramatized portion must be well identified.' Similarly, when reconstruction and simulation are used, 'that fact must be made clear to the audience by audio or visual means.'

In practice, television news consists largely of dramatizations, simulations, and reconstructions that are not identified as such (Epstein 1974; Schlesinger 1978; Altheide 1985; Ericson, Baranek, and Chan 1987). The verbal and visual are entwined into strong metaphors that are representational, and better judged in terms of correctness and incorrectness rather than as true or false. The metaphors of television serve as 'cognitive instruments' that are 'indispensable for perceiving connections that, once perceived, are *then* truly present' (M. Black 1979: 39). Television is not compelled to speak in the figurative language of, say, the witness in court or before a royal commission, for whom questions of evidence, contradiction, lying, and the basis of truth claims are omnipresent. It deals in tropes that do not simply assert that 'things look this way,' but rather urge one to 'look at things this way' (Shearing and Ericson forthcoming). Black's (1979: 39–41) insights in this regard are worth quoting at length.

When I first thought of Nixon as 'an image surrounding a vacuum,' the verbal formulation was necessary to my seeing him in this way. Subsequently, certain kinetic and visual images have come to serve as surrogates for the original verbal formulation, which still controls the sensory imagery and remains available for ready affirmation ... If somebody urges that, 'Nixon is an image surrounding a vacuum,' it would be inept to ask soberly whether the speaker *knew* that to be so, or how he came to know it, or how we could check on the allegation, or whether he was saying something consistent with his previous assertion that Nixon was a shopkeeper ... What lies behind the desire to stretch 'true' to fit some such cases (as when somebody might quite intelligibly respond to the Nixon-metaphor by saying, 'How true!') is a recognition that an emphatic, indispensable metaphor does not belong to the realm of fiction, and is not merely being used, as some writers allege, for some mysterious aesthetic effect, but really does say something (Nixon, if we are not mistaken, is indeed what he is metaphorically said to be). Such recognition of what might be called the representational aspect of a strong metaphor can be accommodated by recalling other familiar devices for representing 'how things are' that cannot be assimilated to 'statements of fact.' Charts and maps, graphs and pictorial diagrams, photographs and 'realistic' paintings, and above all models, are familiar cognitive devices for *showing* 'how things are,' devices that need not be perceived as mere substitutes for bundles of statement of fact. In such cases we speak of correctness and incorrectness, without needing to rely upon those over-worked epithets, 'true' and 'false.' This is the clue we need in order to do justice to the cognitive, informative, and ontologically illuminating aspects of strong metaphors.

RADIO

The task of radio journalists and their sources is especially difficult because they do not have access to the various visual devices of newspapers and television to show things metaphorically or factually. Limited to sound only, radio journalists and their sources must use speech to spark the listener's imagination so that he or she will be able to visualize what is being reported on, to imagine the facts as well as the realities pictured by metaphoric language. Radio journalists and sources must use speech that is 'both typographic and photographic, as the equivalent not only of the newspaper text but in many cases of its photographs' (Crisell 1986: 88).

While the visual capacity of television allows it to use space as well as time as structuring agents for news (Altheide 1985: 104–5), radio news is limited to time as its major structuring device. This makes radio news potentially very evanescent, and radio journalists must work hard to control this potential. Control is effected in part by making talk continuous. Continuous talk is more necessary on radio than on television because only talk is available to set the context, while television journalists can rely in part on visuals for this purpose. Continuity is ensured by preparing scripts that are fluent, precise, orderly, and less diffuse and tautological than ordinary speech (Crisell 1986: 58; Goffman 1981: chap. 5). While radio-news talk must convey the sense that it is ordinary speech from the real world, it is in fact carefully scripted and in this respect has a literary quality (ibid). Control is additionally effected by ensuring that the script is composed with language that is simple, straightforward, and redundant. This means that even more than in television news, radio news presents brief items in a simple manner on recurrent themes. Radio produces distinctive representations of order, offering reassurance and confirmation, because of the limitations of the medium itself.

Sounds

Radio news is not limited to speech. Various sounds are used indexically, to indicate the presence of something else. However, as with visuals in television and newspapers, radio sounds require textual pointing. That is, they are made relevant by the verbal context in which they are placed. Hence it is the words that dominate, while other sounds serve secondary semiotic functions, such as making it evident the reporter is on the scene, giving a sense of immediacy, and providing tertiary understanding of what it is like to be part of the event reported on. 'Radio does not seek to reproduce the chaotic, complex and continuous sounds of actual life: it may tolerate them to a degree, but seeks to convey only those sounds which are relevant to its messages and to arrange them in their order of relevance. Nevertheless the ultimate test of relevance is the verbal context: it is the subject under discussion in the interview which will tell us whether we should be paying any attention to the traffic noise' (Crisell 1986: 49).

An item in RQ illustrates how traffic noises are to be read. Setting the stage for an item regarding anti-nuclear demonstrators protesting on the grounds in front of the legislature, the reporter began his report as follows: '[Traffic 'honking' noises]. The demonstrators here are carrying a variety of anti-nuclear placards. One reads "Nuclear war is bad for life." A second sign attached to a telephone pole advises motorists to honk for peace. Many are honking but others aren't so friendly. One man shouted "Go home, pinkos" and others have advised the group to go to Moscow.'

What cannot be pictured must be visualized in sound and speech. As the above item indicates, radio journalists and their sources can blend words and sounds to make up their stories. While everything must still be left to the listener's imagination, the range of the imaginable can be reduced substantially by imaginative journalists and sources. Such vivid visualizations are evident in another RQ story, this one concerning a company that had designed and manufactured a new truck for dealing with fires in high-rise buildings. Following the anchor's lead and before the reporter's clip, a dramatization was included. This dramatization was manufactured by the company that also manufactured the fire truck.

Unspecified Source: [Sounds of a ladder being raised. Other loud sounds indicating excitement, trouble, clamour. Voices speaking loudly over the sounds.] O.K., Willy, you should be at the 22nd floor now. I'd like to know what, right now what you see.

Willy: A lot of smoke.

Unspecified Source: [Continued loud speech over loud sounds] Are there any rescue possibilities?

Willy: Right

Unspecified Source: You bring these two people off there right now then. Get them down and start pouring water over the blaze. Over.

Voice-clips

A primary device for representing sources in radio news is audio-clips of the source's speech. These provide words not only as symbols of what they represent, but also as an index of the person. The person's attributes and character are revealed by his or her accent, the emphasis he or she conveys in formulating accounts, his or her hesitancy or uncertainty in responding to the journalist's questions, and his or her refusal to answer the journalist's questions when even silence can be made meaningful.

Among the 847 sources cited or referred to in RQ items, 478, or about 56 per cent, were included in a voice-clip. The vast majority of these were journalists, especially RQ journalists. In proportion to the frequency with which they were referred to or cited in RQ, the sources used most often with voice-clips were RQ journalists (99 per cent), other journalists (50 per cent), spokespersons for private corporations (33 per cent), government officials other than those in criminal justice and public administration (30 per cent), members of community organizations (29 per cent), and members of occupational associations (26 per cent). RP used a greater proportion of sources in voice-clips, with a statistically significant difference in comparison with RQ. Among the 629 sources cited or referred to in RP, 388, or 62 per cent, were presented in voice-clips. In proportion to the frequency with which they were cited or referred to in RP, the sources used most often with voice-clips were RP journalists (100 per cent), other journalists (83 per cent), members of community organizations (41 per cent), members of occupational associations (36 per cent), spokespersons for private corporations (35 per cent), and individuals (32 per cent).

These data indicate that in radio news, the voice of journalists was omnipresent. Excluding journalists, only a minority of each type of source was cited in a voice-clip. The majority of sources were simply referred to or cited by the journalist, as is the practice in newspapers. The journalist dominated, referring to the activities of the source or quoting him in her voice rather than his voice. Moreover, similar to the use of talking heads in television, the sources most likely to be represented in voice-clip actualities were members of private-sector organizations and, in RP, individual citizens as well. The authoritative statements of officials in government agencies, especially those in criminal justice, were typically cited or referred to by radio journalists. Proportionate to the frequency with which they were a part of radio news, the voices of the people – individuals, and those organized in terms of particular interests – were more likely to be broadcast than those of officialdom.

Radio Language

The fact that radio news must communicate meaning at first hearing means that its language is at once simple and attention-grabbing. On many dimensions of language use – restrictions on words, number of words used in a clip and in an item, and uses of actuality to make the report seem near to reality and hence authoritative – radio is similar to television and the popular newspaper. Television relies upon popular, vivid, dramatic, as-it-happens language to fit with its visuals. Radio relies upon the same elements of language because it lacks a visual capacity. However there were marked differences between RP and RQ in the use of such language (see also Crissell 1986: chap. 4). Dramatic language was much more evident in RP's items, making the popular-quality differences in this regard much greater within radio than between the television outlets, although much less than between the newspaper outlets (for detailed comparisons, see chapters 4 and 5).

RP's use of language for the 'dramatization of consciousness' (Williams 1989) puts it in the same league as NP and the television outlets. People were described as being 'slapped' with heavy prison sentences and 'slammed' in government enquiry reports. Disputes were frequently depicted as 'battles' and in terms of various other metaphors of war. As did journalists in other news media, radio journalists captured their sources' picturesque phrasings and strong metaphors and blended them into their own voices. An example is provided in the following RQ item regarding the sentencing of two offenders for attempted murder.

> In the words of Crown attorney Paul Culver it was a *'ruthless, callous,* and *cowardly* attempt to murder three people.' He called 32-year-old Falja Singh Baines *'a dangerous religious fanatic'* who would do almost anything to further his cause. The court found that Baines carried a loaded handgun to a protest between rival East Indian factions at Bloor and Yonge last November 14. He shot and wounded two brothers and then *opened fire* on Metro Police

Ethnic Squad officer Chris Fernandes. Nineteen-year-old Giviog Guraj then shot and wounded the constable in the head to help Baines escape. The Crown attorney found it *shocking* that 90 per cent of the Sikh population here in Toronto would stand behind a man like Baines for shooting members of a rival faction. County court judge Hugh Locke said this is not a weapon-oriented society but he noted that the use of guns is also *increasing at frightening speed.* He sentenced Baines to life in prison and Guraj to fourteen years. Judge Locke said, 'They *trampled all over* this country's deep respect for law and order and peaceful protest.' [Sign-off] (emphasis added)

Here crime and punishment is vividly captured in twenty seconds. Those who 'opened fire' are 'ruthless, callous, cowardly' and 'dangerous religious fanatics' who 'trampled all over' fellow citizens. Their crime is indicative of the 'frightening speed' with which guns are proliferating in society, and it is 'shocking' that they should have any organized support at all. The dramatic language casts crime-punishment into a stimulus-response framework. With the offenders captured in such dramatic terms, the severe punishment seems unquestionably appropriate.

Discriminating Source Formats by Media and Markets

The stepwise discriminant analyses presented in tables 7.7 and 7.8 weight and combine three elements of source format (source types, source contexts, and knowledge provided by sources) as independent measures in a way that forces the groups – medium (newspapers, television, radio), and the markets within each medium (quality, popular) – to be as distinct as possible so that one can predict on what criteria the groups are distinguishable.

The stepwise discriminant analysis of source formats by medium is presented in table 7.7. The best predictor of medium is whether the source is a journalist of the news outlet. Additional predictive influence comes from adding, in turn, whether the source was quoted in the following contexts: interviews, media events, reports, other media, and news releases or statements. Following these, some predictive influence comes from adding, in turn, whether the source offered tertiary understanding, a recommendation, secondary understanding, an evaluation, or was referred to in the context of an organizational document. Newspaper stories are distinguished as quoting sources in the context of other media reports, and having their sources offer recommendations, secondary understanding, and evaluations. The television outlets are distinguished as having their own journalists as sources; quoting sources in the contexts of interviews, media events, and formal statements or releases; and having their sources offer secondary

TABLE 7.7
Stepwise discriminant analysis of news formats by medium

Variables	F	Discriminant function 1 standardized coefficients	Discriminant function 2 standardized coefficients
Type of source: Own journalist	284.54	0.87	–0.33
Context quoted: Interview	179.40	0.58	0.62
Context quoted: Media event	132.41	0.59	0.13
Context quoted: Media report	53.90	–0.31	0.33
Context quoted: Statement/release	18.23	0.19	0.18
Type of understanding: Tertiary	10.65	0.01	0.32
Type of assessment: Recommendation	11.44	–0.15	–0.16
Type of understanding: Secondary	4.69	–0.02	0.21
Type of assessment: Evaluation	2.49	–0.02	0.15
Context quoted: Document	2.33	0.08	0.02

Centroids:			
Newspaper	(N = 1784)	–0.58	0.09
Television	(N = 1873)	0.46	0.17
Radio	(N = 1470)	0.12	–0.33

Percentage of cases correctly classified:

Newspaper	70.5%
Television	37.3%
Radio	44.6%
Total	51.0%

Wilk's lambda = 0.7996; chi-square = 1144.60 (d.f. = 20; $p < 0.01$)

understanding and evaluations. The radio outlets are distinguished as having their own journalists as sources and having their sources offer recommendations.

The stepwise discriminant analyses of source formats within markets are presented in table 7.8. From table 7.8a we learn that the best predictor of markets within newspapers is whether the source was quoted in the context of a media event, with some additional influence deriving form whether the source offered tertiary understanding, was a journalist for the outlet, offered an evaluation, was quoted in the context of an interview, was quoted in the context of a media report, was quoted in the context of a document, offered secondary understanding, and offered an assessment. NQ is distinguished as quoting its sources in the contexts of interviews, reports in other media, and documents, and having them offer evaluations and recommendations. NP is distinguished as relying on its own journalists as sources, quoting sources in the context of a media event, and having sources offer secondary and tertiary understanding.

From table 7.8b we learn that the best predictor of markets within television is whether the source was quoted in the context of an interview, with some additional influence deriving from whether the source offered secondary understanding, was quoted in the context of a document, offered an evaluation, offered a recommendation, was a journalist, and was quoted in the context of a formal news statement or release. TQ is distinguished as quoting sources in documents and having them offer secondary understanding and evaluations. TP is distinguished as using its own journalists, citing sources in the context of interviews and news statements or releases, and having sources offer recommendations.

A stepwise discriminant analysis of source formats by market orientation in radio produced results that are not statistically significant.

In this chapter we have established significant components of source formats peculiar to each news outlet. Each news outlet represented sources differently because it operated with medium and market criteria that differed from the others.

NQ items almost always cited outside sources. NQ averaged more sources per item than the other outlets, although NP was at a similar level. The newspapers were especially likely to cite multiple sources: approximately one-third of NQ and NP items cited four or more sources. NQ gave particular emphasis to politicians and civil servants, and approximately one-third of all its sources represented the institutional voices of politics. While the news outlets did not vary significantly in their porportionate use of different types of knowledge, there were significant differences in relation to how each type of knowledge was presented. NQ's government sources were often used to present primary facts, which was not the case for the television stations, in which factuality was primarily constituted by journalists. NQ had a slightly greater tendency than the other outlets to include evaluations and recommendations, especially as offered by their own journalists.

NP, like NQ, used the greater discursive capacity of the print medium to cite more sources per item than the broadcast outlets. NP differed from NQ in giving much greater attention to criminal-justice officials as sources, and in citing lower-ranking as opposed to higher-ranking officials. NP also varied

TABLE 7.8a
Stepwise discriminant analysis of source formats within markets:
newspapers

Variable	F	Discriminant function standardized coefficients
Context quoted:		
Media event	14.98	0.51
Type of understanding:		
Tertiary	14.34	0.49
Type of source:		
Own journalist	9.01	0.39
Type of assessment:		
Evaluation	3.85	−0.25
Context quoted:		
Interview	5.14	−0.29
Context quoted:		
Media report	4.82	−0.28
Context quoted:		
Document	3.92	−0.26
Type of understanding:		
Secondary	3.16	0.23
Type of assessment		
Recommendation	1.82	−0.18

Centroids:	
Quality paper ($N = 1040$)	−0.16
Popular paper ($N = 744$)	0.22
Percentage of cases correctly classified:	
Quality paper	72.7%
Popular paper	42.3%
Total 60.0%	

Wilk's lambda = 0.9658; chi-square = 61.85 (d.f. = 9; $p < 0.01$)

substantially from NQ in giving much more space to the voice of individual
citizens. However, these individual voices were framed in particular ways.
NP joined with the television outlets in the frequent use of individual citizens
to express fear and loathing over serious crime and other threats to their
sense of order. NP was similar to other popular outlets in using individual
citizens in a 'vox pop' format whereby what is at issue has already been
framed by the actions of government officials and the structures of
government institutions. When individuals are given a voice in the news, it
is nearly always to address the institutional practices and arrangements of

TABLE 7.8b
Stepwise discriminant analysis of source formats within markets:
television

Variable	F	Discriminant function standardized coefficients
Context quoted:		
Interview	26.43	0.79
Type of understanding:		
Secondary	6.49	–0.37
Context quoted:		
Document	6.06	–0.37
Type of assessment:		
Evaluation	4.59	–0.32
Type of assessment:		
Recommendation	2.84	0.26
Type of source:		
Own journalist	3.19	0.29
Context quoted:		
Statement/release	2.64	0.24
Centroids:		
Quality television (N = 1159)		–0.13
Popular television (N = 174)		0.22
Percentage of cases correctly classified:		
Quality television		52.5%
Popular television		58.3%
Total		54.7%

Wilk's lambda = 0.9750; chi-square = 47.19 (d.f. = 7; $p < 0.01$)

government. NP pictured its sources in still photographs much more often than did NQ. In particular, individual citizens were pictured in NP. Pictures of individual citizens as sources not only helped to personalize the story, but also provided additional readings of character and context regarding people who were unfamiliar to readers because they were not regular news sources. NP also differed from NQ, but not the broadcast outlets, in its reliance upon citing sources in official-meeting contexts, indicating a greater orientation to scheduled events to generate stories. This component, along with its greater emphasis on pictures, its use of individual citizens as sources in 'vox pop' formats, and its use of dramatic language, made NP distinct from NQ and more similar to the broadcast outlets, especially the television stations.

All of the broadcast outlets used substantially fewer sources per item than did the newspapers. However, this finding must be qualified with the understanding that, in broadcast news, the individual news item is often not discrete. Several items may be 'wrapped' in terms of a theme, with multiple sources cited over the several items. Broadcast news also differs from newspapers in the greater use of its own journalists as central sources. Many broadcast-news reports consist of the anchor being the only source, or the anchor and a reporter combining to make a report.

Journalists dominated TQ's news items, although less so than in TP and the radio stations. Consistent with TP, TQ's journalists were used, in particular, to provide primary facts, while outside sources were used to offer other types of knowledge. Part of the parsimony of broadcast news, especially television, is that the factual object of the story is constituted by journalists; the vast majority of primary knowledge is transmitted by journalists themselves without reference to, or direct citation of, other sources. Television journalists were also more evaluative than radio journalists, although less so than their counterparts in newspapers.

Television visuals provide for the representation of sources in ways not available to newspapers and radio. Visuals provide a context for the quotation of sources without the need for verbal descriptions by reporters, as is the case with newspapers and radio. Nevertheless, most television news sources are simply pictured as talking heads or in voiced-over shots that are similar to still photographs in newspapers. Television news was not 'everywhere' as an eyewitness to reality. Rather, television journalists and their sources were pictured as witnesses to events that occurred at a different time and in a different place. The same witnessing function is provided by still photographs accompanying the accounts of journalists and their sources in newspapers.

In previous chapters we have emphasized that the television-news outlets were least distinct from each other because they were especially constrained by the format requirements of the medium which compel a popular orientation. Nevertheless, TP differed from TQ in a number of the ways in which it represented sources. TP had a greater proportion of news items without any citation of outside sources. TP, in keeping with NP, its counterpart among the newspapers, was much more likely than TQ to cite criminal-justice sources and to use lower-ranking as opposed to higher-ranking officials. Also in keeping with NP, TP gave much more attention to individual citizens as sources in 'vox pop' formats than did TQ. TP used more talking-head interview shots of sources than TQ, and was more likely to use such shots to represent non–government organization sources and individual citizens. This talking-head representation of people outside government is parallel to NP's use of still photographs in that it personalized the story and provided additional readings of character and context regarding people who were unfamiliar to audience members because they were not regular news sources. On all of the above criteria, TP had a greater affinity with NP than with TQ. TP also differed from TQ in the occasional use of 'mood' music as background sound to news items or to particular clips within an item, thereby living up to its reputation as 'disco journalism.'

The radio outlets cited the fewest number of sources per item, although RP was especially low in this regard with RQ more similar to the levels in the television outlets. When RQ and RP did use outside sources, it was usually one person only, and the use of three or more sources was very rare compared to the television outlets and the newspapers. In both radio outlets, journalists predominated, with many items consisting of a statement by the anchor alone, or a combination of statements by the anchor and a reporter with no outside sources. The journalist-centrism of radio is further indicated by the fact that most voice-clips in RQ and RP were of journalists rather than outside sources. RQ used somewhat fewer voice-clips than RP, and when these used outside sources they tended to be government sources. In contrast, RP's outside source voice-clips were mostly of sources representing organizations outside of government as well as individual citizens. As a popular outlet, RP gave emphasis to the voices of the people – individuals, and those organized in relation to particular interests – more than to the voice of officialdom. RP also differed from RQ in its use of distinctive dramatic language. In this respect, it was more characteristic of the 'dramatization of consciousness' evident in the television outlets and in NP.

While our cross-sectional analyses to this point have detailed many components of news formats and source formats, additional components of format are analysed in the following two chapters which address topics in news of crime, law, and justice. In the next chapter, we analyse how topics in crime and deviance varied in terms of the medium and market of news outlets.

8

Crime and Deviance

Stories of Deviance and Control

BAD NEWS AND OTHER NEWS

A concern with deviance and control in social relations and organizations is *the* defining characteristic of newsworthiness (Ericson, Baranek, and Chan 1987). Conceptions of deviance and control not only define the central object and character of news stories, but are woven into the methodology of journalists, influencing their choices from assignment, through the selection and use of sources, to the final composition of the story.

Control is built into designations of deviance since the language we use about deviance and deviants always bears implications for control. Moreover, it is the language used in designating a problem, and the stories told about it, that are crucial for framing and influencing its resolution (Gusfield 1981; Wagner-Pacifici 1986). Thus analysis of stories about problems of deviance, such as those that appear in the news, helps us to understand how they simultaneously frame problem definition and resolution. ' "Problem setting" should indeed be considered the crucial process, as opposed to "problem solving." And the "stories that people tell about troublesome situations" do set up or "mediate" the problem. And "frame conflict" between various stories should be studied in detail, precisely because it is quite often "immune to resolution by appeal to the facts" ' (Reddy 1979: 284; see also Schon 1979).

The emphasis on deviance and control in the news is not new. As Milton (1671) remarked pithily centuries ago, 'Evil news rides post, while good news baits.' Moreover, the news media offer good news, as well as a lot of factual information, such as sports scores and financial results, for which goodness and badness are very much in the eye of the beholder. Scanning items from the news outlets we studied that were not included in our sample of deviance and control stories, we find items to help people avoid troubles and delays: for example, a report that a road crew hit a gas line and this was causing traffic delays. There were announcements of corporate moves and financial strategies: for example, of price 'wars' between competing airlines, of corporate take-overs, of plant closures, and of government grants to bolster employment and local economies. There were reports of citizens and politicians advocating amenities: for example, a city alderman was cited making demands for a new swimming pool. There were reports of archaeological discoveries, scientific discoveries, and medical advances. There were reports of visits by dignitaries: for example, a visit from Prince Philip; and of nice things happening to prominent people, for example, the provincial premier becoming a grandfather. Last but not least there were 'brighteners,' such as a report that a race horse named after a prominent politician had won a race.

Some news articulates with a consensus. It is bad news that a man has raped and tortured five women. It is good news that the premier is becoming a grandfather. But, in other reports, the matter is not straightforward. For example, a price war between airlines may bring cheer among consumers, but indifference or even resentment among those who cannot afford to take trips anyway, and fear among shareholders and employees of the companies concerned.

A further complication in understanding news of deviance and control is that aspects of deviance and control are sometimes included as a minor element in stories that are mainly concerned with other matters. For example, one news outlet we studied ran stories about a small city that was depressed economically and whose officials were searching for a new director of business development. In the course of reporting these matters, the reporter 'dropped in' the fact that the previous director of business development for the city had been dismissed for misuse of funds while in office. This is one example of the general point that news of crime and deviance is sometimes 'blurred' with other news so that it is difficult to categorize an entire item as, say, a 'crime story' as opposed to something else (Ditton and Duffy 1982: 13).

Sensitive to such difficulties, we scrutinized the total output of each news outlet studied over the period sampled in order to ascertain the proportion of stories that were on topics of deviance and control. Our findings are summarized in table 8.1. These data indicate that just less than one-half of all items in the quality newspaper (NQ), the popular newspaper (NP), and the popular television station (TP) were on topics of deviance and control. In contrast, the quality televison station (TQ), quality radio station

TABLE 8.1
The proportion of news items on topics of deviance and control

	News outlets												Sig. diff.
	NQ		NP		TQ		TP		RQ		RP		
	N	%	N	%	N	%	N	%	N	%	N	%	
Deviance and control items	3,438	45.3	2,737	47.5	489	60.2	332	47.0	243	71.5	224	64.2	T
Other items	4,157	54.7	3,022	52.5	323	39.8	374	53.0	97	28.5	125	35.8	
Totals	7,595	100.0	5,759	100.0	812	100.0	706	100.0	340	100.0	349	100.0	

*For NQ and NP, the figures represent 32 days of output.
For TQ, TP, RQ and RP the figures represent 33 days of output.
Tests of significance based on tables with deviance and control items/other items dichotomized into 'yes/no' for each of the categories. The last column indicates comparisons that show significant differences: chi-square statistics significant at the 0.05 level with Cramer's V or PHI ≥ 0.10, when N is large. Significant differences may occur between the newspapers (N); television stations (T); radio stations (R); or among the three types of media (M).

(RQ), and popular radio station (RP) had elements of deviance and control in the great majority of their items. A comparison by medium indicates that, on a proportionate basis, radio was the most likely to include items with elements of deviance and control (68 per cent of all radio items), followed by television (54 per cent of all television items), with newspapers having the least (42 per cent of all newspaper items).

A comparison of market orientation within newspapers indicates that, on a proportionate basis, NP (48 per cent) was only slightly more likely than was NQ (45 per cent) to carry deviance-and-control items. However, in a separate analysis within newspapers we found a substantial difference in crime coverage between the two newspapers. NQ included much less on topics of crime and its control (510/7,595, or 7 per cent of all items) than did NP (765/5,759, or 13 per cent of all items). A comparison by markets within television indicates that, on a proportionate basis, TQ (60 per cent) was much more likely than was TP (47 per cent) to include deviance-and-control stories. Similarly within radio, it was the quality outlet RQ (72 per cent) more than the popular outlet RP (64 per cent) that emphasized deviance-and-control items. TQ and RQ were both affiliates of the national CBC network, and their particular emphasis on deviance and control in public bureaucracies as part of their 'institutional journalism' approach helps explain these findings.

CONCURRENCE

Another consideration is whether a news event included in one outlet was also included in others. To assess the degree of concurrence in items across news outlets, we proceeded as follows. We took as the point of comparison all stories that appeared in RQ from Monday to Thursday of each week sampled, and examined each of the other outlets to ascertain if a story on the same news event was included on the same day or on the following day. Friday of each week was excluded because, except for NQ, there was no comparable publication or broadcast on Saturday that would allow us to undertake a following-day comparison. This procedure yielded a total of 24 days for comparison, during which RQ broadcast 243 items. Among the 243 news events reported by RQ in these items, 35 per cent were also included in RP, 32 per cent in TP, 42 per cent in TQ, 46 per cent in NP, and 58 per cent in NQ. Thus the greatest overlap was between RQ and the quality outlets in television and print, as well as with NP. There was least overlap with RQ's popular counterparts in radio and television.

In a separate analysis, we examined concurrence among deviance and control items in the newspapers. We found that 28 per cent (774/2,737) of the deviance-and-control items in NP also appeared in NQ on the same day or the next day. We found that 23 per cent (792/3,438) of the deviance-and-control items in NQ also appeared in NP on the same day or on the next day. These data indicate that, while there was some overlap, there was substantial variation across news outlets in the events covered. With one exception, there was concurrence in only a minority of instances.⁑This finding of low concurrence is consistent with other studies including those that analyse concurrence in crime news (Hauge 1965; Davis 1973; Ditton and Duffy 1982), as well as those considering concurrence in all types of news items (e.g., Epstein 1974: 367). Moreover, as we proceed to document in the case of deviance-and-control news, there is additional variation among outlets in the specifics of topics, angles, themes, sources, and emphasis. At this juncture it is instructive to offer some general explanations of why there is relatively little concurrence and substantial variation across news outlets.

One explanation is that news outlets do not mirror reality but rather construct it in terms of their own criteria and resources. Newsworthiness is not embedded in the event itself, but in what can be visualized about it in terms of journalists' imaginative capacity and the material tools and organizational resources at their disposal. 'What is newsworthy ... is not the particular act or deed itself so much as what can be done with it, how it corresponds to the criteria of accessibility, visual quality, drama, action, audience relevance, and ease with which it can be encapsulated and given a thematic unity' (Altheide 1985: 20).

Given that news outlets do not reflect events but rather construct them in their own terms, it is still arguable that concurrence is likely because the norms of the craft of journalism are similar regardless of the particular outlet that employs the journalist. Journalists operate with similar occupational values and recipe rules. Moreover, their knowledge is internal to the craft: they look to the news itself to decide what is newsworthy (Ericson, Baranek, and Chan 1987). However, while some concurrence no doubt transpires in these terms, there remains considerable divergence, suggesting that the nose for news is sensitive to many different things.

One source of divergence is the considerable autonomy available to journalists in some news organizations (Ericson, Baranek, and Chan 1987). However, the main reason for diversity in news events covered and how they are covered is the format requirements of each medium and of each particular news outlet. These format requirements often take precedence over the particular events and topics through which they work. It is the formats of the medium and organization to which the journalist must conform, not the particular event or issue that might be covered.

Areas of Crime and Deviance

An enormous range of deviant activities were reported on in our sample of 1,485 news items. We categorized these deviant activities into five general types for analysis: violence, economic, political, ideological/cultural, and diversionary. In table 8.2 we document the proportionate frequency with which these areas of deviance were reported in each of the six news outlets.

VIOLENCE

In the category of 'violence' we included reports on acts of both threatened violence and direct violence. Examples are violent crimes such as murder, attempted murder, kidnapping, and robbery; violent abuse such as child abuse, spousal abuse, and sexual abuse; and harms to health and safety such as impaired driving, unsafe working environments, and unsafe living environments. We also included reports on actions taken to control the means of violence, for example, concerning the use of weapons; and concerning the use of coercive mechanisms of state control such as military intervention, the death penalty, incarceration, deportation, and extradition. Thus 'state violence' and 'state terrorism' are conceptualized in the same way as various acts of violence by citizens.

Table 8.2 records the fact that there is substantial variation among the six news outlets in the proportion of their items that focused on violence. There is significant variation by medium, with television (35 per cent) and radio (36 per cent) giving more attention to violence than did newspapers (25 per cent). However, NQ is the outlier, with only 18 per cent of its items on topics related to violence, while NP, at 35 per cent, is closer to the norm for broadcasting. The broadcasting outlets, and NP, relied more on the dramatic-conflict features of violence that are so fitting to news discourse, while NQ gave greater attention to non-violent deviance in the institutional spheres of the political economy. There is also significant variation in terms of market orientation. Within each medium, but especially within newspapers, there is a much greater focus on violence by the popular than by the quality outlets. This finding is consistent with the view that popular outlets in particular rely on violence as a staple for the dramatic structuring of their news items.

Beyond these general comparisons are many substantial differences in the aspects of violence focused on by the news outlets studied. Examples in the coverage of murder, robbery, and impaired driving illustrate the differences.

On the topic of murder, a comparison between NP and NQ is instructive (see also chapter 4). NQ generally 'briefed' local murders for the record, and ignored the ample supply of murder stories on the wire services, unless such reports were relevant to important local issues or to legal trends. Thus a New York Times Service item that said a nurse in Texas was charged for murdering a child, and noted injury to six other children in the same hospital

TABLE 8.2
Areas of deviance

Areas of deviance	Newspaper		Television		Radio		Sig. diff.
	Q	P	Q	P	Q	P	
Violence	49	74	100	88	82	87	M/N/T
	17.8%	34.9%	31.4%	41.3%	33.7%	39.0%	
Economic	83	43	49	43	63	36	N/R
	30.1%	20.3%	15.4%	20.2%	25.9%	16.1%	
Political	106	71	146	58	86	82	T
	38.4%	33.5%	45.9%	27.2%	35.4%	36.8%	
Ideological	29	11	12	9	3	7	M/N
	10.5%	5.2%	3.8%	4.2%	1.2%	3.1%	
Diversionary	9	13	11	15	9	11	
	3.3%	6.1%	3.5%	7.0%	3.7%	4.9%	
Total stories	276	212	318	213	243	223	1,485

Percentages are by column. Tests of significance based on tables with areas of deviance dichotomized into 'yes/no' for each of the categories. The last column indicates comparisons that show significant differences, i.e., chi-square statistics significant at the 0.05 level with Cramer's V or PHI $\geq$ 0.10, when N is large. Significant differences may occur between the newspapers (N); television stations (T); radio stations (R); or among the three types of media (M). The last column also indicates the presence of significant interactions with the variables being analysed and the coders (C) in a separate log-linear analysis.

setting, was likely published because of its thematic relevance to a long-standing continuing story in NQ and other local-news outlets about suspicious deaths in an area children's hospital. NQ also occasionally published murder stories that included extraordinary elements. Thus NQ published a New York Times Service story about a tax protester in the United States who had a 'shoot-out' with police and who killed a U.S. marshall and a sheriff in the process.

Murder was a staple in NP. As addressed in chapter 6, the lack of local mass murders and dramatic murders was compensated for by stories available from United Press International. NP's inclusion of murders from abroad seemed to be in terms of three criteria. First, NP focused on gruesome mass murders, with the text often accompanied by a photograph of persons involved. Typical is a UPI item with the place line 'Lake Arthur, Louisiana,' and lead, 'A former mental patient who threatened his parents and beat his mother was sought yesterday in the shooting deaths of his father, mother, brother, and two other relatives.' Later in the item the gruesome details are recounted, such as 'Chester Perry's body was found in a crouching position behind his television set and the baby had been decapitated by gunfire.'

Second, NP published UPI murder stories involving prominent people, e.g., the stabbing to death of an Academy Award–winner by his homosexual lover. Third, NP, as did NQ, published murder stories from abroad that were unusual or bizarre in their circumstance, e.g., 'A Catania, Sicily soccer stadium caretaker told police he shot at fans gathered outside his home inside the ground because he couldn't take any more of their insults. One man was killed and 25 wounded.'

Robberies were a staple item in all of the popular news outlets, but in none of the qualities. The three popular news outlets broadcast or published even small-scale robberies, such as those at convenience stores, as well as bank robberies. They also reported tallies, such as 'this is the 133rd bank robbery in Metropolitan Toronto this year,' along with an indication of whether this represented an increase or decrease in bank robberies over the previous year. TP tried to have its police reporter and camera crews at the scene of a robbery when the police arrived, aided no doubt by the use of scanner radios that could pick up the police radio frequency (Altheide 1976; Ericson, Baranek, and Chan 1987). The approach in this regard was to make the police reporter appear to be a part of the investigative process, working *with* police rather than merely reporting on them (see also chapter 4). In one item sampled, this fiction became a reality.

TP Anchor: Quick work by Metro Police and [TP] News collared two bank-robbery suspects this afternoon at Bloor and Dufferin. [Shot of bank] Minutes after two men robbed the Bank of Commerce on the corner, crime specialist [TP reporter] and news cameraman [TP cameraman] arrived on the scene. [Wide shot of bank] [TP reporter] overheard a description of the suspects and alerted an officer in the subway. [Man handcuffed by police-man] Later [TP cameraman] spotted two men who fit the bill on a subway train the police had stopped. [Face of boy, who smiles] The hold-up squad has charged [adult suspect's name and address] with robbery and dangerous use of a firearm. [Man taken outside subway into car] The second suspect is a juvenile. A pellet gun and a paper bag with the money have been re-covered, and both [TP reporter and TP cameraman] will be recommended for civilian citations.

Another criminal-offence type appearing frequently in the popular outlets was impaired driving. However, in most instances, reports of impaired driving were tied into specific control recommendations and control actions (see chapter 9). A social movement aimed at 'cracking down' on impaired driving was in full force at the time (cf Gusfield 1981), and considerable coverage was given to heavy sentences against impaired drivers who had struck innocent victims; police definitions of the problem; the activities of a citizens' interest group called People to Reduce Impaired Driving

Everywhere; and a civil action brought against a hotel that was found liable for not terminating alcohol sales to a person who subsequently drove his car and was involved in an accident that paralysed his fellow passenger.

ECONOMIC

In the 'economic' category we included property crimes (theft; fraud; break, enter, and theft; arson), the economic aspects of organized crime, questionable business practices (e.g., bribery, patronage, nepotism, influence peddling), legal conflict over property (e.g., breaches of contract, property rights, business jurisdiction), and social problems related to economic matters (e.g., poverty and lack of affordable housing).

Returning to table 8.2, we find that there is variation in the coverage given to deviance in the economic sphere. Economic deviance is reported in greatest proportion in newspapers (26 per cent) followed by radio (21 per cent) and television (17 per cent). As was the case with the reporting of violence, NQ is the outlier in the reporting of economic deviance. Almost one-third of deviance and control stories in NQ are in the economic area, reflecting the economic and business orientation of this newspaper. There is a statistically significant difference between NQ (30 per cent) and NP (20 per cent) in the reporting of economic deviance, and between RQ (26 per cent) and RP (16 per cent).

The reporting of economic *crimes* was rare in all news outlets. Ordinary property crimes, such as theft or burglary, were not reported unless there was an unusual twist. Moreover, the reporting of such stories was almost entirely confined to the popular outlets. For example, RQ reported in an anchor-brief that 'in Louisville, Kentucky a woman on welfare was arraigned today on charges that she taught children to shoplift in an alleged scheme from the pages of Oliver Twist ... Police say [the accused], in a role similar to Fagin in the Charles Dickens novel, recruited the children to steal merchandise from department stores and give it to her. She would then return it to the stores for cash refunds.' NP reported that a man who broke into a home and stole $16,000 worth of goods made his escape in a taxi, but ran into difficulty when he tried to pay the taxi fare with some of the goods. This item, headlined, 'Cabby refuses $16Gs booty as fare,' leads with the statement that 'a man who tried to pay a cabby with stolen property has been charged in connection with a $16,000 burglary. The cab driver sped off with a trunkload of stolen goods after a man threatened him with a knife for refusing the property as cab fare.'

Much more common in all news outlets were reports of violation of trust, with or without criminal aspects or criminal charges being laid. The reporting of 'white collar' economic crimes in this regard was much more frequent than the reporting of 'blue collar' theft and burglary. Misleading advertising, forgery of immigration documents, frauds by charities and other fund-raising enterprises, fraudulent airline tickets, dealers turning back the odometer readings on used cars, 'kick-backs' on purchases, income-tax evasion, and fraudulent conversion of funds belonging to an employer were featured in quality and popular outlets alike.

NQ was an outlier because of the particular attention it gave to organized crime, questionable business practices, and legal conflicts over property. Many of these items appeared in the special business section of the newspaper. While NP also had a business section, it was substantially smaller in size and scope than that of NQ, and gave relatively little attention to economic deviance.

POLITICAL

In the category of 'political' deviance we included actions by political authorities (e.g., law-enforcement procedure violations, human-rights violations, jurisdictional disputes), actions by subjects in challenges to political authority (e.g., civil disobedience, violent protests, subversion, sabotage, refusal to submit to controls), and violations of administrative procedures (e.g., professional malpractice).

As documented in table 8.2, there is variation across the news outlets in the coverage given to political deviance. The major differences are between markets in newspapers and television, with quality outlets giving more attention to political deviance. NQ (38 per cent) was somewhat more likely to focus on political deviance than was NP (34 per cent), while TQ (46 per cent) was significantly more likely than was TP (27 per cent) to include items addressing political deviance. This substantial difference within television relates to TQ's institutional focus as a quality outlet within the national broadcasting network, which meant a greater use of feeds from both foreign sources and its own network regarding international and national political events.

The quality outlets, and especially NQ, focused on procedural propriety in government and the professions. All outlets gave attention to serious acts of 'terrorism,' for example, IRA bombings in Ireland, a bombing at Orly airport in Paris, and a shooting during a rally outside the Indian consulate in Toronto. There was also substantial attention by all outlets to local political protests and demonstrations, especially anti–cruise missile protests at the legislature, and pro-choice and pro-life demonstrations outside a free standing abortion clinic.

IDEOLOGICAL

'Ideological' deviance refers to conflicts over political ideologies (e.g., stories or opinion columns framed in terms of capitalism versus socialism or communism), cultural ideologies (e.g., efforts to influence beliefs and values regarding multiculturalism, language rights, ethnic or racial discrimination), and information control (e.g., official secrecy, propaganda, libel actions).

As evidenced in table 8.2, the reporting of ideological deviance was rare, especially in the broadcast outlets. The newspapers gave more attention to this area of deviance, although in very different ways. NQ focused on specific issues in cultural ideology, such as language rights. NQ also had several items relating to freedom of the press, including wire material from abroad regarding serious violations and acts of censorship. Many of NP's items, in contrast, were opinion columns attacking opposing political ideologies, especially socialism and communism.

DIVERSIONARY

'Diversionary' forms of deviance refer primarily to 'morality' crimes or moral regulation regarding the distribution and use of alcohol and other drugs, pornography, gambling, and prostitution. This category also refers to the regulation of leisure activities, such as video games and sporting events.

As indicated in table 8.2, diversionary forms of deviance were reported infrequently. The single most prevalent topic was drug abuse. Items on this topic were typically presented as stories of control, e.g., a major drug 'bust' locally or abroad; the arrest, charging, conviction, or sentencing of someone for a drug-related violation; and features on the levels of drug abuse and efforts at control. Within these drug-related items, the most common were briefs that announced the arrest, charging, conviction, or sentencing of a public figure for illegal possession of drugs, e.g., the son of a politician, members of a football team, and entertainers. The bulk of these items were American-based and off the wires. In these items it is not only the 'personality' or 'powerful figure' who is newsworthy but also what he or she represents in the moral scheme of things. He or she is represented as a fallen idol, someone who carries a particular responsibility to be morally respectable but who has now let people down. His or her failure to signify a commitment to the moral order is used as an occasion to represent what that order is.

Types of Crime and Deviance

Three basic types of deviance traversed the areas of deviance considered in the last section. These types include deviance in interpersonal relations, violations of civil or human rights by the more powerful in relation to the less powerful, and overt challenges to the powerful by the less powerful. In table 8.3 we document the proportionate frequency with which these types of deviance were reported in each of the six news outlets.

INTERPERSONAL

Interpersonal deviance refers to disputes and attendant imputations of deviance arising out of social relations. Most items in this category involve the 'sex and violence' formula that is typical of the news in general and popular news media in particular (Graber 1980: esp. 32ff; Ditton and Duffy 1982). While sexual harassment and assault, and other forms of violent assault, are serious social problems, there are other 'violent' events and conditions – such as those caused by unsafe vehicles and road conditions, unhealthy and unsafe work environments, and unsafe living conditions – that are arguably more harmful to greater numbers of people (Reasons, Ross, and Patterson 1981; Carson 1982). However, these events and conditions are underreported relative to individual acts of violent assault and the arrest, prosecution, and punishment of those who commit them. This suggests that newsworthiness does not reside in the perceived harm caused by an act or condition of deviance. Rather, newsworthiness is a matter of the type of infractions or rules that have been violated and their relation to symbolic order.

As indicated in table 8.3, there is significant variation in the reporting of interpersonal deviance by medium and markets. A medium comparison reveals that on a proportionate basis, television news (24 per cent) paid greater attention to matters of interpersonal deviance than did radio (22 per cent) or the newspapers (17 per cent). In terms of market, the popular outlets emphasize the 'sex and violence' formula of interpersonal-disputes coverage. The difference is considerable in television (31 per cent of TP items and 20 per cent of TQ items) and substantial in newspapers (26 per cent of NP items and 10 per cent of NQ items).

RIGHTS VIOLATIONS

As theorized in chapter 1, contemporary public discourse is centred on the propriety of official actions. The focus on procedural propriety is directed at a determination of whether official actions are arbitrary exercises of power, or, alternatively, indicate that officials are acting properly and therefore that they should be accorded authority (legitimate power). At the core of this discourse is talk about justice, equality, fairness, and rights, often formulated in the terms of law and legal authority.

As documented in table 8.3, 'rights talk' was a feature of deviance-and-control items in all news outlets. There is no significant variation by

TABLE 8.3
Types of deviance

Deviance	Newspaper Q	Newspaper P	Television Q	Television P	Radio Q	Radio P	Sig. diff.
Interpersonal	27 9.8%	56 26.4%	63 19.8%	66 31.0%	49 20.2%	53 23.8%	N/T
Rights violations	60 21.7%	35 16.5%	74 23.3%	26 12.2%	49 20.2%	44 19.7%	T
Challenges to authorities	20 7.2%	26 12.3%	48 15.1%	27 12.7%	30 12.3%	29 13.0%	
Other	169 61.2%	95 44.8%	133 41.8%	94 44.1%	115 47.3%	97 43.5%	M/N
Total stories	276	212	318	213	243	223	1,485

Percentages are by column. Tests of significance based on tables with types of deviance dichotomized into 'yes/no' for each of the categories. The last column indicates comparisons that show significant differences, i.e., chi-square statistics significant at the 0.05 level with Cramer's V or PHI ≥ 0.10, when N is large. Significant differences may occur between the newspapers (N); television stations (T); radio stations (R); or among the three types of media (M). The last column also indicates the presence of significant interactions with the variables being analysed and the coders (C) in a separate log-linear analysis.

medium or market orientation except that TQ (23 per cent) had a much higher level than did TP (12 per cent). This difference between TQ and TP relates to the local-news orientation of TP – with an emphasis on city-based activities including 'street life,' public order, and crime control – as contrasted with the national and international political focus of TQ. Given the institutional-news emphasis of NQ, and its attention to national and international politics, it is surprising that it did not give even greater emphasis to rights violations, especially in comparison to NP, which had a local-news orientation similar to TP's. RQ's level of attention to rights-violations is lower than one would expect for a quality outlet because the RQ newscast sampled was designed for local news. RQ left national and international political coverage, and the rights-violations discourse charac-teristic of such coverage, to the national network news it transmitted at other times.

CHALLENGES TO AUTHORITIES

News also affords considerable coverage to those who challenge official authority, even if such coverage ultimately contributes to the marginalization of the protesters and secures the status quo (Gitlin 1980). Such challenges, whether in the form of violent protest and sabotage or quiet dissent and civil disobedience, obviously overlap with the previous two categories to a degree. Some challenges are violent, the difference here being that the violence is collective rather than individual. Some challenges are with reference to violation of rights, the difference here being that it is a major *policy* that is at issue (e.g., nuclear disarmament; abortion) rather than a specific, individual act of official-procedural deviance leading to a violation of rights. Challenges to authorities involved people in political movements who challenged *concepts* of power as opposed to individuals in power alleged to have violated official procedures. To the extent that members of political movements were violent, it was political collective violence aimed at changing concepts of power (Taylor 1986; Wagner-Pacifici 1986), rather than individual criminal violence aimed at family, friends, sex, or money (Boyd 1988).

As indicated in table 8.3, there are no significant differences in terms of medium or market in the extent to which challenges to authorities were covered. It is perhaps surprising that the popular outlets gave as much attention to this type of deviance as the quality outlets, and in particular that NP emphasized it more than did NQ, given the institutional focus of quality outlets. However, it should be kept in mind that most of the items in this category relate to major social issues at the time – in particular, nuclear disarmament and abortion on demand – which all outlets covered. Moreover, collective violence and disorder that arose in protests over these issues fit squarely with the popular-news emphasis on violence and disorder of all types. The dramatic, conflictual, simple, personalized (through political movement leaders) formula of the 'good guys' versus the 'bad guys' is as easy to format in challenges to authorities as it is in relation to interpersonal disputes. It makes good news.

The category 'other' appearing in table 8.3 is a residual category for all other types of deviance that appeared with less frequency than did interpersonal deviance, rights violations, and challenges to authorities. NQ is the outlier in this category, indicating that it covered much less of the three main types of deviance taken together than did the other five outlets. These data also point to the fact that NQ covered a greater range of types of deviance than did the other outlets. This was partly a function of the greater overall news space available in NQ, meaning it covered what other outlets covered to a degree but other things in addition.

Institutional Context of Person Involved in Crime and Deviance

A major function of news of deviance is the policing of organizational life in important institutions in society. Journalists focus on crime, corruption,

negligence, mismanagement, and procedural impropriety to foster accountability and effect change in the organizations concerned, and to provide
general lessons about institutional order.

Government institutions are the primary locus and focus of news (e.g.,
Sigal 1973; Tuchman 1978: esp. 163–4; Royal Commission on Newspapers
[RCN] 1981c; Herman 1986). Moreover, even when non-governmental
institutions, organizations, and individuals are covered, the reports are
usually framed in terms of official government reactions and categories (e.g.,
Fishman 1980; Gitlin 1980). This framing occurs in particular when an
individual citizen is subject to imputations of deviance, such as allegations
that he or she has committed a criminal offence: such imputations will be
reported only when they have been officially processed and classified by the
police or other official agency (Fishman 1980; Ericson, Baranek, and Chan
1987). This framing also occurs when a community organization mobilizes
for political reform: such mobilization will be reported only when it has
been officially responded to by the appropriate governmental agency.

There is also a special place for the private corporate sector. One aspect
of private corporate power is the ability to stay out of the news (Tuchman
1978: 164; RCN 1981c: 21; D. Schiller 1986; Ericson, Baranek, and Chan
1989: chap. 5). When private corporations are reported on, the coverage is
often more favourable than that accorded to governmental institutions
(Winter and Frizzle 1979). Indeed, business and corporate activity is often
incorporated into the special section of a newspaper that articulates business
interests, including their economic difficulties in face of governmental
interference (Baer 1981: 226). Moreover, a lot of what is included in the
news sections regarding governmental activities, and deviance in official
offices, can be read as useful 'intelligence' for private corporate decisions
and activities (Warshett 1981: 190).

In table 8.4 we document the institutional contexts of persons subject
to imputations of deviance in the 1,485 news items sampled. This table
indicates that, while most deviant designations were in relation to officials
in government, there was also considerable attention to people in private
corporate roles and in community organizations. A substantial number of
individuals, without an organization affiliation relevant to their deviance,
were also subject to reports. Moreover, there was significant variation among
the six news outlets in terms of the institutional locus of their imputations
of deviance.

GOVERNMENT

Table 8.4 shows medium and market variation regarding items that reported
on government officials involved in deviance. The variation by market

254 Representing Order

TABLE 8.4
Institutional context of persons involved in deviance

Institutional context	Newspaper		Television		Radio		Sig. diff.
	Q	P	Q	P	Q	P	
Government	138	60	138	55	82	82	N/T
	50.0%	28.3%	43.4%	25.8%	33.7%	36.8%	
Private corporate	53	47	60	49	69	43	R
	19.2%	22.2%	18.9%	23.0%	28.4%	19.3%	
Community groups	39	33	54	25	27	20	
	14.1%	15.6%	17.0%	11.7%	11.1%	9.0%	
Individuals	19	64	28	48	30	53	N/T/R
	6.9%	30.2%	8.8%	22.5%	12.3%	23.8%	C
Not applicable/ Don't know	27	8	38	36	35	25	
	9.8%	3.8%	11.9%	16.9%	14.4%	11.2%	
Total stories	276	212	318	213	243	223	1,485

Percentages are by column. Tests of significance based on tables with institutional context of persons involved in deviance dichotomized into 'yes/no' for each of the categories. The last column indicates comparisons that show significant differences, i.e., chi-square statistics significant at the 0.05 level with Cramer's V or PHI ≥ 0.10, when N is large. Significant differences may occur between the newspapers (N); television stations (T); radio stations (R); or among the three types of media (M). The last column also indicates the presence of significant interactions with the variables being analysed and the coders (C) in a separate log-linear analysis.

orientation is significant. Within newspapers, NQ (50 per cent) was almost twice as likely as NP (28 per cent) to publish items imputing deviance to officials in government. This divergence underscores the institutional-news emphasis of NQ as a watch-dog of government, while NP focused its news of deviance much more on aberrant individuals outside institutional contexts. Similarly in television, TQ (43 per cent) focused in particular on deviance in government while TP (26 per cent) gave much less attention to government deviance in favour of focusing its gaze elsewhere, including on the portrayal of individual deviance outside institutional contexts. Although TQ was itself an agency of government, its primary search for deviance was in other government agencies. The same pattern did not hold for radio, with RQ (34 per cent) actually giving slightly less attention to the deviance of government officials than did RP (37 per cent). However, this is a reflection of the fact that the RQ newscast we studied was oriented to local and regional events whereas the RP newscast included national and international stories that focused on government deviance at home and abroad. It is likely that a content analysis of the separate national network newscasts picked up by RQ would reveal substantially more items on deviance by government officials in Canada and abroad.

PRIVATE CORPORATE

As documented in table 8.4, while each news outlet gave less attention to deviance in private corporate contexts than in government contexts, there was still substantial attention to the private corporate sphere. Indeed, NP, TP, and RQ gave almost as much attention to deviance by people in private corporate settings as to deviance by officials in government.

In terms of the proportionate coverage of private corporate deviance, the outlier is RQ (28 per cent), which had significantly more items on private corporate deviance than did RP (19 per cent), and much more than any of the other news outlets. NQ (19 per cent) had the second-lowest proportion of items on deviance by persons in the private corporate sector. This finding is noteworthy, given that NQ had a substantial business section and made frequent use of private corporate sources in many other sections. While NQ reported on corporate deviance regularly, it did so with much less frequency than it did on government deviance. What these data suggest is that NQ focused disproportionately on deviance in government as a source of 'intelligence' for its private corporate constituency. While news of private corporate deviance is also of importance to this constituency, it is the daily barometer of the procedural propriety of governments, which is of primary interest to private corporate officials who generally like to keep their own affairs private (Ericson, Baranek, and Chan 1989; Tuchman 1978; Herman 1986; D. Schiller 1986).

COMMUNITY GROUPS

Deviance by persons in 'community groups' was covered much less frequently than government or private corporate deviance (table 8.4). There is no significant medium and market variation in relation to community-organization deviance. While popular news outlets tended to have more of a community-group focus as part of their 'vox pop' orientation (see chapter 7), this did not include a disproportionate emphasis on the deviant actions of members of such groups.

INDIVIDUALS

Deviance by 'individuals' refers to news items that reported on the deviant acts of people who were not acting in an organizational or institutional capacity. Typical of items in this category are reports of violent crime committed by individuals.

As indicated in table 8.4, there is significant variation among the six news outlets in reporting deviance by individuals. While there is little variation by medium, there is substantial variation in terms of market orientation. Within each medium, the popular outlets gave disproportionate attention to deviance by individuals. Within newspapers, NP (30 per cent) devoted almost one-third of its deviance-and-control items to acts of deviance by individuals, whereas NQ (7 per cent) gave very little attention to deviance occurring outside of institutional contexts. Within television, TP (23 per cent) provided many more items on deviance by individuals than did TQ (9 per cent). The same pattern holds for radio, with RP (24 per cent) reporting deviance far more often than did RQ (12 per cent).

These data underscore that the particular focus of the popular outlets, compared to their quality-market counterparts, was on 'sex and violence' and 'street crime' stripped of organizational and institutional contexts. The popular outlets focused in particular on dangerous individuals committing serious crimes, moral-character portraits of them, and fear and loathing about them (see chapter 4). They were less oriented to violence by private corporations and governments, although NP did traffic in items emphasizing the dangers of foreign communist and socialist states, including portraits of their deviant character and characters, and fear and loathing about them. The quality outlets, especially in television and newspapers, focused instead on being watch-dogs of government officials. The specific fields that were subject to their gaze are addressed in the following section.

Institutional Field of Person Involved in Crime and Deviance

While they have all of organized life as their potential sphere of operation, journalists focus more narrowly on particular institutional fields. The news staples are politics, health, and law enforcement, rather than, say, architecture, engineering, and forestry. Fields such as politics, law enforcement, and health are central to the functioning of the news media as participants in the production of social, political, and moral orders, and as barometers of these orders. The price to be paid for being in a field that is subject to the media spotlight is potential exposure of glaring errors as well as glorious achievements.

In table 8.5 we document the institutional fields of persons involved in imputations of deviance in the 1,485 news items sampled. Table 8.5 indicates the six fields in which most deviant designations were made – politics, culture, health, trade/finance, law enforcement/public safety, and military – and the variation in the fields focused on in the news outlets studied.

POLITICS

'Politics' refers to imputations of deviance about persons in political office or in a political party. As shown in table 8.5, there is significant medium

TABLE 8.5
Institutional field of persons involved in deviance

Institutional field	Newspaper		Television		Radio		Sig. diff.
	Q	P	Q	P	Q	P	
Politics	62	37	57	27	26	26	M
	22.5%	17.5%	17.9%	12.7%	10.7%	11.7%	
Culture	35	25	16	19	12	14	M
	12.7%	11.8%	5.0%	8.9%	4.9%	6.3%	
Health	10	21	23	15	32	25	N
	3.6%	9.9%	7.2%	7.0%	13.2%	11.2%	
Trade/finance	31	15	40	20	38	16	R
	11.2%	7.1%	12.6%	9.4%	15.6%	7.2%	
Law enforcement/ public safety	15	14	27	11	27	26	
	5.4%	6.6%	8.5%	5.2%	11.1%	11.7%	
Military	43	11	53	10	10	19	N/T/C
	15.6%	5.2%	16.7%	4.7%	4.1%	8.5%	
Other	36	17	36	24	39	27	
	13.0%	8.0%	11.3%	11.3%	16.0%	12.1%	
Not applicable/ Don't know	44	72	66	87	59	70	
	15.9%	34.0%	20.8%	40.8%	24.3%	31.4%	
Total stories	276	212	318	213	243	223	1,485

Percentages are by column. Tests of significance based on tables with institutional field of persons involved in deviance dichotomized into 'yes/no' for each of the categories. The last column indicates comparisons that show significant differences, i.e., chi-square statistics significant at the 0.05 level with Cramer's V or PHI ≥ 0.10, when N is large. Significant differences may occur between the newspapers (N); television stations (T); radio stations (R); or among the three types of media (M). The last column also indicates the presence of significant interactions with the variables being analysed and the coders (C) in a separate log-linear analysis.

variation in the coverage of deviance in politics, with the newspapers (20 per cent) giving more attention to this field than did television (16 per cent) and especially radio (11 per cent). While there is no significant variation in market orientation, NQ (23 per cent) is the outlier, and TQ (18 per cent) had as much coverage of deviants in politics as did NP (18 per cent) and considerably more than did TP (13 per cent) or the radio stations.

CULTURE

'Culture' refers to designations of deviance against people working in a range of cultural activities or industries, e.g., the mass media, publishing, entertainment, sports, and the arts. This category also incorporates instances in which deviant imputations were made about people working in fields related to culture, such as those concerning language, ethnic and racial equality, religion, and 'multiculturalism.' As table 8.5 indicates, the newspapers (12 per cent) were more likely to include items concerning deviance in the field of culture than was television (7 per cent) or radio (6 per cent). There are no substantial differences in terms of market orientation. NQ focused in particular on deviance in the mass media. In the popular outlets, especially in NP and TP, there was particular emphasis on entertainers and sport figures gone wrong through drug abuse or other disreputable pleasures.

HEALTH

'Health' refers to imputations of deviance against people responsible for various aspects of medical care, and for environmental and occupational health standards and practices. The issue of practices and standards in nursing homes was prominent at the time, and several items in each outlet involved imputations of deviance regarding this specific issue. There were also inquests focusing on deaths of persons while under care of the medical health system. These inquests were covered by all outlets. As detailed in table 8.5, the health field was given more prominence by the radio outlets than by television or the newspapers. Within the newspapers NP (10 per cent) gave significantly more attention to this field than did NQ (4 per cent).

TRADE AND FINANCE

'Trade and finance' refers to imputations of deviance about the activities of persons working in, for example, manufacturing, banking, and construction industries. Table 8.5 records the fact that coverage of deviants in the trade-and-finance field did not vary substantially by medium. However, within markets RQ (16 per cent) gave much more attention to this field than did RP (7 per cent). Furthermore, while NQ devoted substantial space to business news, this space was not taken up with news of deviants in business to a substantially greater extent than space in NP (11 per cent of NQ items and 7 per cent of NP items). Indeed, the quality broadcast outlets were more likely than NQ to focus on deviants in the trade-and-finance field.

LAW ENFORCEMENT AND PUBLIC SAFETY

'Law enforcement and public safety' refers to imputations of deviance against police officers, court officials, prison officials, and others concerned with public safety. Table 8.5 records the fact that the news outlets did not vary substantially in coverage of deviance by law-enforcers. While qualities focus on policing the police and other law-enforcers, the populars also include this material along with their focus on 'normal crime discourse' and its affinity with law-enforcers (Ericson, Baranek, and Chan 1989: chaps. 2, 3).

MILITARY

'Military' refers to imputations of deviance against military officials at home and abroad. As detailed in table 8.5, there is significant variation by markets regarding deviance in the military field. NQ (16 per cent) had far more of such items than did NP (5 per cent), and TQ (17 per cent) had far more than did TP (5 per cent). These substantial differences reflect the fact that both NQ and TQ included far more foreign news items than did their popular counterparts, and a lot of the foreign coverage was of military conflicts. Within radio, RP (9 per cent) broadcast more items in the military field than did RQ (4 per cent). This difference is related to the fact that RP incorporated foreign-news items into the particular show we studied, while RQ did so rarely, leaving such coverage to its national network.

Types of Knowledge about Crime and Deviance

PRIMARY

As evidenced in table 8.6, primary (factual) understanding was an element in all items in all news outlets. Stories of deviance invariably include a description of what is taken to be deviant. Sometimes the description alone is given, although usually it is related to some combination of explanations, expressions of impact, evaluations, and recommendations. As emphasized previously, primary facts are not given in the world but rather are interpreted, constituted, and propounded by those who make use of them. The factual is constituted in terms of intentions and contexts, and therefore the facts blend and bend with explanations and values. Factual descriptions not only denote what happened, but also connote reasons, motives, explanations, justifications, excuses, values, attitudes, and recommendations at the same time (Hartley 1982; Runciman 1983; Geertz 1983). A lot depends on who is espousing the factual description. For example, a core characteristic of news discourse is that the facts are made reputable through having them enunciated by authoritative sources. News discourse uses 'people in the know' to say it is so, to witness normatively the facts so that readers will accept them as facts. How primary factual descriptions mesh with other levels of understanding and assessment is analysed in subsequent sections.

TABLE 8.6
Types of knowledge about deviance

Types of knowledge	Newspaper		Television		Radio		Sig. diff.
	Q	P	Q	P	Q	P	
Primary	276	212	318	213	243	223	
	100.0%	100.0%	100.0%	100.0%	100.0%	100.0%	
Secondary	89	78	103	53	59	43	M
	32.2%	36.8%	32.4%	24.9%	24.3%	19.3%	
Tertiary	16	30	36	35	9	9	M/N
	5.8%	14.2%	11.3%	16.4%	3.7%	4.0%	
Evaluation	145	90	123	75	79	74	M/N
	52.5%	42.5%	38.7%	35.2%	32.5%	33.2%	
Recommenda-tion	97	59	65	46	66	53	M
	35.1%	27.8%	20.4%	21.6%	27.2%	23.8%	
Total stories	276	212	318	213	243	223	1,485

Percentages are by column. Tests of significance based on tables with types of knowledge about deviance dichotomized into 'yes/no' for each of the categories. The last column indicates comparisons that show significant differences, i.e., chi-square statistics significant at the 0.05 level with Cramer's V or PHI ≥ 0.10, when N is large. Significant differences may occur between the newspapers (N); television stations (T); radio stations (R); or among the three types of media (M). The last column also indicates the presence of significant interactions with the variables being analysed and the coders (C) in a separate log-linear analysis.

SECONDARY

Table 8.6 records the fact that secondary knowledge (explanation) was present in only a minority of items in each news outlet. However, there is significant variation by medium, with more explanations in newspapers (34 per cent) than in television (29 per cent) or radio (22 per cent). There are no significant differences by market orientation. What is especially noteworthy in this regard is that NQ (32 per cent) actually had slightly fewer explanations than did NP (37 per cent). The quality newspaper might be expected to include more explanations as part of its lengthier items and claims about offering greater 'analysis' and 'depth.'

Our finding on the extent of secondary understanding is consistent with the view in the research literature that the news downplays explanations. Moreover, when explanations are given, they are typically inseparable from political processes of evaluation and the laying of blame. Causal explanations and political causes are inseparable (for empirical instances, see Tumber 1982; Gusfield 1981; Nelson 1984; Voumvakis and Ericson 1984;

Wagner-Pacifici 1986). As Turney (1988: 11) observes, 'When misfortune strikes, explanation and blame are inseparable. Environmental calamity offers the clearest examples: dead seals, dying trees, flood in Bangladesh, holes in the ozone layer. Debate about causes is inextricably bound up with responsibility, even when the argument is that no one is responsible.'

These observations are applicable to the deviance-and-control items we sampled. Further analysis in this regard is provided in the subsequent section, 'Explanations of Crime and Deviance,' and in the case examples presented in chapters 4 and 5. Both sources and journalists are more concerned with the blaming aspect than with analytical explanations and understandings (Bolton 1986; Ericson, Baranek, and Chan 1989). The result is erasure of certain kinds of explanations, especially those that address process and structure. Indeed, the lack of analytical attention to causation, in combination with other news conventions such as simplification and personalization, largely explains why the news usually fails to question seriously basic values but rather reproduces them in representations of order.

TERTIARY

Tertiary knowledge is empathetic. It transmits experience and plays on emotions. As a matter of the heart as well as the head, tertiary knowledge is sometimes overwhelming, even to the point where the meaning of the item is missed by the consumer. This overwhelming impact is especially likely in television, with its powerful visual capacities.

As documented in table 8.6, tertiary knowledge was not prevalent in any of the news outlets. Television (13 per cent) included significantly more tertiary understanding than the newspapers (9 per cent) or radio (4 per cent). Furthermore, within television and the newspapers, the popular outlets included tertiary understanding more often. The difference was significant between the newspapers, with NP including tertiary understanding in 14 per cent of its items compared to NQ's inclusion of it in only 6 per cent of its items. As discussed in our analysis of types of knowledge offered by sources (chapter 7), TP and NP gave particular emphasis to 'fear and loathing' reactions from citizens about criminal victimization, accidents, and disasters they were involved in or close to (see also chapter 4).

EVALUATION

Evaluations are often embedded in the three levels of knowledge analysed above, and they may also carry recommendations for control action. This explains why evaluations are very often a component of news of deviance and control, appearing in anywhere from one-third to one-half of the items sampled (table 8.6). Evaluations were most prevalent in newspaper items (48 per cent), followed by television (37 per cent) and radio (33 per cent). The higher proportion of evaluative items in the newspapers is explained by their inclusion of formats that are explicitly evaluative, such as editorials, opinion columns, and letters to the editor. Within the newspaper medium, NQ (53 per cent) had significantly more evaluative knowledge in its deviance-and-control items than did NP (43 per cent). This finding may be related to the fact that, by chance, our sampling method yielded an overrepresentation of items on the editorial pages of NQ. However, it is also consistent with the prevailing view in the local news-media culture, including the view of regular news sources we interviewed (Ericson, Baranek, and Chan 1989), that NP's *news* items conveyed a greater sense of factuality than did NQ's, which were perceived as being more evaluative, with multiple connotations.

RECOMMENDATIONS

News discourse tends to present recommendations in terms of opposing interests, and to have the proponents of each interest position formulate their recommendations in terms of competing primary facts. This approach typically results in 'endless' debate and lack of resolution, because the problem is not a matter of factuality but of frame-conflicts. Frame-conflicts cannot be resolved in these terms because each frame already has all of the relevant facts embedded in it.

The data in table 8.6 indicate significant variation by medium in the inclusion of recommendations, with the newspapers (32 per cent) again being highest, followed by radio (26 per cent) and television (21 per cent). There are no significant variations in terms of market orientation, although NQ (35 per cent) is higher than NP (28 per cent), suggesting further that it had more of an interpretive and institutional policing orientation than did NP.

These data are instructive about the formal properties of knowledge of deviance in the news. They address important questions in the research literature concerning the *extent* to which news discourse conveys facts, explanations, empathy, evaluations, and recommendations. However, they fail to provide knowledge about how these types of knowledge are actually employed in news discourse. Such knowledge is offered in the detailed case examples presented in chapters 4 and 5.

Headlines

The headline is an additional and special format for presenting knowledge of deviance. In newspapers, the headline is presented in large and/or bold-face type at the head of the item. In broadcast news, the headline is presented in two ways. At the top of the show there are bulletin-like announcements stating the major items to be reported during the show. In some instances, such as in quality BBC radio newscasts, such headlines are more analogous to 'the table of contents which somewhat inconspicuously runs down the side of the front page of quality newspapers ... [They] are not closely analogous to newspaper headlines and their length implies not sensationalism but quality and depth – a perspective on the news and on current affairs' (Crisell 1986: 89).

In the broadcast outlets we studied, the opening headlines did function more like sensational newspaper headlines, serving as 'teasers' to arouse the interest of readers and to keep them tuned in and turned on for the duration of the show. This was also the function of broadcast-news headlines that appeared during the show, just before a commercial break. These 'teasers' were designed to ensure that the reader would stay tuned in through and after the commercials. Such devices are especially important in broadcast news, which must hold the reader's attention through successive items of news and advertising in order to sustain market share.

In the news outlets we studied, headlines were common in the newspapers but rare in broadcast news. Headlines appeared with 90 per cent of the newspaper items, with more in NQ (93 per cent) than in NP (86 per cent). Headlines or teasers appeared with 22 per cent of television items, with significantly more in TQ (26 per cent) than in TP (15 per cent). Headlines were even more rare in radio, appearing with only 19 per cent of items. Moreover, there was a significant difference between the radio outlets, with RP using headlines with 29 per cent of its items whereas RQ used them with only 10 per cent of its items. The fact that RQ was the outlier among the broadcast outlets is explained by its commercial-free dimension. While it used headlines or teasers at the top of the show to make the listener interested in what was to follow, it did not have to use the same technique to entice listeners to stay tuned over subsequent commercial breaks.

A scrutiny of the headlines that were used in each news outlet reveals the following types of knowledge: control action, primary understanding, background information, evaluations, recommendations, and other. The proportionate frequency with which each of these headline types appeared, and their variation across news outlets, is summarized in table 8.7.

'Control action' refers to statements in headlines that describe actions taken by persons involved in the events reported on. As documented in table 8.7, this was the type of knowledge that appeared most frequently in the headlines of all news outlets, especially the broadcast outlets. Indeed, within radio, the vast majority of headlines described control actions being taken. The television outlets also described control actions in the majority of headlines. Both radio and television used this type of knowledge in headlines to a greater degree than did the newspapers. A description of control action

TABLE 8.7
Types of knowledge in news headlines

Types of knowledge	News outlets NQ		NP		TQ		TP		RQ		RP		Sig. diff.
	N	%	N	%	N	%	N	%	N	%	N	%	
Control action	104	40.5	80	44.0	40	48.8	20	62.5	18	78.3	40	61.5	M
Primary	53	20.6	38	20.9	19	23.2	7	21.8	4	17.4	12	18.4	
Background	33	12.8	17	9.3	7	8.5	1	3.1	0	0.0	4	6.2	
Evaluations	31	12.1	18	9.9	4	4.9	2	6.3	1	4.3	5	7.7	
Recommendations	26	10.1	11	6.0	2	2.4	0	0.0	0	0.0	3	4.7	M
Other	10	3.9	18	9.9	10	12.2	2	6.3	0	0.0	1	1.5	M/N
Totals	257	100.0	182	100.0	82	100.0	32	100.0	23	100.0	65	100.0	

Tests of significance based on tables with types of knowledge dichotomized into 'yes/no' for each of the categories. The last column indicates comparisons that show significant differences: chi-square statistics significant at the 0.05 level with Cramer's V or PHI ≥ 0.10, when N is large. Significant differences may occur between the newspapers (N); television stations (T); radio stations (R); or among the three types of media (M).

is part of the 'aliveness' and 'present-tense' the broadcast media convey in their news items. These elements are, in turn, related to the dramatic-structuring imperatives of broadcast news, and to the need to hold the attention of consumers through successive items. In newspapers, control-action headlines are used to draw the reader's attention to the item as he or she scans the newspaper and selects what seems interesting to read.

'Primary' facts directly relevant to the story were the second most frequently occurring type of knowledge in headlines. Primary knowledge occurred in roughly equal proportion in the headlines of each news outlet, accounting for about 20 per cent of headline material in each case.

'Background' understanding refers to material contained in headlines that was not directly relevant to the story but that nevertheless was designed to contextualize or supplement it in some way. As documented in table 8.7, such material was very rare in broadcast-news headlines. It is too peripheral and uninteresting in the context of how broadcast headlines must function as 'teasers' to keep their stories and consumers 'alive.' The newspapers, however, used background information more frequently.

'Evaluations' in headlines, involving assessments of whether someone or something was good or bad, followed the same pattern as background information in headlines (table 8.7). Evaluations appeared with some frequency in newspaper headlines, and in NQ marginally more than in NP. Many of these evaluative headlines headed editorials, opinion columns, letters to the editor, and other accepted formats for evaluative statements by journalists. In contrast, evaluations were very rare in the broadcast-news headlines. In broadcast news, headlines are in the voice of the anchor, who is to appear neutral. While the anchor can convey primary understanding and a vibrant sense of what is going on, it is out of place for him or her to add moral assessments in the headline context. In broadcast news, evaluations are derived from other sources and are used with a delicate sense of balance (see chapter 7). If evaluations were used frequently in the headline statements of anchors, they would serve to displease rather than tease, turning people off.

For the same reasons 'recommendations' were extremely rare in broadcast-news headlines. Recommendations appeared more often in NP and NQ headlines, although, again, these were frequently in the editorial columns, which are explicitly contextualized to give licence to journalists' recommendations as well as evaluations.

Leads

The lead statement is another important means by which journalists communicate the essence of the story and attract the reader to it. In newspapers, the lead is conveyed in the opening paragraph. In broadcast news, the lead is conveyed by the anchor, either in the opening sentence of an anchor-only story or in introducing an item involving a reporter. As Swope (1958) once remarked, 'the only two things people read in a story are the first and last sentences. Give them blood in the eye on the first one.'

Given the importance of the lead in indicating the angle of the story and the fact that the lead is often read even if other parts of the story are not, we decided to analyse the types of knowledge in leads and how they varied by medium and market. The results are summarized in table 8.8. These data, when compared with the data presented in table 8.7, indicate consistency in the types of knowledge emphasized in headlines and the types of knowledge emphasized in leads. There is also consistency in how the proportionate use of various types of knowledge in headlines and in leads varies by medium and market.

Almost half of the leads in newspapers and the majority of leads in broadcast news describe some control action taken by persons involved in the events reported on. There is substantial variation by medium in this regard, with radio (68 per cent) leads most often conveying control action, followed by television (58 per cent) and the newspapers (46 per cent). As is the case with headlines, control action is prevalent in leads because it conveys a sense that the news is alive, active, dramatic, addressing an event 'as-it-happens.' This sense attracts readers to the item and leads them to read on.

Primary knowledge was the second most frequently occurring type of knowledge in leads in each of the news outlets. Primary understanding was a little more prevalent within television (21 per cent) and newspaper (20 per cent) leads than within radio leads (14 per cent).

Background understanding was not used often in leads, although it appeared significantly more frequently in newspaper leads (11 per cent) than television (6 per cent) or radio (3 per cent) leads. In the newspapers, background information appeared with some frequency in opinion-format leads (e.g., in letters to the editor, editorials, opinion columns) by way of easing the reader into the particular slant.

Evaluations were also more common in the leads of newspapers than in those of radio or television. As with headlines, newspaper leads that were evaluations were frequently part of items in the editorial pages. As with headlines, broadcast-news leads were rarely evaluative because they emanated from the anchor, who is not mandated to evaluate news events, at least until they have been reported on. When evaluations were used in television-news leads, it was usually by way of introduction to special 'panel discussion' or 'commentary' slots explicitly formatted for evaluations.

TABLE 8.8
Types of knowledge in leads

Types of knowledge	News outlets NQ		NP		TQ		TP		RQ		RP		Sig. diff.
	N	%	N	%	N	%	N	%	N	%	N	%	
Control action	123	44.5	101	47.5	177	55.7	133	62.4	169	69.5	145	65.5	M
Primary	54	19.6	43	20.3	77	24.2	36	16.9	29	11.9	34	15.2	M
Background	33	12.0	22	10.4	13	4.1	17	8.0	5	2.1	10	4.5	
Evaluations	35	12.7	19	9.0	19	6.0	12	5.6	17	7.0	17	7.6	
Recommendations	18	6.5	12	5.7	10	3.1	7	3.3	14	5.8	12	5.4	
Other	13	4.7	15	7.1	22	6.9	8	3.8	9	3.7	5	1.8	
Totals	276	100.0	212	100.0	318	100.0	213	100.0	243	100.0	223	100.0	

Tests of significance based on tables with types of knowledge dichotomized into 'yes/no' for each of the categories. The last column indicates comparisons that show significant differences: chi-square statistics significant at the 0.05 level with Cramer's V or PHI ≥ 0.10, when N is large. Significant differences may occur between the newspapers (N); television stations (T); radio stations (R); or among the three types of media (M).

The level of recommendations in leads was very low. What we have said regarding evaluations in leads and headlines applies also to recommendations: it is rarely fitting for them to be a part of an anchor's lead into a broadcast-news item, but more fitting if they are used to introduce an opinion piece in either broadcast news or the newspapers. In general, for headlines as well as leads, in all news outlets, it was control action and/or primary facts that were used to both suggest the angle and hook the consumer.

Explanations of Crime and Deviance

As addressed earlier (pp. 260–1), there is relatively little attention paid to causal explanation in news discourse. For example, crime stories rarely address the causes of crime (Sherizen 1978; Dussuyer 1979; Graber 1980). Graber (1980: 70) reports that causes of crime were mentioned in only 4 per cent of the crime-news items she sampled.

A number of explanations have been given for why explanations are not a routine feature of news discourse. News imperatives work against explanation. The focus is on present-time, specific events, the individuals involved in those events, and the contingencies of the events. One consequence is that often 'what ought to be explained is treated as fact or assumption' (Tuchman 1978: 180). Moreover, the dramatic-structuring imperatives of news discourse reinforce the event-orientation, with the news event being stripped of its structural conditions, context, or linkages with other events. As Chibnall (1977: 79) has observed regarding the portrayal of violence in the news media: 'A violent act is more amenable to dramatization than are the conditions and processes which shape its development ... The causes of violence are more complex and intractable, less open to instant empathetic understanding. They cannot be checked and verified by the established procedures of news reporting because they are theoretical constructs which can only *inform* the collection of empirical material. They cannot themselves be directly observed and recorded by busy journalists in pursuit of 'facts.'' ' Beyond the format constraints of the medium and the organizational constraints of journalists, news sources often wish to eschew causal explanation, especially in terms of the structure and process of their own organizations (Ericson, Baranek, and Chan 1989). When sources do offer explanations, it is typically in pursuit of their own legitimacy and often through a process of blaming others (ibid). In their pursuit of news that is helpful in having social-control effects, sources themselves limit causal understanding and foster blockage or erasure of structural explanations.

There are difficulties in defining and determining what constitutes an explanation. Explanations in news discourse appear subtle in very enclosed forms that do not enhance causal understanding. When an explanation can be read into the news, it 'is more likely to be tacitly evoked by cues in the text or by the powerful master labels such as "violent" and "criminal" which carry unambiguous connotations and meld together disparate phenomena and their meanings' (Chibnall 1977: xi–xii). As such, explanations in the news are political. They are deployed stereotypically. The stereotypes are blended with imputations of motives, whether noble or blameworthy. The imputations of motives, in turn, carry excuses and justifications for behaviour.

It is interesting to note that one of the earliest approaches in sociology was designed as a political communication strategy to combat the labelling of criminals in newspapers. Shaw and Burgess of the Chicago School developed the life-histories approach to provide alternative views of the delinquent that would, in turn, carry different implications for policy. ' "While dramatization of a criminal act may serve to promote the financial interest of the newspaper, it contributes little to an understanding of the nature of the act" [C. Shaw, H. McKay, and J. McDonald, *Brothers in Crime* (Chicago: University of Chicago Press 1938), pp ix–x]. The newspaper usage of the term "The moron" calls up emotional reactions of indignation and vengeance; the phrase "the natural history of a delinquent career" invites a scientific inquiry into the causes of behaviour [C. Shaw *The Natural History of a Delinquent Career* (Chicago: University of Chicago Press 1931), p 235]' (Bennett 1981: 205–6).

This quotation points to another important component in the politics of explanation, namely, what is excluded. Through processes of simplification and stereotyping – which are related to the imperatives of news production, including the need for dramatic structuring – news discourse 'explains away' more than it explains. It 'explains away' deviance as part of the process of reaffirming reality and representing order. In the process, it 'erases' considerations of structure and political economy that may deconstruct reality and thereby destabilize our sense of order (O'Neill 1981). 'By concentrating only on the eruptions on the surface of social life, the news helps to make ... underlying structures invisible. They are simply "common sense" ' (Cayley 1982: 137).

Sensitive to the role of explanations in news discourse as specified above, we analysed explanations of deviance in the items we surveyed and how they varied by medium and market. The results of our analysis are summarized in table 8.9. These data are derived from the sample of sources, and the numbers refer to explanations attributed to sources. These data incorporate the fact that a given item may include multiple explanations attributed to one or more source.

The data in table 8.9 indicate that explanations of deviance were more prevalent in the quality outlets. The most frequently occurring explanations

TABLE 8.9
Explanations of deviance

Explanations	Newspaper		Television		Radio		Sig. diff.
	Q	P	Q	P	Q	P	
Organizational expedience	120 28.9%	68 26.6%	87 22.1%	49 25.3%	59 28.9%	40 26.8%	
Organizational pathology	29 7.0%	8 3.1%	28 7.1%	8 4.1%	7 3.4%	5 3.4%	
Rules and justice	64 15.4%	40 15.6%	87 22.1%	44 22.7%	45 22.1%	29 19.5%	
Dispute settlement	38 9.2%	20 7.8%	26 6.6%	4 2.1%	7 3.4%	9 6.0%	T
Group conflict	32 7.7%	17 6.6%	30 7.6%	13 6.7%	5 2.5%	7 4.7%	
Order maintenance	28 6.7%	12 4.7%	31 7.9%	16 8.2%	14 6.9%	7 4.7%	
Circumstances	16 3.9%	22 8.6%	24 6.1%	20 10.3%	17 8.3%	6 4.0%	N/C
Individual pathology	11 2.7%	20 7.8%	12 3.0%	10 5.2%	5 2.5%	8 5.4%	N
Other	77 18.6%	49 19.1%	69 17.5%	30 15.5%	45 22.1%	38 25.5%	
Total responses	415	256	394	194	204	149	1,612

Percentages are by column. Tests of significance based on tables with explanations of deviance dichotomized into 'yes/no' for each of the categories. The last column indicates comparisons that show significant differences, i.e., chi-square statistics significant at the 0.05 level with Cramer's V or PHI ≥ 0.10, when N is large. Significant differences may occur between the newspapers (N); television stations (T); radio stations (R); or among the three types of media (M). The last column also indicates the presence of significant interactions with the variables being analysed and the coders (C) in a separate log-linear analysis.

dealt with aspects of 'organizational expedience' or efficiency, and questions of 'rules and justice' or legitimacy. Considerations of efficiency and legitimacy dominate public discourse of crime, law, and justice (cf Scheppele 1988), while other explanations are relatively infrequent and are often linked in various ways to those dominant considerations.

ORGANIZATIONAL EXPEDIENCE

'Organizational expedience' refers to mechanisms of bureaucratic efficiency and interest that are said to have precipitated deviant actions. These mechanisms include, for example, cost-reduction measures; expediency in expenditures and practices regarding personnel; and competitive business practices. Such attributions were common in all news outlets, with little variation by medium or market.

Attributions regarding organizational expedience were common in stories on a wide variety of topics. A significant component of public discourse in contemporary society relates to the acquisition and control of resources to promote particular professional and bureaucratic interests. A well-publicized act of deviance, or sustained attention to a social problem, provides the occasion for various bureaucratic and professional interest groups to claim that they can respond better if they are provided with more resources. The modern answer to a lot of problems is 'to throw money at it.' The hope is that the problem will go away, if not literally, at least in the sense that it will be handled by a specialized professional and bureaucratic body who will manage it, keep it relatively invisible, and save everyone else from having to worry about it. For example, the response to the 'drug problem' – often personalized and symbolized through the tragic circumstances or death of an otherwise respectable youth 'on drugs' – is to hire more police, intensify anti-drug education campaigns in schools and mass media, and so on. Ignored are myriad ways in which drugs are promoted and normalized in everyday life (Boyd 1983). Also ignored is the fact that intensified control can facilitate and escalate the very thing it seeks to control, at the same time also intensifying public concern about the problem (Marx 1981, 1988; S. Cohen 1985).

Many of the sources who provided 'organizational expediency' explanations were members of organizations charged with the provision of a public service. They used occasions when there were imputations of deviance regarding the provision of their services to indicate that other problems, related to organizational expedience, explained (or explained away) the deviance; and to suggest explicitly or implicitly that these other problems could be dealt with by the infusion of more resources (for detailed examples, see Ericson, Baranek, and Chan 1989). For example, in the course of a public inquiry into deaths of babies at a local children's hospital – with the belief by many that a hospital-staff member had killed at least some of the babies – the head of the unit concerned attributed the deaths to nursing staff shortages combined with oversubscription of facilities. The audio portion of TP's coverage of the unit head's testimony at the inquiry is illustrative.

Anchor: Babies may have died at the Hospital for Sick Children because of a shortage of nurses. The Grange probe into mysterious deaths at the hospital today heard testimony from [names source], the head of cardiology.

Source: You have to realize that there is a shortage of nurses during that time. There was considerable difficulty in getting replacements for those who're on vacation and those sick, there's a lot – there were a lot of times when I understand that doubling-up of nursing was the case. We also didn't have the same capability of getting patients into the intensive-care unit, not because the intensive wouldn't respond to discussion on that point, but because the intensive-care area was very highly occupied during that particular period of time.

Anchor: [The unit head] says the clustering of infant deaths for a period from one to five o'clock in the morning may have been caused by a lack of close monitoring. During a series of meetings [regarding] about fifteen unexpected deaths at the hospital [the unit head] noted an increase in the number of babies on the ward and they were younger and more ill than previous patients. [The unit head] testified six of the unexpected deaths might have been prevented with respiratory treatment, five children may have needed additional operations, and four babies on the ward were so sick they should have been transferred to intensive care.

ORGANIZATIONAL PATHOLOGY

'Organizational pathology' refers to explanations of deviance in terms of fundamental flaws in an organization's administrative structure, rules, and/or relations (e.g. relationships of trust). This type of explanation is similar to organizational expedience, except here the focus is not on resources and cost-effectiveness but on aspects of organizational structure and interpersonal relations. An organization may create a mandate that is structurally difficult or impossible for its members to achieve, 'causing' them to resort to deviant means. This can occur at the level of workers, who are administratively directed to achieve the impossible, or at the level of executives, who are 'led' to tolerate or engage in corrupt practices to remain competitive or to meet the perceived demands of the wider institutional environment. As documented in table 8.9, explanations of deviance in terms of organizational pathology were relatively infrequent. They were more frequent in the quality television and newspaper outlets, indicating one aspect of the more institutional focus of these outlets and their greater interest in the policing of organizational life. The detailed case example in chapter 5 illustrates that explanations of organizational pathology are typically associated with an advocacy role that includes maintaining certain visions of institutional integrity and associated cultural norms.

RULES AND JUSTICE

In 'rules and justice' explanations, deviance was portrayed in the context of decision processes and/or laws, rules or norms that were said to be unfair, arbitrary, immoral, inhumane, or inapplicable. As documented in table 8.9, these explanations were common, but they varied little across the news outlets. These explanations typically incorporated motivational accounts of the deviance that served to justify or excuse the deviance as a noble act in face of legal or other prohibitions on it (Matza 1964; Brandt 1969; Brodeur 1981). Typical of explanations that appealed to a noble motive is the, following TP item regarding a 'mercy killing.'

Anchor: [Head shot] A 23-year-old Texas man was given three years probation for shooting his comatose father. An attempted mercy killing. This story tonight from [names reporter].

Reporter: [Side view of Clore] Billy Ray Clore was relieved at the sentence. [View of courtroom] Three years probation, no prison. [Family members embracing Clore] Family members never wanted Billy prosecuted and they were over-joyed. [Close-up of grandmother] His grandmother for example had testified Billy shot his terminally ill father out of love. [Family 'huddle' together] The family said Billy Ray, 26, loved his 62-year-old father [still photograph of Clore and father] and wanted, as he had promised his father, to end the suffering from a hopeless coma that resulted from two heart seizures and a kidney failure. [View of courtroom, then judge, then courtroom again] With no backing from the community or family, prosecutors were less than enthusiastic about the case, even reducing the original murder charge to attempted murder when doctors disagreed on whether disease or Billy Ray's bullet killed the father. He died twelve days after the March 21st shooting. [Close-up of Clore] Billy Ray was found guilty of attempted murder. I was legally wrong, he said, but morally right.

Clore: A lot of things have been going through my mind. Mostly I just want to get back to work.

Reporter: To a question Billy Ray answered he had no advice to others whose loved ones are terminally ill, I hope no one else has to face it.

[Sign-off, NBC News, Houston]

DISPUTE SETTLEMENT

'Dispute settlement' is an explanation related to 'rules and justice,' but with specific reference to resistance, the assertion of rights, or justifications of deviance, in the context of settling particular disputes. As with 'rules and justice,' at the core of 'dispute settlement' explanations was the question of the legitimacy of the rules and decision-makers concerned, and by implication, of their organizations and institutions. Explanations in terms of 'dispute settlement' typically addressed deviant acts as an expression of resistance to authority. For example, all six news outlets had continuing stories concerning the resistance of the Polish trade union Solidarity to the laws and practices of the Polish government. Specific acts of resistance were focused on – such as public demonstrations and illegal meetings – along with the personalization of the resistance through the words and deeds of Solidarity leader Lech Walesa. 'Dispute settlement' explanations were more common in the quality outlets in newspapers and television, with significant differences between TQ (7 per cent) and TP (2 per cent).

GROUP CONFLICT

Deviant acts explained in terms of a person's loyalty to a socio-political group were categorized as 'group conflict.' In assessing the presence of this type of explanation, we distinguished between group conflict as a definition as opposed to an explanation. For example, a strike by labour is by definition a conflict between management and labour; therefore, conflict does not explain the strike, it defines it. Similarly a demonstration is a manifestation of conflict, but is not explained by conflict. However, if a striking labourer sets fire to the factory he or she works in, and this action is explained in terms of the strike or conflict between management and workers, then it is considered an explanation in this analysis.

Causes are typically ascribed to group conflict when there is deviant activity on the part of the subordinates in a relationship. For example, in industrial news causes are attributed to the actions of labourers more than to management (Glasgow University Media Group [GUMG] 1980: 178). Furthermore, this type of causal attribution often contains the 'evil causes evil' fallacy (A. Cohen 1966); the conflicts and problems associated with them are said to cause further problems. This is one way in which the news explains away deviance more than it explains deviance, constituting a means not to know while serving to represent order. Group-conflict explanations are also motivational accounts. They account for someone's deviance in terms of a 'higher loyalty' (Matza 1964) to the group than to the law or constituted authority. As such, they blend political causes and causal attribution. This is illustrated in an NP story headlined 'Attempted murder/brothers charged,' in which the police attribute a serious wounding to religious-group conflicts: 'Two brothers have been charged with the attempted murder of a Scarborough man who was stabbed in the chest in the underground parking lot of his apartment building. Police said the attack was a result of "religious problems." The victim, a Christian, is engaged to a Muslim, they said ... [he] is engaged to the brothers' sister, police said.' As documented in table 8.9, 'group conflict' explanations were more prevalent in the newspapers and television than in radio, with little variation in terms of market orientation.

ORDER MAINTENANCE

'Order maintenance' explanations are consistent with social-reaction or labelling theories of deviance (Schur 1971; Ericson 1975). Deviance is explained in terms of the various order-maintenance activities of the authorities in trying to respond to deviance, whether those activities are preventative, investigative, punitive, or stigmatizing. Thus explanation of deviance is part of the 'discourse of failure' regarding the inability of the state to deal with crime and other social problems, which in turn justifies reform efforts (Ericson and Baranek 1982, 1984; Ericson 1987). As documented in table 8.9, this type of explanation did not vary much across the news outlets.

CIRCUMSTANCES

Deviance was also attributed to various situational contingencies or aggravating or mitigating 'circumstances.' These were motivational accounts intended to justify or excuse the deviance as necessary or inevitable in the circumstances but otherwise out of character, e.g., victim precipitation or provocation, self-defence, necessity, duress. These accounts were often accompanied by associated imputations regarding the offender's character and attitude. Table 8.9 indicates that explanations in terms of circumstances varied significantly between NP (9 per cent) and NQ (4 per cent). This finding is related to the previously established fact that NP focused in particular on deviance by individual citizens. Part of this focus included motivational accounts of their deviance and its relation to other indicators of their moral character. As such, it sometimes blended with explanations of 'individual pathology,' as detailed below.

INDIVIDUAL PATHOLOGY

'Individual pathology' explanations attribute deviance to some disability of the individual. Disabilities include those that are conceived as physiological, mental, social, psychological, or some combination of these conceptions. Previous analysts have commented on the prevalence of 'individual pathology' explanations, both in the news and in popular drama on television (Dominick 1973; Chibnall 1977: esp. 79; Barrile 1980; Garofalo 1981). Such explanations fit with the cultural emphasis on individualism and personal success or failure, again shifting consideration away from societal failure and its origins in social structures and processes.

As documented in table 8.9, explanations in terms of individual pathology were infrequent. They appeared with greater proportionate frequency in popular news outlets, especially in NP (8 per cent) compared to NQ (3 per cent). These differences reflect the fact that the popular outlets include more items concerned with individual crimes and their processing through the criminal-justice system. Isolating NP, we have already seen that it used a lot of wire copy regarding acts of mass murder and other serious violence in the United States. Given the nature of these crimes, several of these items included accounts of the psychiatric history and state of the accused, and were sometimes blended with previous failures of the control system to deal with the person (order-maintenance explanations). An illustration is provided by the following NP story, which originated with United Press International, Fort Worth, Texas, and which was headlined, 'Accused of killing 5 – he had visions as he grew up.'

The mother of a man accused of slaying five people said yesterday her son was 'the best little boy who ever lived' but had visions and acted irrationally as he grew older. Larry Keith Robison, 25, is accused in the stabbing and shooting deaths of five people, including his male lover who was decapitated and sexually mutilated. He is on trial for the slaying last Aug. 10 of truck driver Bruce Gardner, 33.

Lois Robison took the stand to bolster the defence claim that her son is insane. 'He was the best little boy who ever lived,' she said. 'He loved animals and babies and he got along with his brothers and sisters. He was easy-going and liked to read books.'

She said as her son began to approach his teenage years, his behaviour began to disintegrate and she knew 'something was wrong with Larry.'

She said that from the age of 15, her son visited various psychiatrists because 'Larry was acting irrational.' He was one of four children from a previous marriage and his father gradually 'lost his mind' because of a brain tumour.

During cross-examination, prosecutor Larry Moore tried to blame Robison's behaviour on drug use.

Mrs. Robison said she knew only that he sniffed glue and smoked marijuana.

Under the pressure of questioning, however, she said it was possible that he used LSD and 'angel dust,' strong mind-altering drugs.

He talked a lot about witchcraft when he returned from a one-year hitch in the air force and an assignment in Amsterdam, she said.

She said she tried to have him admitted to several hospitals but they would not take him because he was not violent. Robison moved often and called for help another time saying 'his room-mates were trying to kill him and all the divorces and tornadoes and bad things in the papers were his fault.'

In another call, her son pleaded: 'Please come and help me. I'm flying out of my body over Camp Bowie Boulevard (a Fort Worth thoroughfare) and seeing the story of my life. I'm all lit up like a neon sign.'

As indicated in this story, explanations in terms of individual pathology were linked to specific recommendations for control. The very language used to describe deviance and the deviant also allows for the assignment of blameworthiness and specific control measures. In the above case, a court hearing is to decide whether the accused should be dealt with further through the criminal process or diverted to the mental-health system. While there is no explicit recommendation in this story to proceed one way or the other, the account leaves little doubt as to what the decision should be.

In other NP items, the account left no doubt because a recommendation for control was stated explicitly. Consider the following American-based syndicated column that tells us to read a woman's self-confessed deviance in one 'obvious,' commonsensical way and no other, leading to the equally 'obvious,' commonsensical recommendation that she requires medical help rather than, say, help from friends, family, church officials, social-welfare officials, or law-enforcement officials, or no help at all.

DEAR ABBY: For the last year or so, when I go into a store I take a few small things and put them in my purse or pocket. I have the money and could easily pay for them, but I still do it. Some of the items I have taken I throw away because I have no use for them.

Why am I doing this? I am a respectable 42-year-old married woman. Please tell me soon, as I'm very much ashamed. Otherwise Honorable

DEAR HONORABLE: You could be afflicted with kleptomania – a compulsion to steal. If you can't bring yourself to ask your physician to recommend a therapist, consult your local mental health facility. It offers confidential counselling.

OTHER EXPLANATIONS

As indicated in table 8.9, a range of 'other' explanations were offered in each news outlet. This category includes explanations that can be termed 'social pathology' – laying the blame on social institutions or macro-level considerations – but these were too rare to justify a separate category. An example is a story reporting on a news conference held by the Children's Aid Society regarding the 'increase' in the number of abandoned babies in the metropolitan area (the 'increase' amounted to four incidents in the previous five years). A spokesperson for the society attributed the 'increase' to the depressed 'economy.' Even when such explanations were offered, there was no analysis. The Children's Aid Society spokesperson was merely cited as saying that people are likely to abandon their babies because they cannot afford to look after them, without any systematic evidence, or even accounts from persons involved, to strengthen the argument.

In place of such understanding, the news offers explanations at the level of individual failure, group conflict, organizational failure, and institutional injustice. These explanations ultimately reflect the focus of the news media on established organizations and institutions and how they formulate deviance and control. As such, news is the discourse of the administered society. To 'raise' explanations to the level of structural tensions involved in the production of deviance would expose how society is 'structurally oriented toward the production of trouble,' and how it 'promotes the very competitive conflict which its lawful controls are designed to solve' (Pfohl 1985: 352). By focusing on events involving exercises of lawful authority in institutional settings, news augments the thrust of legal control. News joins with the law in excluding the deviant because it too 'produces the appearance (or collective representation) that troublesome persons rather than troublesome social structure are at fault. This mystifies the social roots of trouble in a society that is structurally unequal' (ibid: 353). Social order is represented through a silencing of its most fundamental structural dimensions (White 1984).

Discriminating Crime and Deviance by Medium and Market

The following stepwise discriminant analyses weight and combine five elements of deviance (areas of deviance, types of deviance, institutional contexts of deviance, institutional fields of deviance, and types of knowledge of deviance) as independent measures in a way that forces the medium and market groups to be as distinct as possible so that one can predict on what criteria the groups are distinguishable.

The stepwise discriminant analysis of deviance by medium is presented in table 8.10. The best predictor of medium is whether there is tertiary understanding of deviance. Additional predictive influence comes from adding in turn the following elements: evaluative assessments, recommendations, secondary understanding, interpersonal acts of deviance, and deviance in the political area. Newspapers are distinguished as offering evaluative assessment, recommendations, and explanations of deviance. Television is distinguished as offering tertiary knowledge and explanations of deviance, interpersonal deviance, and deviance in the political area. Radio is distinguished as offering recommendations, and interpersonal deviance.

The stepwise discriminant analyses of deviance within markets are presented in table 8.11. From table 8.11a we learn that the best predictors

TABLE 8.10
Stepwise discriminant analysis of crime and deviance by medium

Variables	F	Discriminant function 1 standardized coefficients	Discriminant function 2 standardized coefficients
Knowledge:			
Tertiary	11.94	0.23	0.78
Assessment:			
Evaluation	5.84	0.55	−0.06
Assessment:			
Recommendation	5.44	0.30	−0.45
Knowledge:			
Secondary	5.90	0.52	0.12
Types of deviance:			
Interpersonal	2.37	−0.23	0.33
Area of deviance:			
Political	1.55	−0.11	0.30
Centroids:			
Newspaper(N = 488)		0.23	−0.09
Television (N = 531)		−0.04	0.21
Radio (N = 466)		−0.20	−0.15
Percentage of cases correctly classified:			
Newspaper	41.2%		
Television	28.4%		
Radio	52.6%		
Total	40.2%		

Wilk's lambda = 0.9468; chi-square = 80.96 (d.f. = 12; $p < 0.01$

of market within newspapers are whether interpersonal deviance is being reported on and whether the deviant was a government official, with some influence deriving from the addition of whether there was a recommendation with respect to the deviance. NQ is distinguished as focusing on the deviance of government officials and offering recommendations with respect to deviance. NP is distinguished as reporting on interpersonal deviance, offering tertiary understanding, and focusing on deviance in the political field.

In table 8.11b, it is established that the best predictor of market orientation in television is whether the deviance was in the political area, with some additional influence deriving from whether the deviant was a government official, whether there was an explanation of deviance, and whether there was tertiary understanding of deviance. TQ is distinguished as focusing on deviance in the political area and on government officials

TABLE 8.11a
Stepwise discriminant analysis of crime and deviance within
markets: newspapers

Variables	F	Discriminant function standardized coefficients
Types of deviance:		
Interpersonal	12.43	0.57
Institutional context of deviant:		
Government	13.28	−0.57
Knowledge:		
Tertiary		7.67
	0.42	
Area of deviance:		
Political	1.29	0.18
Knowledge:		
Recommendation	1.20	−0.17

Centroids:		
Quality paper $(N = 276)$		−0.28
Popular paper $(N = 212)$		0.36
Percentage of cases correctly classified:		
Quality paper	56.2%	
Popular paper	67.9%	
Total	61.3%	

Wilk's lambda = 0.9077; chi-square = 46.84 (d.f. = 5; $p < 0.01$)

who are deviant, and as offering explanations. TP is distinguished as offering tertiary knowledge.

A stepwise discriminant analysis of deviance by market in radio produced results that are not statistically significant.

In this chapter, we have established significant components of topics in crime and deviance peculiar to each news outlet. Each news outlet represented crime and deviance differently because it operated with medium and market criteria that differed from the others.

The newspapers had a significantly lower proportion of deviance and control stories than did the broadcast outlets. NQ and NP each devoted slightly fewer than one-half of their columns to stories of deviance and control. However they varied substantially in the specifics of what was presented in these stories. There was a very low rate of concurrence (approximately 25 per cent) in the deviance and control stories covered by

TABLE 8.11b
Stepwise discriminant analysis of crime and deviance within markets: television

Variables	F	Discriminant function standardized coefficients
Area of deviance:		
Political	12.95	0.62
Institutional context of deviant:		
Government	9.19	0.52
Knowledge:		
Secondary	5.07	0.39
Knowledge:		
Tertiary	3.12	–0.30
Centroids:		
Quality television ($N = 318$)		0.22
Popular television ($N = 213$)		–0.33
Percentage of cases correctly classified:		
Quality television	63.2%	
Popular television	60.6%	
Total	62.2%	

Wilk's lambda = 0.9334; chi-square = 36.30 (d.f. = 4; $p < 0.01$)

the two newspapers, indicating that the format requirements of the market orientation clearly take precedence over the particular event and topic as newsworthy to all news media. NP gave much more emphasis to crime, especially serious violent crimes such as murder and robbery. NP had more similarity to the broadcast-news outlets, especially TP and RP, in this regard. NQ focused in particular on deviance in the economic, political, and ideological spheres. Almost one-third of NQ's deviance and control stories were in the economic sphere, compared to about one-fifth of NP's. Moreover NQ's stories in the economic sphere focused more often on policy or the deviance of officials, whereas NP focused primarily on economic crimes.

NQ was especially concerned with the deviance of officials in government, offering stories on this context of deviance twice as frequently as did NP. In contrast, NP, in keeping with the popular broadcast outlets, gave particular attention to deviance by individuals outside of explicit organizational and institutional contexts. Almost one-third of NP's stories dealt with deviance by individuals compared to only 7 per cent of NQ's. NP was replete with stories of individual acts of violence, sexual deviance, and street crime stripped of organizational and institutional contexts, providing a perpetual discourse of dangerous individuals and fear and loathing about them.

The newspapers offered more explanations of crime and deviance than did the broadcast outlets. While the types of explanation offered varied little across the six outlets studied, NP gave much more emphasis to individual pathology explanations as part of its personalization of violent crime by individuals. NQ gave particular emphasis to explicit evaluations of crime and deviance and to recommendations for control. In contrast, NP joined with the television outlets in offering a considerable degree of tertiary knowledge about crime and deviance, including especially fear and loathing over individual acts of serious violent crime.

The vast majority of newspaper items included headlines, and most of these referred to some control action being taken and/or primary facts pertaining to the story. The newspapers also sometimes included background information and evaluations in their headlines, while the broadcast outlets almost never did so because these forms of knowledge were inappropriate to their present-tense action orientation and their need to appear objective. All of the above features of headlines also pertained to what was contained in the leads to each story.

TQ gave much more space to deviance and control stories than did TP and was similar to the radio stations in this regard. TQ and TP also diverged in the aspects of crime and deviance they emphasized. TP was similar to NP and RP in focusing on violence, especially violent crimes committed by individuals. In contrast, TQ gave much more emphasis to political deviance and rights violations, due in part to its reliance on national and international political news provided through network and various news-source feeds that were not available to TP.

TQ focused in particular on deviance by government officials, apparently not constrained by the fact that it was itself government-owned and -operated. TP, in keeping with its popular counterparts in radio and newspapers, gave particular attention to deviant individuals without explicit organizational or institutional affiliation.

Radio news was dominated by deviance and control stories; almost three-quarters of RQ's stories included these elements. RQ gave the greatest proportionate emphasis to deviance in the economic sphere, while RP, like all of the popular outlets, focused in particular on violence. RP was also similar to the other popular outlets in giving considerable attention to deviance by individuals, while RQ emphasized private corporate deviance and deviance in the field of trade and finance more than did any of the other outlets.

RP was also distinguished from RQ in its much greater use of headline 'teases' to draw listeners into the news and particular stories. This difference is related to the fact that RP was a commercial radio station that attempted to hold listeners' attention over advertisements with 'teases,' while RQ did not have such a need because it was non-commercial. While all outlets used headlines and leads to express control actions being taken in respect to crime and deviance, the radio stations were especially likely to emphasize control actions in their 'teases' and leads. This finding is explained by the radio medium's need to convey a sense that the news is alive, active, and dramatic, addressing an event in the 'present tense' and even 'as it happens.'

In the next chapter, we continue our analysis of how topics in deviance and control were covered. Our focus shifts to how acts of social control and, in particular, legal control were represented and how this representation varies in terms of the medium and market of news outlets.

9

Law and Justice

Control, Law, and Justice

LEGAL DISCOURSE AND NEWS DISCOURSE

News is a discourse of efforts to control behaviour through law and to obtain justice. This discourse is evident in the murder story analysed in chapter 4, which focused on the police at work producing evidence, interviewing witnesses, and bringing the accused to justice. The news emphasis on control, law, and justice is central to news sources, who view the news first and foremost as a vehicle for helping them to enact and control their organizational environment (Ericson, Baranek, and Chan 1989).

News of control is marked by dramatic decisions and outcomes, such as an arrest made, a corporation fined, an official dismissed from office, or a law enacted. However, in major continuing news stories, the focus is less on the dramatic decisions and outcomes than on the control procedures used in arriving at outcomes and on the conceptions of justice embedded in the procedures. In a major continuing story, the outcome is sometimes no more than an after-clap of accord regarding the justice of procedures invoked to arrive at the outcome. What is important is the public processes by which the outcome is arrived at and the social authority thereby represented. In reporting on control actions, there is not only a search for facts and truth, but also a quest for justice and authority.

The discourse of control, law, and justice is channelled institutionally. Yearnings for justice and urgings for authority are expressed through the suasive use of institutionally sanctioned words. Often 'an answer is only seen to be the right one if it sustains the institutional thinking that is already in the minds of individuals as they try to decide' (M. Douglas 1986: 4).

News represents the thinking about justice and authority of several institutions involved in efforts at controlling a social problem: the institution that initiated control against another; the institution whose resources are mobilized in control efforts; the institution that is the target of control; the institution of law; and the mass-media institution.

As underscored in previous chapters, the language used to classify disorder and deviance also frames the solutions developed for these problems. The process of problem-setting is fundamental, because it establishes the framework for thinking, including the selection of appropriate generative metaphors, which in turn influence the determination of relevant facts and the recommendation of control actions to solve the problem. Problem-setting is facilitated and routinized through the invocation of established institutional classifications. In particular, the classifications of substantive law are readily available to imprint the reality that an act or person is, for example, criminal, or in violation of compliance regulations under administrative law.

The importance of legal discourse in news of control is not limited to the classification of substantive acts for specific control purposes. As introduced in chapter 1, law is a cultural tool for the production of meaning, not simply a machinery for the administration of justice. Culturally, law offers an imaginative and interpretive capacity for construing behaviour as well as controlling it. As such, law is also an important source of language about social relations, providing 'a vocabulary with which we rationalize our actions to others and ourselves' (Macauley 1987: 185). As a means of visualizing social relations, law also articulates political (power) relations and economic relations. In contrast to the impenetrability of law in its case-book and other professional textual forms, legal discourse in the news makes evident 'power relations within a society in terms of the most general social ideologies available' (Sumner 1979: 271), and functions 'to express, regulate and maintain the general nature of the dominant social relations of a social formation' (ibid: 272). There is nothing fixed or static about these social functions of law. Because 'law is the unsettled product of relations with a plurality of social forms,' its 'identity is constantly and inherently subject to challenge and change' (Fitzpatrick 1984: 138). As a discourse about a plurality of interinstitutional relations that are equivocal and conflictual, law is central to news and news is crucial for the perpetual articulation of legal discourse.

As a cultural tool for the articulation of social, political, and economic relations, legal discourse in the news reaches beyond its institutional boundaries and contributes to public debates about social justice. Like law, justice is also 'an institution we interpret' (Dworkin 1986: 73). As such, it too requires perpetual articulation and elaboration, and the news media provide the essential public vehicle for the task. News of control provides ongoing debates and unresolved choices regarding how particular conceptions of justice can be made workable. 'Our most intense disputes about justice – about income taxes, for example, or affirmative action programs – are about the right tests for justice, not about whether the facts satisfy some agreed test in some particular case' (ibid).

While a 'right test' may be decided upon in a particular instance or at a particular juncture, it is in need of constant retesting and adjustment. This is inevitable since justice itself is not objectively identifiable but rather is an imagined state that varies by events, circumstances, and those who are using their imaginations. This does not mean conceptions of justice cannot be specified, and that procedures for justice cannot be developed and implemented. 'Perhaps no useful statement of the concept of justice is available. If so, this casts no doubt on the sense of disputes about justice, but testifies only to the imagination of people trying to be just' (Dworkin 1986: 74–5). Indeed, it is precisely this inability to make definitive statements about justice, and to point to factual instances of justice, that ensures perpetual imaginative discourse about justice in the legal media, news media, and other social institutions.

THE NEWS AS CONTROL

In the very process of reporting on the control activity of others, the news becomes part of that control activity. News participation in control is obvious in the murder story analysed in chapter 4, with some news outlets featuring their journalists working with police to generate tips from informants. The participation of journalists in control is pervasive, although much more subtle, in most news stories. News involves control through the routine selection and classification procedures of journalists and their sources, through the influence news has on sources, and through the way in which news articulates and influences public opinion about knowledge/ power relations in society.

In the very process of making news, journalists and their sources inevitably participate in and contribute to control (Ericson, Baranek, and Chan 1987, 1989). Control is embedded in the selection of institutions to report on. The news media as an ideological form and apparatus link up with particular other institutions with their ideological forms and apparatuses. These other institutions, in turn, have influence over their link with the news media in terms of the level and nature of their participation. They also have a say in what institutions, organizations, and groups are excluded, joining with the news media in the processing of social opposition. Control action is also embedded in the negotiated selections made by journalists and their sources regarding topics, spokespersons, and formats of presentation. For example, the selection of someone with an identifiable status and organizational affiliation as a spokesperson bears meaning for control action. 'As soon as actors are typified as role performers, their conduct is *ipso facto* susceptible to enforcement' (Berger and Luckmann 1966: 92).

News sources know that being in the news carries not only the potential to have influence over others, but also the potential to be influenced by others. Control over the news is a negotiated matter in which there is the omnipresent possibility of loss of power as well as significant gains. Indeed, control action is built into the process of communicating. 'All transmission of institutional meanings obviously implies control and legitimation procedures' (ibid: 88). The news controls sources in various ways and at different levels (Ericson, Baranek, and Chan 1989). It influences their routines, affects their careers, and contributes to both stability and change in their organizations. The news has a powerful controlling influence over organizations that need to control the level and nature of public awareness of their activities. News entails control because it produces knowledge that has its conditions of possibility in power relations.

The knowledge/power relations through which news is produced are expressed in news content, and in this respect also the news participates in control action. As news texts escape their authors and enter into the contexts of readers, they give shape to readers' opinions and activities in relation to knowledge/power hierarchies and implications for control. In using its own myths and rituals to report on the myths and rituals of other control institutions, the news-media institution provides consumers with a daily barometer of control activity, and moral authority in exercises of control, which the reader can make significant in his or her own institutional contexts of control.

ERASURES OF CONTROL

News-media participation in control is highly selective and partial. The dimensions of this selectivity and partiality, and its variation by medium and market orientation, are specified in the analyses that follow. These analyses also point to the fact that, being selective and partial, news erases a lot of control activity in its accounts and this, too, has control implications for news consumers.

In combination with entertainment programming, news presents images of control institutions that are perceived as real and therefore real in their consequences (Ericson 1991). The emphasis on violence, by both citizens and state agents, can inure people to violence, which in turn yields a passive acceptance of injustice (Gerbner and Gross 1976). The emphasis on the failure of institutions can have the same effect of passive acceptance of injustice, or even fuel contempt for due-process requirements and other aspects of civil liberties (Alley 1982). At the same time, images of the failure of public institutions, including public police, can foster reliance on private security police and hardware mechanisms. As Macauley (1987: 203–4) points out, films and television serials (and we might add, news) frequently perpetuate the Sherlock Holmes theme that society is corrupt and that the public police are part of the scandal or are otherwise simply too weak to cope.

The way in which social problems are defined, framed, and understood also leads to erasure in thought and action. A kind of cognitive myopia is created as a result of presenting issues in terms of a point/counterpoint format as if alternative pragmatic choices and solutions are possible, when in fact they are not. This type of presentation erases more fundamental issues concerning the distribution of power in society by trafficking in a conception of power as a mere limitation on liberty. This conception of power in turn is arguably the principal means by which the distribution of power in society is made acceptable, legitimated as moral authority. Moreover, even when multiple perspectives on a problem are presented, the result may still be depoliticalization, and being inured to injustice. 'Ironically, the "liberalizing" effect of the multiple perspective view may still give a political advantage to conservatives, reactionaries and special interest groups. After all, multiple perspectives often lead many people to an overabundance of empathy, and, therefore, to political ambivalence and inaction' (Meyrowitz 1985: 144).

Ironically, the news media can capitalize on the very ignorance they foster through erasure. It is only when the cultural template available in the news media is used as a guide that the news media exposé of a particular institutional practice is experienced as an exposé. The reader is only shocked by an exposé if he or she relies upon mass-mediated moral lessons about how an institution should operate rather than on systematic analyses of how it does operate, or on first-hand experience in the institution concerned. Macauley (1987: 210) offers an example regarding the legal institution: 'Muckraking rests on the shock in discovering that things aren't as they should be. Those who understand that an American legal system in action typically involves bargaining in the shadow of the law probably find programs such as "Sixty Minutes" less interesting.'

SOURCES AND EVIDENCE OF CONTROL

In the following sections, we analyse the reporting of control in the six news outlets. We initially classify stories in terms of whether they reported on a compliance mode of control, a deterrence mode of control, or some combination of the two. This analysis is based on the sample of 1,485 stories, and addresses the mode(s) of control depicted in each item. The remaining analyses address control actions mentioned in the stories. These analyses are based on all reported control actions ('responses'). However, if multiple control actions were of the same type – for example, it was mentioned three times during a story that a police officer had made an arrest – only one was coded. In other words, multiple 'responses' were coded only if different types of actions were reported. We included control action that had taken place or was taking place, as well as control action that was projected (planned or scheduled to take place), but not recommendations for control action. The vast majority of control actions reported in each outlet had taken place or were taking place, as opposed to being projected, with a range from 79 per cent of the control actions reported in the popular radio station (RP) to 89 per cent of the control actions reported in the quality television station (TQ), and no significant medium and market differences.

In the vast majority of instances, the only evidence of control action taken or projected was a statement by the source. Television was the most likely to offer additional evidence of control action because of its visual capacity. In 25 per cent of the control actions reported on the television stations ($N = 1,151$), there was some visual or sound evidence of the control action taking place, with more in TQ (28 per cent) than in the popular television station (TP) (20 per cent). In addition, in 9 per cent of the television stories, sources who described actions also cited other sources to back up their claims. Radio sources were much less likely to offer additional evidence of control action, and when they did so it was through the citation of additional sources to back up their claims (14 per cent) rather than through the use of sounds of control action taking place (less than 1 per cent) ($N = 988$). Newspaper sources were also unlikely to offer evidence of the control action they participated in, and when they did so it was through the citation of additional sources (13 per cent) rather than through the use of photographs or other visuals (less than 1 per cent) ($N = 982$). The quality newspaper (NQ) (15 per cent) sources cited additional sources regarding the control actions they were involved in proportionately more often than did the popular newspaper (NP) (10 per cent) sources. However, the 8 instances in which some visual evidence was added all occurred in NP (for an example, see chapter 4, p. 78).

Compliance and Deterrence Models

In table 9.1, we present the proportion of items in each news outlet that address control actions in the compliance mode, deterrence mode, or

TABLE 9.1
Proportion of news items on compliance and deterrence modes of control

Modes of control	News outlets NQ		NP		TQ		TP		RQ		RP		Sig. diff.
	N	%	N	%	N	%	N	%	N	%	N	%	
Compliance	132	47.8	77	36.3	118	37.1	73	34.3	131	53.9	94	42.2	M/N/R
Deterrence	41	14.9	68	32.1	66	20.7	64	30.0	48	19.8	57	25.5	N/T
Compliance/ deterrence	87	31.5	56	26.4	123	38.7	68	31.9	44	18.1	60	26.9	M/R
Other	16	5.8	11	5.2	11	3.5	8	3.8	20	8.2	12	5.4	
Totals	276	100.0	212	100.0	318	100.0	213	100.0	243	100.0	223	100.0	

Tests of significance based on tables with modes of control dichotomized into 'yes/no' for each of the categories. The last column indicates comparisons that show significant differences: i.e., chi-square statistics significant at the 0.05 level with Cramer's V or PHI $\geq$ 0.10, when N is large. Significant differences may occur between the newspapers (N); television stations (T); radio stations (R); or among the three types of media (M).

compliance and deterrence modes combined (Reiss 1984; Hawkins 1984; Manning 1987).

A compliance mode of control is based on changing a state of affairs so that an agreed standard is reached and possible risks are reduced. Deviance is embedded more in a state of affairs of organizations than in the acts of individuals. For example, the manufacturing process of a company inevitably results in some pollution. The question is what level of pollution is acceptable, given the likely effects on the environment, and the likely costs to the company and its employees if new standards require additional equipment or cause reduced output. 'Given a distribution of risks, conformity is a matter of selecting a threshold that defines an acceptable risk' (Reiss 1984: 92). As such, compliance typically involves not simply refraining from an act, but doing something positive to remedy a state of affairs.

Compliance is most often sought through regulatory agencies operating in terms of administrative law, an area of law that has experienced rapid growth in the late twentieth century (Law Reform Commission 1986). In regulation for compliance, law is 'a series of instructions to administrators, rather than a series of commands to citizens' (Lowi 1979: 106). Compliance officers, unlike public police officers, are not primarily oriented to detection and proof that violation has occurred. Rather, they are primarily agents of surveillance who monitor an organizational activity to ascertain whether there is effort made to achieve an agreed-upon standard that will enhance the minimization of risks and prevention of serious harms. Moreover, since the standards and risks are uncertain, morally as well as objectively, compliance officers have discretion to draw the boundaries of regulatory deviance. 'Definition and enforcement, a dual authority, are reciprocally related' (Hawkins 1984: 23).

The goal of compliance enforcement is *not* to use the full force of the law or to seek punishment. Indeed, to the degree the system works, it is because it does not use the formal process of law (prosecution) or seek punitive assessments through the courts. To take a punitive approach is to risk damage to the relationship between the compliance officer and the organization, which will prevent effective monitoring and prevention work. The goal is regulation rather than repression, not whether to allow a deviant activity but how much of it is tolerable and not unduly risky. A relationship of trust and reciprocity between the enforcer and the deviant allows enforcement to be performed in a serial, incremental, and continuous manner. If there is any routine 'punishment,' it is in the process of having to expend material and human resources in negotiating a workable and acceptable level of deviance.

Publicity is a crucial component of compliance enforcement. Since the primary aim of compliance enforcement is prevention through an ongoing dialogue about standards, risks, and control capabilities, the role of publicity as an educational tool is especially important. Increasingly, regulatory agencies seek publicity through news outlets and paid advertisements in order to educate as well as to 'pressure' organizations they regulate (Ericson, Baranek, and Chan 1989: chap. 5; Braithwaite 1989). Publicity is also valuable to organizations subject to regulation if they are able to give off signs that they are good corporate citizens striving for new standards of safety, health, and welfare that benefit everyone (ibid).

Publicity is also of value in the rare instances when compliance mechanisms fall apart and it is deemed necessary to take formal proceedings against the deviant organization. In compliance enforcement, 'what is sanctionable is not rule-breaking as such, but rule-breaking which is deliberately or negligently done, or rule-breaking accompanied by an uncooperativeness which amounts to a symbolic assault upon the enforcer's and the agency's authority and legitimacy' (Hawkins 1984: xiv). Compliance officers take formal action when they have been symbolically assaulted, and their formal action consists of symbolic assaults on the deviant organization. That is, prosecutions or other formal actions are taken to obtain publicity that 'punishes' the deviant organization. Most companies fear the sting of publicity much more than they do any fine or penalty that might be levied in law (ibid: 116–17; Ericson, Baranek, and Chan 1989: chap. 5; Braithwaite 1989). Moreover, publicity about successful prosecutions or other formal actions can enhance the regulatory agency as a credible enforcement authority. Ultimately the cases that are publicized provide occasions for dramatic displays of the agency's good work and moral authority (Manning 1987).

While the significance of the publicity component is explicitly in the minds of regulatory agents, and those subject to regulation, as they go about their work (Hawkins 1984), it is also sometimes revealed in what is actually publicized. A number of compliance control actions in the news items we sampled underscored the dual educational and control value of publicizing compliance work. For example, the quality radio station (RQ) broadcast an item reporting the first Ontario case in which a doctor had been prosecuted under the Child Welfare Act for failing to report a case of child abuse. Excerpts from this item reveal that the prosecution was seen to have publicity value for gaining compliance among other doctors to report instances of child abuse.

Reporter: Under a law which has been in effect for several years now all professionals, including teachers, social workers, and physicians, have an obligation to report suspected cases of child abuse. The chairman of the Ontario Medical Association's Committee on Child Welfare ... says that while he is not familiar with the details of the case against the doctor he's glad there has been a change under this act.

Source: Many people are unaware that this really applies to them and that the law means business and I personally, while I feel sorry for the individual physician who's been charged, I am damned pleased that somebody has been because then hopefully we will get this message across more strongly that this, this is a problem that cannot be overlooked, cannot be ignored, and that we all have a responsibility to address ourselves to it.

Reporter: Dr. [names doctor] says the fact that a fine for failing to report a case of abuse is on the books has improved reporting and he hopes the new publication to be issued by the OMA [Ontaro Medical Association] and authored by a Hamilton paediatrician will also help, at least in the awareness doctors have, particularly of sexual abuse.

In some news items, there was an explicit admission that direct enforcement of regulations is too difficult and that the only hope is to educate people about the risks involved through publicity. For example, a TQ item reported on the fact that the city health department had declared beaches unsafe for swimming because of high bacterial counts. After noting that warning signs had been posted on the beaches, and citing a health-department official concerning the health risks involved in swimming in the polluted waters, the reporter added, 'Although the signs are now up bathers can ignore them if they want to and life guards are still on patrol. Mr [health official] says closing the beach would be impossible to enforce.'

Other items made it explicit that governmental agencies want publicity as part of the grants they give to help other agencies achieve better standards in equipment and safety. Thus, NQ reported on the fact that a municipal government had refused a substantial grant from a federal agency regarding improvement of its gas-distribution system because of a stipulation in the contract that the municipality must hold a 'media event' to publicize the grant. The 'project manager for the program said from Ottawa that Kitchener is the only municipality that she knows of to balk at a provision in the contract with the Department of Energy, Mines and Resources requiring municipalities to hold media events in exchange for grants. The event, whose timing, setting, and other details must be approved by the department, is intended "to strengthen awareness of the federal contribution to extend natural gas service." '

Another sign of the importance of publicity to the compliance-control mode is the high proportion of stories dealing with compliance in all news outlets. As documented in table 9.1, in each news outlet, there was a higher proportion of stories on compliance-control topics alone than on deterrence-control topics alone. Furthermore, a substantial proportion of items in each outlet had a combination of compliance and deterrence elements. The quality outlets had a particularly high proportion of items reporting on the compliance mode of control. Indeed, the compliance mode of control was included in approximately one-half of the items in each of NQ and RQ. The contrast between NQ and NP is especially marked: NQ emphasized compliance items (48 per cent) over deterrence items (15 per cent), while NP had almost equal proportions of compliance (36 per cent) and deterrence (32 per cent).

The deterrence mode of control is directed primarily at the deviant acts of individuals rather than the states of affairs of organizations. It is associated more with criminal law than with administrative law. While prevention or general deterrence is a major consideration, deterrence-enforcement agencies such as the public police are organized to react to deviant events once they occur. Enforcement officers working within the deterrence mode adopt a penal style in which detection, proof of violation, and punishment are paramount. 'Deterrence law enforcement's principal objective is to ensure conformity by detecting violations, determining who is responsible for them, and penalizing violations in order to deter the offender or others from committing violations in the future' (Reiss 1987: 25).

While the compliance-enforcement officer is successful if he or she establishes a working agreement regarding the achievement of standards and *avoids* formal prosecution and legal sanctions, the deterrence-enforcement officer measures success in terms of the full force of the law: arrests, convictions, and sentences of the court. In deterrence law-enforcement, the outcomes are meant to be final and dramatic, as opposed to the gradual and shifting nature of compliance agreements and standards. While, in the compliance mode, the main 'punishment' is in the process of having to commit resources to meet standards, in the deterrence mode, the main punishment is in the application of legal penalties by the courts even though offenders may experience the prosecution process as punitive (Feeley 1979; Ericson and Baranek 1982). In the deterrence mode, publicity has assumed general deterrent effects as well as punitive stigmatic effects on the offender (Ericson, Baranek, and Chan 1989: chaps. 2 and 3). Publicity is also a means of mobilizing public assistance to law-enforcement agencies and functions to reproduce the organizational and occupational ideologies of those agencies (ibid). Publicity in this regard is arguably more potent in the case of deterrence law-enforcers than of compliance officers because the former operate with the moral authority of the criminal law and its centrality to the state. In contrast, compliance officers are usually on morally ambiguous ground (Manning 1987), with the result that publicity is more likely to work against them.

As indicated in table 9.1, the deterrence mode of enforcement was given greater proportionate attention in the popular news outlets. The popular outlets all had full-time crime reporters working the police beat who ensured a steady supply of deterrence items, while none of the quality outlets had such specialists (Ericson, Baranek, and Chan 1989: chaps. 2 and 3). Moreover, as shown previously (chapter 6), the popular outlets, but especially NP, used wire copy as an additional major source of crime-control stories in the deterrence mode. While the quality outlet samples also included wire stories in the deterrence mode, these were more likely to address military deterrence and other aspects of international conflict rather than crime control.

Table 9.1 indicates that in many news items there was a combination of compliance and deterrence modes of control, ranging from about 18 per cent of the items in RQ to almost 39 per cent of the items in TQ. Examples of combined modes are evident in areas of public police work in which the main enforcement effort is directed at crime containment and management rather than at punitive deterrence. For example, prostitution is usually regulated so that practitioners can operate in designated times and places (Reiss 1984). Thus the items in our sample regarding prostitution mainly focused on regulation of the times and places of practice rather than on arrests, convictions, and punishments. One item reported on how residents and police had arranged for a change in traffic signs, including the alteration of one-way street signs, in an effort to influence the traffic flow of 'johns' trolling for street-walkers so that they would not pester local residents. While the police also vowed to make arrests where possible, the main effort was regulation through traffic-engineering.

Similarly compliance officers were reported to have resorted to penal methods in the face of persistent and wilful non-compliance. For example, a major continuing story accounting for multiple items in each news outlet involved the prosecution of a company that caused serious pollution to a river affecting not only recreational fishing but the livelihood of native people in the area. As Hawkins (1984) points out, it is only in the face of blatant violations showing negligence or wilful disregard that prosecution is likely, and these prosecutions depend on publicity to condemn the company's disregard for the public interest and at the same time to reinforce the legitimacy of the enforcement agency.

The most remarkable finding regarding modes of control represented in news items is the fact that the deterrence mode is in the minority, even in popular outlets and on television. Most news items are not dramatic displays of the penal apparatus at work. This finding does not support the claim that compliance modes of control with a conciliatory style and negotiation mechanisms are not treated as newsworthy (e.g., E. Black 1982: 139–40;

Evans and Lundman 1983; Braithwaite 1989: esp. 178–9). Furthermore, this finding is contrary to claims of researchers studying regulatory agencies and practices that 'regulatory deviance rarely possesses the emotive properties of many traditional crimes. The latter also more regularly invite the attention of the press and therefore the organized resentment of the public' (Hawkins 1984: 13). At least statistically, and without regard to play, the compliance mode, and compliance blended with deterrence, dominate control actions in the news. The greater emphasis is on the less dramatic, procedural aspects of regulation and control.

One dimension of the focus on compliance through regulation and negotiation is that many of the activities of deterrence law-enforcers are depicted in compliance terms. For example, the police are shown in one context to be engaged in dramatic feats of crime detection and penal suppression, while in another context they are shown in negotiations with management over working conditions. 'Police who negotiate with the city "through the media," for example, can no longer distinguish their front region image of dedication as selfless protectors of the people from their back region haggling for more sick days, vacation time, and higher salaries' (Meyrowitz 1985: 149). News items directed at policing the police also depict the compliance mode of control. For example, some items reported on the activities of a newly established Public Complaints Commission for civilian review of police activities, which was explicitly designed to institutionalize policing the police in a compliance mode (McMahon and Ericson 1984, 1987; McMahon 1989). Other items addressed what special commissions of inquiry, such as one concerned with violence against women, sought in terms of police compliance. Moreover, the news organizations themselves, and especially NQ, took the initiative to detect procedural strays in the police and to write stories about them with the aim of 'policing the police' to the point of compliance (Ericson, Baranek, and Chan 1989: chap. 3).

The emphasis on compliance modes of control in the news may be explained by several developments. There has been a significant growth in administrative law and compliance mechanisms (Law Reform Commission 1986). This is coincident with the development of huge corporations and the need to regulate their private orders (Unger 1976; Shearing and Stenning 1981, 1987). It is also connected with the evolution of the welfare state and its myriad regulatory forms and requirements (Unger 1976). The news-media institution and its organizations are paying increasing attention to these trends. Journalists, especially in certain news outlets such as NQ, are ferreting out and documenting the activities of regulatory agencies in keeping with trends in law and society (cf Roscho 1975: 122). At least one study in the American context indicates that journalists favour more governmental regulation (Lichter and Rothman 1981). This tendency may lead journalists to focus on procedural deviance and police organizational life in ways that encourage governmental intervention and enhanced regulation in an amplifying spiral.

At the same time, news sources in regulatory agencies increasingly seek publicity because it is central to their mandate to achieve compliance through education. As seen in the examples cited previously (pp. 292–3), the news media are used routinely to tell people how to behave in the face of designated risks and dangers (avoid swimming in polluted waters; report suspected cases of child abuse, etc.). Just as there is 'normal crime discourse' (Fishman 1980, 1981; Wheeler 1986; Ericson, Baranek, and Chan 1989: chap. 3) routinely supplied by the police, so there is 'normal compliance discourse' routinely supplied by a range of regulatory agencies. Ultimately the effect of being bombarded with such instruction day in and day out is that a 'belief context' (Mathiesen 1987) is created whereby the citizen is likely to accept not only the specific control instructions, but the necessity for such regulation and the 'administered society' (Giddens 1979). That is, the news consumer accepts the 'normal compliance discourse' as an instruction not only of what to *do*, but also of what to *be*, as part of his or her identity within the administered society.

The focus on compliance in terms of procedures is also consistent with what we have identified previously (Ericson, Baranek, and Chan 1987, 1989), following Habermas (1975), as characteristic of legitimation work in the administered society. The legitimacy of organizations and institutions is increasingly dependent upon their ability to show that they are acting with procedural propriety, and willing to work towards improved standards in the public interest. This is the essence of the compliance mode of control, and it is this essence that has become a major focus of news.

Styles of Law and Justice

In table 9.2 we present an analysis of how styles of control action, law, and justice varied by medium and market orientation. These styles are based on the typology developed by D. Black (1976).

PENAL

In the penal style, the focus is on efforts to punish wrongdoing. Penal control actions include, for example, law-enforcement officers and officials engaged in investigations, making arrests, charging people, conducting trials, conducting sentencing hearings, and administering penal sanctions. Also included in this category are various law-and-order campaigns such as crack-

TABLE 9.2
Styles of law and justice

Style	Newspaper		Television		Radio		Sig. diff.
	Q	P	Q	P	Q	P	
Penal	201	243	348	245	323	255	M/N
	35.1%	57.3%	50.2%	53.0%	57.7%	59.3%	
Conciliatory	327	120	283	174	184	123	M/N
	57.2%	28.3%	40.8%	37.7%	32.9%	28.6%	
Therapeutic	9	19	14	5	10	9	
	1.6%	4.5%	2.0%	1.1%	1.8%	2.1%	
Other	35	42	47	38	43	43	C
	6.1%	9.9%	6.8%	8.2%	7.7%	10.0%	
Total actions	572	424	693	462	560	430	3,141

Percentages are by column. Missing cases = 1. Tests of significance based on tables with styles of law and justice dichotomized into 'yes/no' for each of the categories. The last column indicates comparisons that show significant differences: chi-square statistics significant at the 0.05 level with Cramer's V or PHI ≥ 0.10, when N is large. Significant differences may occur between the newspapers (N); television stations (T); radio stations (R); or among the three types of media (M). The last column also indicates the presence of significant interactions with the variables being analysed and the coders (C) in a separate log-linear analysis.

downs on trade in prohibited drugs, impaired driving, and security of psychiatric facilities and prisons. Penal law-reform efforts, sometimes overlapping with law-and-order campaigns, are also included here (e.g., efforts to reform the law with respect to dangerous offenders). Another dimension is punitive control actions in international conflicts, for example, military intervention or attacks, as well as direct economic sanctions. The penal style is most closely associated with the deterrence mode but it is by no means coincident with it. As indicated previously, there is often a blend of compliance and deterrence elements in stories of control, with punitive sanctions pursued for their symbolic 'publicity' value when the normal means of compliance regulation have failed.

As documented in table 9.2, the penal style of control action was dominant, except in NQ. While the penal style was attributed to 50–60 per cent of the control actions in NP and all of the broadcast outlets, it constituted only 35 per cent of the control actions in NQ. NQ's place as an outlier in this regard accounts for the fact that there is significant variation by medium, and between the newspapers.

These data do not reveal more subtle aspects of variation among the news outlets in reporting control actions. While there was little statistical variation between TQ and TP, there was qualitative variation in that TP gave more emphasis to the penal control efforts of local law-enforcement officials, whereas TQ included more penal control efforts in international conflicts through the use of news-service feeds. The newspapers also differed in the specific areas of penal control actions they focused upon. NP used both local stories and foreign wire feeds to give emphasis to the control actions of police and other criminal law-enforcers, whereas NQ gave particular attention to penal actions associated with failures in compliance, and to penal control efforts in international conflicts. There were also subtle differences in the language of penal-control action. The popular outlets and TQ were much more reliant than was NQ or RQ on dramatic language to depict control actions. Differences in this respect are evident in the murder story analysed in chapter 4.

CONCILIATORY

In the conciliatory style of control, the focus is on the resolution of a problem or conflict through concessions and reconciliations that restore harmony between the parties concerned. The conciliatory style was reported with respect to a wide variety of control actions by sources. A partial list of examples includes efforts by labour to achieve better working conditions from management; the conduct of special commissions of inquiry regarding the failure of a particular institution to deliver its service or products properly; the conduct of established commissions, such as a human-rights commission or a police public-complaints commission, regarding particular complaints of rights violations or official misconduct; the handling of ongoing protest demonstrations, such as a 'peace camp' demonstration outside the Parliament Buildings; regulation of private security operatives regarding the use of *agents provocateurs* in industrial disputes; and the regulation of professional misconduct, especially on the part of lawyers and doctors. The conciliatory style is most closely associated with the compliance mode. The focus is on regulating social relationships within and between organizations and institutions rather than on punishing wrongdoers for individual acts of deviance. However, the deterrence mode can also incorporate elements of concession and reconciliation for the restoration of harmony as part of conflict resolution.

As documented in table 9.2, the depiction of conciliatory control actions by sources varied significantly by medium. NQ is again the outlier. While NP had far more penal control actions than did NQ, the reverse is true regarding conciliatory control actions with the proportion in NQ (57 per cent) far exceeding that of NP (28 per cent). The broadcast outlets are closer to the level of NP, although television is significantly higher than radio. Far more than any of the other news outlets, NQ gave emphasis to the conciliatory style and the modes and mechanisms of control associated with it.

Indeed, this is one of the features that most distinguishes a quality print news outlet from its popular counterpart and from most broadcast news.

The language of conciliation was different in NQ and RQ compared to TQ and popular outlets in all media. Especially in the coverage of demonstrations connected with the conciliatory efforts of social movements (e.g., peace protesters, labour unions on strike), the popular outlets and TQ emphasized confrontation and conflict to indicate that actual conciliation was a long way off. Even in coverage of commissions of inquiry, dramatic language was used to describe procedural conflicts between the parties and their legal representatives. In contrast, NQ gave particular emphasis to conflicts over the language of deviant designations and control itself. Letters to the editor in NQ frequently focused on the political meaning of deviant designations. For example, one letter advised the newspaper not to use the word 'dissident' as though it meant 'rebel' regarding the actions of groups reported in previous stories of political conflict in both Zimbabwe and Nicaragua. Other NQ items reported on language contests between groups as the conflict that was subject to a conciliatory process. For example, one story headlined 'Indians deny pressure in dropping "powwow"' addressed a previous news report that said a government grant to a native group to hold a Canada Day celebration was dependent upon the event being advertised as a 'native heritage day celebration' rather than as a 'powwow.'

Sometimes items reporting on conciliatory actions in relation to a social problem or conflict also reported on problems and conflicts within the conciliatory process itself. Thus there were reports of conciliatory actions taken to control the procedures by which other conciliatory actions would be taken. For example, reports of the proceedings of a commission of inquiry regarding suspicious deaths at a hospital repeatedly focused on arguments among the lawyers for the various parties regarding procedural detail (e.g., witnesses allowed, order of witnesses, video and audio recording of the proceedings), and on the head of the inquiry's repeated complaints that the lawyers were causing unnecessary delay. In these items, the procedural obsession of the administered society and the news media reached almost absurd proportions. Nevertheless, such procedural concern in the resolution of conflicts and achievement of compliance is the very essence of the conciliatory style.

THERAPEUTIC

In the therapeutic style of control action, the focus is on helping the wrongdoer through medical, welfare, or other provisions that might restore the person to normality. As indicated in table 9.2, this style of control action was not represented often enough in any of the news outlets to indicate significant variation among them. Therapeutic control action did appear with greater proportionate frequency in NP, a finding consistent with the fact that NP dwelt more on acts of serious violent crime and psychiatric designations of those acts as pathological.

Mechanisms of Law and Justice

In table 9.3 we enumerate the specific mechanisms of control action engaged in, and how these mechanisms varied by medium and market.

Support mobilization refers to organizing efforts (e.g., publicizing, petitioning, lobbying, demonstrating) directed at securing public sympathy or assistance (e.g., general 'public opinion' pressure, specific help, membership, donations) to achieve political aims. Support mobilization was the control mechanism represented most often in each of the news outlets except for RP, which represented coercion more often, and NP, which represented coercion as often.

Coercion refers to control actions imposed unilaterally by one party against another, e.g., acts of military intervention, martial law, economic sanctions, deportation or expulsion, strikes or lock-outs, civil lawsuits, and criminal procedural actions including prosecutions. NQ is the outlier, with only 16 per cent of its sources' control mechanisms being coercive compared to 25 per cent of NP's, and similar proportions in the broadcast media.

Investigation was also a mechanism of control that was represented frequently in each news outlet, with a narrow range between 13 per cent in NQ and 17 per cent in RP. Investigations included not only police searches for witnesses and physical evidence, as analysed in chapter 4, but also the search for deviants and knowledge about them through regulatory agencies, inquests, and special and permanent commissions of inquiry. In the case of inquests and commissions of inquiry, there were continuing stories of investigative discoveries and the investigative procedures involved. Often these stories presented the law and law-enforcers not as agents of certainty – as in the quickly concluded continuing story analysed in chapter 4 – but as equivocal, uncertain, lacking in the ability to settle facts, and lacking in the ability to settle claims.

As documented in table 9.3, the remaining types of control mechanisms were represented relatively infrequently, and did not vary significantly by medium or market orientation. *Negotiation* – deliberations between two or more parties to reach an agreement affecting each of them – was represented most often in the newspapers, especially NQ, and least often in the popular broadcast outlets. *Adjudication* – dispute-settlement actions conducted by a third party with power to enforce an outcome – was most prevalent in radio, especially RP, followed by television, especially TP, and the newspapers. The

TABLE 9.3
Mechanisms of law and justice

Mechanisms of law and justice	Newspaper Q	Newspaper P	Television Q	Television P	Radio Q	Radio P	Sig. diff.
Support mobilization	171 29.9%	110 25.9%	227 32.8%	168 36.4%	164 29.3%	103 24.0%	
Coercion	95 16.6%	107 25.2%	149 21.5%	116 25.1%	142 25.4%	118 27.4%	N
Investigation	76 13.3%	64 15.1%	105 15.2%	64 13.9%	86 15.4%	71 16.5%	
Negotiation	35 6.1%	22 5.2%	33 4.8%	11 2.4%	19 3.4%	10 2.3%	
Adjudication	31 5.4%	25 5.9%	45 6.5%	33 7.1%	45 8.0%	49 11.4%	
Rule creation	20 3.5%	10 2.4%	16 2.3%	7 1.5%	20 3.6%	14 3.3%	
Resource control	23 4.0%	8 1.9%	12 1.7%	4 0.9%	10 1.8%	7 1.6%	
De-escalation of control	6 1.0%	4 0.9%	10 1.4%	2 0.4%	3 0.5%	2 0.5%	
Other	85 14.9%	52 12.3%	72 10.4%	41 8.9%	57 10.9%	41 9.5%	
Total actions	572	424	693	462	560	430	3,141

Percentages are by column. Missing cases = 6. Tests of significance based on tables with mechanisms of law and justice dichotomized into 'yes/no' for each of the categories. The last column indicates comparisons that show significant differences: chi-square statistics significant at the 0.05 level with Cramer's V or PHI ≥ 0.10, when N is large. Significant differences may occur between the newspapers (N); television stations (T); radio stations (R); or among the three types of media (M). The last column also indicates the presence of significant interactions with the variables being analysed and the coders (C) in a separate log-linear analysis.

greater emphasis on adjudication processes in broadcast news may be related to the tendency of broadcast journalists to cover scheduled hearings regarding the settlement of conflicts. *Rule creation* – regarding legislation, legislative amendments, regulation, standards *vis-à-vis* regulation, and administrative procedures of organizations – appeared infrequently as a control mechanism. *Resource control* – practices regarding the allocation and condition of funding – was also infrequently represented, although NQ represented it twice as frequently as any other outlet. *De-escalation of control* – the lifting of sanctions, such as decriminalization and diversion from the criminal-justice system – was rarely included as a control mechanism in any of the news outlets.

Institutional Contexts of Control Agents

In this section, and the following five sections, we analyse the institutional contexts and fields in which control action took place and how these vary by medium and market. We consider the institutional contexts and fields 1 / of the persons engaged in control actions; 2 / of the organizations or people whose resources these persons mobilized in taking control actions; and 3 / of the organizations or people subject to control actions.

GOVERNMENT

In table 9.4, we analyse the institutional context of those who participated in control actions as this varied by medium and market orientation. The majority of control participants represented in each news outlet were government officials. This finding is in keeping with the established fact that the main focus of the news media is on governments and the control activities of their officials.

The radio outlets focused on the control actions of government officials more so than did the newspapers, while television did so least. This finding is related to the fact that with comparatively limited news resources, radio is especially likely to use the predictable supply of newsworthy material available from a range of official government sources. This material inevitably centres upon government officials at work taking control actions. RP, the outlier, with 72 per cent of its control participants functioning in a governmental capacity, was also the news outlet that had the least news resources of any of the outlets studied. It relied in particular on anchor briefs, typically incorporating wire feeds or clips, and on reporters who covered the basic local beats such as police, courts, city hall, and provincial legislature.

PRIVATE CORPORATE

Actors in the private corporate institutional context were depicted as participants in control action in only a small minority of instances. Several items cited private corporate sources who were resisting or failing to comply with government regulations. For example, an item reported that a cinema operator was defying a censor-board ruling by continuing to show a censored film. There were also many items that addressed control actions taken by

TABLE 9.4
Institutional context of control agents

Institutional context	Newspaper		Television		Radio		Sig. diff.
	Q	P	Q	P	Q	P	
Government	385	265	410	269	352	311	R
	67.3%	62.5%	59.2%	58.2%	62.9%	72.3%	C
Private corporate	55	47	73	53	68	30	
	9.6%	11.1%	10.5%	11.5%	12.1%	7.0%	
Community	88	59	134	73	92	50	C
	15.4%	13.9%	19.3%	15.8%	16.4%	11.6%	
Individual	33	45	55	47	30	23	
	5.8%	10.6%	7.9%	10.2%	5.4%	5.3%	
Total actions	572	424	693	462	560	430	3,141

Percentages are by column. Missing cases = 94. Tests of significance based on tables with institutional context of control agents dichotomized into 'yes/no' for each of the categories. The last column indicates comparisons that show significant differences: chi-square statistics significant at the 0.05 level with Cramer's V or PHI $\geq$ 0.10, when N is large. Significant differences may occur between the newspapers (N); television stations (T); radio stations (R); or among the three types of media (M). The last column also indicates the presence of significant interactions with the variables being analysed and the coders (C) in a separate log-linear analysis.

private corporate officials against various community groups, especially trade unions. Several items in this category were derived from a particular continuing story regarding the withdrawal of a corporation's sponsorship of a symphony orchestra that had given a benefit concert for groups committed to disarmament. Another area of control depicted with frequency was actions taken by landlords against individual citizens who were tenants.

COMMUNITY ORGANIZATIONS

Persons participating in control actions in the context of community organizations were represented frequently. The representation of control actions by community-group members focused on resistance to government regulation, policies, and decisions. Resistance was depicted in the actions of members of a wide variety of community organizations in terms of the specific interest-group politics they were engaged in. For example, there were items on the resistance of doctors to a proposed federal act that would restrict further their ability to bill patients beyond the fee schedule of provincial health plans; items on the efforts by residents of a particular street to withhold payment of their property taxes until the government took action to deal with contaminated soil on their properties that the government was responsible for; and items on a civil-liberties group holding protest meetings with respect to the excessive powers being proposed for security and intelligence police under a draft federal security bill. Other control actions resistant to government policies and regulations were less specific. For example, all news outlets gave substantial coverage to 'peace protests' conducted by a range of groups in different places and contexts.

The control actions of community-group members were not limited to resistance against government policies and regulations. Also represented were people from one community group trying to control other community groups relevant to their sphere of operation. For example, members of one trade union were reported to be trying to recruit members away from a second union, with counter-control moves from the second union. There were also control moves reported *within* a particular community organization, for example, regarding which faction within a private club would gain control of the organization. Community-organization members were also depicted in control actions against individual citizens, as in an RP item that reported that 'in Pennsylvania the local Girl Scout troop is getting tough over unpaid Girl Scout cookie bills. The council has filed lawsuits against the parents of 14 girl scouts allegedly owing $1,100 in unpaid cookie bills.'

In many reports on the control actions of community-group members, it is evident that journalists themselves were taking control action on behalf of their community source. For example, a TP report on a civil-liberties group protesting the excessive powers in a proposed security bill (see pp. 174–5) included not only a text sympathetic to the group and its leader, but even the telephone number of the group, encouraging citizens to join the group and thereby to join in the protest. There were many more subtle instances in which journalists contextualized and interpreted the control actions of community-group sources in a sympathetic manner. The provision of media access to community groups engaged in resistance to government actions or regulations is itself a form of journalistic participation in control action. Similar aspects of journalistic participation in control action appear in the coverage of control activity by individual citizens.

INDIVIDUALS

A few persons were said to be taking control actions individually, rather than in the context of an institutional role. The depiction of control actions by individuals without an institutional role was infrequent, ranging from just over 5 per cent in the radio outlets to just over 10 per cent in NP and TP. The slightly higher proportion in both NP and TP is related to their greater focus on the activities of individual citizens as a part of their popular format. Compared to NQ and TQ, NP and TP focused less on organizational and institutional relations *within* government, and more on the activities of individual citizens. As documented in chapter 7, one dimension of this emphasis on individuals in NP and TP was greater attention to acts of individual deviance outside of institutional contexts. Another dimension is the one noted here (table 9.4), with NP and TP being somewhat more attentive to individuals taking control actions on their own, outside of an institutional role. Attention to individual control actions was consistent with their 'vox pop' orientation, and in particular the 'little guy versus bureaucracy' theme within this orientation.

Individual control actions in all outlets most often focused on the individual citizen 'fighting' bureaucracy with respect to an alleged violation of individual rights or an unfair decision. Typical is a TQ story about a man on a hunger strike to protest a decision by a municipal land-division committee not to allow him to subdivide and sell off some of his acreage. An excerpt from this story shows the citizen's control efforts in his struggle with the authorities.

Reporter: [Shot of citizen drinking from a cup and smoking a cigarette] ... In protest Ramsey is on a hunger strike. He's living on coffee and cigarettes. He claims he's lost fifteen pounds in the last five days. Ramsey also claims he's willing to starve himself to death.

Source: [Head shot, vista 'Fred Ramsey hunger striker'] If I starve myself to death the severance which I have requested would be automatically granted.

Reporter: [Reverse to reporter and the back of the source] Some would say you're a publicity seeker, that you're grandstanding, what would be your response to that?

Source: [Head shot] No, I'm not. You don't go without eating for five days just to grandstand or make an impression on somebody.

Reporter: [Reverse to the reporter and the back of the source] Do you think your hunger strike will get you anywhere?

Source: [Head shot] Yes. It will get me a severance.

This excerpt not only depicts the little guy 'fighting' bureaucracy, it also signifies the fact that publicity itself is an important part of the 'battle' for control. The reporter raises the question of 'grandstanding,' suggesting that the man might be dramatizing his plight in the hope that the pressure of publicity will be too much for the authorities to bear and they will give in. The journalist is taking control action in his decision to report on the control actions of others.

There were institutionalized dimensions to reporters taking control actions on behalf of individual citizens. For example, TP's municipal-beat reporter adapted a populist format whereby he regularly 'took to the streets' to present citizens 'fighting city hall' on regulatory matters such as noise complaints and parking problems. In these items the reporter explicitly took the side of individual complainants, and/or a local community, in efforts to remedy what they interpreted as incursions on their privacy and enjoyment.

Newspaper columnists also used their space as a designated place for one-sided opinion to advance the grievances of individuals against the authorities. This was frequently a feature of the opinion columns in NP. Some of these columns took up particular grievances, for example, the case of a penitentiary inmate who was initiating a civil suit against guards regarding the way in which they had conducted searches of his family members when they came to visit him at the penitentiary.

Another institutionalized format for control action on behalf of individuals was the regular columns in the newspapers, and a slot on TQ, devoted to consumers' complaints about the goods and services provided by either government agencies or private corporations. While these mechanisms are typically limited to individual complaints rather than systematic wrongdoing, they do offer some scope for individuals to use the power of publicity to achieve specific remedies for their troubles with bureaucracy (Hannigan 1977; Palen 1979; Pfuhl and Altheide 1987).

NP had an 'Action Line' column in which letters of complaint from consumers were published along with the columnist's account of the action she had taken to achieve a remedy. Typical was an item in which a woman complained that she and her husband had to cancel a trip abroad because the authorities had not responded to her application for the birth certificate that she needed to apply for a passport. The 'action line' columnist said she called the appropriate bureaucrat who was in charge of issuing birth certificates, and he 'told us a new set of birth certificates has been rushed via special delivery to the [woman], who confirmed receiving them.'

TQ had a citizen-advocate who received complaints and then showed himself to be acting on them on the citizen's behalf. Typical was a letter of complaint about postal service regarding a parcel that never arrived, and a letter of complaint about rail service regarding a train that arrived seven hours later than scheduled. Among the remedies offered by TQ's action-line journalist was 'raspberries': he was pictured taking a spoonful of raspberries from a jar, and dumping it on the letter of complaint to the bureaucracy concerned, as an expression of the sentiments he was visualized as sharing with the aggrieved citizen.

NQ had a regular 'Consumer Game' column in which the columnist reported on an individual's alleged problem with a company or government agency offering a good or service. As with NP's 'Action Line,' this column was comparable to a letters-to-the-editor format except that the topic was restricted to specific consumer complaints. However, while the NP columnist reproduced an edited letter from the individual citizen stating the complaint, the NQ columnist wrote the complaint up herself with selected quotations from the citizen's letter. Moreover, unlike the NP columnist, the NQ columnist reported no investigation in search of a remedy to the problem. The negative publicity alone was assumed to be sufficient to evoke a responsive chord in the organization that had offended. On occasion, the NQ columnist did encourage others to take action, in effect using the column as the basis for a 'petition' against a particular regulation or practice. This approach is illustrated in the following 'Consumer Game' item from NQ:

> 'We retired persons who receive a significant portion of our income from Canada Savings Bonds are required to prepay tax on March 31, June 30 and Sept. 30 on interest we don't receive until Nov. 1,' writes J.H. Layne of Islington, Ont. 'If we don't prepay on time, we are fined!
>
> 'The problem is greater now because many of us have diverted savings away from the prevailing instability of deposit-taking institutions toward CSBs.
>
> 'This is not a petty-cash problem. The fine is substantial. It can be a real problem to come up with the money on time. The net negative after-tax and inflation return on these bonds is further reduced.'
>
> Mr. Lane thinks the demand is 'unreasonable and unjust' and suggests that retirees who agree with him should clip this column and forward it to Revenue Canada requesting credit for the interest on the prepayments.

This item illustrates how journalists take control action in the very process of giving space to an individual to publicize his or her control action. Action-line slots highlight what journalists do routinely in other formats: they select and represent sources in ways intended to have control effects on organizations whose procedures have been brought into question. While journalists are much more likely to participate in control action along with community organizations, private corporations, and especially governmental agencies, they do offer a little space and some assistance to the individual citizen acting in his or her own interest.

Institutional Fields of Control Agents

In table 9.5, we analyse the institutional field of people depicted in control action as this varied by medium and market orientation.

In all news outlets except NQ, law-enforcement and public-safety agents were represented more than any other type. Accounts of law-enforcers taking control actions were especially prevalent in radio (47 per cent), compared to television (36 per cent) and the newspapers (27 per cent). There is also

TABLE 9.5
Institutional field of control agents

Institutional field	Newspaper		Television		Radio		Sig. diff.
	Q	P	Q	P	Q	P	
Law enforcement/ public safety	124 21.7%	144 34.0%	241 34.8%	178 38.5%	246 43.9%	219 50.9%	M/N
Politics	162 28.3%	59 13.9%	124 17.9%	55 11.9%	65 11.6%	73 17.0%	N C
Health	27 4.7%	48 11.3%	51 7.4%	43 9.3%	69 12.3%	22 5.1%	N/R C
Trade/finance	45 7.9%	14 3.3%	45 6.5%	14 3.0%	30 5.4%	18 4.2%	N C
Culture	49 8.6%	42 9.9%	44 6.3%	45 9.7%	18 3.2%	13 3.0%	M
Military	46 8.0%	11 2.6%	52 7.5%	18 3.9%	15 2.7%	21 4.9%	N
Other	83 14.5%	43 10.1%	75 10.8%	36 7.8%	58 10.4%	24 5.6%	
Total actions	572	424	693	462	560	430	3,141

Percentages are by column. Missing cases = 232. Tests of significance based on tables with institutional fields of control agents dichotomized into 'yes/no' for each of the categories. The last column indicates comparisons that show significant differences: chi-square statistics significant at the 0.05 level with Cramer's V or PHI ≥ 0.10, when N is large. Significant differences may occur between the newspapers (N); television stations (T); radio stations (R); or among the three types of media (M). The last column also indicates the presence of significant interactions with the variables being analysed and the coders (C) in a separate log-linear analysis.

variation by market orientation, with the popular outlets in each medium focusing more on the control actions of law-enforcement agents than their quality-outlet counterparts. The difference is especially marked within the newspapers, with NP (34 per cent) giving substantially more coverage to the control actions of law-enforcers than did NQ (22 per cent).

NQ is also the outlier in depicting control actions by politicians and others in the field of politics. NQ (28 per cent) cited control actions by those in politics twice as often as did NP (14 per cent), with the broadcast outlets being at roughly similar levels to NP.

Persons in the health field were depicted in control action with some frequency, especially in NP, TP, and RQ. NP (11 per cent), compared to NQ (5 per cent), and RQ (12 per cent), compared to RP (5 per cent), were much more focused on the control actions of health officials and medical professionals. All outlets included the control actions of government health officials in their efforts to regulate the medical profession, and the control moves of the medical profession to counter these efforts. In addition, NP and TP were particularly committed to depictions of medical personnel working hard to help people in emergency situations. This was a staple component of their popular format, consistent with, and frequently a part of, their focus on the diligence and heroic efforts of the police. Cathected scenarios of law-enforcement and medical-emergency personnel taking control actions for the public good, whether in news or other programming, offers the blend of disaster, crime, legal accomplishment, and scientific accomplishment that is at the core of popular sensibility in the administered society (O'Neill 1981).

The control actions of people in the field of trade and finance were not depicted frequently relative to other fields. The quality outlets included control actions in trade and finance more often than did the popular outlets within each medium. The difference was most marked between the newspapers, with NQ (8 per cent) including a much greater proportion of accounts about the control actions of people in trade and finance than did NP (3 per cent). This is explained by the much larger amount of space NQ devoted to its business section, and to the fact that control actions within private corporate circles or between government regulatory officials and private corporate actors also permeated other sections of NQ.

Control actions by people in the field of culture, including media operatives, appeared infrequently, especially in radio (3 per cent), compared to television (10 per cent) and newspapers (9 per cent). NQ differed from the other outlets in the extent to which it included control actions taken by members of the media institution *vis-à-vis* regulatory efforts by government and associated freedom-of-the-press issues. NP and TP focused more on control actions within the entertainment industry, for example, regarding contracts for entertainers.

The control actions of military personnel were represented more often in those outlets that focused on international stories through the use of wire feeds (NQ, TQ, and RP). While NP (3 per cent) very rarely provided accounts of control actions by military personnel, NQ (8 per cent) did so with some frequency.

Institutional Contexts Mobilized in Control Action

In table 9.6, we analyse the institutional contexts mobilized to carry out the control action as these varied by medium and market orientation. While the institutional context of the person participating in the control action referred to the control actor's institutional 'home,' the present consideration is the institutional context mobilized by the control agent in effecting his or her

TABLE 9.6
Institutional context mobilized in control action

Institutional context	Newspaper		Television		Radio		Sig. diff.
	Q	P	Q	P	Q	P	
Government	403	307	462	329	427	359	
	70.5%	72.4%	66.7%	71.2%	76.3%	76.5%	
Private corporate	77	57	95	45	64	46	
	13.5%	13.4%	13.7%	9.7%	11.4%	10.7%	
Community	58	34	67	61	37	25	
	10.1%	8.0%	9.7%	13.2%	6.6%	5.8%	
Individual	2	7	8	6	1	2	
	0.3%	1.7%	1.2%	1.3%	0.2%	0.5%	
Total actions	572	424	693	462	560	430	3,141

Percentages are by column. Missing cases = 192. Tests of significance based on tables with institutional context mobilized in control dichotomized into 'yes/no' for each of the categories. The last column indicates comparisons that show significant differences: chi-square statistics significant at the 0.05 level with Cramer's V or PHI ≥ 0.10, when N is large. Significant differences may occur between the newspapers (N); television stations (T); radio stations (R); or among the three types of media (M). The last column also indicates the presence of significant interactions with the variables being analysed and the coders (C) in a separate log-linear analysis.

control action. For example, a person representing a community interest group might mobilize a government ministry in efforts to deal with a problem, or vice versa. Similarly, an individual might mobilize a community group in helping with a particular problem or lobbying effort, or mobilize the police in controlling a deviant person. Of course, people within a particular institution can mobilize the resources of that institution in taking control action, an approach that was especially typical for depictions of government control agents.

As documented in table 9.6, the resources of government were depicted as being mobilized in a substantial majority of instances in all news outlets. A comparison of tables 9.6 and 9.4 makes evident that government resources were cited as being mobilized more often than government officials were cited as being the principal actors in control action. This suggests that control actors in other institutional spheres – private corporations, community groups, and individuals – were frequently depicted as mobilizing the resources of government, a fact underscored when we also compare tables 9.6 and 9.4 regarding these other institutional spheres.

The resources of the private corporate sector were depicted as being mobilized in control action to a relatively minor degree. A comparison of tables 9.6 and 9.4 reveals that in all outlets except TP and RQ, the mobilization of private corporate resources was depicted more often than the control actions of private corporate actors. This finding indicates that, in these outlets, there were frequent depictions of private corporate power being mobilized by people in institutional roles outside the private corporate sphere.

The resources of community groups were not often depicted as being mobilized in control action. The incidence of such depictions by TP is somewhat higher because its popular format included items depicting control actions taking place through local community organizations and interest groups. However, a comparison of tables 9.6 and 9.4 reveals that overall, the mobilization of community-resources was depicted much less often than the control actions of people based in community organizations or interest groups. In all outlets, community organization members were frequently depicted mobilizing the resources of other institutional spheres, especially government.

Table 9.6 indicates that it was very rare, indeed, to find depictions of an individual being mobilized in control actions. While individuals were depicted as control agents with some frequency (table 9.4), they were very rarely mobilized by others to serve as a resource for control action. In all news outlets, the power resources for control were shown to reside in institutions, and especially in the institutions of government.

Institutional Fields Mobilized in Control Action

In table 9.7, we analyse the institutional fields mobilized to carry out the control action as this varied by medium and market orientation.

LAW ENFORCEMENT AND PUBLIC SAFETY

Table 9.7 indicates that, in all news outlets, law enforcement was depicted most often as the field being mobilized in control action. However, the degree to which the use of law-enforcement resources dominated depictions of control action varied substantially among the news outlets. In terms of medium, it was the radio outlets (61 per cent) that were especially likely to depict the mobilization of law-enforcement agencies in control action, followed by television (48 per cent) and the newspapers (37 per cent). In terms of market orientation, there is significant variation between the quality and popular newspapers, with NQ (30 per cent) depicting mobilization of law-enforcement resources much less often than NP (46 per cent). A comparison of tables 9.7 and 9.5 reveals that, while law-enforcers were very frequently the persons said to be taking control action, law-enforcement mechanisms were mobilized to an even greater degree. This indicates that

TABLE 9.7
Institutional field mobilized in control action

Institutional field	Newspaper		Television		Radio		Sig. diff.
	Q	P	Q	P	Q	P	
Law enforcement/ public safety	169	195	312	244	339	263	M/N
	29.5%	46.0%	45.0%	52.8%	60.5%	61.2%	C
Politics	120	52	127	52	68	68	N/T
	21.0%	12.3%	18.3%	11.3%	12.1%	15.8%	C
Health	23	41	32	20	38	13	N
	4.0%	9.7%	4.6%	4.3%	6.8%	3.0%	C
Trade/finance	35	9	29	15	20	13	N
	6.1%	2.1%	4.2%	3.2%	3.6%	3.0%	
Culture	58	36	49	47	25	16	
	10.1%	8.5%	7.1%	10.2%	4.5%	3.7%	
Military	58	15	42	16	8	11	M/N
	10.1%	3.5%	6.1%	3.5%	1.4%	2.6%	
Other	73	38	43	36	28	20	M
	12.8%	9.0%	6.2%	7.8%	5.0%	4.7%	
Total actions	572	424	693	462	560	430	3,141

Percentages are by column. Missing cases = 125. Tests of significance based on tables with institutional field mobilized in control action dichotomized into 'yes/no' for each of the categories. The last column indicates comparisons that show significant differences: chi-square statistics significant at the 0.05 level with Cramer's V or PHI $\geq$ 0.10, when N is large. Significant differences may occur between the newspapers (N); television stations (T); radio stations (R); or among the three types of media (M). The last column also indicates the presence of significant interactions with the variables being analysed and the coders (C) in a separate log-linear analysis.

control agents in other fields were often depicted as mobilizing law-enforcement agencies as part of their control actions.

There are several dimensions in the mobilization of law enforcement that are not evident from the data categorized in these general terms. NQ differed from the other outlets not only in the lesser degree to which it depicted the mobilization of law enforcement, but also in the areas of law enforcement mobilized. It included relatively more mobilizations of regulatory agencies and less on the public police compared to the other outlets. Moreover, while the public police were dominant as the law-enforcement resource mobilized most often, there was considerable variance in the depiction of how they were mobilized and in the value of such mobilization.

In spite of considerable police effort to patrol publicity so that it works in their favour (Ericson 1989), there were many signs of the inability of the police to deal with problems. The police were said to be unresponsive to some efforts at mobilization and/or unwilling to commit additional resources to handle a particular problem or type of problem. For example, their handling of complaints by victims of rape was said to be discouraging complainants from mobilizing police. The police were frequently depicted as having minimal detection capabilities. For example, an item in NP focused on the inability of police in British Columbia to solve sixty occurrences of rape against children over a six-year period. In the following RQ item, a woman is said to be taking control action of her own after having mobilized the police. Not only were police unable to capture the man who attacked her, they admitted their limited detection capabilities in this regard and that 'it will be a fluke if the man is caught before he strikes again.'

Anchor: [Tease] A Toronto woman warns her neighbours that a dangerous attacker is loose.

Anchor: A Toronto woman is posting notices alerting women to a dangerous attacker. The 24-year-old woman was beaten on Saturday night shortly after midnight just doors from her ... home ...

Reporter: [Loud traffic noises in background conveying that the reporter is 'on the street'] This woman is five foot seven. She's slim but she's strong. Today she has a swollen black eye and puffy cheeks. She says she's lucky she had the reflexes to try and fight back. On the sidewalk here at Wellesley and Sackville a man approached her from behind and brutally attacked her.

Woman: One arm encircled my both arms across my chest. One leg crossed over my ankles holding those straight. He leaned us both forward supporting himself with the fence that was behind us and then leaned my head forward so when his fists came up he would have dead impact on my face.

Reporter: Her attacker put his hand over her mouth to muffle her screams for help. She fought back with her teeth.

Woman: And then when the first thing came available for me to bite or hit or anything else, which was his hand, I grabbed it as fast as I could and I just bit as hard as I could.

Reporter: Eventually neighbours came to help. The police arrived and the woman's attacker fled. He bolted north over backyard fences and then scaled a tall barrier to get into the neighbouring graveyard. The woman hopes her poster campaign will help find her attacker.

Woman: I'm doing this because I was hurt, I was attacked, I was beaten, and I was scared and it's happened to other people in the neighbourhood. And it has to be stopped and I don't think the police are doing the best they can do to stop it. And so until the time they catch that person the public has to be made aware that it's happening in this neighbourhood.

Reporter: What more should the police be doing?

Woman: As I said, once you get into the graveyard they told me that the game's up, he's away now, he's gone, whereas I feel if that had been another policeman who'd been attacked it would have been floodlights galore, search dogs, and everything else. I mean this man's a potential killer and if they can't put out that little bit of extra energy to get him then we're in bad shape. We're never going to be safe in that case because this guy was really in shape. He ran, he was much faster than the police. So he can do it as much as he wants as they can't catch up with him.

Reporter: Police admit a young man on the run wearing light clothing has it over older officers in uniform weighed down by guns and batons but Sergeant [names him] at 51 Division says more attention will be paid to the neighbourhood. The description of the woman's attacker could match thousands of men. He's believed to be about 20, with a medium build and blond hair. He's about five feet, eight inches tall. Teeth marks on his right hand could be the best clue. Police say it will be a fluke if the man is caught before he strikes again. [Sign-off]

The police were regularly depicted as being heavily dependent on citizens' input in order to detect and solve crimes. This view was conveyed routinely through stories that emphasized that an alert witness or secret informant had provided the crucial 'tip.' Typical were accounts stating that the return of treasures stolen from a synagogue resulted from an anonymous informant's tip and the arrest of a bank robber resulted from a bank customer noticing employees were agitated, leading him to call the police. In all such accounts, it was evident that police detection capabilities were dependent on citizens, a view that is in accord with research literature on police mobilization (Reiss 1971b; Manning 1988), and with the movement toward 'community policing' as an attempt to foster more citizen input into surveillance and crime control (Murphy 1988; Carriere and Ericson 1989).

POLITICS

In all news outlets, politics was second only to law enforcement and public safety in frequency of reported mobilization for control action. There is substantial variation by market orientation within newspapers and within television. NQ (21 per cent) much more than NP (12 per cent), and TQ (18 per cent) much more than TP (11 per cent), depicted the mobilization of politics in control actions. A comparison of tables 9.7 and 9.5 indicates that, in all outlets except NQ, there are similar levels of political actors engaged in control action as politics being a field mobilized for control action. In NQ, political actors engaged in control action were depicted with greater frequency than the field of politics being mobilized for control action. This indicates that, in NQ, more than in the other outlets, people in politics were frequently said to be mobilizing resources in other fields as a part of their control actions.

HEALTH

Table 9.7 shows that the field of health was said to be mobilized in control actions more in newspapers than in radio or television. The outlier is NP (10 per cent), which cited mobilization of health resources much more than NQ (4 per cent), and somewhat more than the broadcast news outlets. A comparison of tables 9.7 and 9.5 reveals that, in the broadcast outlets in particular, there were more depictions of people in the health field taking control actions than of the health field itself being mobilized for control actions. This indicates that many health officials and professionals were depicted mobilizing the resources of other institutional fields in their control efforts.

TRADE AND FINANCE

The mobilization of resources for control in the realm of trade and finance was most frequently depicted in NQ (6 per cent), which is not surprising, given its emphasis on business interests. In contrast, NP (2 per cent) very rarely depicted the mobilization of resources in trade and finance as a part of control action. A comparison of tables 9.7 and 9.5 reveals that, although the differences are small, in all outlets except TP more trade-and-finance actors were depicted taking control actions than was the trade and finance field said to be mobilized in control actions. This indicates that persons in trade and finance were frequently shown to be mobilizing the resources of other fields in taking control action.

CULTURE

Resources within the field of culture were more often depicted as being mobilized in the newspapers than in television and radio, although the difference is not statistically significant. Included here are instances in which the news media were *explicitly* mobilized to assist in control action. Such explicit accounts of the use of the news media in control action were sometimes featured as part of the 'vox pop' orientation of a popular outlet. This was especially typical of TP, whose reporters often made reference to the fact that they were publicizing the cause of a particular person or group as part of a control effort to achieve a remedy to a problem, and who reported successful outcomes to such efforts, including expressions of gratitude from sources. The 'media moves mountains' approach was also institutionalized in the regular 'action line' or consumer slots in the newspapers and TQ. The radio outlets did not have institutionalized 'action line' slots as part of the newscasts we studied, nor did they explicitly take a 'radio moves mountains' approach to their stories of control. This partly accounts for the fact that the radio outlets depicted the mobilization of resources in the field of culture much less often than did the television outlets and newspapers.

As argued previously, in the very act of news communication the media institution can function as a resource for control even if its role in this regard is not made explicit. The data presented here are silent on the fact that, in myriad ways, regular sources in all institutional fields use the news media as a crucial component of their everyday control work (Ericson, Baranek, and Chan 1989). These data do not account for the fact that the news media are a resource in control action in the very reporting of control actions.

MILITARY

Table 9.7 reveals that focus on the mobilization of military resources was most common in NQ (10 per cent) and TQ (6 per cent), with very little attention to this field in the other outlets. The higher frequency in NQ and TQ is related to their greater attention to foreign news that included international hostilities involving military threats, mobilization, or actual armed conflict.

Institutional Contexts Targeted in Control Action

We have analysed the institutional contexts and fields of control actors, and of the resources they mobilized in control action. It remains to consider the institutional contexts and fields that were subject to control action. In this section, we analyse the institutional contexts subject to control action and how these varied by medium and market orientation. The results of our analysis are summarized in table 9.8.

GOVERNMENT

Government organizations were depicted as being subject to control action much more frequently than were organizations in the private corporate or community sectors. There is significant variation by medium and market orientation in this regard. Government organizations were targeted for control much more frequently in the newspapers (45 per cent) than in television (35 per cent) or radio (24 per cent). Within the newspapers, NQ

TABLE 9.8
Institutional context targeted in control action

Institutional field	Newspaper		Television		Radio		Sig. diff.
	Q	P	Q	P	Q	P	
Government	307	137	275	123	163	161	M/N/T
	53.7%	32.3%	39.7%	26.6%	29.1%	37.4%	C
Private corporate	84	75	144	91	144	76	R
	14.7%	17.7%	20.8%	19.7%	25.7%	17.7%	
Community	87	58	112	81	100	145	R
	15.2%	13.7%	16.2%	17.5%	17.9%	10.5%	C
Individual	75	147	150	163	131	144	N/T/R
	13.1%	34.7%	21.6%	35.3%	23.4%	33.5%	C
Total actions	572	424	693	462	560	430	3,141

Percentages are by column. Missing cases = 68. Tests of significance based on tables with institutional context targeted in control action dichotomized into 'yes/no' for each of the categories. The last column indicates comparisons that show significant differences: chi-square statistics significant at the 0.05 level with Cramer's V or PHI $\geq$ 0.10, when N is large. Significant differences may occur between the newspapers (N); television stations (T); radio stations (R); or among the three types of media (M). The last column also indicates the presence of significant interactions with the variables being analysed and the coders (C) in a separate log-linear analysis.

(54 per cent) gave particular emphasis to the control of governmental organizations compared to NP (32 per cent), which tended to focus much more on the control of individuals without an institutional affiliation. These aggregate data confirm our field observations regarding the emphasis of NQ journalists on policing government (Ericson, Baranek, and Chan 1987). What is especially noteworthy in this regard is that, while NQ had a major business section and had a self-proclaimed focus on business interests, it was the least likely of the six outlets to depict control actions taken in relation to private corporations. This fact underscores the point that NQ policed governmental operations on behalf of the private sector, providing a form of intelligence about governmental activity useful to business interests (ibid). Among the most valuable functions of public bureaucracies for the private corporate sector is the provision of information that reduces risk and uncertainty (Warshett 1981). The news media, and especially newspapers such as NQ, not only help transmit such information to the private corporate sector, but also provide information about, and police, the information-production activities and procedures of government on behalf of private corporate interests.

There is also a significant difference between the television stations in the representation of control actions against government organizations. TQ

(40 per cent) depicted control actions involving the policing of government much more than did TP (27 per cent). This is consistent with our observations in the TQ newsroom regarding the particular commitment of this state-owned network affiliate to policing governmental operations (Ericson, Baranek, and Chan 1987). In contrast, TP, like NP, was much more committed to portrayals of government officials policing individual citizens.

RQ, part of the same state-owned network as TQ, did not show a similar level of commitment to portraying control actions aimed at government. Indeed RQ (29 per cent) was lower in this regard than its popular counterpart RP (37 per cent). This finding may be related to the fact that the RQ newscast we studied adopted a local focus. While RQ included many items involving control actions taken against municipal and provincial organizations, it left concerns about the federal government and governments abroad to other newscasts it picked up from the national network. However, RP, as well as TQ and the newspapers, included a lot of material, usually off the wire services, regarding national and international governmental operations.

Comparisons with some of our previous analyses are also revealing. Comparing tables 9.8 and Table 7.4, we find similar levels in each news outlet regarding the representation of deviant persons in government and government organizations being subject to control action. Deviants in government, and the control of government operations, are much more frequent in NQ and TQ than in NP and TP. Comparing tables 9.8 and 9.4, we discover that all outlets depicted more governmental officials taking control action than government operations being subject to control action. The difference in this regard is least in NQ, followed by TQ. The remaining outlets were about twice as likely to depict government officials taking control action as government operations subject to control actions. Comparing tables 9.8 and 9.6, we find a similar pattern: all outlets gave much greater attention to the mobilization of governmental resources in taking control action than to control actions taken against government operations.

PRIVATE CORPORATE

Compared to the depiction of control actions against government operations, control of private corporations had a relatively minor place. The exception is RQ, which gave only slightly more attention to policing actions against government (29 per cent) than against the private sector (26 per cent). RQ is the outlier in giving the greatest proportionate attention to private corporations as they were subject to control action, while NQ (15 per cent) had the lowest incidence of this attention among the outlets. While NQ focused on control actions against private corporations to some degree in absolute terms, its proportionate focus in this regard is low, given its overall substantial coverage of private corporate activity.

Comparing tables 9.8 and 7.4, we can see that the level at which each news outlet designated deviants in private corporate contexts is similar to the level at which they depicted control actions taken against private corporations. A wider gap is evident in the case of NQ, which focused somewhat more on corporate deviants than on control actions against corporations. Comparing tables 9.8 and 9.4, we discover that for each news outlet, but especially in the broadcast outlets, there was a greater focus on control actions against private corporations than on corporate actors taking control actions. Similarly, in comparing tables 9.8 and 9.4, we find that for all news outlets, but especially the broadcast outlets, there were many more depictions of private corporations being subject to control than of private corporate resources being mobilized in control action.

A comparison of the depiction of government and private corporate organizations subject to control action supports the prevalent claim that the news media are primarily oriented to the policing of government. However, it is rather extreme to claim that the 'search for truth, which now demands that governments at least project an image of openness and honesty, left virtually untouched precisely that sector which is the principle source of newspaper financing – the business world ... though they sometimes have a greater influence over the destinies of modern societies than the public authorities do' (Royal Commission Newspapers [RCN] 1981c: 21). Our data indicate that private corporations are hardly 'untouched' in news accounts of control actions, although admittedly they are underrepresented in this regard *vis-à-vis* their dominant influence in society. The news polices private corporate life, but to a much lesser degree than it polices government (Ericson, Baranek, and Chan 1989: chap 5).

COMMUNITY ORGANIZATIONS

There is not a great deal of variation in the proportionate extent to which community organizations were depicted as being subject to control action. However, within radio, RQ (18 per cent) offered a greater proportion of such depictions than did RP (11 per cent). Comparing tables 9.8 and 7.4, we learn that the newspapers, TQ and RP had similar levels of deviant persons in community groups as control actions taken against community groups, while TP and RQ gave greater attention to community groups subject to control action than to the deviance of members of community groups. Comparing tables 9.8 and 9.4, we find that all outlets had very similar levels of control actions taken by members of the community and community organizations subject to control actions. Comparing tables 9.8 and 9.6, it is evident that in each outlet there was much greater attention to control actions taken in relation to community organizations than to control actions involving the mobilization of community resources, especially in the radio outlets. This is another indication that news discourse is dominated more by government officials and governmental resources being mobilized to control non-state organizations and individuals than vice versa. This trend is evidenced further in analysing accounts of control actions taken in relation to individuals without an institutional affiliation.

INDIVIDUAL

Table 9.8 reveals significant variation among the news outlets in the extent to which individuals without an institutional affiliation were depicted as targets of control action. Within each medium, the popular outlets had a significantly higher proportion of individuals being subject to control action than did the quality outlets. The difference is especially marked between the newspapers, with NP (35 per cent) including control actions against individuals far more often than NQ (13 per cent). However, the gap is also quite wide in television (35 per cent in TP compared to 22 per cent in TQ) and in radio (34 per cent in RP compared to 23 per cent in RQ). While quality outlets focus more on institutions subject to control actions, the popular format accords relative priority to control actions taken against individuals without an institutional affiliation.

A comparison with previous analyses reveals additional significant insights regarding how individuals were represented. Comparing tables 9.8 and 7.4, we find that in all outlets there was an even greater emphasis on the control of individuals than on depictions of deviance by individuals. The quality outlets gave far more attention to individuals being subject to control action than to individual deviants. This finding indicates the greater focus in quality outlets on the institutional procedures of control (e.g., in relation to criminal control, investigation, accusation, trial and sentencing) than on attributions regarding the deviant actor and his or her act (e.g., portraits of the criminal offender).

Comparing tables 9.8 and 9.4, it is clear that all news outlets focused much more on control actions taken against individuals than by individuals. The citation of control action against individuals as compared to control actions taken by individuals was two times greater in NQ; three times greater in NP, TQ, and TP; four times greater in RQ; and five times greater in RP. The powerlessness of individuals in news accounts of control action is underscored even more in comparing tables 9.8 and 9.6. While the news outlets very often depicted individuals being subject to control action, they almost never depicted the resources of individuals being mobilized in control action.

Power for control resides in institutions. In news accounts, institutions take a lot of their control actions in relation to individual citizens, but almost never mobilize the individual citizen as a resource in control actions.

Our data on institutional contexts of control generally support the claim that government organizations dominate the news. 'News organizations are more apt to report about public institutions than about powerful private ones' (Tuchman 1978: 163), both as initiators of control action and as the subjects of control action. News organizations are also more apt to report about private individuals than about powerful private institutions, but these individuals are usually portrayed as being subject to control. News of crime, law, and justice does allow some space for control action by non-state organizations and individuals, but it gives much greater emphasis to non-state organizations and actors being subject to control at the hands of state agencies and agents.

Institutional Fields Targeted in Control Action

In table 9.9 we summarize our analysis of the institutional fields that were depicted as being subject to control action, and how these varied by medium and market orientation. The large number of missing cases in this analysis is accounted for by the fact that, in the case of all individuals and some community organizations subject to control action, no particular field was specified. Thus our analysis focuses on accounts of the major institutional fields that were targeted in control action and excludes individuals as well as community groups that did not fall within these fields.

LAW ENFORCEMENT AND PUBLIC SAFETY

Table 9.9 documents significant variation among the news outlets in the proportionate degree to which they included accounts of control actions taken in relation to law-enforcement agencies. Such accounts occurred much more frequently in radio (16 per cent) than in television (10 per cent) or the newspapers (8 per cent). A comparison with previous analyses provides additional insight. Comparing tables 9.9 and 7.5, we find that all outlets had more accounts of control actions taken against law-enforcers than of deviant law-enforcers. Comparing tables 9.9 and 9.5, we learn that control actions taken by law-enforcers were depicted far more often than were control actions against law-enforcers: by a multiple of three in NQ, TQ, and RQ; a multiple of four in NP and RP; and a multiple of five in TP. Comparing tables 9.9 and 9.7, we discover that the mobilization of law enforcement was also depicted with much greater frequency than were control actions against law-enforcers: by a multiple of four in each of NQ, TQ, RQ, and RP; a multiple of

TABLE 9.9
Institutional field targeted in control action

Institutional field	Newspaper		Television		Radio		Sig. diff.
	Q	P	Q	P	Q	P	
Law enforcement/	45	33	85	32	89	71	M
public safety	7.9%	7.8%	12.3%	6.9%	15.9%	16.5%	C
Politics	125	70	127	63	50	59	M
	21.9%	16.5%	18.3%	13.6%	8.9%	13.8%	C
Health	23	48	63	30	71	54	N
	4.0%	11.3%	9.1%	6.5%	12.7%	12.6%	
Trade/finance	65	29	74	29	57	19	R
	11.4%	6.8%	10.7%	6.3%	10.2%	4.4%	C
Culture	46	35	50	46	46	24	T
	8.0%	8.3%	7.2%	10.0%	8.2%	5.6%	
Military	99	26	59	17	11	24	M/N/T
	17.3%	6.1%	8.5%	3.7%	2.0%	5.6%	R
Other	72	44	72	51	79	36	
	12.6%	10.4%	10.4%	11.0%	14.1%	8.4%	
Total actions	572	424	693	462	560	430	3,141

Percentages are by column. Missing cases = 893. Tests of significance based on tables with institutional field targeted in control action dichotomized into 'yes/no' for each of the categories. The last column indicates comparisons that show significant differences: chi-square statistics significant at the 0.05 level with Cramer's V or PHI $\geq$ 0.10, when N is large. Significant differences may occur between the newspapers (N); television stations (T); radio stations (R); or among the three types of media (M). The last column also indicates the presence of significant interactions with the variables being analysed and the coders (C) in a separate log-linear analysis.

six in NP; and a multiple of eight in TP. All outlets, but in particular the popular outlets, depicted law-enforcers controlling others far more often than law-enforcers being subject to the control actions of others.

These aggregate data on control actions against law-enforcers do not reveal other dimensions of difference among the news outlets. For example, while NQ and NP had the same level of accounts in which law-enforcers were subject to control action, the specific targets were different. Almost one-third of the NP accounts were directed at the criminal courts, and almost one-half at the prison system. Few were directed at the public police or regulatory agencies. In contrast, NQ's accounts were primarily directed at policing the police, regulatory agencies, and court procedures. Moreover, NP's accounts tended to convey a view that the courts and prison system were too lenient within a law-and-order ideology, while NQ focused more on procedural propriety of law enforcement within a framework of institutional accountability.

All three quality outlets had depictions of their journalists involved in policing the police, while none of the popular outlets did so. For example, in an item on public demonstrations outside a free-standing abortion clinic, a TQ reporter included the fact that his outlet was conducting surveillance of police surveillance. The reporter said that the outlet's camera crew had discovered a hidden police surveillance camera and a communications antenna in a shop across from the clinic, and backed up his words with visuals of these police surveillance devices. The proportion of policing the police depictions in RQ was swelled by the fact that one of its reporters was doing a continuing investigative story about wrongdoing in a particular police force. Perhaps because this was the featured investigative piece in RQ at the time of our sampling, RQ also included many other items on wrongdoing in neighbouring police forces.

All outlets focused on officially mediated control actions against the police made possible by a new state mechanism for civilian review of complaints against the police. NQ not only focused on the 'policing the police' activities of this agency, but included stories from other jurisdictions regarding mechanisms for complaints against the police. For example, NQ included coverage of a Supreme Court of Canada case regarding the issue of whether citizens' complaints against members of the Royal Canadian Mounted Police could be heard by a provincial human-rights board.

Items depicting court officials subject to control action typically involved one member of the court system taking action against another, for example, an abuse of process ruling by a judge against a Crown attorney, and a decision by the Manitoba attorney general that a judge would not be disciplined for saying that 'any woman who needs an abortion should be given a razor blade.' In the prison setting, control actions were typically those taken on behalf of prisoners. Examples include a legal challenge to disciplinary procedures in the Ontario prison system, a legal suit in which the lawyer argued that the punishment imposed on his client while in custody was a violation of rights and principles of fundamental justice, and criminal action against guards accused of assaulting inmates. There were also depictions of direct control action by prisoners themselves, for example, accounts of a prisoners' hunger strike protesting harsh sentences and solitary confinement.

POLITICS

The depiction of control actions against people in politics was especially prevalent in the newspapers (20 per cent) compared to television (17 per cent) and radio (11 per cent). Comparison with previous analyses reveal additional insights. Comparing tables 9.9 and 9.5, we find that in each outlet there was a roughly similar level of imputations of deviance about people in politics as depictions of control action against those in political office. Comparing tables 9.9 and 9.5, we find that in the radio outlets and in NQ, in particular, there was more attention to politicians taking control actions than to control actions against politicians. In the television outlets and NP, this pattern is reversed, although the differences are not great. Comparing tables 9.9 and 9.7, it is evident that, in each news outlet, there is a roughly similar level of control actions involving the mobilization of the political institution as control actions directed at that institution.

HEALTH

The items dealing with control actions in the health field were dominated by continuing stories on a few major topics. These included the regulation of nursing homes operated by the private sector; the regulation of medical professionals, especially regarding a practice in which doctors were billing patients for amounts beyond the fee schedule established in the state health-care scheme; and the regulation of unauthorized medical services that were striving to achieve legitimacy (e.g., a free-standing abortion clinic; the practice of midwifery). The depiction of control actions in these continuing stories and other items pertaining to the health field varied between the newspapers. NP (11 per cent) gave much more attention to control actions against members of the health field than did NQ (4 per cent). Comparisons with previous analysis shed additional light on how the health field was covered in deviance and control news. Comparing tables 9.9 and 7.5, we find that within each news outlet there are similar levels of coverage given to deviance by persons in the health field and accounts of control actions taken in relation to the health field. Comparing tables 9.9 and 9.5, we see that generally there are similar levels of health officials taking control action and health officials being subject to control action. However, in RP, there were almost twice as many depictions of the health field being subject to control action as health officials taking control action. Comparing tables 9.9 and 9.7, we find that all of the broadcast outlets were much more likely to depict the health field being subject to control action than the health field being mobilized to take control action: by a multiple of one and one-half in TP, a multiple of two in TQ and RQ, and a multiple of four in RP. These outlets in particular focused on the voices of interest groups, politicians, and other political forces outside of the health field bringing their institutional resources to bear on health procedures and professionals, especially regarding the above-noted topics of regulating medical professionals, unauthorized medical services, and private-sector nursing homes.

TRADE AND FINANCE

Control actions aimed at the field of trade and finance primarily involved government officials as control agents and the mobilization of their regulatory resources. A dominant regulatory mechanism at the time was the so-called 6 and 5 anti-inflationary program of the federal government, which restricted most employers to granting wage and benefit increases of 6 per cent in the first year and 5 per cent in the second year. A large number of items in each news outlet focused on exercises of these '6 and 5' controls as well as disputes about them. Other regulatory agencies depicted in control actions *vis-à-vis* trade and finance were agricultural marketing boards, combines investigations, income-tax investigators, banking and financial-service regulators, and various officials responsible for government subsidies to industry in exchange for meeting standards of compliance.

As evidenced in table 9.9, there is significant variation among the news outlets in the depiction of the trade-and-finance field being subject to control action. Such depictions were most frequent in NQ (11 per cent), which is to be expected, given its orientation to business interests and its monitoring of governmental regulation in this regard. In contrast, RP (4 per cent) had very few accounts of those in the trade-and-finance field being subject to control action, especially when compared to RQ (10 per cent) and the other quality outlets. In general, the quality outlets within each medium were more likely to focus on control actions in relation to trade-and-finance operations.

Comparing tables 9.9 and 7.5, we find that imputations of deviance against those in the trade-and-finance field were more common in TP and the radio outlets than were accounts of the trade-and-finance field being subject to control action. Comparing tables 9.9 and 9.5, we see that, in each outlet, with the exception of RP, there were far fewer accounts of trade-and-finance people taking control action than of control actions taken against people and practices in the trade-and-finance field. Similarly, a comparison of tables 9.7 and 9.9 indicates that, in each outlet, there were much fewer depictions of trade-and-finance resources being mobilized in control action than of control actions against trade-and-finance operations. In the news, the trade-and-finance field is depicted more often as being regulated than as being mobilized in regulation.

CULTURE

The representation of people in the field of culture being subject to control action varied significantly between the television stations. Comparing tables 9.9 and 7.5, we discover that, in the newspapers and RQ, there were more items focusing on deviants in the field of culture than accounts of control actions taken in relation to the field of culture. However, this trend is reversed in the television outlets and RP. Comparing tables 9.9 and 9.5, we see very similar levels in the depiction of those in the field of culture taking control action and being subject to control action, with the exception of RQ, which has much fewer instances of the former than of the latter. Comparing tables 9.9 and 9.7, it is evident that the same pattern exists, with similar levels in the depiction of cultural resources being mobilized in control action and the depiction of the cultural field being subject to control action, except for RQ, which has much fewer instances of the former than of the latter.

These aggregate data do not reveal the differential emphasis in the news outlets regarding what parts of the cultural field were depicted as being subject to control action. TP in particular focused on deviants in the entertainment industry and on regulation of that industry as part of its greater proportionate attention to entertainment news. NQ paid particular attention to governmental actions at home and abroad that restricted freedom of the press. It also included items on the regulation of reporting practices, such as decisions by the Ontario Press Council, and law suits against reporters elsewhere regarding conflicts of interest. The newspapers also accommodated specific control actions directed at their operations through letters to the editor that corrected their errors. The television outlets focused on particular control actions pertaining to their medium, such as the issue of television in the courtroom. However, a few control actions against the media were cited across a number of the outlets studied. For example, there was an investigation, including a search and seizure, by the Combines Investigation Branch against the Thomson newspaper chain that not only received considerable play in the newspapers (NQ was a member of this chain) but also in the broadcast outlets. All outlets covered specific instances of legal control, such as publication bans on media coverage of court cases, and specific law suits, such as libel actions against a member of the media institution. Similarly there was coverage in several of the outlets regarding an incident in which police arrested ten journalists for trespassing on airport property to obtain a closer view of an airplane crash site. In this context, some reporters decided to make their arrest newsworthy along with their account of the airplane crash. TQ's reporter closed his item with the statement, 'The arrests were unfortunate, but trying to get the best for you, our viewers, is our responsibility. We were doing our job. The police were doing theirs.'

The news focus on control actions taken against journalists is another sign of how journalists portray themselves as *part of* the stories they report on. News discourse does not exclude its own operatives from accounts of their being subject to control actions, any more than it disguises the fact that journalists are active control agents in the very events and relationships they report on. The reflexivity of journalistic control practices is evident not only in the low-visibility conditions of back-region negotiations between journalists and their sources, but in the high-visibility conditions of news content itself.

MILITARY

Table 9.9 reveals a wide spread among the news outlets in depictions of control action taken in relation to the military field. Such depictions were most prevalent in the newspapers (13 per cent), followed by television (7 per cent) and radio (4 per cent). However, NQ (17 per cent) is the outlier, having significantly more accounts of the military field being subject to control action than did NP (6 per cent) or any of the other outlets. There is also a significant market-orientation difference in such depictions in television (9 per cent in TQ and 4 per cent in TP) and in radio (6 per cent in RP and 2 per cent in RQ). NQ, TQ, and RP were higher in the depiction of control actions *vis-à-vis* military operations because they gave more attention to international conflicts abroad.

Comparing tables 9.9 and 7.5, we find that, within each outlet except TQ, there was a roughly similar level of items depicting deviance by military personnel and accounts of targeting the military field in control action. However, in TQ, there was a proportionately much greater focus on military deviants than on control actions regarding military operations. Comparing tables 9.9 and 9.5, we see that in the newspapers, although not in the broadcast outlets, there was far greater attention to accounts of control actions taken against military operatives and operations than of military operatives themselves taking control actions. This reflects the particular focus in these outlets on international peace efforts against military activities as initiated by governments and peace activist groups. Comparing tables 9.9 and 9.7, we see a similar trend with the same explanation. In all outlets, but especially the newspapers and RP, there was a greater emphasis on accounts taken against military operatives and operations than on depictions of military resources being mobilized in control efforts.

Justification of Control Actions

In the course of depicting control actions, sources sometimes made direct statements about why such actions were being taken. These statements were essentially justifications of the control action. As justifications, they typically incorporated a designation of the deviance being responded to, the person's motivation in responding, and the purpose of the control response. Such explicit statements of justification appeared in only a small minority of the

TABLE 9.10
Justification of control actions

Institutional	Newspaper		Television		Radio		Sig.
field	Q	P	Q	P	Q	P	diff.
Rules, justice	21	9	30	8	24	7	R
	22.1%	12.9%	25.0%	14.5%	30.0%	10.8%	
Dispute	18	7	32	12	10	7	M
settlement,	18.9%	10.0%	26.7%	21.8%	12.5%	10.8%	
rights							
Organizational	11	8	4	6	10	10	M
expedience	11.6%	11.4%	3.3%	10.9%	12.5%	15.4%	
Organizational	7	7	6	5	4	7	
pathology	7.4%	10.0%	5.0%	9.1%	5.0%	10.8%	
Order	21	25	24	15	22	13	
maintenance	22.1%	35.7%	20.0%	27.3%	27.5%	20.0%	
Other	17	14	24	9	10	21	R
	17.9%	20.0%	20.0%	16.4%	12.5%	32.3%	
Total	95	70	120	55	80	21	485

Tests of significance based on tables with justifications of control action dichotomized into 'yes/no' for each of the categories. The last column indicates comparisons that show significant differences: chi-square statistics significant at the 0.05 level with Cramer's V or PHI $\geq$ 0.10, when N is large. Significant differences may occur between the newspapers (N); television stations (T); radio stations (R); or among the three types of media (M). The last column also indicates the presence of significant interactions with the variables being analysed and the coders (C) in a separate log-linear analysis.

accounts of control action, and they were much less common than explanations of deviance (chapter 7). However, it should be kept in mind that justifications of control action were often implicitly embedded in news items through what was stated elsewhere about the deviance being subject to control and through subtleties of language use. Our data on justifications of control action refer only to explicit statements in the course of depictions of control, not to the more implicit justifications embedded elsewhere in the items or in other items in a continuing story.

As evidenced in table 9.10 and in our subsequent interpretation of these findings, justifications of control action were not only limited in number, they were stated within a limited discourse. Essentially the justifications were in the terms of equality ('rules, justice' and 'dispute settlement'), efficiency ('organizational expedience' and 'organizational pathology'), and public order ('order maintenance' in the public interest). This is even more restricted than the range of explanations given for deviance (compare table 7.9).

The restricted level and range of justifications for control action is explained by the nature of news discourse, the influence of sources on the terms of that discourse, and the practices of journalists.

The focus in news discourse on describing current exceptional events, on the contingency of those events rather than their historic or structural necessity, and on dramatizations of those events limits the range of explanations and justifications to a narrow repertoire that accords with prevailing sensibilities in the dominant culture.

As we pointed out with respect to explanations of deviance, sources themselves eschew explanations that touch upon the structure and processes of their own organizations. The justifications they offer tend to have a singular general purpose, to legitimate their activities in the public sphere. Already powerful and legitimate organizations in society have little need to state justifications of their control actions in a routine case. They can exercise control with silence as to the reasons for their actions. Channelling reporters into already-legitimated forms and classifications, powerful bureaucratic sources receive 'automatic' justification of what they have been up to. 'By focusing on bureaucratically appropriate dispositions in their everyday reports, journalists' stories leave invisible the agency procedures and social conditions which give rise to these dispositions' (Fishman 1980: 71).

Journalists contribute to the erasure of explanations in terms of structure and process through their own social organization and cultural conventions. An orientation to the exceptional event and its dramatization fixes journalists in the descriptive mode, rather than leading them to search for the everyday, routine structural features that might explain how the exceptional event came about. Additionally, as Gitlin (1980: 53) noted regarding news accounts of the control actions of demonstrators, when journalists ask, '"Why are you here?" they are looking for singular reasons, not political logic.' Moreover, regardless of who is depicted taking control action, the singular reason must be in accordance with dominant cultural criteria of rational acceptability. In the items we sampled, the criteria of rational acceptability for control actions were within the limits of equality ('rules, justice' and 'dispute settlement'), efficiency ('organizational expedience' and 'organizational pathology'), and public order ('order maintenance').

RULES, JUSTICE

Control actions that were justified in terms of the need to uphold or correct laws, rules, norms, and/or decision processes were classified as 'rules, justice' justifications. These justifications included related depictions of rules and/or decision processes in terms of fairness, arbitrariness, morality, applicability, rights, and freedoms. At the heart of these depictions was the value of equality in socio-political relations. Typically the control action was said to be necessary to ensure greater procedural propriety in decision processes to the point where equality of treatment in those processes seemed apparent. This is the discourse of due process and procedural propriety that is at the heart of legitimation work in the administered society. The achievement of justice itself is inextricably linked with justifications of control in procedural due-process terms. That is, justice is primarily a matter of justification in these terms.

Table 9.10 reveals that rules and justice justifications vary significantly in radio (30 per cent in RQ compared to 11 per cent in RP), but there is also a substantial difference between the television stations (25 per cent in TQ and 15 per cent in TP) and between the newspapers (22 per cent in NQ compared to 13 per cent in NP). As we have shown through ethnographic materials (Ericson, Baranek, and Chan 1987, 1989), it is characteristic of quality outlets to focus more on the discourse of equality and rights in procedure than on the discourse of law-and-order via dramatic depictions of serious crime, investigation, and capture.

DISPUTE SETTLEMENT, RIGHTS

Justifications classified as 'dispute settlement, rights' refer to instances in which sources said they were taking control action to resolve a conflict in a way that would better the conditions, rights, and/or freedoms of an aggrieved party. This justification is akin to 'rules, justice' in that both address issues in rights and freedoms, including the legitimacy of rulers and rules, in terms of the value of equality. The difference is that 'dispute settlement, rights' justifications focus not so much on procedural due process in the administrative apparatus as on a particular political group resisting authority and asserting its rights for a resolution to a dispute that is in accordance with its claims.

In table 9.10, it is evident that justifications for control action in terms of 'dispute settlement, rights' were far more common in television (25 per cent) than in the newspapers (15 per cent) or radio (12 per cent). The 'dispute settlement, rights' justifications were more frequent in the quality outlets within each medium than in their popular-outlet counterparts, although the differences in this regard are less marked than is the case for justifications in terms of 'rules, justice.' The particular emphasis of the television outlets on 'dispute settlement, rights' justifications for control actions is related to the greater tendency of this medium to represent control action in terms of dramatic conflicts. Television carried proportionately more clips of aggrieved parties struggling to achieve their rights – through demonstrations, protests, news conferences, etc. – including their justifications for taking such action.

ORGANIZATIONAL EXPEDIENCE

In offering 'organizational expedience' justifications, sources said their control actions were in the interest of bureaucratic efficiency. Bureaucratic-efficiency criteria included not only cost-effectiveness in economic terms but also non-economic costs relating to such matters as working conditions and welfare provision. For example, a source representing the management of a company might justify firing employees in cost-effectiveness terms while the employees' union might justify their subsequent strike action in terms of working conditions and welfare. Justifications in terms of organizational expedience were more common in radio (14 per cent) and the newspapers (12 per cent) than on television (6 per cent).

ORGANIZATIONAL PATHOLOGY

Sources who said they were taking control action to correct a defect in an organization's structure, roles, or relationships were classified as giving an 'organizational pathology' justification. As indicated in Table 9.10, such justifications were rare and did not vary significantly by medium or market orientation.

ORDER MAINTENANCE

Control actions such as crime-prevention measures, investigations, and punishment were sometimes justified in terms of maintaining the existing state of affairs, a status quo, in the public interest. We refer to these as 'order maintenance' justifications. In these accounts, sources were preoccupied with law-and-order as a solution to the problems they were facing. This contrasts with order maintenance as an explanation of deviance (see chapter 5), in which law-and-order was seen as a possible cause of the deviance sources were facing. As evidenced in table 9.10, order-maintenance justifications occurred with considerable frequency in all news outlets. While there are no statistically significant differences by medium and market, order-maintenance justifications were proportionately more common in NP (36 per cent) compared to NQ (22 per cent), TP (27 per cent) compared to TQ (20 per cent), and RQ (28 per cent) compared to RP (20 per cent). The greater frequency of such justifications in NP and TP relates to their greater focus on police and other law-enforcement agents engaged in control action and their tendency to obtain accounts from these agents concerning the purposes of the control activity.

The quality outlets focused on justifications of control actions that emphasized rules and justice, as well as dispute settlement and rights. The popular newspaper and television outlets gave more attention to order maintenance and organizational pathology as justifications of control action. While control actions were justified in only a small minority of instances in which they were depicted, these data suggest that quality outlets were more oriented to the discourse of due process and procedural propriety of control agents, while popular outlets focused more on law-and-order justifications of control activity.

Discriminating Control Action by Media and Market

The following stepwise discriminant analyses weight and combine eight elements of control action (styles of control, mechanisms of control, institutional contexts of control agents, institutional fields of control agents, institutional contexts mobilized in control action, institutional fields mobilized in control action, institutional contexts targeted in control action, and institutional fields targeted in control action) as independent measures in a way that forces the groups – media, and the market orientation within each medium – to be as distinct as possible so that one can predict on what criteria the groups are distinguishable.

The stepwise discriminant analysis of control action by medium is presented in table 9.11. The best predictor of medium is whether the control agent is acting on behalf of government. Additional predictive influence comes from adding, in turn, the following elements: whether government is the context targeted, law enforcement is the field mobilized, law enforcement is the field of the control agent, and law enforcement is the field targeted. Newspapers are distinguished as offering accounts of the control actions of government officials, and of governmental operations being subject to control. Television stations are distinguished as offering accounts of law-enforcement officers taking control actions. Radio stations are distinguished as depicting the mobilization of law-enforcement resources in taking control action, and as emphasizing control actions against law-enforcement agencies and agents.

The stepwise discriminant analyses of control actions within market are presented in table 9.12. From table 9.12a, we learn that by far the best predictor of market orientation within newspapers is whether a conciliatory style of control is depicted. Additional predictive influence comes from adding whether government is the target of control action, and whether control actions are being taken by government officials. NQ is distinguished as depicting the conciliatory style of control, focusing on control actions against government, and emphasizing the control actions of government officials. In table 9.12b, it is established that the best predictor of market

TABLE 9.11
Stepwise discriminant analysis of control action by medium

Variables	F	Discriminant function 1 standardized coefficients	Discriminant function 2 standardized coefficients
Context of control agent:			
Government	12.46	−0.19	0.99
Context target:			
Government	8.75	−0.35	0.33
Field mobilized:			
Law enforcement/safety	10.79	0.50	0.34
Field of control agent:			
Law enforcement/safety	5.04	0.34	−0.46
Field target:			
Law enforcement/safety	12.15	0.41	0.33
Centroids:			
Newspaper (N = 966)		−0.30	0.07
Television (N = 1,154)		0.02	−0.12
Radio (N = 990)		0.28	0.08
Percentage of cases correctly classified:			
Newspaper	48.3%		
Television	26.3%		
Radio	51.7%		
Total	41.3%		

Wilk's lambda = 0.9415; chi-square = 188.97 (d.f. = 10; $p < 0.01$)

orientation in television is whether the context targeted was government. Some additional predictive influence comes from adding in turn the following elements: whether a government official is the control agent, governmental resources are mobilized, law enforcement is the field targeted, law enforcement is the field mobilized, and the style of control is conciliatory. TQ is distinguished as focusing on control actions against government, government officials as control agents, and control actions against law-enforcement agents and agencies. TP is distinguished as emphasizing government resources being mobilized in control action, law-enforcement resources being mobilized in control action, and the conciliatory style of control. A stepwise discriminant analysis of control action by market orientation in radio produced results that are not statistically significant.

In this chapter, we have established significant components of the topics in control, law, and justice peculiar to each news outlet. Each news outlet

TABLE 9.12a
Stepwise discriminant analysis of control action within markets: newspapers

Variables	F	Discriminant function standardized coefficients
Style of control:		
Conciliatory	60.81	0.79
Context target:		
Government	15.31	0.41
Context of control agent:		
Government	4.13	0.20
Centroids:		
Quality paper (N = 572)		0.29
Popular paper (N = 424)		−0.39
Percentage of cases correctly classified:		
Quality paper	57.2%	
Popular paper	71.7%	
Total	63.4%	

Wilk's lambda = 0.8985; chi-square = 106.27 (d.f. = 3; $p < 0.01$)

represented control, law, and justice differently because it operated with medium and market criteria that differed from the others.

While the research literature has suggested that the main news emphasis is on dramatic aspects of deterrence law-enforcement under criminal law, our data show that there is far greater emphasis on the less dramatic aspects of compliance law-enforcement under administrative law. The news is articulating the enormous growth in administrative law and compliance mechanisms in the late twentieth century. News of administrative law, compliance, and regulation has become predominant in conjunction with developments in law and society, including the proliferation of powerful corporations and efforts to regulate their private orders; the elaboration of welfare-state mechanisms with their myriad regulatory forms and require-ments; the increasing significance of norms of procedural propriety to the legitimation of bureaucratic practices; and the mandate of regulatory agencies to seek compliance through publicity and education.

While all news outlets emphasized a 'normal compliance discourse' more than a 'normal crime discourse,' there was considerable variation. NQ gave relatively little play to deterrence law-enforcement, especially compared to the popular outlets, and almost one-half of its items pertained to compliance alone. Following from this especially strong emphasis on

TABLE 9.12b
Stepwise discriminant analysis of control action within markets: television

Variables	F	Discriminant function standardized coefficients
Context target:		
Government	11.87	0.71
Context of control agent:		
Government	3.53	0.41
Context mobilized:		
Government	2.84	−0.41
Field target:		
Law enforcement/safety	4.29	0.39
Field mobilized:		
Law enforcement/safety	1.85	−0.33
Style of control:		
Conciliatory	1.71	−0.29
Centroids:		
Quality television (N = 692)		0.14
Popular television (N = 462)		−0.21
Percentage of cases correctly classified:		
Quality television	56.6%	
Popular television	59.1%	
Total	57.6%	

Wilk's lambda = 0.9716; chi-square = 33.05 (d.f. = 6; $p < 0.01$)

compliance modes of control, NQ was the most likely to include items representing a conciliatory style of dispute resolution and the least likely to include items representing a penal style.

All news outlets gave prominence to government officials as control agents, although considerable space was also given to control agents in private corporations and community organizations, and to individuals without organizational affiliation. In NQ, two-thirds of control agents were government officials, with more emphasis on control agents in political office and those in the field of trade and finance than NP, and less emphasis on law-enforcement officers than any of the other outlets.

All news outlets gave even greater prominence to government as the institutional context mobilized in taking control actions, indicating that when people outside government were represented as taking control action, it frequently involved mobilization of government resources. Non-government organizations, and especially individuals, were rarely depicted as being mobilized in control actions. In all news outlets, the power resources for control were shown to reside in institutions, and in particular the institution of government.

There was considerable focus on government operations as the target of control actions, especially in NQ. In NQ, there was particular emphasis on control actions against holders of political office, those in the field of trade and finance, and foreign governments engaged in military actions. However, in keeping with all of the other outlets, NQ gave much greater emphasis to non-state organizations and individuals being subject to control at the hands of state agents and agencies than to control actions taken by non-state organizations and individuals against government.

Explicit justifications of control action were rare. The focus in news of crime, law, and justice on current exceptional events, on the contingency of those events rather than their historic or structural necessity, and on the dramatization of those events limits the range of justifications to a narrow repertoire that accords with prevailing cultural sensibilities about equality, efficiency, and public order. NQ, in keeping with the other qualities, gave somewhat more emphasis to 'rules and justice' and 'dispute settlement and rights' justifications for control actions, while the popular outlets focused more on 'organizational pathology' and 'order maintenance' justifications. These trends are in keeping with the greater emphasis in the quality outlets, and NQ in particular, on the discourse of equality and procedural rights, in contrast to the popular outlets' emphasis on the discourse of law-and-order via dramatic depictions of serious crime, investigation, and capture.

Focusing on NP, we find a much greater emphasis on deterrence law-enforcement than in NQ. Hence NP, along with the other popular outlets, was much more likely to represent the public police as control agents, and to show them as being mobilized as a resource in the control actions of others. NP also represented individuals differently than did NQ. Along with TP, NP was the most likely to represent individuals as control agents. Typically this involved the 'vox pop' format in which the journalist was shown as being actively involved with an aggrieved citizen in taking control action against an offending bureaucracy. However, NP was also far more likely than was NQ to depict individuals as being control targets of major institutions, especially the government's law-enforcers. NP's emphasis on the control of individuals is largely accounted for by its greater attention to the control of the individual criminal.

The television outlets frequently used their visual capacity to provide evidence of control actions taking place. However, with rare exceptions, the newspapers and radio stations provided evidence of control action only through the citation of sources saying what the control action was.

On most dimensions the two television stations did not vary from each other a great deal because in television the medium format constraints are especially strong. Both television outlets gave more emphasis to compliance than deterrence law-enforcement stories, although deterrence stories appeared more frequently in TP. TP gave greater attention to the mobilization of the public police. There was more divergence between the television outlets regarding the institutional contexts of control work. TQ was similar to NQ in representing control actions that targeted government much more than individuals. As a government-owned station, TQ was especially vehement in representing, and taking part in, the control of government. In contrast, TP was similar to NP in focusing much more on control actions against individuals, especially the individual criminal. TP was also similar to NP in giving much more space to individual citizens taking control actions against organizations within a 'vox pop' format. Both television stations were similar in their emphasis on 'dispute settlement and rights' justifications for control action. This was part of television's representation of control action in terms of dramatic conflicts: aggrieved parties struggling to achieve their rights through demonstrations, protests, news conferences, and other formats that included their justifications for taking such actions.

Both of the radio stations gave far greater emphasis to compliance than deterrence law-enforcement. Both stations emphasized law-enforcers as control agents, and as being mobilized in the control efforts of others. The radio stations diverged somewhat in their representation of control targets. RQ gave roughly equal attention to individuals, non-state community organizations, and government organizations being subject to control. RP gave much greater emphasis to control actions against government and against individuals. RP's focus on individuals being controlled was parallel to what appeared in NP and TP, with particular attention to the control of the individual criminal. Both radio outlets focused on control actions against those in law enforcement and the health field and were similar to NP in this respect. RQ, RP, and NP gave regular attention to efforts to regulate medical professionals, unauthorized medical services, and private-sector nursing homes.

This chapter completes our cross-sectional analysis of how news of crime, law, and justice varies by medium and market. The remaining task is to conclude the longitudinal and cross-sectional analyses presented in parts II and III by linking them more directly to the theoretical and methodological dimensions raised in part I.

PART IV

Conclusions

10

Conclusions

In this book, we have explored news content in order to advance understanding of the mass-media institution and its place in society. Our previous research was based in operational data concerning how journalists and their sources produce meaning from the flow of events. In the present work, we analyse the presentational data of news content, the meanings that journalists and their sources have already fixed from the flow of events. This analysis has required our own fixing of what journalists and sources produce. We have frozen the perpetual rush of news in order to subject it to sustained thought, to take apart what is normally taken for granted. We have included both longitudinal and cross-sectional analyses of news formats, sources, knowledge, and topics as these vary by medium and market orientation. These analyses provide systematic descriptions of the language, rituals, and classifications routinely available in news texts. These descriptions offer a view of sign or symbol use in action, showing texts as human action. These descriptions also present an aggregate view of the news system. Finally, these descriptions provide a portrait of Canadian public culture as drawn and drawn upon by journalists and their sources.

Our analyses do not incorporate all news content, only that which focuses on aspects of crime, law, and justice. As documented in chapter 8, such items are predominant: they constituted just under one-half of all news coverage in newspapers and popular television, well over one-half of all news coverage in quality television, and approximately two-thirds of all news coverage on radio.

Why this obsession with stories of crime, law, and justice? One explanation is that law has become the primary cultural device for defining acceptable behaviour, identity, and reality. News operatives pick up on these culturally definitive aspects of law because they are especially helpful in pursuing their own cultural tasks. News operatives use the law as a tool of cultural construction, as one of the predominant means by which the authority system instructs people on what to *be* as well as what to *do*.

In relying upon both the constructive and the instructive capacities of law, news operatives appreciate that law is a kind of conceptual device for order, an imaginative and interpretive tool for construing social relations and co-ordinating institutional activities. They also appreciate that law is an important source of language about social relations, that it provides 'a vocabulary with which we rationalize our actions to others and ourselves' (Macauley 1987: 185). In other words, news operatives rely on law's cultural pre-eminence as a map of normative order and as a language of social relations, bonding culture to social organization (Unger 1976: 250–1). News organizations and operatives join with legal agencies and agents in turning 'stories about what is into stories about what ought to be' (Scheppele 1988: 316). These stories are an important source of contemporary myths – narratives that at once describe and justify – that help us to make sense of, and express sensibilities about, social order. Stories of legal control are central to representing order.

There are several shared goals of the law and mass-media institutions that help explain the dominance of legal control and justice stories in the news. Both the law and news media are disciplinary and normalizing social discourses that are intertextually related to each other as part of continuing dialogue about the terms and conditions of social order. As such, both of them are agencies of policing regarding fundamental activities such as the allocation of resources, the regulation and resolution of conflict, and keeping the peace.

As agencies of policing, the news media and law prompt discourse about symbolic boundaries, power relations, and rules that relate to organizing and organizational order. As instruments of organizing, they also provide for controlled reform and social change. They both focus on bad news – on what has gone wrong, on failure – to offer openings for what may be done to improve things, to achieve progress.

As documented in our previous work, processes in deviance and control, law and policing, are central to the production of news stories about deviance and control, law and policing. News texts exhibit the fact that they are part of ongoing discursive struggles between key players in major institutions for whom 'what is at stake is ultimately quite a lot more than either words or discourses' (Macdonnel 1986: 51). News inevitably incorporates aspects of deviance and legal control because they are central to the hierarchical roles and power relations that news operatives themselves participate in while accomplishing their reporting tasks. Analytically, the concern is not truth, but how news emerges from and plays back into power relations and serves to legitimate or undermine them.

The murder story in chapter 4 and the law-reform story in chapter 5 illustrate that news provides an active discourse about the legal control and justice activities of the people and organizations reported on, including journalists themselves. In these stories there is a lot more at stake than the resolution of a particular tragedy or injustice. The society's system of institutional authority is at stake. A murder provides the occasion not simply for a primary factual account of what happened, but for a morality play of how what happened fits into the order of things. A new law provides the occasion not simply for a statement of its provisions, but for the expression of conflicting ideologies with respect to the law's implications for social control and justice.

The law and news-media institutions join in perpetuating public conversations about justice and authority. For both institutions, justice, as the primary cement of social institutions, is even more important than truth, which is the primary cement of systems of thought. Justice is articulated in particular through a focus on the control procedures used in arriving at outcomes. For the news media, as for law, the resolution of a dispute is often no more than the after-clap of accord regarding the justice of procedures invoked to accomplish the resolution. The procedural obsession relates to core values such as equality, liberty, and efficiency. These values are perpetually contested because what is seen as an instance of justice by one party is often seen by the other party as an injustice (e.g., liberty for one party entails loss of liberty for another). The inevitably unsettled nature of such core values yields news stories that are themselves inevitably unsettled, even though they too give weight to whose liberty should be strengthened and whose weakened in the particular case. It is precisely the inability to make factual statements about justice that perpetuates imaginative discourse about law and justice in the news media.

The fixation on procedural justice is also the primary means by which the news media and law join in helping to constitute the legitimacy of institutions, including their own. Moral authority is always subject to consent, and legitimacy is always something that is granted. Law is crucial to making convincing claims to moral authority because, in modern administered society, questions of legitimacy revolve around procedural norms, procedural propriety, and the search for and sanctioning of procedural strays. Especially regarding the legitimacy of the state, this procedural emphasis is expressed in terms of the legality and constitutionality of decisions. News media are crucial in communicating these claims, the most pervasive and persuasive means by which the powerful can perform their authority and seek consent. Moreover news operatives do not just act as passive communicators but actively interpret, shape, and constitute authoritative claims based on legal procedure.

As illustrated in particular by the murder story in chapter 4 and the law-reform story in chapter 5, the news media ultimately display justice as the fulfilment of institutional needs for authority. Ultimately it is the authoritative strength of institutions and 'the system' that is on view. Even while particular authorities are shown to be hard at work – the police investigating, judges judging, legislators legislating – it is *authority*, more than the particular authority of these actors, that is reproduced. *Authority* defines how to see the world, including what is just. *Authority* and justice no longer embody particular social relations but cultural mythologies about those relations. Through these cultural mythologies the law and news media represent order.

The murder story in chapter 4 and the law-reform story in chapter 5 also show the affinities between the methodologies of law and news media. Through well-established conventions – an event-orientation, personalization, a focus on procedure, realism, and precedent – legal operatives and news operatives provide the essential ingredients for visualizing justice and its connection to authority and social order.

The law and news media both have an event orientation. They examine conflict on a specific, case-by-case basis. They derive their conceptions of justice from the specific and concrete conflict, rather than expressing them in the abstract.

The law and news media read the event through the specific individual involved in it. 'It is the very essence of legal rhetoric that it individualizes the issues before the court. Legal meaning is always to be attached to individual acts and legal explanation is correspondingly biographical and moral rather than sociological and contextualizing' (Goodrich 1986: 204). Individualization and personalization provide the attribution of individual responsibility and accountability. Likewise, in the news, events and problems are isolated to the individual and personalized. Moral-character portraits are drawn not only as a dramatic technique for presenting news stories as serial narratives involving leading actors, but also as a political means of allocating responsibility for actions and attributing accountability as these justify legal control.

The law and news media not only focus on orderly procedure as an end, they also incorporate it as a part of their methodology for expressions of morality. An emphasis on procedural propriety is in keeping with the decreasing significance of absolute values or tradition in sustaining legitimacy (Habermas 1975), and with the focus on moral responsibility and accountability of individuals.

Both the law and news media use formats of realism to produce the truth of their respective discourses. While both news and legal discourse are politically and socially constructed, include aspects that are fabricated and fictive, and present evaluative differences as differences in fact, they try to erase these aspects through realistic packaging. Staged performances in both the courtroom and newsroom are packaged as if they are based on more 'natural' events and therefore represent unmediated reality. The realism helps them to constitute the truths of their discourses, as if they are presenting the whole truth rather than the truth reduced to their genre capacities; as if their procedures and knowledge are the same; as if theirs is not *one* way of seeing but *the* way of seeing.

The event orientation, personalization, procedural emphasis, and realism contribute to the fact that news and legal discourse both offer precedent, the repetition of a discourse or way of life and mode of belonging. Precedent provides a vocabulary for institutional classification, and authority for that vocabulary, that people use commonsensically and comfortably in their everyday tasks (Ericson, Baranek, and Chan 1987: 133–8; Shearing and Ericson forthcoming).

While all news outlets share the goals and methodologies specified above, they also vary a great deal in the specifics of what they pursue and how they go about their pursuits. While the news-media institution's 'whole vision of the world is its own program' (M. Douglas 1986), the news organizations that constitute the institution vary considerably in their programming. A central focus in this book has been on how news of crime, law, and justice varies in terms of the medium and market characteristics of different news outlets.

Newspaper, television, and radio each have distinctive medium characteristics that fundamentally influence the formats, sources, knowledge, and topics of their communications. News content must always fit the format requirements of the particular medium and is therefore always secondary to it. The medium is the primary consideration for journalists and sources in their efforts to 'arrange, define and communicate meaning' (Altheide 1985: 39), and therefore it has a relatively autonomous function in both framing and accomplishing news discourse.

News outlets also vary substantially in the market to which they direct their communications. Quality news outlets see themselves as communicating to the élite authorized knowers who are regular sources, and to other persons who are influential because of their political purchase and up-market purchasing power. Popular news outlets see themselves as communicating to the less elevated officials (such as police officers) and other people who are their regular sources, and to people who buy into their particular popular ideologies and advertisers' products. The popular/quality dichotomy is a useful analytical distinction as it addresses how news operatives perceive their consumers and the particular formats required to attract and hold them (Crisell 1986). The distinction does not imply that particular news outlets are perceived by consumers as genuinely exhibiting quality, or as exhuming popular appeal (Williams 1976).

The medium has a significant bearing on market orientation. On many dimensions, the distinction between quality and popular is less marked in television news than it is in radio news, and especially in newspapers. The medium characteristics of televisions mean that practitioners operate mostly in the popular mode. In contrast, radio, and especially the newspaper medium, allow choice with respect to market possibilities because they are more suited to market segmentation. However, the market choice of radio and newspaper operatives is itself restricted by the imperialism of the television medium. Television has fundamentally influenced the formatting of radio and newspapers, including how they choose to slice into the market. This influence is exemplified by the popular newspaper we studied, which relied on the visual to the point of being characterized within the industry as the closest thing to television in print.

Our focus on variation in news of crime, law, and justice by medium and market was a necessary component of our broader effort to document the ways in which the news media are more pluralistic than given credit for in recent research by both structuralists (e.g., Hall et al. 1978) and ethnographers (e.g., Tuchman 1978; Fishman 1980). Our previous ethnographic studies documented considerable variation at the level of discursive struggles among journalists and sources producing news (see also Murdock 1982; Schlesinger 1988, 1989; Morrison and Tumber 1988). In the present study we document systematic variation in selected aspects of formats, sources, knowledge, and topics at the level of news products.

Formats are the devices by which journalists and sources are able to categorize, choose, organize, and represent knowledge as news. Some aspects of formats, for example, those pertaining to medium characteristics, are essentially invariant and autonomous features of news communications and therefore of the very ability to communicate. While format considerations permeate our analysis of news content, we highlighted particular aspects of format and how those aspects varied by medium and market orientation.

Our reading of news content confirmed our ethnographic observations that news rarely presents an event 'as it happens.' As it happens, a great deal of news is of selected *news* events that have already been formatted into news discourse by sources. Such scheduled events were covered more often by broadcast outlets, including television, in spite of its frequently touted 'live eye' capability. Continuing stories about previous events were also common, especially in newspapers, although much less so in radio. In contrast, radio, with a medium capacity that allows reporters to be relatively mobile and to report quickly, was the most likely to cover unscheduled events more or less as they happened.

News media also have a differential ability to create the *fiction* that they are reporting events as they happen. In particular, the murder story analysed in chapter 4 indicates how television, and to a lesser extent newspapers, are able to combine their picture and language-use capacities to visualize the present-tense aliveness of events. For example, the police investigation of the murder was shown as active and real through iconic elements such as simple themes; brief, poignant scripts or texts; striking language; and pictures. The popular television station provided an even greater sense of active realism by personalizing the investigative process through its crime-specialist reporter. As a familiar, credible, and authoritative person working with a public institution and through a medium that had the same characteristics, he pictured himself as part of the community and its ordering activities.

As fictive as this murder story was, it was a 'natural' for television. It was a 'real life' example of rituals, dramas, and tragedies also shown endlessly in entertainment programming on television. In contrast, radio news could do relatively little with this story because radio lacks a visual capacity, and because dramatic devices in particular contexts of this story would have seemed inappropriate on radio. If radio journalists had constructed connotative meanings through dramatic language, juxtaposition of actuality clips, and background music and other sounds, their items would have been perceived as out of place and in bad taste, perhaps to the point of seeming even more bizarre and disordered than the events reported on. Radio was limited to bulletin-like announcements and only particular actuality clips, such as the fear and loathing of a resident in the small town where the woman was murdered.

The news claim to be reflecting reality more or less as it happens is also based on the range of *places* it is able to cover. News of crime, law, and justice is derived from a large number of places locally, nationally, and internationally, especially in newspapers and quality television. The question is begged as to whether such broad coverage geographically makes a qualitative difference. For example, we found that the popular newspaper had considerable foreign-news coverage, but most of it played upon the same themes and ideologies the newspaper trafficked in regarding events closer to home. Most foreign-news coverage was of serious crime, to augment what its crime reporters were able to cull locally; and of events or official statements that conveyed the anti-left ideology the newspaper also trafficked in through its editorial pages and regular columnists. In this respect, the place mattered little, if at all: the material is best characterized as 'eternally recurrent' (Rock 1973), 'news from nowhere' (Epstein 1974), yielding 'no sense of place' (Meyrowitz 1985).

News outlets also have formats for demarcating facts and values, news and opinions. Newspapers are more explicitly opinionated than broadcast-news outlets in that they provide greater space for features, opinion columns, and editorials that allow interpretive latitude and language that is more loaded and less laundered. While broadcast outlets make some use of 'commentary' slots, they shy away from too much explicit opinion in their news to avoid appearing too idiosyncratic, propagandistic, dramatic, or lacking in seriousness. However, as illustrated in the law-reform story in chapter 5, the news and opinion format categories are in fact used inter-dependently, with facts and values blended in each format to sustain preferred versions and visions of order.

News outlets also try to maintain a sense of balance through presenting different sides of an issue or event. Our data indicate that, in a substantial majority of instances, a single news item contained only one side. One has to look to follow-up or continuing stories for additional sides and a greater sense of balance. When sides were presented within a single item, it was more likely to be in the newspapers, and to a lesser degree in the quality broadcast outlets, than in the popular broadcast outlets. If sides were presented in any news outlet, it was almost invariably two sides only, the classic point/counterpoint version of journalistic objectivity. In any event, as documented in the law-reform story in chapter 5, such expressions of objectivity and sensibilities about balance simply enhance the ideological strength of news outlets. While juggling successive news and opinion format items within the point/counterpoint format of news objectivity, the news outlet can also conjure up its own ideological predilections and subjectivity.

The format requirements of a particular medium and market orientation also influence the representation of news sources. Formats not only bear on journalists in their selection of source organizations and individuals, but also on sources in their selection of news organizations and individual journalists. Sources choose news outlets with the medium and market orientation most suited to their need for knowledge control and expressions of authority. For example, court officials are oriented to newspapers, the police to radio, and politicians to television (Ericson, Baranek, and Chan 1989).

Newspapers used the most sources, radio news the least. This is one indication that newspapers have a greater discursive capacity than television and especially radio. Newspapers frequently cited a large number of sources within a single item. While broadcast news limited the number of sources in a single item, it sometimes extended the range of sources addressing a particular event or issue by wrapping successive items in a segment of the newscast.

Journalists and government officials were the source types cited most frequently in all news outlets. Indeed, they were so dominant that it is reasonable to conclude that news is primarily a public conversation among journalists and government officials, with others left to make only occasional utterances and to eavesdrop.

In broadcast news, journalists are the font. Often journalists are the only source of knowledge, as the entire item consists of the anchor's account; the anchor interviewing a reporter who is a member of his or her news outlet; the anchor interviewing a reporter who is a member of another news outlet; and/or a reporter who is a member of one news outlet interviewing a reporter who is a member of another news outlet. While ethnographic studies have documented the substantial extent to which journalists informally rely on each other and previous news reports to make more news (e.g., Schlesinger 1978; Tuchman 1978; Fishman 1980; Ericson, Baranek, and Chan 1987, 1989), the present research shows that the self-referential nature of journalism is also evident in news content.

Government officials were a dominant source type in all news outlets, but especially in newspapers, and the quality newspaper in particular. A consideration of specific types of government sources also revealed that there was significant variation between the quality and popular outlets, especially in the newspapers and on television. Taking the example of how police officials were cited, we found that the popular newspaper cited police twice as often as did the quality newspaper, and that the popular television station cited the police twice as often as did the quality television station. Moreover, the police officials cited in the popular newspaper and popular television station were mainly lower-ranking officers, while the police officials cited in the quality newspaper and quality television station were mainly higher-ranking officers. With respect to all source bureaucracies, the quality outlets tended to use senior officials for a top-down view, while popular outlets also focused on lower-ranking officials to provide a view from below.

Private-sector organizations, whether corporations or community interest groups, were cited infrequently compared to journalists and government officials. Most private corporations probably want it this way. Their power over the news is power to stay out of the news, especially the bad news of crime and legal control (Ericson, Baranek, and Chan 1989: chap. 5).

Individuals without an organizational affiliation or status also appeared infrequently relative to journalists and government officials. Individuals were cited much more frequently in the popular news outlets, especially the popular newspaper and television station. This is because they are an important ingredient of the 'vox pop' format characteristic of popular news outlets. It is significant that, in this format, the accounts of individuals were still framed institutionally. Individuals were asked for their reaction to events that had already been framed by official sources. Often they appeared in the news only because they had been assigned an official role by a government institution, for example, the legally defined role of victim, accused, or witness in a criminal case. They were sometimes asked for their opinion on official policies and practices, especially as they may have affected the individual. Individuals often functioned as 'normative witnesses' to an event, or regarding people more directly involved in the event, for example, providing character testimonials about victims or accused persons. They were called upon to express emotions, such as fear and loathing with respect to serious crime. Individual sources were also portrayed as peculiar deviant characters, seen against the cultural template of official classifications and responses.

Individual sources were also used for the purposes of a news outlet's institutional format and frame. For example, in chapter 5 we saw how the popular newspaper used its 'You Said It' citizens' opinion column for its own ideological purposes in advancing the story. In this instance, individuals were used to represent the consensus about proposed legislation to restrict the use of electronic lie-detectors in the work place, to express the after-clap of accord with what the government had done in the legislature. The newspaper used this column to set up a subsequent editorial in which it, in turn, denounced these same people for following the government's justification of the legislation, and thereby asserted itself as a minority voice against both political and popular opinion on the matter.

All sources are framed in limited news contexts. Most material we surveyed derived from interviews tailored to news-media formats: direct quotations or reference to statements in newspapers; talking heads, voice-clips, or reference to statements in television; and voice-clips or reference to statements in radio. Underscoring the point that news is rarely presented 'as it happens,' broadcast-news outlets rarely presented sources actually engaged in the event reported on in spite of their technological capacity to do so and their advertised claims to be doing so. For example, less than 2 per cent of the popular television station's sources were shown as actually involved in the event reported on, in spite of advertised claims by the station that it was 'everywhere' with its 'live eye' to bring people events spontaneously and instantaneously. The popular television station was not different from the other news outlets in presenting sources as normative witnesses to events occurring elsewhere and previously.

Sources of all types were mainly called upon to provide primary, factual understanding. Secondary understanding or explanation was infrequent. When explanations did appear, they were mostly offered by journalists or individuals. Official government sources were rarely called upon to offer explicit explanations. They primarily offered a discourse of factuality embedded in their official forms and classifications as released routinely to the news media. Of course, on another level, this discourse of factuality functioned precisely to justify, excuse, and otherwise explain or explain away their behaviour (Scott and Lyman 1968; Brandt 1969; Fishman 1980, 1981; Wheeler 1986; Ericson, Baranek, and Chan 1989).

Tertiary (empathetic, affective) understanding was rare. It appeared most often on television, and in the popular newspaper. It was especially frequent among individuals, compared to other source types. Individuals were called upon to express their emotions, while those acting in official bureaucratic capacities usually appeared emotionless, even stoic. The visualization of emotional individual citizens helps news operatives to represent the social impact of calamitous events that government officials are responsible for controlling, and of laws, official rulings, and official decisions.

Explicit evaluations by sources appeared frequently. In particular, individuals were called upon to offer evaluations regarding the impact of laws and official policies on their everyday life. In contrast, sources were rarely represented in making recommendations with respect to legal control, although the newspapers allowed greater scope for recommendations.

In the vast majority of instances (about 90 per cent in all news outlets), sources offered no evidence to support their statements or claims. Accounts from sources are overwhelmingly 'performative' (Fishman 1980) in character and, as such, are based on their credibility. Their credibility is most often based upon their organizational affiliation and status, which combines with the credibility of the news organization and the medium itself to make them appear truthful. Thus source accounts are not as much a matter of *truth* as what consumers accept as organizational, institutional, and mass-media criteria of knowledge and truth (Altheide 1985). This is so even when the debate depends upon scientific evidence. As evidenced in chapter 5, a debate about the reliability and validity of polygraph devices was not based upon the presentation of detailed scientific evidence, but rather on the performatives and promotional rhetoric of sources representing different political and ideological positions on such devices.

Visuals function as a source of evidence, especially as they provide a reading of the moral character and context of sources. Television is obviously superior in this regard, as its visuals can 'impose meaning at one stroke' (Barthes 1972). In fact, most visuals in television news simply picture sources in talking-head shots or in voiced-over videos or stills of sources (which were about as frequent as talking heads with respect to all sources except journalists). These 'head shots' have a similar function to newspaper still photographs of sources. They provide a reading of moral character and context beyond what is said, or can be said, in the script. Similar to newspapers also, the written narrative or script in television news provides textual pointers on how to read the visuals. The verbal and visual are entwined into strong metaphors that are representational, and are best judged in terms of correctness and incorrectness rather than in terms of being true or false. As strong metaphors they are not mere fictions, but cognitive, informative, and ontologically illuminating.

Newspaper pictures of sources were relatively rare. In our survey, photographs of sources appeared five times more often in the popular newspaper (used with respect to about 10 per cent of all sources) than in the quality newspaper (used with respect to about 2 per cent of all sources). This finding is in keeping with the fact that the popular newspaper generally gave more emphasis to the visual, including not only photographs but graphics, display headlines, and colour. In the popular newspaper's major stories, the visual aspects usually combined to take up far more space than the written narrative.

The lack of a visual capacity is radio's major limitation in comparison to television and newspapers. However, the radio outlets did not even make extensive use of their capacity to represent sources in voice-clips. Excluding journalists, only a minority of each source type was cited in a voice-clip actuality that could provide social cues from speech, tone, language use, and silences. Most sources in radio news simply had their activities, statements, or claims referred to by journalists. In radio news, journalists are necessarily the central sources. They work hard to control radio's evanescence via their own prepared scripts, continuous talk, and simple language. It is the limitations of the radio medium itself that narrow radio-news stories into the grooves of highly redundant representations of order.

One common thread across media is that visuals and actuality clips – newspaper photographs, television talking heads and voice-overs of pictured sources, and radio voice-clips – were much more likely to be used with respect to non-governmental sources. Visuals and actuality clips were an important ingredient of the 'vox pop' representations of individuals and community interest groups being affected by law or fighting bureaucracy. They were apparently deemed more necessary in representing and providing moral-character readings of unknown or lesser-known persons, especially those who had no relevant organizational affiliation or status to support their claims. Visuals and actuality clips help to provide a reading of the source's character and status, which blends with their other functions, including personalization, a sense of realism, and a sense of factuality regarding the unknown person and the events he or she is involved in. In contrast, officials are already known, authenticated, and credible, and their familiarity in these respects can be used to have them make a statement without the additional readings available in a visual and/or actuality clip. When known officials were pictured or cited in voice-clips, it was more often to show them at work, performing their legal authority in actions such as legislating (see chapter 5) and investigating (see chapter 4).

News topics of crime, law, and justice varied substantially by medium and market. There was a low rate of concurrence in items among the six news outlets studied. There was significant variation among the outlets in the coverage they gave to specific aspects of crime, law, and justice.

Interpersonal conflict, including violence, was particularly dominant in the popular newspaper, the popular radio newscast, and both television newscasts. The particular focus in the popular news outlets was on individual acts of violence, especially violent crime. This focus meant that the popular outlets paid particular attention to deviant acts by individuals without an organizational affiliation or status relevant to their deviance. The quality newspaper, and to a lesser extent the quality radio newscast, focused more on economic deviance and how it was classified and regulated by governments. While all outlets paid attention to deviance by government officials, the quality outlets, and especially the quality newspaper, focused on official deviance. The quality newspaper functioned as a police of government on behalf of the private sector. The quality television station was part of the government broadcasting corporation, yet also focused its attention on deviance by government officials. In contrast, the popular newspaper and the popular television newscast not only stressed deviance by individuals outside of organizational contexts but gave as much attention to private corporate deviance as to deviance by government officials.

Explanations of deviance were infrequent, although they appeared significantly more often in the newspapers than in television newscasts, and least often in the radio newscasts. The explanations were typically low-level accounts that erased consideration of social structure and process. Given their focus on acts of violence by individuals, the popular outlets, and the popular newspaper in particular, favoured individual-pathology explanations. Given their focus on economic deviance and deviance by government officials, the quality outlets, and the quality newspaper in particular, favoured explanations related to organizational expedience (efficiency) and 'rules and justice' (legitimacy). Regardless of the explanations offered, all outlets used explanations to blend causal explanation with political causes. Deployed stereotypically, explanations of deviance in the news are political. They impute motives, whether noble or blameworthy, which in turn bear justifications and excuses for deviant behaviour with specific control implications.

Our qualitative content analyses also reveal that the failure to seek explanation of deviance erases a lot (see also Ericson, Baranek, and Chan 1987, 1989; Voumvakis and Ericson 1984). For example, in the murder story analysed in chapter 4, there was no apparent effort to seek explanation of the murder in terms of a possible previous relationship between the accused and the victim. This erasure sustained the impression of a stranger-stranger attack motivated by robbery, which in turn sustained the popular narrative and its subplots of police prowess and popular fear.

While subtleties of knowledge use are best appreciated through qualitative analyses, our quantitative analyses revealed that tertiary understanding with respect to deviant acts was most common in the television newscasts (especially in the popular outlet), followed by the newspapers (again especially in the popular outlet), and least common in the radio newscasts. Evaluations of deviance were proportionately greater in the newspapers (especially in the quality newspaper) than in the television newscasts, and least in the radio newscasts. Recommendations with respect to the control of deviant activity were also most common in the newspapers, followed by the radio newscasts, and least in the television newscasts.

We also examined the types of knowledge most commonly found in headlines, teases, and leads. In general, all of these devices were used in all news outlets to convey a sense of direct action taking place and/or to offer primary facts that would suggest the angle and, it is hoped, hook the reader. However, the newspapers offered more background information, evaluations, and recommendations as part of their headlines and leads. The broadcast-news outlets tended to rely more on a sense of direct action taking place as central to their teases and leads. This emphasis was consistent with the sense of aliveness and present-tense required in broadcast-news accounts.

With respect to legal-control efforts depicted in the news, we found that the compliance mode of legal regulation appeared more frequently than did the deterrence mode of law enforcement. This finding held across all news outlets, although the emphasis on compliance was especially strong in the quality outlets while the popular outlets gave more attention to deterrence-based law enforcement. Reflecting its particular emphasis on the compliance model of legal regulation, the quality newspaper stressed control efforts that were conciliatory, whereas the other outlets gave greater emphasis to penal and coercive control efforts.

The greater emphasis on legal control through compliance signifies a number of developments in law and legal regulation. There has been a very significant increase in administrative law, and its compliance and regulatory mechanisms, associated with the welfare state and enhanced corporate regulation. Journalists have become as much participating agents of the government's regulatory apparatus as they have been traditionally of the government's police and criminal-court law-enforcement apparatus. Furthermore, particular regulatory issues have become dominant in the public political agenda, some of which are seen as more significant than the crime problem, or indeed as part of the crime problem. For example, environmental regulation is a continuing major issue, prompting perpetual public discourse about legal regulation as it might accomplish compliance.

In all news outlets, the control agents depicted most often were government officials. However, government officials were especially predominant in radio newscasts, followed by the newspapers, and then the television newscasts. This finding is explained by the fact that radio-news operatives have the least resources and therefore are especially reliant upon official accounts of government control agents at work. The particular focus in radio, as well as in the popular outlets generally, was on the control actions of law-enforcement officers, especially the police. The popular newspaper and the popular television station also focused especially on the control actions taken by health officials, while the quality newspaper concerned itself more with control actions taken by politicians and senior civil servants.

The control actions of community-interest organizations also appeared with some frequency, especially in the popular outlets and in the quality television newscast. This emphasis signifies that the popular format, including the television format, features journalists joining with community groups in 'fighting bureaucracy.' Similarly individuals without an organizational affiliation and status relevant to the control action were depicted as control agents more often in the popular outlets, especially in the popular newspaper and the popular television newscast. The 'vox pop' of these outlets included a continuous stream of items that imaged up the 'little guy versus bureaucracy' theme.

We also examined what institutional contexts and resources were depicted as being mobilized by people involved in social-control efforts. All outlets showed that it was primarily the resources of government that were mobilized in control action. Moreover, it was the resources of law enforcement more than any other field of government that were most often shown to be mobilized, especially in radio, followed by television (particularly popular television), and the newspapers (particularly the popular newspaper). In contrast, the mobilization of community-group resources in taking control action was depicted very rarely, and the mobilization of an individual's resources in taking control action was depicted in only a few instances. In all news outlets, the power resources for control were shown to reside in institutions, especially the institutions of government and particularly its law-enforcement apparatus.

Paralleling our findings with respect to crime and deviance, government officials were also the most likely to be depicted as the targets for control action. The targeting of government for control action was especially dominant in the quality newspaper. The popular outlets in each medium gave considerable attention to control actions taken against individuals without an organizational affiliation or status relevant to the matter. All news outlets paid far greater attention to control actions taken against the individual than by the individual. In news accounts, government institutions are frequently depicted as taking control actions in relation to the individual, but almost never mobilize the individual as a resource in control action. Moreover, 'news organizations are most apt to report about public institutions than about powerful private ones' (Tuchman 1978: 163), both as initiators of control action and as the targets of control action.

Explicit justifications of control action were infrequent. Institutional sources are not usually called upon to explain, justify, or excuse what they do beyond what is already embedded in the official forms and classifications of their news releases. They have already accounted for their explanations, justifications, and excuses in their textually mediated bureaucratic forms. When explicit justifications were given, it was typically in the terms of equality, efficiency, and public order. The quality outlets emphasized justice and rights around the norm of equality, while the popular outlets emphasized order maintenance. It was characteristic of the qualities to foster the discourse of equality and rights in procedure, while the populars promoted the discourse of law-and-order available through dramatic depictions of serious crime, investigation, and capture. For all news outlets, however, the focus on current exceptional events, on the contingency of those events rather than their structural necessity, and on dramatizations of those events, limited the range of explanations and justifications given to a narrow repertoire that accorded with dominant cultural values.

In choosing among possible stories, journalists, sources, and consumers reveal the cultural templates of their understanding. Cultural templates are neither uniform nor fixed. There is no such thing as a conduit in organizational communications. When knowledge moves, it is always through a process of constructive interpretation. Visions of what ought to be frame stories of what is, and these stories in turn communicate to others what ought to be. That is, interpretation involves a mutual construction of factual accounts, norms, and values, a fact made especially evident in the longitudinal analyses in chapters 4 and 5 and in our previous research (Ericson, Baranek, and Chan 1987, 1989).

While cultural templates are shifting and plural, they are not free-floating and completely relative. A main focus of our present inquiry is that they are circumscribed by medium formats and market considerations. There is 'medium power' and 'market power' beyond the interpretive power to construct the particular accounts that journalists, sources, and consumers may give to the news with the aid of their cultural templates. News content must always fit the particular news outlet's medium and market format requirements, and is therefore always secondary to these requirements. Particular medium and market format requirements foster different means of knowledge flow and result in different knowledge systems. In themselves, they are a source of valuing facts, metaphorically reconstituting the world in ways that surface particular moral and political realities. In that sense they are ideological. In sum, the meanings that journalists, sources, and consumers give the news are formatted not only culturally, but also technologically and economically.

In the very process of constructive interpretation within medium and market format requirements, news texts are objectified and commodified. As such, they escape their authors and become autonomous as they are interpreted, understood, and used in other contexts. News texts have many uses. They provide a stream of diagnostic symbols on the basis of which people take action in the circumstances of their daily lives. As such, news texts are human action and they constitute human action, including especially efforts to effect legal control, accomplish justice, and envision order (Ericson 1991). They provide a familiar discourse, based in common sense and precedent, that makes the world plausible. The sense of plausibility in turn provides a structure of reassurance, a tool for acknowledging the familiar and silencing alternatives. News texts also provide a sense of knowledge structure, and therefore of social structure. Social structure emerges from patterns in secrecy and publicity (Scheppele 1988; Ericson, Baranek, and Chan 1989), the public representation of élite authorized knowers (Tuchman 1978; Ericson, Baranek, and Chan 1987), and what these reveal about the social distribution of knowledge. Knowledge of structured inequality in knowledge in turn creates awareness of how other power resources in society are unequally distributed, and of how these other dimensions of inequality are in part attributable to knowledge inequality.

Operating with three media, in distinctive market orientations, and in all spheres of organized life involving myriad source organizations, news organizations, and consumers, the news-media institution is bound to be plural and fluid. It is too unitary and fixed to conclude that news is structurally predetermined (Hall et al. 1978), technologically determined (McLuhan 1962, 1964), reduced to the condition of entertainment (Postman 1985), and therefore that the broadcasting tower is the modern-day equivalent of the Tower of Babble (Reddy 1979). There is no doubt that determined journalists and sources provide a rush of amusing babble in the news. None the less, as our trilogy of research studies has shown in fine-grained detail, there is a lot more to the news than that. News is *the* most available, serious, and powerful means by which we represent our social organization and aspirations. News is also one of the most available, serious, and powerful means by which each of us orders our daily life. As such, news touches everyone. It soothes some, pricks others, and wounds a few. While news is clearly 'programmed' within the economic, political, social, cultural, and technological criteria of the news-media institution, its programs can be used in myriad ways to visualize deviance, negotiate control, and represent order.

References

Adorno, T., and M. Horkheimer. 1979. 'The Culture Industry: Enlightenment as Mass Deception,' in J. Curran et al., *Mass Communication and Society*. Beverly Hills: Sage

Alley, R. 1982. 'Television Drama,' in H. Newcomb, ed., *Television: The Critical View*. New York: Oxford University Press

Altheide, D. 1976. *Creating Reality: How TV News Distorts Events*. Beverly Hills: Sage

– 1985. *Media Power*. Beverly Hills: Sage

– 1987a. 'Ethnographic Content Analysis,' *Qualitative Sociology* 10: 65–77

– 1987b. 'Format and Symbols in TV Coverage of Terrorism in the United States and Great Britain,' *International Studies Quarterly* 31: 161–76

Altheide, D., and J. Johnson. 1980. *Bureaucratic Propaganda*. Boston: Allyn and Bacon

Ames, A. 1960. *The Morning Notes of Adelbert Ames*. Hadley Cantril, ed. New Brunswick, NJ: Rutgers University Press

Annan, Lord. 1977. *Report of the Committee on the Future of Broadcasting*. London: HMSO

Atiyah, P. 1982. *Law and Modern Society*. New York: Oxford University Press

Baer, D. 1981. 'Cultural Indicators Research: Canadian Prospects,' in L. Salter, ed., *Communication Studies in Canada*, pp. 212–31. Toronto: Butterworths

Baldwin, J., and M. McConville. 1977. *Negotiated Justice: Pressures on Defendants to Plead Guilty*. London: Martin Robertson

Barrile, L. 1980. 'Television and Attitudes about Crime,' PHD thesis, Department of Sociology, Boston College

Barthes, R. 1972. *Mythologies*. London: Cape

– 1977. *Image – Music – Text*, trans. S. Heath. Glasgow: Fontana

Bates, A. 1984. *Broadcasting in Education*. London: Constable

Bell, E. 1927. *Life and Letters of C.F. Moberly Bell*. London: The Richards Press

Bennett, J. 1981. *Oral History and Delinquency: The Rhetoric of Criminology*. Chicago: University of Chicago Press

Bennett, T. 1977. *The Mass Media as Definers of Reality*. Milton Keynes: Open University Course, 'Mass Communication and Society,' Unit 13

Berger, P., and T. Luckmann. 1966. *The Social Construction of Reality: A Treatise in the Sociology of Knowledge*. Harmondsworth, Middlesex: Penguin

Berry, C. 1983. 'Learning from Television News: A Critique of the Research,' *Journal of Broadcasting* 27: 359–70

Bishop, Y., S. Feinberg, and P. Holland. 1975. *Discrete Multivariate Analysis: Theory and Practice*. Cambridge, Mass.: MIT Press

Black, D. 1976. *The Behavior of Law*. New York: Academic Press

Black, E. 1982. *Politics and the News: Political Functions of the Mass Media*. Toronto: Butterworths

Black, M. 1979. 'More about Metaphor,' in A. Ortony, ed., *Metaphor and Thought*, pp. 19–43. Cambridge: Cambridge University Press

Blumler, J., and M. Gurevitch. 1986. 'Journalists' Orientations to Political Institutions: The Case of Parliamentary Broadcasting,' in P. Golding, G. Murdock, and P. Schlesinger, eds., *Communicating Politics: Mass Communications and the Political Process*, pp. 67–92. Leicester: Leicester University Press

Blumler, J., and E. Katz, eds. 1974. *The Uses of Mass Communications: Current Perspectives on Gratifications Research*. Beverly Hills: Sage

Blumler, J., and D. McQuail. 1969. *Television in Politics: Its Uses and Influence*. Chicago: University of Chicago Press

Blyskal, J., and B. Blyskal. 1985. *PR: How the Public Relations Industry Writes the News*. New York: William Morrow

Bok, S. 1979. *Lying: Moral Choice in Public and Private Life*. New York: Vintage

Bolton, R. 1986. 'The Problems of Making Political Television: A Practitioner's Perspective,' in P. Golding, G. Murdock, and P. Schlesinger, eds., *Communicating Politics*, pp. 93–112. Leicester: Leicester University Press

Boorstin, D. 1962. *The Image: Or What Happened to the American Dream*. New York: Atheneum

Boyd, N. 1983. 'The Dilemma of Canadian Narcotics Legislation: The Social Control of Altered States of Consciousness,' *Contemporary Crises* 7: 257–69

– 1988. *The Last Dance: Murder in Canada*. Toronto: Prentice-Hall

Boyd-Barrett, O. 1979. 'Media Imperialism: Towards an International Framework for the Analysis of Media Systems,' in J. Curran et al., eds., *Mass Communication and Society*, pp. 116–35. Beverly Hills: Sage

Brandt, R. 1969. 'A Utilitarian Theory of Excuses,' *Philosophical Review* 78: 337–61

Braithwaite, J. 1989. *Crime, Shame and Reintegration*. Cambridge: Cambridge University Press

Brannigan, A. 1981. *The Social Basis of Scientific Discoveries*. Cambridge: Cambridge University Press

Bridson, D. 1971. *Prospero and Ariel*. London: Gollancz

Brodeur, J.-P. 1981. 'Legitimizing Police Deviance,' in C. Shearing, ed.,

Organizational Police Deviance, pp. 127–60. Toronto: Butterworths

Burns, T. 1979. 'The Organization of Public Opinion,' in J. Curran et al., eds., *Mass Communication and Society*, pp. 44–69. Beverly Hills: Sage

Canadian Broadcasting Corporation. 1978. *The C.B.C. – A Perspective*. Submission to the C.R.T.C. in Support of Applications for Renewal of Broadcast Licences. 3 vols. Ottawa: CBC

– 1982. *Journalistic Policy*. Ottawa: CBC Information Centre

Cardiff, D. 1980. 'The Serious and the Popular: Aspects of the Evolution of Style in Radio Talk, 1928–1939,' *Media, Culture and Society* 2.

Carey, J. 1979. 'Mass Communication Research and Cultural Studies: An American View,' in J. Curran et al., eds., *Mass Communication and Society*, pp. 409–25. Beverly Hills: Sage

Carriere, K., and R. Ericson. 1989. *Crime Stoppers: A Study in the Organization of Community Policing*. Toronto: Centre of Criminology, University of Toronto

Carson, W.G. 1982. *The Other Price of Britain's Oil*. Oxford: Martin Robertson

Cayley, D. 1982. 'Making Sense of the News,' *Sources*, Spring: 126–8, 130–3, 136–7

Chibnall, S. 1977. *Law-and-Order News*. London: Tavistock

Clarke, D. 1981. 'Second-Hand News: Production and Reproduction at a Major Ontario Television Station,' in L. Salter, ed., *Communication Studies in Canada*, pp. 20–51. Toronto: Butterworths

Clarke, M. 1987. 'Prosecutorial and Administrative Strategies to Control Business Crimes: Private and Public Roles,' in C. Shearing and P. Stenning, eds., *Private Policing*, pp. 266–92. Beverly Hills: Sage

Clement, W. 1975. *The Canadian Corporate Elite*. Toronto: McClelland and Stewart

Cohen, A. 1966. *Deviance and Control*. Englewood Cliffs, NJ: Prentice-Hall

Cohen, S. 1985. *Visions of Social Control*. Cambridge: Polity

Collins, R. 1975. *Conflict Sociology: Toward an Explanatory Science*. New York: Academic Press

Crisell, A. 1986. *Understanding Radio*. London: Methuen

Davis, F. 1973. 'Crime News in Colorado Newspapers,' in S. Cohen and J. Young, eds., *The Manufacture of News*, pp. 127–35. London: Constable

Dell, S. 1971. *Silence in Court*. London: Bell

Diamond, E., and S. Bates. 1984. *The Spot: The Rise of Political Advertising on Television*. Cambridge, Mass.: MIT Press

Ditton, J., and J. Duffy. 1982. *Bias in Newspaper Crime Reports: Selected and Distorted Reporting of Crime News in 6 Scottish Newspapers during March, 1981*. Background Paper Number 3, Department of Sociology, University of Glasgow

Dominick, J. 1973. 'Crime and Law Enforcement on Prime-Time Television,' *Public Opinion Quarterly* 37: 241–50

Doob, A. 1984. 'The Many Realities of Crime,' in A. Doob and E. Greenspan, eds., *Perspectives in Criminal Law*, pp. 61–80. Toronto: Canada Law Book

Douglas, J. 1976. *Investigative Social Research*. Beverly Hills: Sage

Douglas, M. 1986. *How Institutions Think.* Syracuse: Syracuse University Press
Draper, R. 1986. 'The Faithless Shepherd,' *New York Review of Books*, 26 June, pp. 14–18
Dussuyer, I. 1979. *Crime News: A Study of 40 Ontario Newspapers.* Toronto: Centre of Criminology, University of Toronto
Dworkin, R. 1986. *Law's Empire.* Cambridge, Mass.: Harvard University Press
Edelman, M. 1988. *Constructing the Political Spectacle.* Chicago: University of Chicago Press
Eliot, G. [1863]. *Romola.* Harmondsworth, Middlesex: Penguin
Elliott, P. 1978. 'Professional Ideology and Organizational Change: The Journalist since 1800,' in G. Boyce et al., *Newspaper History.* London: Constable
– 1979. 'Media Organizations and Occupations: An Overview,' in J. Curran, ed., *Mass Communication and Society*, pp. 142–73. Beverly Hills: Sage
Epstein, E. 1974. *News from Nowhere.* New York: Vintage
Ericson, R. 1975. *Criminal Reactions: The Labelling Perspective.* Westmead, Hants: Saxon House (D.C. Heath)
– 1981. *Making Crime: A Study of Detective Work.* Toronto: Butterworths
– 1982. *Reproducing Order: A Study of Police Patrol Work.* Toronto: University of Toronto Press
– 1987. 'The State and Criminal Justice Reform,' in R. Ratner and J. McMullan, eds., *State Control: Criminal Justice Politics in Canada*, pp. 21–37. Vancouver: University of British Columbia Press
– 1989. 'Patrolling the Facts: Secrecy and Publicity in Police Work,' *British Journal of Sociology* 40: 205–26
– 1991. 'Mass Media, Crime, Law and Justice: An Institutional Approach,' *British Journal of Criminology* forthcoming
Ericson, R., and P. Baranek. 1982. *The Ordering of Justice.* Toronto: University of Toronto Press
– 1984. 'Criminal Law Reform and Two Realities of the Criminal Process,' in A. Doob and E. Greenspan, eds., *Perspectives in Criminal Law*, pp. 255–76. Toronto: Canada Law Book
Ericson, R., P. Baranek, and J. Chan. 1987. *Visualizing Deviance: A Study of News Organization.* Toronto: University of Toronto Press; Milton Keynes: Open University Press
– 1989. *Negotiating Control: A Study of News Sources.* Toronto: University of Toronto Press; Milton Keynes: Open University Press
Evans, S., and R. Lundman. 1983. 'Newspaper Coverage of Corporate Price-Fixing,' *Criminology* 21: 529–41
Fairhurst, T. 1983. 'Making Stories: A Study of Social Construction in a Television News Room.' MA thesis, Department of Political Science, York University
Feeley, M. 1979. *The Process Is the Punishment.* New York: Russell Sage Foundation
Fishman, M. 1978. 'Crime Waves as Ideology,' *Social Problems* 25: 531–43
– 1980. *Manufacturing the News.* Austin: University of Texas Press
– 1981. 'Police News: Constructing an Image of Crime,' *Urban Life* 9: 371–94

Fiske, J. 1987. *Television Culture*. London: Methuen
Fiske, J., and J. Hartley. 1978. *Reading Television*. London: Methuen
Fitzpatrick, P. 1984. 'Law and Societies,' *Osgoode Hall Law Journal* 22: 115–38
Foucault, M. 1977. *Discipline and Punish: The Birth of the Prison*. New York: Pantheon
– 1981. [1971]. 'The Order of Discourse,' in R. Young, ed., *Untying the Text: A Post-Structuralist Reader*. London: Routledge and Kegan Paul
Fuller, L. 1967. *Legal Fictions*. Stanford: Stanford University Press
Gadamer, H. 1975. *Truth and Method*. New York: Seabury
Gans, H. 1979. *Deciding What's News*. New York: Vintage
Gardner, M. 1987. 'Giving God a Hand,' *New York Review of Books*, 13 August, pp. 17–23
Garnham, N. 1986. 'The Media and the Public Sphere,' in P. Golding, G. Murdock, and P. Schlesinger, eds., *Communicating Politics*, pp. 37–53. Leicester: Leicester University Press
Garofalo, J. 1981. 'Crime and the Mass Media: A Selective Review of Research,' *Journal of Research in Crime and Delinquency* 18: 319–50
Geertz, C. 1983. *Local Knowledge*. New York: Basic Books
Gerbner, G., and L. Gross. 1976. 'Living with Television: The Violence Profile,' *Journal of Communication* 26: 173–99
Giddens, A. 1979. *Central Problems in Social Theory: Action, Structure, and Contradiction in Social Analysis*. London: Macmillan
Gitlin, T. 1980. *The Whole World Is Watching*. Berkeley: University of California Press
Glaser, B., and A. Strauss. 1967. *The Discovery of Grounded Theory: Strategies for Qualitative Research*. Chicago: Aldine
Glasgow University Media Group. 1976. *Bad News*. London: Routledge
– 1980. *More Bad News*. London: Routledge
– 1982. *Really Bad News*. London: Writers and Readers
Goffman, E. 1981. *Forms of Talk*. Philadelphia: University of Pennsylvania Press
– 1983. 'The Interaction Order,' *American Sociological Review* 48: 1–17
Golding, P., and P. Elliott. 1979. *Making the News*. London: Longman
Golding, P., G. Murdock, and P. Schlesinger. 1986. *Communicating Politics: Mass Communications and the Political Process*. Leicester: University of Leicester Press
Goodrich, P. 1986. *Reading the Law*. Oxford: Blackwell
Graber, D. 1980. *Crime News and the Public*. New York: Praeger
Greenberg, D. 1979. *Mathematical Criminology*. New Brunswick, NJ: Rutgers University Press
Gunter, B. 1987. *Television and the Fear of Crime*. London: John Libbey
Gusfield, J. 1981. *The Culture of Public Problems*. Chicago: University of Chicago Press
Habermas, J. 1975. *Legitimation Crisis*. Boston: Beacon
– 1979. 'The Public Sphere,' in A. Matterlart and S. Siegelaub, eds., *Communication and Class Struggle*, Vol. 1. New York: International General
Hall, S. 1975. 'Introduction,' in A. Smith, E. Immirzi, and T. Blackwell, eds.,

Paper Voices: The Popular Press and Social Change, 1935– 1965, pp.
11–24. London: Chatto and Windus

– 1979. 'Culture, the Media, and the "Ideological Effect,"' in J. Curran et al.,
eds., *Mass Communication and Society*, pp. 314–48. Beverly Hills: Sage

– 1981. 'The Determinations of News Photographs,' in S. Cohen and J.
Young, eds., *The Manufacture of News*, pp. 226–43. London: Constable

– 1982. 'The Rediscovery of Ideology: The Return of the Repressed in Media
Studies,' in M. Gurevitch et al., eds., *Culture, Society and Media*, pp. 56–90.
London: Methuen

Hall, S., C. Critcher, T. Jefferson, J. Clarke, and B. Roberts. 1978. *Policing the
Crisis*. London: Macmillan

Hannigan, J. 1977. 'The Newspaper Ombudsman and Consumer Complaints: An
Empirical Assessment,' *Law and Society Review* 11: 679–99

Hartley, J. 1982. *Understanding News*. London: Methuen

Hauge, R. 1965. 'Crime and the Press,' in N. Christie, ed., *Scandinavian Studies
in Criminology*, Vol. 1. London: Tavistock

Hawkes, T. 1977. *Structuralism and Semiotics*. London: Methuen

Hawkins, K. 1984. *Environment and Enforcement: Regulation and the Social
Definition of Pollution*. Oxford: Clarendon Press

Hayman, R. 1983. 'The Invisible Performance,' British Broadcasting Corporation
Talk, Radio 3

Herman, E. 1986. 'Gatekeeper versus Propaganda Models: A Critical American
Perspective,' in P. Golding, G. Murdock, and P. Schlesinger, eds., *Communicating Politics*, pp. 171–95. Leicester: Leicester University Press

Hirsch, P. 1977. 'Occupational, Organizational, and Institutional Models in Mass
Media Research: Toward an Integrated Framework,' in P. Hirsch et al., eds.,
Strategies for Communication Research, pp. 13–42. Beverly Hills: Sage

Hoover, S. 1988. *Mass Media Religion: The Social Sources of the Electronic
Church*. Beverly Hills: Sage

Inbau, F., and J. Reid. 1967. *Criminal Interrogation and Confessions*. 2d ed.
Baltimore: Williams and Wilkins

Jones, E. 1976. 'The Press as Metropolitan Monitor,' *Public Opinion Quarterly*
40: 239–44

Kermode, F. 1966. *The Sense of an Ending: Studies in the Theory of Fiction*.
Bloomington: Indiana University Press

Knight, G., and T. Dean. 1982. 'Myth and Structure of News,' *Journal of
Communication* 32: 144–61

Knight, S. 1980. *Form and Ideology in Crime Fiction*. Bloomington: Indiana
University Press

Law Reform Commission. 1986. *Policy Implementation, Compliance and
Administrative Law*. Working Paper 51. Ottawa: Law Reform Commission of
Canada

Levy, M., and S. Windahl. 1985. 'The Concept of Audience Activity,' in K.
Rosengren et al., eds., *Media Gratifications Research: Current Perspectives*.
Beverly Hills: Sage

Lichter, S., and S. Rothman. 1981. 'Media and Business Elites,' *Public Opinion*
4: 42–6

Lowi, T. 1979. *The End of Liberalism: The Second Republic of the United States*, 2d ed. New York: Norton

Macauley, S. 1987. 'Images of Law in Everyday Life: The Lessons of School, Entertainment and Spectator Sport,' *Law and Society Review*, 21: 185–218

McBarnet, D. 1981. *Conviction: Law, the State and the Construction of Justice*. London: Macmillan

McCormack, T. 1982. 'Content Analysis: The Social History of a Method,' in T. McCormack, ed., *Studies in Communications*, 2, pp. 143–78. Greenwich, Conn.: JAI Press

Macdonnel, D. 1986. *Theories of Discourse*. Oxford: Blackwell

McLuhan, M. 1962. *The Gutenberg Galaxy: The Making of Typographic Man*. Toronto: University of Toronto Press

– 1964. *Understanding Media: The Extensions of Man*. New York: McGraw-Hill

McMahon, M. 1989. 'Police Accountability: The Situation of Complaints in Toronto,' *Contemporary Crises* 12: 301–27

McMahon, M., and R. Ericson. 1984. *Policing Reform*. Toronto: Centre for Criminology, University of Toronto

– 1987. 'Reforming the Police and Policing Reform,' in R. Ratner and J. McMullan, eds., *State Control: Criminal Justice Politics in Canada*, pp. 38–68. Vancouver: University of British Columbia Press

McQuail, D. 1986. 'Diversity in Political Communication: Its Sources, Forms, and Future,' in P. Golding et al., eds., *Communicating Politics*, pp. 133–47. Leicester: Leicester University Press

McWhinnie, D. 1959. *The Art of Radio*. London: Faber and Faber

Manning, P. 1982. 'Organizational Work: Structuration of Environments,' *British Journal of Sociology* 33: 118–34

– 1987. 'Ironies of Compliance,' in C. Shearing and P. Stenning, eds., *Private Policing*, pp. 293–316. Beverly Hills: Sage

– 1988. *Symbolic Communication: Signifying Calls and the Police Response*. Cambridge, Mass.: MIT Press

Marx, G. 1981. 'Ironies of Social Control: Authorities as Contributors to Deviance through Escalation, Non-Enforcement, and Covert Facilitation,' *Social Problems* 28: 221–46

– 1988. *Undercover: Police Surveillance in America*. Berkeley: University of California Press

Mathiesen, T. 1987. 'The Eagle and the Sun: On Panoptical Systems and Mass Media in Modern Society,' in J. Lowman et al., eds., *Transcarceration: Essays in the Sociology of Social Control*, pp. 59–75. Aldershot: Gower

Matza, D. 1964. *Delinquency and Drift*. New York: Wiley

Menzies, R. 1989. *Survival of the Sanest: Psychiatric Order and Disorder in a Pre-trial Forensic Clinic*. Toronto: University of Toronto Press

Merton, R. 1946. *Mass Persuasion*. New York: Harper

Meyer, J., and B. Rowan. 1977. 'Institutionalized Organizations: Formal Structure as Myth and Ceremony,' *American Journal of Sociology* 83: 340–63

Meyrowitz, J. 1985. *No Sense of Place: The Impact of Electronic Media on Social Behavior*. New York: Oxford University Press

Midgley, M. 1982. 'Moral Melodrama,' *Times Higher Education Supplement*, 16 April, p. 10

Milton, J. 1671. *Samson Agonistes*

Molotch, H., and M. Lester. 1975. 'Accidental News: The Great Oil Spill,' *American Journal of Sociology* 81: 235–60

Monaco, J. 1981. *How to Read a Film: The Art, Technology, Language, History and Theory of Film and Media.* Oxford: Oxford University Press

Morrison, D. 1969. 'On the Interpretation of Discriminant Analysis,' *Journal of Marketing Research* 6: 156–63

Morrison, D., and H. Tumber. 1988. *Journalists at War.* London: Sage

Mulkay, M. 1979. *Science and the Sociology of Knowledge.* London: Allen and Unwin

Murdock, G. 1973. 'Political Deviance: The Press Presentation of a Militant Mass Demonstration,' in S. Cohen and J. Young, eds., *The Manufacture of News*, pp. 156–75. London: Constable

– 1982. 'Disorderly Images: Television's Presentation of Crime and Policing,' in C. Sumner ed., *Crime, Justice and the Mass Media*, pp. 104–21. Cambridge: Institute of Criminology, University of Cambridge

Murphy, C. 1988. 'Community Problems, Problem Communities, and Community Policing in Toronto,' *Journal of Research in Crime and Delinquency* 25: 392–410

Nelson, B. 1984. *Making an Issue of Child Abuse.* Chicago: University of Chicago Press

Ng, Y. 1982. 'Ideology, Media and Moral Panics: An Analysis of the Jacques Murder,' MA thesis, Centre of Criminology, University of Toronto

O'Neill, J. 1981. 'McLuhan's Loss of Innis-Sense,' *Canadian Forum* 61(May): 13–15

Ortony, A., ed. 1979. *Metaphor and Thought.* Cambridge: Cambridge University Press

Palen, F. 1979. 'Media Ombudsmen: A Critical Review,' *Law and Society Review* 13: 799–850

Palmer, M. 1978. 'The British Press and International News, 1851–99: of Agencies and Newspapers,' in G. Boyce et al., eds., *Newspaper History*, pp. 205–19. London: Constable

Paulu, B. 1981. *Television and Radio in the United Kingdom.* London: Macmillan

Pearson, G. 1983. *Hooligan: A History of Respectable Fears.* London: Macmillan

Pfohl, S. 1985. *Images of Deviance and Social Control.* New York: McGraw-Hill

Pfuhl, E., and D. Altheide. 1987. 'TV Mediation of Disputes and Injustice,' *Justice Quarterly* 4: 99–118

Phillips, B. 1977. 'Approaches to Objectivity: Journalistic versus Social Science Perspectives,' in P. Hirsch et al., eds., *Strategies for Communication Research*, pp. 63–77. Beverly Hills: Sage

Pietropaolo, D. 1982. 'Structuring "Truth": The Uses of Drama in "Information" Radio,' *Canadian Theatre Review* 36: 52–6

Postman, N. 1985. *Amusing Ourselves to Death: Public Discourse in the Age of Show Business.* New York: Viking

Putnam, H. 1981. *Reason, Truth, and History*. Cambridge: Cambridge University Press

Putnam, L., and M. Pacanowsky, eds. 1983. *Communication and Organization*. Beverly Hills: Sage

Raphael, F. 1980. 'The Language of Television,' in L. Michaels and C. Ricks, eds., *The State of the Language*. Berkeley: University of California Press

Rawls, J. 1971. *A Theory of Justice*. Cambridge, Mass.: Harvard University Press

Reasons, C., L. Ross, and C. Patterson. 1981. *Assault on the Worker*. Toronto: Butterworths

Reddy, M. 1979. 'The Conduit Metaphor – A Case of Frame Conflict in Our Language about Language,' in A. Ortony, ed., *Metaphor and Thought*, pp. 284–310. Cambridge: Cambridge University Press

Reiss, A. 1971a. 'Systematic Observation of Natural Social Phenomena,' in H. Costner, ed., *Sociological Methodology*. San Francisco: Jossey-Bass

– 1971b. *The Police and the Public*. New Haven: Yale University Press

– 1984. 'Consequences of Compliance and Deterrence Models of Law Enforcement for the Exercise of Police Discretion,' *Law and Contemporary Problems* 47: 83–122

– 1987. 'The Legitimacy of Intrusion into Private Space,' in C. Shearing and P. Stenning, eds., *Private Policing*, pp. 19–44. Beverly Hills: Sage

Robinson, J. 1976. 'Interpersonal Influences in Election Campaigns: Two-step Flow Hypothesis,' *Public Opinion Quarterly* 40: 304–19

Robinson, J., and M. Levy. 1986. *The Main Source: Learning from Television News*. Beverly Hills: Sage

Rock, P. 1973. 'News as Eternal Recurrence,' in S. Cohen and J. Young, eds., *The Manufacture of News*, pp. 28–39. London: Constable

– 1986. *A View from the Shadows*. Oxford: Oxford University Press

– 1988. 'On the Birth of Organizations,' *Canadian Journal of Sociology* 13: 359–84

Roscho, B. 1975. *Newsmaking*. Chicago: University of Chicago Press

Roshier, B. 1973. 'The Selection of Crime News by the Press,' in S. Cohen and J. Young, eds., *The Manufacture of News*, pp. 28–39. London: Constable

Rowland, W. 1983. *The Politics of TV Violence*. Beverly Hills: Sage

Royal Commission on Newspapers. 1981a. *Canadian News Sources*. Ottawa: Research Studies on the Newspaper Industry, Supply and Services Canada

– 1981b. *Final Report*. Ottawa: Supply and Services Canada

– 1981c. *The Journalists*. Ottawa: Research Studies on the Newspaper Industry, Supply and Services Canada

– 1981d. *Labour Relations in the Newspaper Industry*. Ottawa: Research Studies on the Newspaper Industry, Supply and Services Canada

– 1981e. *The Newspaper and Public Affairs*. Ottawa: Research Studies on the Newspaper Industry, Supply and Services Canada

– 1981f. *Newspapers and Computers: An Industry in Transition*. Ottawa: Research Studies on the Newspaper Industry, Supply and Services Canada

– 1981g. *Newspapers and Their Readers*. Ottawa: Research Studies on the Newspaper Industry, Supply and Services Canada

Runciman, W.G. 1983. *A Treatise on Social Theory*. Vol. 1: *The Methodology of Social Theory*. Cambridge: Cambridge University Press

Ryle, G. 1949. *The Concept of Mind*. London: Hutchinson

Scheppele, K. 1988. *Legal Secrets: Equality and Efficiency in the Common Law*. Chicago: University of Chicago Press

— 1990. 'Facing Facts in Legal Interpretation,' *Representations*, forthcoming

Schiller, D. 1986. 'Transformations of News in the U.S. Information Market,' in P. Golding, G. Murdock, and P. Schlesinger, eds., *Communicating Politics*, pp. 19–36. Leicester: Leicester University Press

Schiller, H. 1989. *Culture, Inc.: The Corporate Takeover of Public Expression*. New York: Oxford University Press

Schlesinger, P. 1978. *Putting Reality Together: BBC News*. London: Constable

— 1988. 'Rethinking the Sociology of Journalism: Source Strategies and the Limits of Media Centrism.' Paper to the Economic and Social Research Council Workshop on Classic Issues of Mass Communication Research, Madingley Hall, Cambridge

— 1989. 'Crime and Mass Media: Theoretical Issues.' Paper to the British Criminology Conference, Bristol

Schon, D. 1979. 'Generative Metaphor: A Perspective on Problem-Setting in Social Policy,' in A. Ortony, ed., *Metaphor and Thought*, pp. 254–83. Cambridge: Cambridge University Press

Schur, E. 1971. *Labeling Deviant Behavior*. New York: Harper and Row

Scott, M., and S. Lyman. 1968. 'Accounts,' *American Sociological Review* 33: 46–62

Seaton, J. 1980. 'Politics and Television,' *Economy and Society* 9: 90–107

Shearing, C., and R. Ericson. 1991. 'Culture as Figurative Action,' *British Journal of Sociology*, forthcoming

Shearing, C., and P. Stenning. 1981. 'Modern Private Security: Its Growth and Implications,' in M. Tonry and N. Morris, eds., *Crime and Justice: An Annual Review of Research*, Vol. 3, pp. 193–245. Chicago: University of Chicago Press

— 1987. 'Reframing Policing,' in C. Shearing and P. Stenning, eds., *Private Policing*, pp. 9–18. Beverly Hills: Sage

Sherizen, S. 1978. 'Social Creation of Crime News: All the News Fitted to Print,' in C. Winick, ed., *Deviance and Mass Media*, pp. 205–24. Beverly Hills: Sage

Shibutani, T. 1966. *Improvised News*. Indianapolis: Bobbs-Merrill

Sigal, L. 1973. *Reporters and Officials*. Lexington, Mass.: D.C. Heath

Silvey, R. 1974. *Who's Listening?* London: Allen and Unwin

Singer, B. 1973. *Feedback and Society*. Lexington, Mass.: D.C. Heath

— 1986. *Advertising and Society*. Don Mills: Addison-Wesley

Smith, A. 1978. 'The Long Road to Objectivity and Back Again: The Kinds of Truth We Get in Journalism,' in G. Boyce et al., eds., *Newspaper History*, pp. 152–71. London: Constable

— 1979. 'Technology and Control: The Interactive Dimensions of Journalism,' in J. Curran et al., eds., *Mass Communication and Society*, pp. 174–94. Beverly Hills: Sage

- 1980. *Goodbye Gutenberg: The Newspaper Revolution of the 1980s*. New York: Oxford University Press

Smith, D. 1984. 'Textually-Mediated Social Organization,' *International Social Science Journal* 36: 59–75

Snow, R. 1983. *Creating Media Culture*. Beverly Hills: Sage

Sumner, C. 1979. *Reading Ideologies*. London: Academic Press

- 1981. 'Race, Crime and Hegemony,' *Contemporary Crises* 5: 277–91

Swope, H. 1958. 'Statement Recalled in Obituaries after His Death,' cited in R. Tripp, *The International Thesaurus of Quotations*. Harmondsworth, Middlesex: Penguin, 1978

Tatsuaka, M. 1971. *Multivariate Analysis: Techniques for Educational and Psychological Research*. New York: Wiley

Taylor, P. 1986. 'The Semantics of Political Violence,' in P. Golding et al., eds., *Communicating Politics*, pp. 211–21. Leicester: Leicester University Press

Thorngate, W. 1976. 'Must We Always Think before We Act?' *Personality and Social Psychology Bulletin* 2: 31–5

Towler, R. 1984. 'Television and Its Audiences,' Mass Communication and Modern Culture Seminar Series, Social and Political Studies Committee, Cambridge, England

Tracey, M. 1984. 'Does Arthur Scargill Have a Leg to Stand On? – News,' *The Sunday Times*, 28 August, p. 43

Tuchman, G. 1978. *Making News*. New York: Free Press

Tumber, H. 1982. *Television and the Riots*. London: Broadcasting Research Unit, British Film Institute

Turney, J. 1988. 'Out of Tune with the Rest of the Group,' *The Times Higher Education Supplement*, 25 November, pp. 11, 13

Unger, R. 1976. *Law in Modern Society: Toward a Criticism of Social Theory*. New York: Free Press

Voumvakis, S., and R. Ericson. 1984. *News Accounts of Attacks on Women: A Comparison of Three Toronto Newspapers*. Toronto: Centre of Criminology, University of Toronto

Waddington, P. 1986. 'Mugging as a Moral Panic: A Question of Proportion,' *British Journal of Sociology* 37: 245–59

Wagner-Pacifici, R. 1986. *The Moro Morality Play: Terrorism as Social Drama*. Chicago: University of Chicago Press

Warshett, G. 1981. 'The Information Economy in Late Capitalism,' in L. Salter, ed., *Communication Studies in Canada*, pp. 178–95. Toronto: Butterworths

Weber, M. 1954. *On Law and Economy in Society*. Trans. by Max Rheinstein. Cambridge, Mass.: Harvard University Press

Weick, K. 1979. *The Social Psychology of Organizing*, 2d ed. Reading, Mass.: Addison-Wesley

- 1983. 'Organizational Communication: Toward a Research Agenda,' in L. Putnam and M. Pacanowsky, eds., *Communication and Organizations*, pp. 13–29. Beverly Hills: Sage

Wheeler, G. 1986. 'Reporting Crime: The News Release as Textual Mediator of Police/Media Relations,' MA thesis, Centre of Criminology, University of Toronto

White, J. 1984. *When Words Lose Their Meaning: Constitutions and Reconstitutions of Language, Character, and Community*. Chicago: University of Chicago Press

Williams, R. 1961. *Communications*. Harmondsworth, Middlesex: Penguin

– 1976. *Communications*, 3rd ed. Harmondsworth, Middlesex: Penguin

– 1977. *Marxism and Literature*. Oxford: Oxford University Press

– 1989. *Raymond Williams on Television: Selected Writings*. Toronto: Between the Lines

Winter, J., and A. Frizzle. 1979. 'The Treatment of State-owned versus Private Corporations in English Canadian Dailies,' *Canadian Journal of Communication* 6: 1–11

Wuthnow, R., J. Hunter, A. Bergesen, and E. Kurzweil. 1984. *Cultural Analysis*. London: Routledge

Index

Adorno, T., 18
advertising: and compliance mode of control, 292; and mass-market effects on news media, 36–42, 44, 107–8; and news columns, 153–4; and public relations, 14, 218; similarity of broadcast news to, 29, 221; and source selection, 40–1
Albertan (Calgary), 40
Alley, R., 288
Altheide, D., 4, 19, 20, 21, 28, 34, 35, 37, 55, 57, 62, 149, 151, 162, 185, 217, 220, 223, 227, 228, 243, 246, 307, 345, 351
Ames, A., 52
analysis, qualitative, 54–8, 61–2; advantages of, 62, 65, 73–4
analysis, quantitative, 50–4, 62–9; limitations of, 51–4, 57, 73–4, 150, 205
anchorperson: framing role of, 81–4, 90–3, 103, 104, 133, 170–1, 173–4, 227, 265–6; as news source, 188–90, 200–1; and per-sonalization, 27
angles, 27, 38, 266, 354; and con-notative meanings, 23, 85, 225; and media ideology, 112, 133; and use of previous news stories, for, 14
Annan Committee, 175, 196

Associated Press, 159
Atiyah, P., 182
audio: manipulation of tertiary understanding, 34; and radio and television formats, 20–30, 38, 84–5, 218, 220–32; recordings of court procedures, 102; use of voice-clips, 226, 230–1, 238, 352; use of voice-overs, 222, 223–5, 237; *see also* language
authority, role of news media in establishing, 5–8, 14–15, 30–2, 81, 85–6, 214–18, 284–8, 343–4, 348, 357
autonomy: of journalists 16–17, 168–9, 243; of news text, 33, 52–3, 57, 218, 287, 357

Baer, D., 253
Baldwin, J., 125
Barrile, L., 275
Barthes, R., 24, 351
Bates, A., 25
Bates, S., 218
Bell, E., 163–4
Bennett, J., 175, 269
Berger, P., 287
Berry, C., 18
Bishop, Y., 66
Black, D., 297
Black, E., 175, 295
Black, M., 227–8